THE PUNK READER.
RESEARCH TRANSMISSIONS FROM THE LOCAL AND THE GLOBAL

RUSS BESTLEY
MIKE DINES
ALASTAIR 'GORDS' GORDON
PAULA GUERRA

intellect Bristol, UK / Chicago, USA

Published in the UK in 2019 by
Intellect, The Mill, Parnall Road, Fishponds, Bristol, BS16 3JG, UK

Published in the USA in 2019 by
Intellect, The University of Chicago Press, 1427 E. 60th Street,
Chicago, IL 60637, USA

Produced in collaboration with the Punk Scholars Network

First published in Portugal in 2017 by
Universidade de Porto, Faculdade de Letras,
Via Panorâmica, s/n, 4150-564,
Porto, Portugal
www.letras.up.pt

A catalogue record for this book is available from the British Library.

Designer: Russ Bestley
Cover image: Andrew Morgan

Print ISBN: 978-1-78938-129-0
ePDF ISBN: 978-1-78938-131-3
ePUB ISBN: 978-1-78938-130-6

Printed and bound by Gomer, UK.

This is a peer-reviewed publication.

THE PUNK READER.

RESEARCH TRANSMISSIONS FROM THE LOCAL AND THE GLOBAL

RUSS BESTLEY

MIKE DINES

ALASTAIR 'GORDS' GORDON

PAULA GUERRA

CONTENTS

The Punk Reader.

CONTENTS

INTRODUCTION: THE PUNK NARRATIVE TURNED UPSIDE DOWN: RESEARCH TRANSMISSIONS FROM THE LOCAL TO THE GLOBAL

RUSS BESTLEY, MIKE DINES, ALASTAIR 'GORDS' GORDON & PAULA GUERRA

The Editors

Russ Bestley is a designer and writer, specialising in graphic design, punk and humour. His publications include *Action Time Vision: Punk & Post Punk 7" Record Sleeves* (2016), *The Art of Punk* (2012) and *Visual Research* (2004, 2011, 2015). He has contributed articles to *Punk & Post-Punk, Eye, Zed, Emigré, Street Sounds* and *Vive Le Rock* and curated exhibitions in London, Southampton, Blackpool, Leeds, Birmingham and Newcastle. He is editor of the journal *Punk & Post-Punk* and leads the Graphic Subcultures Research Hub at the London College of Communication. E-mail: r.bestley@lcc.arts.ac.uk

Mike Dines joined the West Sussex Institute of Higher Education in the early 1990s. After writing a thesis on Crass and the anarcho-punk scene of the 1980s, Mike continued his research at the University of Salford, completing a PhD on *The Emergence of the Anarcho-Punk Scene of the 1980s*. Mike has recently co-edited *Tales From the Punkside* (2014) and *Some of Us Scream, Some of Us Shout* (2016) with Greg Bull, and has also written on punk pedagogy and Krishnacore. His co-edited *The Aesthetics of Our Anger: Anarcho-Punk, Politics, Music* (2016) is published by Minor Compositions, an imprint of Autonomedia. E-mail: miked71uk@gmail.com

Alastair 'Gords' Gordon is Senior Lecturer in Media and Communications at Leicester De Montfort University. His current research is based around genre authenticity and hierarchy across international networks of DiY punk with specific focus on Japan and Europe. He researches and teaches modules on introduction to media and communication studies, youth subcultures and paranormal media. In 2012, Gords co-founded the Punk Scholars Network with Mike Dines and records and tours internationally with band, Endless Grinning Skulls. Gords hates Tories, neoliberals and collects old Barry Manilow autographs. E-mail: agordon@dmu.ac.uk

Paula Guerra is Assistant Professor of Sociology at University of Porto (FLUP), Researcher in the Institute of Sociology of the same university (IS-UP) and Invited researcher at the Centre for Geography Studies and Territory Planning (CEGOT). She is also Adjunct Professor at Griffith Centre for Social and Cultural Research, Australia (GCSCR). Founder and coordinator of KISMIF Project/Conference, she coordinates/participates in several other research projects in the field of youth cultures and sociology of art and culture, having published in the last few years inumerous works on those themes. E-mail: pguerra@letras.up.pt

THE PUNK NARRATIVE TURNED UPSIDE DOWN: RESEARCH TRANSMISSIONS FROM THE LOCAL TO THE GLOBAL

From dehumanisation　　　　　　*Reject the system*
To arms production　　　　　　　*That dictates the norm*
For the benefit of the nation?　　　*From dehumanisation*
Or its destruction　　　　　　　*To arms production*
Power is power　　　　　　　　*For the benefit of the nation*
It's the law of the land　　　　　*Or its destruction*
Those who live by death　　　　　*It's your choice*
Shall die by their own hand　　　　*Peace?*
Life is no ordeal　　　　　　　　*Or annihilation?*
If you can come to terms

Crucifix, *Dehumanisation* (1983, Corpus Christi Records)

Editing a book on global punk has its obvious challenges. For, as any punk (let alone punk scholar) would tell you, there are too many scenes to document even in a short set of edited volumes. Now forty years on from its inception, punk has traversed international boundaries and the legacy of the events of 1977 towards a global reach: where the original United Kingdom and United States scenes are now accompanied by complex and important global counterparts. Indeed, most Western cities on the planet have some variation on punk as a culture in their respective undergrounds. This manifestation is a consequence of networks existing through decades of uneven flows among music distribution, tape trading, friendships, and touring bands that fleetingly appear as scenes rise and fall with membership demographics. Long-standing diverse punk scenes are to be found in Japan, South East Asia, China, the Middle East, Scandinavia, East, West, and South Europe, Russia, Australia, India, and Africa. Each scene, rather than adopting traditional interpretations of the punk filter, hybridise and assimilate, and in turn reflect national, regional, and local identities. In such ways, punk culture represents new and historical approaches to challenging and disrupting cultures of hegemony. While it is beyond both its scope and remit to document the complete global punk scene, this first collection reflects a range of current and timely research investigating the topic. Contained in this edited book are the research transmissions from a number of scholars seeking to explore and critically interrogate punk culture's place in the radicalized globalization in which we live.

We know that a complex process, generally called globalization, is underway, involving accelerated social changes in a plurality of dimensions (Lash and Urry 1999). This means that globalization refers to the network of interdependencies and interconnections that is rapidly growing. This growing density characterizes, in modern societies, the social, economic, and

11

cultural life (Guerra 2010). Thus, there is a world globally connected by financial flows, information, commodities, and people, but also by beliefs, fashions, images, and multiple appropriations. Nevertheless, increasing global connectivity does not necessarily imply that the world is becoming politically and economically unified. Above all, it must include the contrary tendencies of social, political, and even cultural division. However, it should be noted that globalization does not destroy localities. On the contrary, localities thrive on globalization. It is with youth culture that we can find some of the most significant changes in the cultural sphere, for example Paul Gilroy's concept of hybrid cultural identifications (Gilroy 1993a; 1993b; Guerra and Quintela 2016). Following an *active deterritorialization* (of the dissolution of the links between cultures and place, of escape from tradition) a reterritorialization arises, with the globalized culture to be integrated and retranslated in terms of localized versions of the canons of the international scene. Contrary to the traditional idea of cultural identity, which spoke of a solid and fixed self, umbilically related to a territory and collective history, nowadays we must take into account the volatility of these identities. More and more, this volatile nature proceeds from a flux of social uprooting, permanent technological innovation, and the physical mobility of goods and ideas, all of which are deeply rooted in late modernity (Giddens 1990; 1991). This volatility is often put into focus by the plastic nature of the human being and the provisional character of social roles and bonds (Hall 2003; Hall and Du Gay 1996; Hall and Jefferson 1993; Featherstone 1995). Crane's (2002) perspective on this is, of course, of the utmost importance. The global music culture, spread by the media conglomerates, is mostly centred in English language countries, with the repertoires of major labels focusing ever more on a small number of international stars. There is then a renovated model of 'media imperialism based on global capitalism' (Crane 2002, 6). Therefore, we have globalization and localization simultaneously in a complex web of network flows, showing progressive cultural homogeneity while assuring that identity and specific values are ever more crucial to understanding popular music (Huq 2003, 2006).

From a personal perspective, Gordon (notes), as a participant in the UK anarcho and hardcore scenes, notes that the international dimensions of punk were initially registered along three lines. The first was Dead Kennedys, Black Flag, the Minutemen, and Toxic Reasons touring Europe and the United Kingdom, in addition to GBH, Discharge, and the Exploited touring the United States and Scandinavia.[1] Such connections, alongside Crass records releasing bands like MDC, KUKL, and the Sleeping Dogs, added a clear DIY connection to the development of the early international scenes. In addition, the release of the Crucifix LP *Dehumanisation* (1983) on the Crass Records imprint label Corpus Christi and their UK tour in 1984 were landmark examples of the international connections of the burgeoning global connections of punk.[2] Equally, Chaos UK were among the first UK bands to tour Japan in 1985, setting up contacts with that scene that were subsequently developed

---

1 For an insider's account of the unease, conflict, and direct hostility that American bands faced from the English and European audiences and bands see Rollins (1994).
2 For a discussion of how attendance at shows on the Crucifix 1984 tour became a badge of authenticity and an important step in the formation of the later UK hardcore scene see Gordon (2015) and Glasper (2009).

the bands, the songs...

Side 1
1. ARTICLES OF FAITH--"Up Against a Wall" U.S.
2. GISM--"Endless Blockade for Pussyfooter" JAPAN
3. NEON CHRIST--"Ashes to Ashes" U.S.
4. KALASHNIKOV--"Schluters Kabinet" DENMARK
5. CAUSE FOR ALARM--"Time Will Tell" U.S.
6. LOCAL DISTURBANCE--"No U.S.A." HOLLAND
7. UNWARRANTED TRUST--"Honour's Calling" CANADA
8. WRETCHED--"Mai Arrendersi" ITALY
9. O.D.F.X.--"Drop the A Bomb On Me" U.S.
10. AFFLICTED--"Here Come the Cops" U.S.
11. DECLINO--"Inutile Trionfo" ITALY
12. DICKS--"Hope You Get Drafted" U.S.
13. BGK--"Arms Race" HOLLAND
14. CRASS--"It's You" U.K.

Side 2
1. UPRIGHT CITIZENS--"Swastika Ratss" W. GERMANY
2. FALSE PROPHETS--"Banana Split Republic" U.S.
3. MOB 47--"Nuclear Attack" SWEDEN
4. OFFENDERS--"Face Down in the Dirt" U.S.
5. CONTRAZIONE--"Sbarre" (Bars) ITALY
6. SCUM--"So Much Hate" CANADA
7. LOS VIOLADORES--"Viejos Pateticos" ARGENTINA
8. DEADLOCK--"Sometimes" HOLLAND
9. P.P.G.--"Will It Ever End?" U.S.
10. TRASH--"Peace of What" U.S.
11. VICIOUS CIRCLE--"Police Brutality" AUSTRALIA
12. CONDEMNED TO DEATH--"Gartlands Pit" U.S.
13. NEGAZIONE--"Non Mi Dire" (Don't Tell Me) ITALY
14. DOA--"America the Beautiful" CANADA

Side 3
1. DIRTY ROTTEN IMBECILES--"Snap" U.S.
2. PORNO PATROL--"Jump Back" W. GERMANY
3. TREASON--"Drop Out" U.S.
4. SHIT S.A.--"Abortos" SPAIN
5. SEPTIC DEATH--"Silence" U.S.
6. CHEETAH CHROME AND THE MOTHERFUCKERS--"Life of Punishment" ITALY
7. PEGGIO PUNX--"No Mai" ITALY
8. PROLETARIAT--"An Uneasy Peace" U.S.
9. CONFLICT--"Bomb" U.K.
10. ICONOCLAST--"Battlefield (Nightmare)" U.S.
11. PANDEMONIUM--"Pay for Shit" HOLLAND
12. DEAD KENNEDYS--"Kinky Sex Makes the World Go Round" U.S.
13. BOSKOPS--"Skorbut" W. GERMANY

Side 4
1. SUBHUMANS--"Rats" U.K.
2. WHITE LIE--"Peace Officer" U.S.
3. WARGASM--"R.A.T./Pentagone" HOLLAND
4. SLAUGHTERHOUSE 4--"Four More Hours" U.S.
5. EXECUTE--"Finale" JAPAN
6. REAGAN YOUTH--"Reagan Youth" U.S.
7. IMPACT--"The Man Goes On" ITALY
8. BUTTHOLE SURFERS--"100 Million People Dead" U.S.
9. KANGRENA--"Ataque" SPAIN
10. PORCELAIN FOREHEAD--"Will Amerika" CANADA
11. BARELY HUMAN--"No Mercy No War" U.S.
12. RAF PUNK--"Contro la Pace Contro la Guerra" ITALY
13. ZENZILE--"Moment By Moment/Exiled Shadows" SO. AFRICA
14. M.D.C.--"Missile Destroyed Civilization" U.S.

Credits:
Thanx: Kent, Ruth Schwartz, Tim Yohannan, Jeff Bale, Tabb Rex, all the bands, China, Felix, and JBAKC, Prairie Fire, Women Against Imperialism, David Solnit, Gil Scott Heron, Sun Ra, Holly Near, S.F. and Dallas WAR CHEST demonstrators, London's Stop the City protestors, squatters, all the musicians and artists who have made it their lives to speak out on nuclear catastrophe, Mobilization for Survival, LAG, Alameda Womens Peace Camp.

Dana F. Smith--album cover art
Quill--magazine cover art

Typesettings:
Rikki Sender

Distributing:
Tabb Rex, USA
John Loder, Europe

Dedication:
for: Karen Silkwood, Vancouver Five, Helen Caldicott, Noam Chomsky, Daniel Ellsberg, all the people everywhere standing up and speaking out against nuclear power, nuclear weapons, and nuclear war, for Jenny Jo, Rosie and Jesse . . .and all the children.

Special Thanx
Kent Jolly, Christy Robb, Alan Thompson and all the RAR crew, Tim Y., Jeff B., Ruth S., MRR, Tabb Rex Enterprises, Andreas Seguro, Nina Serrano, Paris Williams, Ron Glass, James Lewis, George Sams, squatters from all over the world, Hilary, Georgiana, Carmen Cumba and all at Rainbow General and Grocery Store, S.F., Big Jim, Kevin Olish, the Small Free Inn Commune, and to our parents, families and friends for love, understanding, inspiration and support.

R RADICAL RECORDS—2440 16th St. (103)—S.F. Ca. 94103—USA

Figure 0.1: International punk band track list on Various (1984). *P.E.A.C.E/War.* R. Radical Records.

by Kalvin Piper and Digby Pearson's Earache Records (later splitting into Piper's In Your Face Records and Pearson's Earache Records). From the mid-1980s, a clear international network was developed aided by the international-facing *Maximumrocknroll* fanzine, with its inclusion of global scene reports documenting and publicizing the international punk communities' activities beyond the hegemony of the United States and United Kingdom.

Such connections were also publicised on a number of compilation records. Three key examples are the vitally important *P.E.A.C.E* compilation (Radical Records 1984). The latter double LP compilation, with international distribution, was an iconic introduction to the international punk networks. The *Maximumrocknroll* compilation *Welcome to 1984* (Maximumrocknroll Records 1984) and *Cleanse the Bacteria* (Pusmort Records 1985), in addition to the *Putrid Evil* and *Anglican Scrape Attic* international 7" flexi disc compilations (Earache Records 1985), were accessible testimonies to the international global connections of hardcore punk bands in the 1980s. Finally, *The North Atlantic Noise Attack* compilation (Manic Ears Records 1989) demonstrated the development and increasing hybridity of international punk scenes (see Figures 0.1–0.4 for the track lists detailing the international scope of these records). Previous examples of do-it-yourself compilations documenting the collaboration of scenes largely featured bands within a strict geographic location, for example the Crass Records *Bullshit Detector* compilation records (1980, 1982, and 1984) and the numerous American hardcore compilations that documented the national scene networks (see Gordon 2016b and Blush 2010 for accounts of the impact and legacy of these networks and compilations).[3] One of the consequences of these international compilations and associate musical collaborations was the addresses supplied in the reader notes, allowing bands and scene participants to forge new international connections and enhance new avenues and touring destinations for bands and friendships. Thirdly, these connections ensured that bands would begin to move beyond their national boundaries and tour. In pre-Internet days, tape and record trading and call-box phone conversations allowed a number of UK and European bands to set up tours for each other. During the late 1980s and 1990s, many bands forged new touring networks across Germany, Netherlands, Scandinavia, Japan, and the United States. The most notable UK bands pioneering these networks were Antisect, Amebix, Heresy, Disorder, Concrete Sox, Generic, Doom, Napalm Death, Chaos UK and the Varukers, with reciprocal gigs and tours set up for Toxic Reasons, Bad Brains, DRI, Government Issue, and Fugazi (United States); Larm and BGK (Netherlands); SOB and Gauze (Japan); Negazione, Wretched, and CCM (Italy); and Anti Cimex and Agoni (Sweden).[4] Admittedly this is only one aspect of the punk scene framed through Gordon's memories of the time, and thus only partial in scope. There are obviously numerous global examples of more established touring networks above and beyond the anarcho, early crust, and UK European punk scenes.

It is also important to highlight – and Paula Guerra's (2013; 2014; 2015) work has helped to understand this – the role and position of punk in today's society as a result of this inflated context of globalization. The first answer tells us that punk is a musical form (Guerra and Silva 2015), but also an aesthetic, cultural, political, and symbolic form. Punk is a hyper word. Punk is holistic, hybrid, opportunistic, and Dadaist, and holds a very particular

---

3 There are numerous geographical LP compilations from Scandinavia, Japan, Australia, Germany and the United States. All serve as testimonies to the growing international punk scenes of the 1980s.

4 For a biographical insight see Gordon's account of the 1986 Anti Cimex tour in the US fanzine *Negative Insight* issue 4 (2017).

symbolism in contemporary Western culture. Two key characteristics contributed to this relevance. First, punk was an innovation in a period in which the rock of the 1960s and 70s was in a process of institutionalization, incorporated by the great record industry and accepted by several instances of cultural legitimization. Punk was exactly defined as dissent from this logic of co-optation, prefiguring the underground and extending to the street and to clothing, fashion, design, and illustration. Second, punk describes itself as the music that anyone can do. In this sense, the process of performing punk is available to everyone, and anyone can do the lyrics, instruments, recordings, concerts, distribution, clothes, record covers, cassettes, and fanzines. Punk is 'do it yourself' (Guerra and Bennett 2015).

But punk is also a cultural movement. Since the end of the Cold War, punk has been part of the successive generations of young people who live and interpret the great historical processes of mass schooling, the development of mass production and consumption, and the emergence of the mass media and cultural industries. At the same time, we underline the functions of marketing, publicity and fashion, the Welfare State, the political-military polarization, and the antagonistic ideologies. Finally, we highlight the Western challenges modelled by decolonization, anti-imperialism, and the Cold War (Guerra and Bennett 2015). Punk, along with the broader DIY underground, came to define itself as a form and an aesthetic movement. The difference that punk brought is based in a set of lines drawn: its positioning on the fringe or underground of what is perceived to be the institutionalized system, even when punk became its own sphere of influence through its economic, political, social, and musical extensions; its constant defiance of that order, built on a systematic questioning and deconstruction of its core tenets, however naturalized those might have become; and the search for personal coherence, for the articulation of what one says with what one is and what one wears, and, especially, with the ways in which one lives music.

Punk is a scene, or several scenes or sub-scenes. It is a network of connection between different protagonists: bands, publishers, promoters, critics, disseminators, consumers, fans. In addition, we highlight other resources such as records and other recordings, concerts and other events, bars, cellars, rooms, and other exhibition and meeting spaces, newspapers, fanzines, clothing stores, accessories, discos, and the streets, along with physical and digital platforms. This structure has spatiality and a territoriality. It is embedded in a social (physical or, more recently, virtual) environment that it recreates and uses as a constitutive dimension, enhancing economies of agglomeration and scale (Guerra and Silva 2015). Yet, what is important to note from the discussion thus far are the select examples cited of the formation of international touring and 'Networks of Friends' (Heresy 1987) that have continued and expanded to this day. There are now thousands of music compilations, label collaborations, festivals, venues, and touring routes, record and fanzine distributor mail order sites, and record shops all tied into the various seams of a global punk network. The advent of the Internet and social networking sites destabilised the hegemony of Western notions of a 'punk centre.' More is said on this below, though presently we note that reciprocal band touring and musical collaborations have now spread into China, Japan, Indonesia, Scandinavia, Russia, Latin America, East and South Europe, and the Balkans. The globalised free market competition offering cheap flights and the drop of prices in both producing records and procuring and borrowing backline, in addition to the hypermobility of communications via email and social networking messaging services, has accelerated and facilitated international punk network collaborative activities.

There are three important things to say about the general motifs of theorizing global and local punk. The general issues of cultural transmission loom large across all the chapters in the present reader. Firstly, the international connections from the local to the global have been previously discussed in the work of Hannerz (1996), who raised important issues regarding how and in what ways key subcultures traverse international communication boundaries. Such debates follow classic cultural and media sociological debates and theoretical approaches to global communication such as Tomlinson (1991), who critiqued notions of cultural imperialism as a one way process, arguing that Western capitalist ideological messages were uncritically accepted and adopted by host countries. The broad argument is concerned with how dominant Western ideologies were not accepted in blanket terms by host cultures and were instead negotiated, resisted, and assimilated in complex ways that reflected their indigenous norms, values, and cultural practices. Tomlinson rightly noted that arguments of linear ideological and cultural transmission are essentially patronizing, treating host cultures as passive cultural recipients of Western messages and victims of Western ideological control. With dominant narratives of the formation of punk arising from the United States and United Kingdom, such arguments are easily mapped onto the case studies within the chapters in this book. Indeed it is easy to suggest that punk media was imported and traded by the fledgling punk friendship networks and record companies into host countries, and the youth simply danced to the tune of the ideological messages regardless of the pre-existing cultural structures.

What is evident in the following chapters is that such claims are weak. One of the clear narratives linking the chapters is the notion of mimesis. This term claims that recipients of punk merely mimic the original Western punk model. Such claims are clearly naïve and reductionist and have more in common with what Canclini (2001) described as 'hybrid cultures.' Such descriptors open the discussion up to how and in what ways punk culture has been assimilated into host countries yet clearly reflects their cultural, linguistic, social, and aesthetic practices. More importantly, this model has clear explanatory value for explaining how and in what ways new punk styles developed in Japan, Scandinavia, Latin America, etc. in turn influence and shape contemporary Western punk cultures. In short, cultural transmission is certainly not a one-way core of the peripheral process of punk cultural transmission. For example, if we take the current genre of raw punk, the influence of early 1980s bands Discharge from Stoke-on-Trent and Disorder from Bristol in addition to a host of Scandinavian bands (influenced by

Discharge's tours in those countries in the early 1980s) can be noted in that such bands had their records licensed in Japan via VAP records. This influence in Japan, with anti-nuclear sentiments and antagonism to mainstream culture, influenced Japanese punk bands such as Disclose (1991–2007), who took the extreme musical style of Discharge to new sonic levels. In contrast, over the last ten years this style has been assimilated into and influenced a number of bands who have more in common with Disclose than Discharge, yet retain traces of their lyrics and aesthetics. Examples of the latter are the following bands: Aspects of War (Boston, US), Besthoven (Brazil), Go Filth Go (Greece), Liberty, Crisis and Democracy (Portugal), Electric Funeral, Paranoid, (Sweden), and Skitvarld (UK). Indeed, this example of hybrid style conflation is just one subset of influences arising out of the Japanese inflection and interpretation of the Discharge sound, and serves as a clear example of how and in what ways punk culture is always a historical hybrid culture already.

Secondly, the above examples of early cross-cultural music compilations demonstrate these punk connections, yet we must not lose sight of the common links that group punk culture together in spite of the plethora of styles, aesthetic differences, language barriers, and scenes. The recent work of O'Connor (2009), following Bourdieu's landmark sociology (1995) and some chapters in this volume, reflects the term 'field.' This approach usefully describes the total range of global punk scenes, their respective participants, histories, cultural practices, cultural productions, ethical, and political conduct, global or otherwise. The model of 'field' offers new and instructive ways for new and existing scholars to circumnavigate Western dominant assumptions of culture yet equally contemplate notions of relative cultural issues of similarity, authenticity, and difference (Guerra 2015; Haenfler 2004). Indeed, any cultural practice remotely resembling punk practice is already part of this taxonomy. Equally, such an approach dispenses with patronizing assumptions that original Western punk models have been inauthentically 'copied' by their respective 'hosts' (Duncombe and Tremblay 2011) previously noted as mimesis.

Thirdly, such proclamations of an 'authentic/original' form serve to assert a hegemonic cultural dominance whilst equally eclipsing and homogenizing other global punk scenes. Indeed, the work of the late Edward Said (1978; 1994) is most instructive and useful in this respect, noting how Western modes of explaining oriental and cultures of 'the Other' both distort and misrepresent non-Western culture. Here it is important to note who is speaking of the punk cultures described in the following reader. These are research transmissions yet they are equally reflective of the previous subcultural models pioneered by the corpus of writing comprising the CCCS of the 1970s and 1980s and post-subcultural work of the 1990s and early 2000s. The latter models are inescapably Western, embodying Western theoretical discourses. Hence, while the notion of linear cultural transmissions of punk can be problematized, the Achilles heel of the following discussions is that many of the Western theoretical models inadvertently retain the hegemony of Western modes of understanding subcultures. Here lies the poverty of the following accounts. While the application of CCCS and post-subcultural accounts by researchers regarding 'other' punk cultures works in principal, the original over-determinism and pitfalls of these models are hence reproduced. For example, when using theoretical models such as Hebdige (1979) the tropes presented in that model are also reproduced. Punk cultures are represented as void of internal squabbles and differences regarding age, gender, aesthetics, and authenticity, reproduced as uniform blocs appearing out of thin air (Gordon 2014). Equally, while deploying post-subcultural models of ethnographic inquiry (Thornton 1995; Muggleton 2000), problems with the latter theoretical methods are inadvertently imported into the explanatory account as contained in this reader. In many ways, such pitfalls are unavoidable and stand as testimony to the power and influence of those original approaches to studying subcultures and, in our case, punk culture. Yet, such accounts still retain implicit theoretical power relations that echo Said's (1978; 1994) notion of the hegemony of Western theoretical explanatory accounts. In short, there is a hegemony of Western theory holding sway over accounts of global punk culture. There is no immediate solution save calling for current punk researchers to generate new explanatory theoretical models arising out of the data collected.

The central task of this work, therefore, is to explore the emergence of punk rock in both a contemporary and global sense. Drawing upon the rich diversity of the global, this volume will examine punk rock in settings such as Iran, China, Holland, Spain, Portugal, Brazil, and Canada. More specifically, it will adopt an essentially analytical perspective so as to raise questions over the origins of those scenes and subsequently over their form, structure, and cultural significance. There are obvious notable omissions from the present volume: Japan, Scandinavia, Russia, Australia, Africa and India. These absences will certainly be addressed in future volumes of this work. Presently, we hope the following research transmissions, read in tandem with this introduction, inspire a new creative wave of punk research, one where new, generalizable explanatory theories are germinated from such ventures. The editors' own profile and their journey reflect this: on the one hand, we have the Punk Scholars Network participation, based in the United Kingdom, carrying a reflective project in the face of punk and its pedagogy; on the other, we have the KISMIF project based in Portugal and founded around the approach of the Portuguese punk manifestations that emerged in 2012. We believe in the cross fertilization of perspectives, approaches, and data in a heuristic necessary balance between the local and the global, the periphery and hegemony, and cultural dissidence. Alastair Gordon's 'Sell-Out Bastards! Case-Study Accounts of the Dilemmas of Authenticity in UK/US Punk 1984–2001 and Beyond' begins the present volume. Here, the author explores the intricate debates of authenticity and DIY in UK and US punk scenes, a hotly debated topic since punk's inception. Complex debates surrounding notions of 'selling out' (in particular, signing to large record companies) as the opposite of the authenticity inherent within DIY practice have been inherent in the practice of punk, and Gordon cites the signing of the anarcho-punk band Chumbawamba as a key moment in punk wrestling with the authentic and the commercial. Gordon's chapter is useful in that it contextualizes a key practice that is core to the identity of punk in the twenty-first century. It draws upon many key areas that are covered in this book, including the importance of DIY practice, the debates around authenticity, and the links between the beginnings of punk and the present day.

Gordon's chapter is followed by Kirsty Lohman's outline of Dutch punk and, in particular, the Groningen scene. Lohman looks at the links between geographic periphery, local identity, and what she believes as the connection of bands 'beyond' this particular scene. Lohman's chapter illuminates the apparent dichotomy between the fluidity of Dutch punks and the relative locality of the Groningen scene, meaning that, although local, it is also one of mobility and global connectivity. Indeed, these debates continue in Augusto Santos Silva and Paula Guerra's chapter 'The Global and Local in Music Scenes: The Multiple Anchoring of Portuguese Punk.' Here, geography is interrogated. Questions are raised about local and international, looking at the importance of the complex relationship between local scenes – and indeed, in this case, what the authors identify as sub-scenes – and the simultaneity of local, translocal, and international. What is the geography of punk? How do we articulate the global scene of punk with its various local manifestations? Is it a real transnational movement? Or are there as many punk scenes as the national figurations it can take? This chapter addresses these issues by considering the Portuguese punk scene. The analysis is based on (1) 70 interviews with punk protagonists, (2) a database of bands, records and songs, and (3) a database of fanzines. First, the authors take account of the balance between the international influences in the Portuguese scene and their specific characteristics. Then, the meaning of global is redefined, taking into account the new information and/or communication technologies. Likewise, the local nature of the Portuguese punk scene is rebalanced through sub-scenes identified and established in different places within the country, pointing to the general feelings the punk activists express with respect to Portuguese society. Finally, Silva and Guerra explore the dialectic between the global dimension of punk culture and the sense of community that inspires its members, concluding that the multiple anchorage of punk – simultaneously national and international, local and global, macro and micro – is particularly linked to its ability to survive and spread.

Tommaso Gravante and Alice Poma's chapter '"Crack in the System": A Bottom-up Analysis of the Anarcho-Punk Movement in Mexico' explores the changing environment of the Mexican anarcho-punk scene (1984–2014). Using Guadalajara and Mexico City as their backdrop, the authors draw upon the experiences of those who were involved in the scene, exploring how anarcho-punk in Mexico has appropriated and re-elaborated the anarcho-punk identity of the United Kingdom. To further facilitate this research, Gravante and Poma look at how anarcho-collectives have responded to the political, drawing upon the experiences of the Zapatista movement, vegetarianism, and grassroots organizations. As a useful counterpart, this is followed by Paula Guerra and Débora Gomes dos Santos' contribution looking at the importance of scene and the localization in the context of the São Paulo subway system. Although concentrating on the years between 1975 and 1985, the importance of this chapter lies in the illustrating of urbanization on the formation of punk and other subcultures. Here, the authors look to lyrical content as a means of understanding and unpicking the beliefs, ideologies, and specific practices that are part of punk's spatial relationship with space and place. In other words, how a narrative of the everyday through movement (in this case the subway) has an effect on the transience, fragmentation, and mobility in the emergence of this punk scene.

Space remains central to Carles Feixa and Paula Guerra's chapter on youth culture in Spain since the 1960s. Feixa and Guerra begin this outline with the *golfos* and *jipis*, moving onto the transition of democracy and the emergence of *punkis* and *progress*. This overview continues into the post-transitional period with the *pijos* and *makineros* the 1990s (*okupas* and *pelaos*), the beginning of the twenty-first century (*fiesteros* and *alternativos*), the *Latin kings* and *ñetas* (2005–10), and finally the *ninis* and *indignados* in the present. What is useful here is the contextualization of punk within subcultures *per se*; the blurring of boundaries with hackers, skinheads, and what the authors call 'urban tribes.' It is a debate that continues with Edward Avery-Natale's chapter 'Narratives of Transition Within a Subculture: A Case Study of Nomadic Punks,' which looks at notions of identity and the fluidity of 'traveller' punk as a means of situating individuals within a larger punk and/ or anarchist identity. In particular, Avery-Natale raises the question of how one maintains identity and its corresponding label ('punk' or 'anarcho-punk') whilst moving away from particular behavioural traits that are related to the still-existing identity.

Benjamin van Loon's chapter 'Powerviolence, or How to Play Punk with a Hammer' looks specifically at the sub-genre of 'Powerviolence.' Drawing upon bands such as Man is the Bastard, Infest, and Iron Lung, the author first examines its musical and social beginnings, moving onto the global impact of the scene through bands such as Yacøpsæ, Fuck on the Beach, and Merda. Van Loon's chapter is followed by Brian Fauteux's documentation of the punk scene in Vancouver, Canada. Pulling upon notions of the city – urban renewal, municipal restrictions, and concerns around noise pollution from venues – the author looks at ways in which bands and participants have made use of 'tactical spaces' such as warehouses, basements, and parking garages. By exploring the creative output, in particular the *Emergency Room Vol. 1* compilation album, Fauteux argues that the city's weird punk scene formed in response to and has effectively challenged restrictive municipal policies that favour middle-to-upper class residential and commercial development.

'"We Just make Music": Deconstructing Notions of Authenticity in the Iranian Underground' by Theresa Steward follows. Starting from the 1979 Iranian revolution, where the decline and temporary fall of the established music industry gave way to the beginnings of a new underground DIY culture, Steward notes how the scene drew upon the influence of the West – in particular tape distribution, underground gigs, and graffiti – as a means to flourish. As is covered elsewhere in the book, Steward looks at the ways in which punk has been transformed in an specifically Iranian context, raising questions of the ways in which punk in Iran has been shaped by both the local and the global. Steward continues her analysis of the post-2000 scene, looking at ways in which the Iranian underground is often perceived as negative by both Western media and Iranian youth. Indeed, DIY practice is key to Sean Martin-Iverson's chapter on punk in Indonesia. Here, Martin-Iverson argues that the DIY scene of the small city of Bandung acts according to what he notes are anti-capitalist principles, instead expressing and realizing alternative ways of organizing cultural production and social life. What Martin-Iverson notes as 'radical social creativity' echoes what many other chapters within this current work are saying, and defines the values of DIY punk in a succinct manner.

This is also captured in the work of Marco Ferrarese and his chapter on anarcho-punk in Malaysia. Ferrarese's chapter highlights the complex relationship between the local and the global. For Ferrarese, the increasing fostering of the external means is hindering the self-reflective development of Malaysian punks who prefer to seek outside influences rather than develop their own sense of scene. As a case study, Ferrarese looks at Kuala Lumpur's punk house *Rumah Api* and the fanzine *Shock and Awe*. As a conclusion, Jian Xiao's chapter explores the complexities of punk and China. In particular, Xiao uses the notions of space and place to uncover dress, performance, political aspirations, and interactions in the scene. Although she finds that Chinese punk musicians are often constrained within their practices, Xiao highlights the importing of Western punk culture as a means of expressing anti-government feelings and dissatisfaction. The chapter also explores the relevance of sub-groups and genres in this complex scene.

In conclusion, the purpose of this book is to present the first collection of academic studies on the contemporary (post-2000) global punk scene. As a means of contextualization and meaning, some chapters point back to the origins and the roots of punk. As Gordon (2016b) suggests, placing end points in punk culture presents a number of problems. One, it disrupts historical continuity, two it privileges the original protagonists of punk in hierarchical terms, and three it offers a nostalgic view of punk that undermines the originality and authenticity of contemporary punk scenes and networks (Silva and Guerra 2015). The editors are also aware of the selectivity of the global and thus the need for further editions to include those countries not discussed here (Tomlinson 2004). Punk is not perfect and neither is this book. Instead, it is concerned more with immediacy and international scope, which raise clear issues regarding translation and the importation, understanding, and application of theoretical models and ideas.

In conclusion, our approach demonstrates the timeliness of punk as a set of diverse but confluent values and appropriations, contradicting Hebdige's early approaches to a subcultural logic defined in a very narrow sense (Hebdige 1979). While we're on the subject it is important to mention that Hebdige himself admits that things today would perhaps have to be done differently, and would probably 'give out many of the structural oppositions around which the book is organized: authentic versus commercial culture, street versus market, resistance vs. incorporation, fact (event) versus media representation, etc.' (2012, 409), advocating the need to challenge 'the rigidity of the binary structures of the main arguments.' Hebdige's balance highlights the purpose of this book, showing the influence of time and context in approaching youth cultures with a focus on punk.

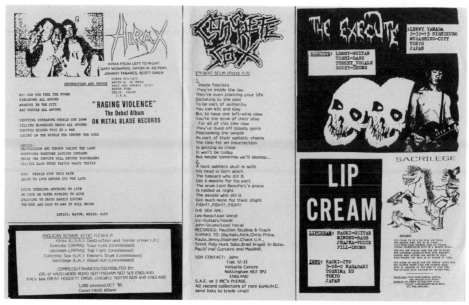

Figure 0.2: Flexidisc UK/Japan compilation insert taken from Various (1985), *Anglican Scrape Attic*, Nottingham: Not on label.

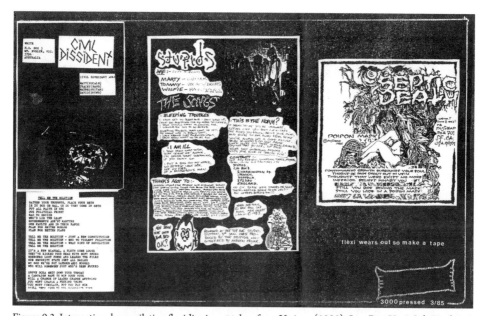

Figure 0.3: International compilation flexidisc insert taken from Various (1985), *Live Dirt Up A Side Track Is A Putrid Evil*, Nottingham: Not on label.

Figure 0.4 (opposite): International band names and addresses from, Various (1985), *Cleanse the Bacteria*, Pusmort Records.

WRITE! PLEASE INCLUDE I.R.C. OR STAMPS!

C.O.C.
c/o Reed Mullin
118 Hawthorne
Raliegh, N.C.
U.S.A. 27605

THE EXECUTE
c/o Lemmy Yamada
2-32-15 Nishikubo
Musashino City
Tokyo Japan

HOLY DOLLS
Box 51
Tampere 21
Finland

INSTIGATORS
5, St. Michael's Close
Thornhill, Dewsbury
W.Yorks WF12 0JU
England

EXTREM
c/o Peter Zinner
Quadenstr. 65-67/17/14
1220 Wien
Austria

CRUDE SS
c/o Peter Ahlqvist
Floravagen 20 c
773 00 Fagersta
Sweden

7 SECONDS
c/o Kevin Seconds
1790 Silverada Bl. #237
Reno, Nevada
U.S.A. 89502

CIVIL DISSIDENT
c/o Tracey
p.o. box 3
Mt. Evelyn Victoria
Australia 3796

INFERYO
c/o Bernard Hlava
L.Ottler st. No. 13 c
8900 Augsburg
W. Germany

ENOLA GAY
c/o Brian Hansen
Banehegnet 14st. T.H.
2620 Albertslund
Denmark

SEPTIC DEATH
c/o Pushead
p.o. box 701
San Francisco, Ca,
U.S.A. 94101

SIEGE
c/o Kurt Habeit
30 Stoney Brook Ln.
Weymouth, Mass.
U.S.A. 02188

ZYKLOME A
c/o VZW Punk etc.
Mottestr. 12
1870 Wolverton
Belgium

AKUTT INNLEGGELSE
c/o Thomas Seltzer
Dalbovei 12
1458 Fjellstrand
Norway

MOB 47
c/o Ake Henriksson
Grindtorpsvagen 31 I
183 32 Taby
Sweden

POISON IDEA
c/o Tom Roberts
1515 S.E. 44th
Portland, Oregon
U.S.A. 97215

GENOCIDE EXPRESS
c/o Tos N.
p.o. box 14570
1001 LB Amsterdam
Holland Netherlands

CREATED & PRODUCED... PUSHEAD
ENGINEERED & MIXED @ PETER MILLER STUDIOS
MASTERED & SPECIAL HELP   JOHN LODER

References

Blush, S. (2010). *American Hardcore: A Tribal History*. Port Townsend, WA: Feral House.

Bourdieu, P. (1995). *Rules of Art: Genesis and Structure of the Literary Field*. Stanford, CA: Stanford University Press.

Canclini, N. G. (2001 [1995]). *Culturas híbridas [Hybrid Cultures]*. Buenos Aires: Paidós.

Crane, D. (2002). 'Culture and Globalization: Theoretical Models and Emerging Trends.' In D. Crane, K. Kawasaki, and K. Kawashima (eds.), *Global Culture: Media, Arts, Policy, and Globalization*, 1–25. New York: Routledge.

Duncombe, S. and J. Tremblay (eds.). (2011). *White Riot: Punk Rock and the Politics of Race*. London: Verso.

Featherstone, M. (1995). *Undoing Culture: Globalization, Postmodernism and Identity*. London: Sage.

Giddens, A. (1990). *The Consequences of Modernity*. Stanford: Stanford University Press.

Giddens, A. (1991). *Modernity and Self-identity: Self and Society in the Late Modern Age*. Stanford, CA: Stanford University Press.

Gilroy, P. (1993a). *Small Acts: Thoughts on the Politics of Black Cultures*. London: Serpents Tail.

Gilroy, P. (1993b). *The Black Atlantic: Modernity and Double Consciousness*. London: Verso.

Glasper, I. (2009). *Trapped in a Scene: UK Hardcore 1985–1989*. London: Cherry Red.

Gordon, A. (2005). *The Authentic Punk: An Ethnography of DiY Music Ethics*. Unpublished PhD thesis. Loughborough University. Department of Social Sciences.

Gordon, A. (2014). 'Distinctions of Authenticity and the Everyday Punk Self.' *Punk and Post Punk* 3 (2). Doi: 10.1386/punk.3.3.183_1.

Gordon, A. (2016a). 'They Can Stuff Their Punk Credentials 'Cause It's Them That Take The Cash': 1980s Anarcho-Punk: Ethical Difference and Division.' In M. Dines and M. Worley (eds.), *The Aesthetic of Our Anger: Anarcho Punk, Politics and Music*, 227–50. Brighton: Autonomedia.

Gordon, A. (2016b [1996]). *Crass Reflections*. Portsmouth: Itchy Monkey Press.

Guerra, P. (2010). 'A instável leveza do rock: Génese, dinâmica e consolidação do rock avouredve em Portugal (1980–2010)' ['The Unstable Lightness of Rock: Genesis, Dynamics and Consolidation of Alternative Rock in Portugal (1980–2010)']. Unpublished PhD thesis. Faculdade de Letras da Universidade do Porto, Porto.

Guerra, P. (2013). 'Punk, ação e contradição em Portugal: Uma aproximação às culturas juvenis contemporâneas' ['Punk, Action and Contradiction in Portugal: An Approach to Contemporary Youth Cultures']. *Revista Crítica de Ciências Sociais* 102/103: 111–34.

Guerra, P. (2014). 'Punk, Expectations, Breaches and Metamorphoses: Portugal, 1977–2012.' *Critical Arts* 28 (1): 111–22.

Guerra, P. (2015). 'Keep it Rocking: the Social Space of Portuguese Alternative Rock (1980–2010).' *Journal of Sociology*. Doi:10.1177/1440783315569557.

Guerra, P. and A. Bennett. (2015). 'Never Mind the Pistols? The Legacy and Authenticity of the Sex Pistols in Portugal.' *Popular Music and Society* 38 (4): 500–21.

Guerra, P. and P. Quintela. (2016). 'From Coimbra to London: To Live the Punk Dream and "Meet My Tribe".' In J. Sardinha and R. Campos (eds.), *Transglobal Sounds: Music, Youth and Migration*. New York/London: Bloomsbury.

Guerra, P. and A. S. Silva. (2015). 'Music and More than Music: The Approach to Difference and Identity in the Portuguese Punk.' *European Journal of Cultural Studies* 18 (2): 207–23. Doi: 10.1177/1367549414563294.

Haenfler, R. (2004). 'Rethinking Subcultural Resistance: Core Values of the Straight Edge Movement.' *Journal of Contemporary Ethnography* 33 (4): 406–36.

Hall, S. (ed.) (2003). *Representations: Cultural Representations and Signifying Practices*. London: Sage.

Hall, S. and P. Du Gay (eds.). (1996). *Questions of Cultural Identity*. London/Thousand Oaks: Sage.

Hall, S. and T. Jefferson. (1993). *Resistance through Rituals: Youth Subcultures in Post-war Britain*. London: Routledge.

Hannerz, U. (1996). *Transnational Connections: Culture, People, Places*. London: Routledge.

Hebdige, D. (1979). *Subculture: The Meaning of Style*. London: Methuen.

Hebdige, D. (2012). 'Contemporizing "Subculture": 30 Years to Life.' *European Journal of Cultural Studies* 15 (3): 399–424.

Heresy (1987). *Thanks!* (Vinyl, EP). Germany: Limited Edition Records.

Heresy (1987). *Face Up To It* (Vinyl, LP). Nottingham: In Your Face Records.

Huq, R. (2003). 'Global Youth Cultures in Localized Spaces: The Case of the UK New Asian Dance Music and French Rap.' In D. Muggleton and R. Weinzierl (eds.), *The Post-subcultures Reader*, 195–208. Oxford: Berg.

Huq, R. (2006). *Beyond Subculture: Pop, Youth, and Identity in a Postcolonial World*. London: Routledge.

Lash, S. and J. Urry. (1999). 'Accumulating Signs: The Culture Industries.' In S. Lash and J. Urry (eds.), *Economies of Signs and Space*, 111–44. London: Sage.

Muggleton, D. (2000). *Inside Subculture: The Postmodern Meaning of Style*. Oxford: Berg.

Negative Insight (2017) #4

O'Connor, A. (2002a). *Who's Emma?: Autonomous Zone and Social Anarchism*. Toronto: Confused Editions.

O'Connor, A. (2002b). 'Local Scenes and Dangerous Crossroads: Punk and Theories of Cultural Hybridity.' *Popular Music* 21 (2): 225–37.

O'Connor, A. (2003). 'Anarcho-punk: Local Scenes and International Networks.' *Anarchist Studies* 11 (2): 111–21.

O'Connor, A. (2008). *Punk Record Labels and the Struggle for Autonomy: The Emergence of DIY*. Lanham: Lexington Books.

O'Connor (2009).

Rollins, H. (1994). *Get in the Van: On the Road with Black Flag*. Los Angeles: 2.13.61.

Said, E. (1978). *Orientalism*. London: Penguin.

Said, E. (1994). *Culture and Imperialism*. London: Vintage Books.

Silva, A. S. and P. Guerra. (2015). *As palavras do punk* [*The Words of Punk*]. Lisbon: Alêtheia.

Thornton, S. (1995). *Club Cultures: Music, Media and Subcultural Capital*. London: Polity.

Tomlinson, J. (1991). *Cultural Imperialism: A Critical Introduction*. London: Pinter Publishers.

Tomlinson, J. (2004). 'Global Culture, Deterritorialization and the Cosmopolitanism of Youth Culture.' In G. Titley (ed.), *Resituating Culture*, 21–9. Strasbourg: Council of Europe.

Albums

Crucifix (1983). *Dehumanisation* (Vinyl LP). UK: Corpus Christi Records.

Various (1980). *Bullshit Detector* (Vinyl LP). London: Crass Records.

Various (1982). *Bullshit Detector Two* (Vinyl LP). London: Crass Records.

Various (1984). *Bullshit Detector Three* (Vinyl, LP). London: Crass Records.

Various (1984). *P.E.A.C.E/War* (Vinyl LP). R. Radical Records.

Various (1984). *Welcome to 1984* (Vinyl LP). San Francisco: Maximumrocknroll Records.

Various (1985). *Anglican Scrape Attic* (Flexi disc). Nottingham: Earache Records.

Various (1985). *Cleanse the Bacteria* (Vinyl LP). San Francisco: Pusmort Records.

Various (1985). *Putrid Evil* (Flexi disc). Nottingham: Earache Records.

Various (1989). *The North Atlantic Noise Attack* (Vinyl LP). Bristol: Manic Ears Records.

Various (2008). *Emergency Room Vol.1* (Vinyl LP). Canada: Nominal Records.

1. SELL-OUT BASTARDS! CASE-STUDY ACCOUNTS OF THE DILEMMAS OF AUTHENTICITY IN UK/US PUNK 1984–2001 AND BEYOND

ALASTAIR 'GORDS' GORDON

Abstract

This chapter critically reflects and reframes Hebdige's (1979) notion of subcultural commodification onto the terrain of punk bands engaging with major labels. It maps the critical intersections of punk dilemmas of authenticity in the UK and US punk scenes from 1984–2001. Drawing from ethnographic field data with key members of New Model Army, Chumbawamba and participants in Bradford's 1in12 anarchist club/venue, the central argument is mapping the fraught borders of the ethical transgression of perceived selling-out. The principal discussion revolves around punk bands signing to major labels and the subsequent backlash from self-described authentic scene members. The chapter concludes that the enduring issue in punk culture is one that cannot be realistically resolved and continues to fuel tense discussion beyond the historical timeframe discussed.

Keywords: Subculture, Postsubculture, Punk, Ethnography, Anarchism, DIY, Authenticity

This chapter is dedicated to the memories of Robert Heaton and Martin 'Protag' Neish.

Alastair 'Gords' Gordon is Senior Lecturer in Media and Communications at Leicester De Montfort University. His current research is based around genre authenticity and hierarchy across international networks of DIY punk with specific focus on Japan and Europe. He researches and teaches modules on media and communication studies, youth subcultures, and paranormal media. In 2012, Gords co-founded the Punk Scholars Network with Mike Dines and records and tours internationally with his band, Endless Grinning Skulls. Gords hates Tories and neoliberals, and collects old Barry Manilow autographs. E-mail: agordon@dmu.ac.uk

SELL-OUT BASTARDS! CASE-STUDY ACCOUNTS OF THE DILEMMAS OF AUTHENTICITY IN UK/US PUNK 1984–2001 AND BEYOND

> HMV, in their moral righteousness, refuse to sell records which contain four letter words as they are regarded as obscene and in bad taste. Yet Thorn-EMI, their parent company, manufacture and export weapons of war and instruments of torture worldwide. Does that cause a public outcry? Does it fuck! (Chumbawamba, *Revolution*, 1985)

The principle aim of this chapter is to examine the role of the dilemma in punk. The interview data is admittedly dated, yet the role of endless discussions of authenticity in punk is certainly not. Indeed, such discussion transcends national boundaries and an endemic discursive feature of international punk practice. The concluding section of this chapter examines anecdotal examples of how such endless punk debates continue.

In 1979 Dick Hebdige offered a detailed, theory-preoccupied hermeneutic account of UK punk, one of the fledgling works in the earlier literature of punk rock. For Hebdige, the control of the punk subculture was enacted in two specific ways. Firstly, in a similar vein to Cohen's (1980) work on moral panics, punk was controlled through denigration in the mass media (the ideological form) or through buying it out (the commodity form) in an Adornoesque manner so to manage, control, and negate subversive qualities (1979, 92–9). From Hebdige's point of view, it appears all too easy to negate a subculture. This portrays subculturalists as willing participants in their own fate.

The present chapter will advance this position by asserting that DIY punk constitutes itself in opposition both to ideological and commodity forms while retaining clear examples of *wilful* subcultural transgression of this perceived ethical rule. As I shall discuss at length, the reaction and response from those who claimed in the 1980s to 2001 to be authentic players within the UK DIY punk have been ones of self-exclusion from the culture industry (Adorno and Horkheimer 1995); the identity of DIY underground punk is centrally constituted through such righteous abstinence. In short, there is a deep-seated commitment to remain authentic in both the underground and also from the platform of a major record label. These two groups mutually antagonize and support each other.

While Hebdige's account was groundbreaking it was equally reductionist, following the general CCCS narrative of subcultures as unified blocs, sealing off internal argument and division beyond the term 'poseur.' This forgivable early oversight was the catalyst for what follows. Within this chapter, the general longstanding debate of commodification and 'selling out' is problematized along the lines of subverting commodification from within to notions of musicians' willing complicity with such decisions. Countering this are examples of some of the disciplinary and supportive comments from within the UK scene. While the work of Hebdige is not afforded significant discussion below, his influence on what follows is, I hope, clear.

Disaffection and disapproval to a perceived other, cultural structure, social norm, and aesthetic practice are the weapons of the authentic punk. Such resistance creates a number of dilemmas. Chief among these is the drive to remain 'authentic' and not succumb to the temptations to 'sell-out.' While such antagonism clearly predated punk, it is central to its practice. Since the 1970s, well-trodden debates have raged around the Sex Pistols, the Clash, and other first-wave punk groups 'selling out' and so losing the cardinal value of authenticity. Such debates represent a complicated intersection of views and remain a constant source of subcultural tension. By dropping the Sex Pistols from their label in 1977, EMI inadvertently established a suspicious link between themselves and punk culture. This has now become a longstanding issue, with a spate of perceived sell-outs to EMI over the last twenty years.[5] This multinational company has a bad ethical track record. Zero (1994, 2) points out that:

> Thorn EMI was, and is, a major defense contractor; they manufactured components for such missile systems as the Pershing, Cruise and Trident; they supported the nuclear industry; and they would not divest from South Africa when there was a public outcry for companies to do so. One of the industries that EMI has connections to is the record industry – they own EMI Music, Virgin Records, Capitol, Chrysalis, etc. Recently, Virgin Records purchased Caroline, a record production and distribution company, effectively making this once independent company a part of a sprawling multinational.

Similarly, *Profane Existence* (1992) criticized EMI in 1992:

> EMI is typical of major labels with its links to the most evil parts of the capitalist system. Thorn EMI the parent company is a major investor and constructor of weapons systems, nuclear weapons, guidance systems, vivisection and security control equipment avoured by countries like Chile and South Africa. They are also major contributors to the Conservative Party.

Critical opposition to capitalist values and institutions is central to DIY, but there is an enduring tension between political activism in punk, which involves directly challenging such values and institutions, and cultural production in punk, which involves expressing opposition to such values through music and/or organizational practice. This tension leads to a dilemma between, on the one hand, utilizing capitalist products (guitars, drums, shops, studios) or becoming annexed to capitalist institutions (signing a recording contract, doing promotion) for the sake of a wider audience, and, on the other, rejecting these strategies in favour of localist cultural autonomy and a more purist sense of identity, practice, and solidarity. Both share the same end result, however: they leave the actual

5   See figures below for examples of the documents of selling-out in punk.

political and economic institutions of capitalism intact. This does not mean that each path as represented in the dilemma should be followed, and many honest, well-intentioned people have done both. But it does perhaps guard against inflated subcultural self-regard and what we might call punk hubris. In 2001 I conducted ethnographic field research as part of my Loughborough University-funded doctoral research. The principle research intention investigated how and in what ways punk authenticity was reciprocally constructed between the dual scenes in the Leeds and Bradford punk scenes. In all, forty semi-structured interviews of core, semi-peripheral, and marginal female/male scene members aged 18–44 were undertaken. The latter inquired how punk was initially encountered, what people do in their scenes; how they *may* exit such groupings, and, of particular relevance to the present chapter, how they encountered, navigated, and espoused longstanding dilemmatic debates of punk authenticity (Gordon 2005). Many of the 2001 fieldwork interviews and observations raised the issue of dilemmas, and they seem centrally contingent on what it is that DIY punk genuinely tries to achieve. DIY punk is a cry for a return to making music for its own sake, for its intrinsic pleasure and satisfaction, rather than for the sake of profit above and beyond any other value. It is equally about creating a sense of trust and concord between people rather than reducing the social relations of music to what is allowed or not allowed in the small print of the recording contract.

Since the whole issue of 'sell-out' was central to DIY punk and what it opposes, attaining the quality of a dilemma for so many of its practitioners, and affecting passages of subcultural entrance and exit as well as practice, it is appropriate to explore it in greater detail. My 2001 research *reflexively* reflected the scene my participants existed in and practiced – DIY punk. This is not to say that other versions of punk replete with competing views on punk authenticity do not exist. To say otherwise is absurd. Indeed, the existence of competing 'other' punk scenes is the fuel of the dilemma. They act as sounding boards from which to present one's own practice as authentic over and above the inauthentic and sell-out 'other.'

To clarify, DIY punk is the production of music by the artist and label with no links to a major label organization. Under the DIY rubric, the writing, recording, promotion, and distribution is done by the bands and labels themselves.[6] At the level of performance, shows, tours, and promotions are undertaken in this manner through international scene networks of likeminded people. In terms of the literature (reviews in fanzines), there are safeguards in place to ensure corporate music finds no mouthpiece there. For example, *Maximumrocknroll* stated in its review submission guidelines:

> We will not accept major label or related ads, or ads for comps and eps that include major label bands. (*MRR* 174, 1997)

---

6   Distribution is a further area of dilemma for the DIY label. Since the number of independent distribution companies collapsed in the early 1990s (Red Rhino, The Cartel, Revolver), major labels have sought to control distribution in the UK. Alternatives arose with Ph.D. and Shellshock. However, those dedicated to DIY in a strict sense view the distribution of records with the latter as selling-out. One of the most respected DIY distributors in the UK is Active (www.activedistribution.org).

And at the start of the reviews section:

> Don't send wimpy arty metal corporate rock shit here. Don't have your label give
> us follow up calls as to whether we received and are reviewing your record. Specific
> criticisms aside, it should be understood that any independent releases deserve credit
> for all the work and money that goes into it. (*MRR* 174, 1997)

Likewise, *HeartattaCk* stated:

> We will not review any record with a UPC or bar code or UPC bar code sticker on it,
> and we will not review any record that is financed by one of the so called independent
> giants as in Dutch East India, Caroline, Cargo. We are only interested in supporting the
> underground do-it-yourself scene, and it is our opinion that UPC codes along with
> 'press and distribute' (P&D) are not fitting with the do-it-yourself ethic of hardcore.
> (*HeartattaCk* 7, 1995)

Such asseverations are not confined to DIY zines. Labels, distributors, distros, and
promoters can all experience a reaction should they walk towards the corporate world. But
the price of apparent authenticity may simply be anonymity, while so-called selling-out
may have the benefit of bringing punk values to a much greater number of people. What's
involved in the dilemma is nothing like as straightforward as is sometimes assumed. Let us
turn to some historical examples. In 1985, Bradford band New Model Army (NMA) signed
to EMI after four years of DIY and independent record releases:

> We were approached by all the majors. The reason we went with EMI was because
> we decided that we had the best record deal. We were offered total control of the
> producers, total control of the product, in inverted commas. It's a hard word to say.
> We were basically signed by a guy called Hugh Stanley-Clarke, who was less than sort
> of compos-mentis at the time, and all record companies were looking for the next
> U2. This was really the thing they wanted. We didn't know. They hated us. We made a
> horrible row, which we did up until we split … We made a horrible noise but, because
> we were selling out gigs, they wanted to sign us. So the EMI thing came along, we were
> offered the greatest amount of freedom, and after research into all the other major
> labels, where the money came from all the rest of it, we decided that everybody was
> as bad as each other. (New Model Army drummer Robert Heaton, interview with
> author, July 2001)

NMA's signing prompted the London anarchist band Conflict to release a record
Only Stupid Bastards use EMI! As a comment on its perceived hypocrisy. This was a play
on NMA's 1984 anti-drug statement 'Only Stupid Bastards use Heroin!' It resulted in
NMA shows being picketed and boycotted by anarcho-punks. A leaflet handed to me at
a NMA concert in Guildford cited the band as 'supposedly an anti-Establishment band,'
and accused them of having 'sold their credibility when they signed to EMI.' Yet, as Robert
Heaton noted in response:

You weren't even aware that you were affiliated with a band anyway from a point of view of artistic freedom. You know that's your only connection. I don't know fuck all about Conflict. I mean, I have never met any of them so I don't know what to fucking say: but from the aspect of what we were talking about earlier, the punk thing, as long as you are doing what you want to do then that's, you know, the essence, innit? I presume Conflict's view would be that if you are signed to a global conglomerate, you know, a corporate nightmare, then you are helping to destroy the world, which is a fair point. But how do you remain separate from that? In any aspect of your life? You know, one well-known band from Leeds [Chumbawamba] came to see us and they used to boycott our gigs and, you know, they were giving out leaflets outside, and we said 'come in and chat to us,' you know, for fuck's sake! I hold my hats off to them because they were doing their damnedest to not be part of the system. You know, I'd go, 'I admire you totally,' but the weak link was we don't make records, we make our own clothes, we don't do such and such. We release tapes. So who makes the tapes? Now there are like four companies in the world that make tapes.

There have been similar targets of abuse in the United States, with Orange County punk bands Rancid, Social Distortion, the Offspring, and Green Day in addition to Bad Religion, L7, All, DRI, Jello Biafra, and NOFX, along with the United Kingdom's Blaggers ITA and Back to the Planet.[7] These bands all signed to the majors in the early-to-mid 1990s and felt the wrath of the DIY scene. Perhaps the most notorious case of a band charged with selling-out is the Leeds band, Chumbawamba.

After a significant period of DIY production, very much in a similar vein to Crass with their DIY label Agit Prop records, Chumbawamba signed a distribution deal firstly with Southern Records before moving to the former Flux of Pink Indians bass player's label One Little Indian from 1991–7. All of Chumbawamba's records continued with the theme of refusal and DIY anarchist resistance, although they had considerably shifted position from their original intentions with the 1985 record *Revolution* (as cited in the epigraph to this chapter). After over fifteen years as DIY and independent anarchists, they signed to EMI Europe and Universal Entertainment in America. Most of the respondents in the interviews commented on this when asked about what they considered as selling-out.

Chumbawamba were responsible, alongside Crass, for producing music framed in anarchist politics. After becoming notorious for throwing red paint over late Clash front man Joe Strummer and their critiques of Live Aid with the record *Pictures of Starving Children Sell Records*, their credibility was irretrievably damaged when they did the unthinkable: sign to EMI in 1997. Since then, they have used their position to rally people to the anarchist cause, among other things through their hit 'Tubthumper.' A series of stunts ensued, including the changing of the latter's song lyrics to 'Free Mumia Abu Jamal' at the 1998 Brit Award ceremonies and throwing a bucket of water over the Deputy Prime Minister John ('Two Jags') Prescott. Ann Widdecombe also received a cream pie in the

---

7   See Arnold (1997) for an account of Green Day, Rancid, and the Sex pistols selling-out punk.

face. They have donated large amounts of their earnings to political causes, including the studio I helped to build during my 2001 fieldwork at the 1in12 Club, Bradford (Gordon 2012). In spite of these stunts, they have come in for some serious criticism from those who claim they have sold out. Hebdige (1979) noted that when commodification fails to control subversive musical/subcultural transgressions then ideological media forces discipline in order to re-present the offending group as a threat to the moral order.

While essentially correct, Hebdige overlooked the subcultures' own media use, their fanzines and own channels of communication (Thornton 1995; Muggleton 2000), examples of how and in what ways such ideological control from within a subculture was left out of these landmark discussions. To return to the present discussion, such an example of this discipline would have been the US fanzine *Maximumrocknroll* simply rerunning an old interview where they were quoted as saying: 'The time has come to take a choice, stop taking orders from his master's voice!' Chumbawamba put out their first record under DIY principles, financing, recording, producing, and screen printing the covers themselves. Their record *Revolution* concentrated on the theme of EMI and the retail outlet HMV. A Chumbawamba flyer distributed at the time of the record's release in 1985 made the point that 'every time you buy from Thorn-EMI you put your cross in their money box, you support the death-lines.' They believed that 'we have to start delving deeper than the glossy high street packet – start reading the small print.'

When I interviewed Chumbawamba member Danbert Nobacon in October 2001, he took up the issue of signing to EMI, which is worth quoting at length:

> Ideologically, it was a massive leap to go onto a major label, 'cos for years we'd said we would never do it, but we had come to a point where we just thought we have done our own label, we've been with indies, small indies, big indies, why not give it a chance? I mean, we talked about it for like a month, going backwards and forwards, and in the end we thought we should just do it. We'll probably have a really good year where they throw loads of money at us and just have a great time and get our records out. Then they'll probably dump us. So it actually lasted a bit longer than that, to our surprise, and being dumped didn't happen till after the next record. But because they knew, and people in the business knew, that that song ['Tubthumper'] was going to be a hit, then it was a really safe bet for 'em. It meant that we could finance subversive projects by other people again, so for a time there was another ideological thing. We got offered an advert and we had always said 'no way!' And we would never let our music be on an advert, but we'd never ever been offered one, and suddenly Renault in Italy said 'ohh,' you know, 'we'll give you twenty thousand quid, or whatever, if you let us use "Tubthumper",' and in the end we said 'yes.' We gave the money to two pirate radio stations, which financed them for like five years each, and while all the hype was going on we got a few offers like that. You are suddenly presented with all these opportunities and you just have to take each one as it comes. We got quite a few letters saying, 'how could you do this? We supported you all these years and you just throw it back in our faces.' I know in America we got

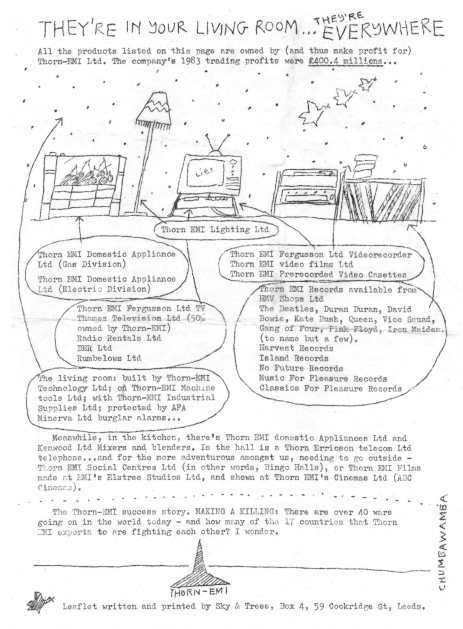

Figure 1.1: Chumbawamba – anti EMI information flyer UK circa 1985 (author collection).

into some arguments with some people in Philadelphia, and they'd been to the gig and that, but they were just stating: 'Yer appealing to ten year olds.'

Chumbawamba were one of the loudest voices in the 1980s and 1990s UK anarcho-punk scene, raising issue with EMI's arms manufacturing connections, but their move to this label was met with mixed views by members of the 1in12 Club. For example, Carol had this to say:

I know them and I totally respect them because even though they did sign for the major label and everything, they stayed in this scene as well … But they have given money to this place [1in12]. They've helped build this place. Alice [Nutter] having a party on Friday, everyone from here is invited, no matter who you are, you know it's the 1in12 … You know they sing about EMI, slag 'em off … it is really hard, it's not black and white is it? You can't say I'm never going to do it, but it would be good if people could get the message across within the DiY scene, but maybe that's just too idealistic.

Interviewees Jen and Martin both took this issue up:

Jen: The EMI thing? It's just them trying to pull a stunt, isn't it? And it backfired on them. Well Danbert's thing about that was that they felt that they were somewhat being exploited by One Little Indian, and because of the level and the amount of coverage they were getting. If you are gonna be exploited, be exploited by someone that can do it efficiently. What pissed me off, though, was their whole slagging of the punk subculture. Fair enough, but then to turn around and do something like that is sort of … If you've got something to say, I think the punk scene doesn't stand a lot of criticism.

Martin: Alice Nutter got bit in the fucking face and the band wrote articles to the papers slagging crusties and travellers and punks off. They basically said they are nothing and propagating their message was more important. 'Our medium is the message,' you know; 'we are gonna go to EMI we're going to get this message across.' The whole fucking contradiction is political. You know, it's the same thing with the Clash, isn't it? Fucking brilliant, I think. I agreed with a lot of what they had to say and then they turned into a bunch of twats. Whether they signed to CBS is fucking incidental, 'cos every fucking punk band around at the time was doing the same.

Jen: Chumbawamba totally went out on a limb and signed to EMI. Fuck knows why EMI signed them. I could never understand why. It's kinda like they were co-opted or something.

Martin: It's like allowing you. The whole DIY thing is that us three are in a band, we do everything DIY. The only executive decisions are made by us, right? You get to sign to someone like EMI, or any of these big record companies. All of a sudden our band actually is no longer three people, its twenty, it's a crew of twenty-five, and the decisions we make then become very difficult. Here's our record, 'well I'm sorry you can't say that.' Eh? What? 'No, no you can't have that picture, no I'm sorry, you will have to do this.' What the fuck is this?

Jen: This whole commodification thing is … like killing the fucking band, and a band is an expression of our culture, isn't it? And then to have that expression of your culture taken by someone else and sold as an expression of culture ceases to become an expression of our culture. It becomes a contradiction.

These responses reveal, in full discursive detail, many of the ins and outs of the dilemma faced by Chumbawamba as this was taken up, debated, and turned around from every conceivable angle by DIY punk subcultural members at the time. Each member faced the dilemma themselves and acted it out vicariously. This was a measure of how deeply it struck into the heart of what DIY punk is about, ethically and politically. The final point can be made by Nick:

> For a band that sells out and doesn't have anything to say, why am I going to be bothered? I'm not. It doesn't affect me at all. Green Day? Who cares? Chumbawamba – different story, you know it is a different story. I am saddened by what they did. I think the best thing I can do is pity them because that is a harsher human emotion to lay into someone with. At one time I would have been angry. Chumbawamba had a long history with the anarcho-punk scene and did the dirty. They went on *Top of the Pops*.

For any self-respecting punk, going on *TOTP* was the *ultimate* sell-out, with even the Clash refusing this opportunity. Nothing could be calculated as a worse way of 'doing the dirty' – that is, not acting 'cleanly' in respect of ethics and politics. This raises the question of why?

The key point to be made in their defence was that Chumbawamba used their post-EMI signing period to fund DIY activities *across* the political and cultural production spectrums. They made donations to pirate radio stations, gave £70,000 to Corporate Watch, and put money into the 1in12, so helping to fund the studio project I worked on back in 2001.[8] The actions of Chumbawamba in signing to a major label encapsulate the tug-of-war that pulls people in DIY punk in contrary directions.

The justifications offered by artists for signing with a major record label can be reduced to two popular arguments. Firstly, it I to gain a realistic income ('I am sick of being poor and putting all this effort in, we can't afford to do anything'), though this is highly unlikely for the vast majority of musicians, who sign to labels and remain unsuccessful.

Secondly, in terms of artistic recognition and progression there is the desire to transcend the already converted autonomous spaces and enter new and previously unexplored spaces in order to reach (and duly inspire) a wider audience. From this perspective, DIY punk is, by default, considered to be inward-looking. To become (in) famous and subvert such new spaces were part of Chumbawamba's strategy: to manipulate the music industry as noted above, to voice previously unheard or suppressed political views (for example, showing videos made by the striking Liverpool Dockers at the Brit Awards) and spread these views around a much wider base than that achievable by the DIY punk purist.

However successful such attempts may be, responses from the hardcore DIY adherents offer inevitable scorn, resentment, and anger after a band that was once DIY is regarded as having sold out. As Nick stated above: 'Green Day? Who cares? Chumbawamba

---

8   See 'Chumbawamba's Tune Turns the Tables on US Car Giant,' *The Observer* (27 January 2002), 11.

– different story, you know it is a different story.' The hostile side of the dilemma levels such accusations as: they 'did the dirty,' are 'not punk,' and are 'hypocritical money grabbers' (Chumbawamba boycotted NMA shows then went and signed to a major label themselves), and represent 'mainstream sell-outs that have become part of the system.' Selling-out to a major label often means facing a boycott and the withdrawal of support from inside the DIY community. As outlined by Heaton, the boycotts and pickets by Chumbawamba outside NMA shows in the 1980s provided bad publicity, yet he maintained that they had never been a part of the DIY philosophy to begin with. NMA were not dedicated to that philosophy, had never held the anarcho-punk torch, and simply viewed the transition from DIY to independent to major as a *natural* progression that allowed them to spread their subversive message to a wider audience. The justifications he offered were that the band cost the label more than they signed for, and that they were a 'thorn in the side of EMI' by negotiating a record deal that allowed them *total* artistic freedom: in short, they retained their integrity; at minimum, an argument based on the retention of their artistic integrity could certainly be mounted. This may be a legitimate argument, but the view from the DIY camp can be unforgiving and austere. A very dim view is taken of any contact with major labels. Such contact is seen as diluting the power and solidarity of underground culture. Here, Boff from Chumbawamba is explicit:

> [*Maximumrocknroll*] stopped reviewing our records because they decided that they weren't punk anymore. That's such a bizarre project – to judge punkness on the basis of style. (Sinker 2001, 124)

However, not all of the interviewees were as militant on the matter of Chumbawamba selling out. Pete and Martin both stated that they could totally understand why they had signed. They said that Chumbawamba had been exploited by a number of independent record labels and, as a consequence, were tired of being ripped off. The only solution was to sign with a major and be exploited effectively. This offered the bonus opportunity of being able to subvert the company from the inside. Protag also revealed sympathetic views towards bands who sign to major labels:

> If bands are important, if groups and music are important, which they might be, then I think it's obviously better if they do it themselves. But I mean if some major corporation band rang up and said, you know, we're fucked on a Wednesday night, the gig's fallen through and we want to play at the 1in12 club. Provided I knew they weren't a bunch of sexist, racist assholes, if I thought they were going to say something reasonably interesting, some people want to be here, I'd be more than willing to bring them here and go: look, this is how you can do it without the major corporations.

> It's like doing a DIY label, but still driving around in your Mercedes truck, filling up, or risking driving past Shell. It didn't make that much difference, you're still filling at some major petrochemical corporation, you're still totally up to your neck in a sort of deep environmental death kind of ecosystem.

Figure 1.2: Various Artists (1998) *Bare Faced Hypocrisy Sells Records*, Propa Git Records.

This is the central key to the punk dilemma. The majority of the system is controlled and monopolized through corporate entities, so the spaces for potential political subversion are shrinking. They exist only in small pockets. Protag similarly suggested that DIY activity is necessary, yet there are few spaces where one can be completely DIY; from the oil used to produce the vinyl, through the chemicals in the plasterboard and insulation used in the 1in12 studio project, to the technology patents in the recording equipment, there are very few spaces where everyday contact with multinational corporations can be avoided. As Zero (1994) points out:

> A percentage of every CD made is paid to the Phillips Corporation because they have the copyright on the format. Does this mean that everyone that makes CDs is bad and part of the evil arms-making empire? If I drink Coke, wear Nike shoes, drive a Volvo or any foreign car … should I be chastised for it? Is it worse to support arms builders or destroy the environment by wasting paper or driving my car? This politically correct stuff is usually too dogmatic and, believe me, fighting with people who use Caroline to

distribute independent records is fighting with your own team. Know your enemy. Plus, once again, where is the punk rock rule book and does everyone have to play by it?

Nevertheless, the DIY spaces that operate beyond corporate control and funding are extremely valuable and play a central role in offering a space virtually free from corporate dictum and control, where political voices can be raised, free of control. Yet, because this space is delimited, the effectiveness of these voices is questionable.

As I have noted elsewhere (Gordon 2016), there is a distinct ironic elitism involved in the dedicated practice of DIY. Claiming that DIY cultural production is the only authentic form of culture means that exclusivity is just around the corner: 'only' quickly becomes translated into 'elite.' Creating a set of scene 'rules' (not signing to majors, not working to contracts, keeping prices cheap, etc.) and applying these in an absolute manner in the production of DIY flies in the face of the original intentions of such core punk rock freedoms as breaking down said rules and challenging boundaries. Anti-elitism can end up, via an awful loop, in the position it so radically opposes. There is an equally absolutist reaction to those who are deemed to have sold-out above and against those still practicing and involved in DIY. This presents a fiercely unforgiving critique by those who cling to stringent DIY ethics. Such an unrelenting, inflexible stance is itself condemned by others in and around the scene. 'Cliquey,' 'PC,' and 'elitist' were some of the denunciations expressed in interviews towards this stance in the DIY community.

Other interviewees noted that the 1in12 are a bunch of 'punk police' and 'language fascists.' Such views were often aimed at the 1in12 back in 2001, although I observed on many occasions behaviour that were far from what could be described as politically correct, even though the club was viewed as a bastion of political correctness. Indeed, Doug provocatively described the 1in12 as often populated not by hippies but by a crowd of 'footie hooligans.' However, the open-ended status of the DIY ethic maintains that if there is a *perceived* problem with being DIY, then being negative towards it will achieve nothing. The preference instead is to get involved, think positive and do something about it. With DIY there is always the opportunity for anybody to get involved in activities and to change the existing state of affairs from within. In reality, due to the lack of available funds and the relatively small numbers of people involved, the capacity for large-scale DIY action in the UK is limited and the knock-on effect is that attendance fluctuates at DIY functions. The justification for Chumbawamba in signing to EMI was that they could increase their financial resources in order to properly fund DIY projects. As Boff noted:

> Obviously we could say 'No we won't have an advert with our music on it,' but when we are offered forty thousand dollars for thirty seconds of music every day for four weeks, then what we do is give that money to an anti-fascist organisation, social center or community group. (Sinker 2001, 128)

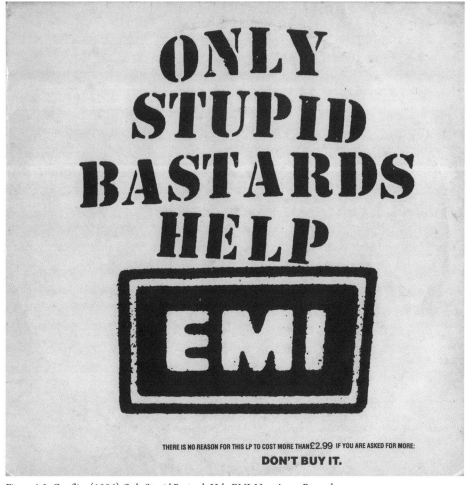

Figure 1.3: Conflict (1986) *Only Stupid Bastards Help EMI*, New Army Records.

Turning their money towards small-scale DIY projects has allowed Chumbawamba to retain their moral and ethical integrity, even though the DIY community remains divided over their actions.[9] The positive and negative views of their signing to EMI remain largely irreconcilable inside the Leeds and Bradford DIY punk scenes of the 1990s and 2000s.

There are those who are militant on the non-DIY front and hail DIY purists as hypocrites. Jello Biafra, one-time singer with the San Francisco band Dead Kennedys, whose record label, Alternative Tentacles, is the second longest-running independent label in the United States, was severely beaten up in 1990 by 'crusty punks' for allegedly selling-out punk rock (Sinker 2001, 33). He chastised the American fanzine *Maximumrocknroll* as 'little Ayatollahs' for creating a new set of divisive rules in the punk community and called those who criticize musicians who sign to major labels 'small-minded and righteous.' Sinker and Biafra said in their exchange:

---

9   It would be unfortunate for me to present Chumbawamba as disconnected from the 1in12. They have maintained constant contact with the club since its inception. The last event they played there was an acoustic show in November 2004

Sinker: *Maximumrocknroll* seems dead set on this line of sectarian purity, where anything that creates a base for mass support is looked upon with suspicion and ultimately rejected as a sellout.

Biafra: It's the same kind of fundamentalist mind-set that makes fundamentalist Christians so dangerous, and the same mind-set that has isolated the animal rights and vegan movements. You take one step out of line and they bite your head off. Young people who are curious about the politics spend ten minutes with people like that and they decide that they would rather be apathetic. This is what has turned a lot of people off punk politics. (Sinker 2001, 44)

Such harsh criticism reflects the often-polarized views that exist in punk on selling-out. The problem is at the centre of DIY politics. DIY purists have been accused of being inward-looking, preaching to the converted and being subculturally elitist with little chance of ever reaching the broader body of people whose support would make DIY a significant political tool of empowerment. The purists in turn accuse those with the defects of intellectual slack-mindedness, political populism, and ethical bankruptcy. The dilemmas strike deep.

Indeed, the historical dilemmas outlined above are still prevalent in relative forms across current global punk scenes. The broad arguments originally set out on selling-out (Adorno and Horkheimer 1995; Becker 1963; Hebdige 1979) are certainly still of relevance. Hebdige's argument certainly loomed large in many of the above accounts. He was broadly correct in terms of the mainstream commodification and ideological control of punk, yet equally wrong in terms of how and in what ways dilemmatic boundaries have shifted over subsequent decades. Punk, in its fortieth year, is now officially sanctioned and vindicated as mainstream media comment that sanitizes and removes elements that are politically salient or threatening to a broadly apolitical narrative. Posters, souvenirs, and concerns in established venues celebrate punk's historical significance, yet ideologically overlook the vibrant global punk scenes active in 2016. Clearly, Hebdige's' explanatory account applies to the latter example, yet the central issue of dilemmatic divisions *within* local punk scenes are of equal importance. This chapter has gone some way to illuminate dilemmatic historical divisions within my original fieldwork, though much more empirical and theoretical scrutiny is required both globally and locally, and equally in provincial and urban scenes. Indeed, Donaghy's (2013) research has saliently illustrated divisions and similarities between punks who choose political change as its central locus compared to those participants who use punk for artistic, aesthetic, and sartorial expression. While punk already inhabits both of these distinctions, dilemmas of what form is most preferable simmer in all punk scenes and are intrinsically relative to the geopolitical, historical and local cultural contexts in which the scenes exist.

However, one of the notable comparative differences between the original 2001 research and the current context of global and local punk scenes is the rise of digital communication technologies. The latter technological fundamentally altered the power of major label control of punk, allowing global DIY punk to rapidly expand as a mode of cultural production, yet the stringent dilemmas of authenticity, while changing in terms of major label versus underground DIY, have presented new issues of punk authenticity. Equally, such developments have added a new punk space in which punk dilemmas can be discussed, communicated, and enacted. In tandem with this development is the growth of intersectional political notions of 'safe spaces' in punk. Such examples are of 'safe space' politics from which internal scene debates regarding the implementation of inclusive spaces within punk communities function as a springboard for disciplinary dilemmatic debates regarding gender, race, ethnicity, ableism, cultural appropriation, vegetarianism, veganism, and punk musical styles, genres, and modes of expressions, which have developed new areas of research interest for current punk scholarship.

This article has attempted to establish the general basis for these ethical dilemmas as it existed in and between two cities in the north of England in 2001. Whilst this world was shot-through with divisions and peppered with elitism both in its rhetorical distinctions of authenticity (Gordon 2016) and badges of countercultural authenticity, what it achieved, albeit unsung and unnoticed out of the mainstream, was of immense cultural value, informing the present discussions of punk dilemmas. It was a rare example of what can be created beyond the confines of an administered culture. In some ways, the scenes described formed a virtual minefield of arbitrary rules of conduct. On the other hand, there was a felt sense of achievement and empowerment: whether it was through making a studio, starting a record shop, setting up a record label, putting on a show at a squat or in someone's front room, or through sheer determination in making some venture succeed against the odds, the subculture provided certain distinct spaces of freedom. Such spaces are rare and impressive.

The dilemmas described in this chapter retain a sharp, at times corrosive, quality which helps to shape and inform subcultural conduct. Such conduct is fraught with a collection of thorny issues which will not be readily resolved or made amenable to any off-the-hook remedy, not least because they are bound up in wider issues of global monopoly capitalism and its stranglehold over (mass) popular culture. Whether or not resistance is best produced from inside the major labels or from the global temporary autonomous spaces of small record labels, squats, or DIY gigs remains an open question, especially in relation to the abiding issue of cultural authenticity. Do you choose DIY anarcho-direct-action-punk, or DIY cultural production, or another version of punk to frame your own authenticity? Are these mutually exclusive or can they be made compatible? Can effective political statements or actions be made from within the culture industry? Perhaps the most difficult issue of all is whether there has ever been, or can ever be, an authentic punk. In the 'true spirit of DIY,' the response to this issue must finally reside with the reader.

References

Adorno, T. W. and M Horkheimer (1995 [1944]). *Dialectic of Enlightenment.* London: Verso.

Arnold, G. (1997). *Kiss This: Punk in the Present Tense.* New York: Pan Books.

Becker, H. (1963). *Outsiders: Studies in the Sociology of Deviance.* New York: The Free Press of Glencoe.

'Chumbawamba's Tune Turns the Tables on US Car Giant.' *The Observer* (27 January 2002).

Cohen, S. (1980). *Folk Devils and Moral Panics: The Creation of the Mods and Rockers.* Oxford: Martin Robertson & Co.

Donaghy, J (2013). 'Bakunin Brand Vodka. An Exploration into Anarchist-punk and Punk-anarchism.' *Anarchist Developments in Cultural Studies* 1.

Frank, T. and M. Weiland (eds.). (1997). *Commodify Your Dissent: Salvos from The Baffler.* New York: W. W. Norton.

Gordon, A. (2005). *The Authentic Punk: An Ethnography of DIY Music Ethics.* Unpublished PhD thesis. Loughborough University. Department of Social Sciences.

Gordon, A. (2012). 'Building Recording Studios While Bradford Burned.' In Z. Furness (ed.), *Punkademics: The Basement Show in the Ivory Tower.* New York: Minor Compositions/Autonomedia.

Gordon, A. (2015). 'Distinctions of Authenticity and the Everyday Punk Self.' *Journal of Punk and Post Punk* 3 (2).

Gordon, A. (2016), '"They Can Stuff Their Punk Credentials 'Cause It's Them That Take The Cash." 1980s Anarcho-Punk: Ethical Difference and Division.' In M. Dines and M. Worley (eds.), *The Aesthetic of Our Anger: Anarcho Punk, Politics and Music.* Brighton: Autonomedia.

Hebdige, D. (1979) *Subculture: The Meaning of Style.* London: Routledge.

HeartattaCk 7. (1995). Fanzine.

Sinker, D. (ed.) (2001). *We Owe You Nothing Punk Planet: The Collected Interviews.* New York: Akashic Books.

Thornton, S. (1995). *Club Cultures: Music, Media and Subcultural Capital.* London: Polity.

Maximumrocknroll 174 (1997). Fanzine.

Muggleton, D. (2000). *Inside Subculture: The Postmodern Meaning of Style.* Oxford: Berg.

Profane Existence 23 (1992). Fanzine.

Zero, B. (1994). 'Major Labels: Some of your Friends are This Fucked.' *Maximumrocknroll* 133.

Discography

Back to the Planet (1993) *Mind and Soul Collaborators,* Parallel: London Records.

Bad Religion (1993) *Recipe For Hate,* Epitaph Records.

Blaggers ITA (1993) *Abandon Ship,* EMI Parlophone Records.

Chumbawamba (1985) *Revolution,* Agit Prop Records.

Chumbawamba (1986) *Pictures of Starving Children Sell Records,* Agit Prop Records.

Chumbawamba (1997) *Tubthumping,* Universal Records.

The Clash (1977) *The Clash*, CBS Records.

The Damned (1977) *Damned Damned Damned*, Stiff Records.

Conflict (1982) *It's Time to See Who's Who*, Corpus Christi Records.

Conflict (1983) *To a Nation of Animal Lovers*, Corpus Christi Records.

Conflict (1984) *Increase the Pressure*, Corpus Christi Records.

Conflict (1984) *The Serenade is Dead*, Mortahate Records.

Conflict (1985) *Only Stupid Bastards Help EMI*, New Army Records.

Converge (2001) *Jane Doe*, Equal Vision Records.

Crass (1978) *The Feeding of The Five Thousand*, Small Wonder Records.

Flux of Pink Indians (1981) *Neu Smell*, Crass Records.

Green Day (1987) *Sweet Children* E.P, Skene! Records.

Green Day (1997) *Nimrod*, Reprise, Records.

Jello Biafra (2000) *Become the Media*, Alternative Tentacles Records.

New Model Army (1984) *Vengeance*, Abstract Records.

New Model Army (1985) *No Rest For The Wicked*, EMI Records.

NOFX (1994) *Punk in Drublic*, Epitaph Records.

Rancid (1995) *… And out Come the Wolves*, Epitaph Records.

Sex Pistols (1977) *Never Mind The Bollocks*, Virgin Records.

Social Distortion (1996) *White Light, White Heat White Trash*, Epic Records.

Various Artists (1998) *Bare Faced Hypocrisy Sells Records*, Propa Git Records.

2. 'NOTHING LIKE THE REST OF HOLLAND': THE GRONINGEN PUNK SCENE

KIRSTY LOHMAN

Abstract

Many Dutch punks are highly mobile. The regularity with which punks travel between towns in the central Netherlands for gigs has led to little sense of local scene identities. This fits with postmodern models of fluidity which look beyond the bounds of locality. The Groningen punk scene, however, flouts this trend. This chapter will argue that this is due to its location in the far north of the country which results in a geographic peripherality to the rest of the Dutch punk scene. Groningen punks are, as a result, more invested in their own local identity and work actively to build and support a *local* punk scene.

Despite this emphasis on locality, Groningen's punk scene is highly connected *beyond* the Netherlands. Groningen bands regularly tour Germany and beyond, and the city is home to the GGI Festival, an annual celebration of the links between punk scenes in Groningen, Glasgow, and Ireland. Groningen's punks therefore position themselves both as connected to a global scene *and* as highly local. This example highlights the geographic complexities that are brought by the mobility and connectivity of a globalized punk scene.

Keywords: Dutch punk, the Netherlands, Groningen, local identities, centre/periphery

This chapter is dedicated to Phil Vane, Andrew Loomis, and Colin McQuillan, RIP.

Kirsty Lohman is a Research Assistant at the University of Warwick. Her research interests include musical/cultural participation, feminism, and political engagement. Her AHRC-funded PhD was an ethnography of punk in the Netherlands, focusing on the political and lifestyle choices of participants in this geographic context. She has played in the UK midlands-based punk bands Not Right, Die Wrecked, and Fear and Slothing, and helps to run Coventry's punk night Revolt. E-mail: kirsty.lohman@warwick.ac.uk

'NOTHING LIKE THE REST OF HOLLAND': THE GRONINGEN PUNK SCENE

A Tribute to Phil Vane

I arrived at the venue, Viadukt, at 7 pm, just as the soundcheck began. I was there early to interview Bram, who would be playing that night. It was a warm, sunny evening in early April, and punks were sitting around the car park drinking beers and chatting, but the palpable pre-gig excitement was tinged with sad nostalgia.

The event was a tribute to recently deceased Phil Vane, co-vocalist of legends Extreme Noise Terror. Originally, ENT themselves had been due to play as part of a small Dutch tour; the preceding night in Amsterdam, and on 2 April 2011 in Groningen. Upon the news of Phil's death in February, the members of the disbanded Groningen-based Extreme Noise Error decided to reform to play the gig that ENT could not. The band had been named as a tribute to ENT, and were their contemporaries, having played gigs together in the 1980s. Although ENE were never strictly a tribute band, for this gig they rehearsed ENT covers to play in honour of Phil. Hearing of this, ENT's other vocalist, Dean Jones, decided to join ENE for two Dutch gigs.

This was my third day in Groningen, and everyone I met had been long awaiting this event. Over the course of the evening, I would meet many more of the current, the ex-, the new, the young, and the old punks of Groningen and the surrounding area. 'Everyone' was there that night. As I sat on the door for the first hour of the gig, helping with admission and interviewing Ruben, he regularly stopped to greet and introduce me to old friends – members of the 'old scene' whom he had not seen for a long time, and who had made a special effort to come tonight.

The Phil Vane tribute night was a significant gig. It was a big event in the Groningen punk calendar, third only to GGI Festival and the Simplon Punks Reunion. It brought various strands of the contemporary and the historical punk scene[10] together. Groningen has a number of different groups of punk fans. There are/were the squatter punks, the beer punks, the old punk rock crew from '77, the farm punks, the skater punks, the hardcore kids, and the straight edge punks (as explained by participants Bram and Henk). Nowadays the distinctions have eroded,[11] with many of those who had previously been in different groups hanging out together, especially in the Crowbar (according to Lotte). Beyond this generational coming together, there was a geographical connectivity too.

The audience were mostly from Groningen or nearby residents. However, these residents were not all long-time Groningers; over the years, Groningen's punk scene has attracted an impressive number of individuals from elsewhere in the Netherlands, as well as from other countries such as France or Scotland. Moreover, for many this gig was worth travelling for: 'I travelled over just for the concert,' said Wim.

Indeed, since Extreme Noise Error had disbanded, some members of the band had moved away from Groningen and were also travelling for the gig. '[T]hat whole tribute thing has got people from all over the place, you know, so that's cool!' (Bram). This highlights issues around locality and global connectivity in the Groningen punk scene, which this chapter seeks to unpick.

Also playing at the gig were Noodweer, a contemporary Groningen band featuring a mix of the generations of the local punk scene, Suicide State, a band from Limburg in the south of the Netherlands, and N.F.F.U., who were on tour from the United States. Touring bands are common at gigs both across the Netherlands and in Groningen. Whilst (as this chapter will argue) Groningen is not as well connected to other cities in the Netherlands as they are with each other, the city *is* well established on the international touring circuit. It regularly hosts international touring bands, which helps foster the connections needed for home-grown bands to tour internationally.

10 I follow O'Connor's definition of 'scene' as being rooted in the way in which it is used by participants of the subculture themselves; 'the active creation of infrastructure to support punk bands and other forms of creative activity' (O'Connor 2002, 226).

11 The modern melodic hardcore scene is still separate from the core of the Groningen punk scene; the participants, who were more involved with it, were not involved with or aware of the Phil Vane tribute gig. Also separate is the straight edge scene, of which neither I nor any participants had any knowledge other than of its existence.

The Groningen Punk Scene

Punk has taken many forms in the Netherlands, and some bands have become highly regarded in the global underground and commercial spheres. Its roots lie in Amsterdam in the 1960s and early 1970s with the Provos and the Kabouters – groups formed by the anarchist/artistic milieu (Kempton 2007). Their 'happenings' – cultural gatherings which usually carried a political message – often focused on issues of squatting, and drew international attendees. This bolstered the squatting movement in Amsterdam and the Netherlands as a whole. As punk spread throughout Europe, Dutch punks became closely related to the squatting movement. The Dutch punk scene has therefore developed to be particularly politically-minded (Lohman 2013; 2015). Punks throughout the Netherlands found space to develop their music, ideas, and lifestyle within these autonomous spaces, and multiple different styles of punk emerged. In Groningen, the scene spawned a variety of successful underground bands such as crust punks Fleas and Lice, ska band the Boegies, and garage punks Moonlizards.

Little is written about the earliest Groningen punk scene, with punk histories focusing more on the Amsterdam, Wormer, or Rotterdam scenes (Goossens and Vedder 1996). However, there were bands active in the late 1970s, including Subway (previously a hippy-blues band from 1969–72, but who reformed as a punk band in 1976–83), The Boobs (1978–81), and Two Two 79 (1979–82).

The first signs of a larger scene in Groningen were apparent with the Rood, Wit, Zwart[12] punk collective (Berkers 2012), encompassing the bands Massagraf (1980–unknown), Fahrenheit 451 (1980–3), JET$ET (1980–5), Bloedbad (1982–5), and Vacuüm[13] (c. 1983–unknown) (Groningen Pop Archive n.d.). The Rood, Wit, Zwart collective were based around the Oude Rooms Katholieke Ziekenhuis[14] (ORKZ, squatted in 1979).

The other key venue for the early Groningen punk scene was Simplon. Established as a youth centre in 1977, it hosted many early punk gigs (Groningen Pop Archive, n.d.). It was the social nexus of the Groningen punks, and all those involved with it remember it fondly – Henk, Lotte, Jacob, Maarten, and Bram all discuss the 'Simplon times.' In 1980, Café Vera also began to host punk gigs, although the bands that played there tended to be more New Wave oriented (according to Maarten). Divides in the Groningen punk scene became apparent in the late 1980s with the spread of hard drug use at Simplon. Around this time, many of the punks drifted to Café Vera, volunteering there as well as, or instead of, at Simplon (such as Lotte, Jacob, and Maarten). In 1993, Simplon closed its doors temporarily due to insufficient sound proofing (Groningen Pop Archive, n.d.); this signalled the end of Simplon as *the* 'punk centre' (according to Lotte). Café Vera remained the centre of the punk scene until 2008 when Crowbar, a small 'punk pub' with a stage, opened its doors.

This chapter is based on a subset of data collected for a project on Dutch punk. Data was collected across the Netherlands between July 2010 and April 2011, and in Groningen between 31 March 2011 and 4 April 2011. Semi-structured and unstructured

---

12 Transl. 'Red, White, Black.'
13 Utrecht-based but part of the Groningen collective.
14 Transl. 'Old Roman Catholic Hospital.'

interviews were conducted with thirteen individuals during that long weekend, and with a further two who had previously lived in Groningen but were now elsewhere in the Netherlands (see the appendix for demographic details).[15] Participants were connected both contemporaneously and/or historically to punk. The data set was augmented with participant observation and document analysis. Names of bands and locations are retained, but individual participants are referred to by pseudonyms.[16]

Locality

The role of the 'local' is today a hotly debated subject in understandings of subcultures such as punk. That multiple locally-based scenes existing around the world, drawing upon similar practices, show an interplay between the global and local aspects of punk. Whilst musical styles, social practices, attire, and methods of production and consumption may be recognizable wherever punk is found, there is still value in understanding that locality will give rise to particular forms and distinctive practices (O'Connor 2002), often based around venues or groups of bands (Shank 1994). These debates have led to various proposed terms, including the 'glocal' (Robertson 1995; Pilkington 2004) and 'translocal' (Peterson and Bennett 2004; Hodkinson 2004) subcultures.

'Glocal' emphasizes the interaction between the global ('central') influences of punk and local ('peripheral') interpretations (Pilkington 2004). However, this does not adequately take into account the multiplicity inherent in a subculture such as punk, which is constantly reimagined and altered (Sabin 1999), or the fact that the underground punk is scene is well connected.

'Translocal' allows for a more nuanced understanding of patterns of cultural flow and interactions between subcultural participants. In his account of the UK goth subculture, Hodkinson (2004, 144) argues that:

> rather than consisting of a series of highly separate, distinctive, and clearly bounded local scenes, [UK goth] comes across more as a singular and relatively coherent movement whose translocal connections were of greater significance than its local differences. While locality remained highly important to everyday participation, the identities, practices, values, and infrastructural elements of the goth scene usually operated beyond the bounds of particular towns or cities.

This interpretation is broadly applicable to the Netherlands' punk scene, which is characterized by a high level of mobility between participants, both producers and fans. Bands (e.g. Vitamin X, Human Corrosion, and Planet Eyelash) can be based 'translocally,' with

15 A few participants who were interviewed in Groningen were originally from or were living in Leeuwarden at the time. Leeuwarden is the closest large city to Groningen and there was a great deal of connectivity between punks in both cities. Groningen has a larger and more active scene, drawing participants regularly from Leeuwarden. Leeuwarden punks have been included in this data-set due to the location of the interview and their knowledge of the Groningen scene, and as part of situating the Groningen scene in a more general northern context. Where necessary, a distinction will be made when participants are discussing Leeuwarden or the north rather Groningen.
16 Occasional quotes are unattributed to protect anonymity as far as possible, where requested by the interviewee or where the context would reveal the participant's identity.

members living in multiple cities and travelling for weekly practices. However, I will argue in this chapter that the Groningen punk scene is distinct from the rest of the Netherlands in that it lies both literally and metaphorically on the periphery of the Dutch scene, which imbues it with a heightened sense of locality when compared to the rest of the country.[17]

Kennedy (2010) has discussed the multifaceted way in which the local lives function in relation to globalized cultural flows. He argues that globalization debates have not placed enough emphasis on the role of the local in affecting individuals' interaction with the global, nor how this then impacts global flows. Individuals need to be recognized as micro-actors in both constructing and understanding their place in a local and global world.

A useful way to understand cultural flow, then, is as having a rhizomic character based on biological rootstocks: '[t]he wisdom of the plants: even when they have roots, there is always an outside where they form a rhizome with something else' (Deleuze and Guattari 2003, 11). This model can be understood on varying levels as allowing cultural flow between different locations, different forms of culture, and different understandings of one form of culture – for example, punk. It allows for high levels of connectedness, whilst the possibility remains for differences in form. Greater importance need not be attributed either to local or global actors within cultural forms: culture forms a complex network in which any social phenomena can be, and is, connected to any other. We are therefore able to break with hierarchical understandings of global cultural flow as necessarily linked to transmission from the centre to a periphery (Hannerz 1992).

The Netherlands' punk scene does not enjoy a similarly high profile to that of 'origin' countries such as the United Kingdom and the United States, and could be located as 'peripheral' to them in a similar way that Groningen might be seen to be 'peripheral' to the rest of the Dutch scene. However, as this chapter will demonstrate, the Groningen (like the Dutch) scene is highly connected to the international underground punk scene; it is one node of the rhizomic network.

The contested importance of locality within globalized musical praxis, and the relationship between a city and the production and promotion of its 'sound,' have been discussed in depth by Cohen in relation to Liverpool (2007). These themes have been further explored in Lashua, Spracklen, and Wagg's (2014) *Sounds and the City*, which recognizes that these localities affect the global praxis just as the globality affects the local: 'the increasing mobility of individuals, cultural practice, and ideas, and the emergence of global networks such as the Internet, made popular music places more common and yet more diverse. In this century, popular music has become a leisure form that seems to transcend borders and it has reshaped the postmodern city' (2014, 5). Whilst this chapter discusses the production of locality within the Groningen punk scene, it maintains a focus on the scene's place within a rhizomatic and global underground punk network. In doing so, it traces participants' understandings of themselves as both 'separate from the rest of the Dutch punk scene' and as highly connected and mobile international punk actors.

17 For a discussion of northern peripherality affecting locality in punk, see Pilkington (2014) in relation to punks in Vorkuta, Russia.

The Groningen punk scene is affected by its geographical position in the far north of the Netherlands. The majority of large Dutch cities lie in close proximity to one another, with travel time between the 'big four' of the 'Randstad' (Amsterdam, Utrecht, The Hague, and Rotterdam) rarely exceeding one hour; Groningen lies at least two to three hours from most other cities. For punks in more central areas of country, travelling forms a key part of their scene participation; it is normal to travel to see or play gigs. Sander, who lives in Amsterdam, will often travel to 'Nijmegen, Utrecht, Tilburg. If there's a cool band then we'll hop in the car, or on a train, no problem!' However, this is more of a problem for those who live further away; interviewees describe the city as 'isolated' (Kosta), and this being a cause of less travelling by Groningen's punks (Lisa). Whilst participants do still travel in order to play and occasionally attend gigs, this is not as normalized as it is for those who live in the better-connected south. Whilst Jasper was considering a trip to Hamburg for a gig around the time of the interview, this was noted as something he did not do regularly.

Whereas city or regional boundaries between scenes do not affect the majority of the Dutch scene (Lohman 2013; 2015), in Groningen the participants talked of the existence of a 'Groningense' or 'northern' punk scene (Bram, Kosta, Lotte, Ruben).[18] It is through these discursive patterns that we can understand the production of and pride in their locality. Interviews with Groningen punks often became an exercise in 'storytelling,' with a number of recurrent themes between interviews through which they construct their local identities. This in part echoes the practices of young people in Vorkuta, Russia in their construction of local community and identity, as highlighted in Pilkington's discussion of the relationship between people and place. Part of this process is through the telling of 'insider stories' (2012, 272).

An important part of the punk scene's local identity is its squatter history and the battles they fought with the government. A significant number of participants of this research discussed the 'stories' of the Wolters-Noordhoff Complex (WNC, squatted 1984) and/or the ORKZ. Both the ORKZ and the WNC were large squat complexes which provided housing, practice rooms, gig venues, pubs, cafes, and more. These venues, alongside a few other squats and the Simplon club, were key social spaces for the Groningen punks in the 1980s. Whilst the ORKZ went through a squat legalization process, the WNC was targeted for demolition. The eviction turned into a 'huge fucking riot, it was a two-day riot and something like 150 people (of our side) got arrested for that and most of them were in jail for a month or more' (Bram).

This event, and subsequent discussions of it, helped cement the Groningen punks' local identity, and their stereotyping in the eyes of the rest of the Netherlands. Bram says that after the WNC eviction it was 'kind of known throughout Holland that we didn't give a fuck so, you know, so they always put us up at the front of the demonstration so even if there's like fights with cops or with skinheads or something we'll just fucking kick the shit of them you know!' Another participant confirms that, to this day, the Groningen punks are considered 'loud, drunk, noisy, troublemakers' by their peers in Amsterdam,

---

18 Also discussed by participants who had connections to Leeuwarden was the 'Frisian' scene (Tom, Erik, Jasper).

whilst Henk recognizes that 'people in Amsterdam, you know, [have always] looked down upon us.' To Bram, the stereotype is a mark of pride:

> I think everybody here will tell you the same, [the] Groningen punk scene is nothing like the rest of Holland. It's always been a bit *more*. More drugs, more drink, more bands, more partying; but also more fights – we've had a fucking rough time here in squats with cops and students but also with hooligans, you know.

The Groningen scene is characterized by strong connections between punks and other groups. This is something which is particularly noticeable as a recent development, with both Lotte and Bram discussing how the diminishing size of the punk scene in Groningen has led to greater hybridism, keeping punk alive and 'keeping it interesting':

> Well if you go to the bars here where we hang out, or the gigs, you [now] get a lot of different people, you know. It's not just [the] punks, it's also the metal guys, and rock and roll, rockabilly, even the proper normal looking people, middle age[d] people. It's not always like that but it has been perhaps for the last ten to fifteen years. And I like that. It's also because the subcultures are getting smaller so it mixes a bit more. You can't run a pub with just 10 fucking metalheads showing up, you know, you need to get all the other people in as well! And it works really well 'cos it turns out that we all get on really well, a lot better than we expected! (Bram)

The unity between subcultures is a recent development in the Groningen scene, noted by multiple individuals as particularly important to their survival. 'Unity' becomes another discursive tool in the construction of the Groningen punk scene.

Henk explains that this happens not just at a social level, but also at a musical level: 'I think for all music and all musicians in Groningen there's a difference; because the city's pretty small. So whether you play jazz, or whether you play funk or hardcore, punkrock or pop; whatever you do, we all know each other! All these people, they're all musicians and they all gather at the Viadukt rehearsal space.' Kosta believes that this improves the quality of the music made in Groningen: 'in Groningen musicians are for real, they really go for it and everybody plays tight, I like that! [For example] if the band from Groningen plays with a band from Amsterdam you can see the difference straight away. Groningen guys gonna blow the other guys away. No! [I'm] serious! [It's the difference between] the nuclear plant and the battery!'

Jolanda describes both the importance of the DIY scene and the squat scene to the Groningen punks, and how well these work together with the more 'normal' music circuit in the city. 'There really is a collaboration between DIY, punk and squatter scenes and the more normal places … These are [now] per se two different worlds, but if needs be then they work together. I think that it's lovely to see.' Again, in describing what is unique about Groningen, Jolanda raises discourses of 'unity.'

Indeed, these 'normal' venues often work so well with the punk scene due to their shared values. Café Vera is a larger venue (having a capacity of 450 people), and usually plays host to established, touring bands; some play punk but most do not. However, Café Vera's history and those who work and volunteer there are firmly rooted in DIY traditions and alternative politics, which are reflected in their desire to support the local underground punk scene. All participants who were engaged in organizing shows in the north mentioned 'helping people out' (Erik) or supporting the 'local' scene as key motivators for what they did. Local bands are often offered support slots on Café Vera's main stage, or in the smaller 'Cellar bar.' Jaap believes that most local punk bands have played at Café Vera. Another participant who was involved in the opening of the Crowbar says that the idea to open this 'punk pub' stemmed explicitly from a desire to support the local music scene. 'We thought that we need[ed] a small venue for alternative bands because there wasn't anything like that, especially for local bands.'

The emphasis that organizers place on making sure to provide for and support the local scene shows a pride in the bands that it has produced. Moreover, it is a sign of recognition that, in lieu of easy, quick access to the venues across the rest of the Netherlands, it is resourcefulness and self-reliance that keep the scene in Groningen vibrant.

One final way in which local identity was produced and negotiated by the Groningen punks was in how a great number of them were engaged in processes of reminiscing about their punk pasts as well as their present. Whilst I was in Groningen, many punks talked excitedly about the upcoming 'Simplon Punks Reunion.' The 'old' crowd which had coalesced around Simplon in the 1980s were, at the time of the fieldwork, planning to all get together later that year (2011) in Café Vera. This was prompted by a spate of nostalgia as a number of them (particularly Jacob and Henk) began to upload old photos to their Facebook accounts and a recently created (December 29, 2010) Facebook page 'Simplon Punks.' Jacob noted that this was the first time such a thing had happened, and he was looking forward to seeing those who had left the Groningen punk scene, with people planning to travel from as far as France in order to attend.

Their identity as 'Simplon' punks, rather than just 'Groningen' punks, shows super-locality: an identity tied to one specific venue. Furthermore, not only is it related to just any location but to a specific location in history; for most participants, the 'Simplon' of which they talked existed only from the late 1970s to the mid/late-1980s. Whilst the venue is still in existence, changes in management and direction meant that the 'Simplon punks' became an identity no longer associated with the venue from which they took their name.

Connectivity
Whilst there was a sense of isolation and difference from the rest of the Dutch punk scene, the Groningen punks were not lacking in mobility and connectivity. On an individual level, compared to other Dutch punks, Groningen punks travelled less often in order to attend gigs; however, Groningen bands maintained extensive tour networks, and Groningen's punk venues were very well connected internationally.

Mobility in the punk scene is often founded upon personal, translocal, or transnational relationships, which both reaffirm these connections and allow new ones to form. This process is the basis of another element of the transmission of cultural practices which may influence the individuals involved and their understandings of what it might mean to 'be' punk. Hodkinson suggested that just as 'travelling participants [of UK goth] were all liable to influence and be influenced by their counterparts in other areas of the country ... The national and sometimes international tours of even small goth bands provided further translocal influence' (2002, 106–7). This travelling is one element in the way punk cultural praxis is communicated translocally, affecting its rhizomic global flow.

As discussed above, in terms of gig-going opportunities Groningen is relatively isolated from the rest of the country. Whilst a few participants did report travelling to attend gigs outside Groningen (Lotte), the majority did not do this very often. Travelling was something that was more likely to be undertaken if the participant was invited to play a gig elsewhere. For example, Jolanda said that, beyond travelling to Leeuwarden regularly for band practice, 'if I travel further it's usually if I'm playing myself. And then I'll get to see other bands play too.'

Bands in Groningen often find themselves playing international gigs. This is partly due to the small nature of both the scene and the country; 'Holland is too small [to do shows every weekend]' (Theo). Playing gigs elsewhere is made possible by good connectivity within an international DIY punk scene. Indeed, in this regard Groningen bands' touring opportunities are similar to those of the rest of the country. Nijmegen-based Larry describes his band's touring pattern as being similar to many Dutch punk bands:

> After the first demo we started playing outside of our own town. And then after our
> first album we started playing all over the country and eventually we went to other
> countries ... our first gig abroad was in Belgium in Oostende and we really did a lot
> of gigs in Belgium ... So we went to England, we had some shows in France, mostly
> in Paris and Northern France ... But we also went to Germany, Austria, Slovenia, Italy,
> Switzerland, Hungary, Poland, Romania one gig, Slovakia, Norway and Sweden.

A Groningen-based band would, by contrast, often skip playing in Groningen straight to playing abroad. Groningen's proximity to Oldenburg in Germany[19] enables especially close links between the cities, which affects bands' touring opportunities. Compared to other Dutch bands, Groningen punks tend to tour internationally in Germany before they have toured as much in the Netherlands itself:

> You can compare [Groningen] a lot more with I suppose the German punk scene,
> which is not that weird because we're more or less on the border. When the first big
> city in Germany is Oldenburg, which is a lot closer than the first big city in Holland,
> you know, so. We've always – we're a bit more international – none of our bands
> played a lot in Holland either, we always went over the border straight away (Bram).

Bram notes how this specific proximity affects not only touring chances but also Groningen punks' self-perception, being closer in identity as well as in distance to Germany's punks. Local identity and transnational connections both affect the rhizomic network.

---

19 It is 130 km from Groningen to Oldenburg, compared to 180 km between Groningen and Amsterdam.

Bram's observation was backed up by the frequency with which the participants Suzanne, Maarten, Jacob, Ruben, Jaap, Henk, Bram, and Wim discussed touring in Germany and other neighbouring countries. Even a short-lived band such as Jolanda's first, who never recorded their music, had toured for 'five days in the Netherlands and Belgium. And we went once for a couple of days to Germany.'

Extending touring schedules across Europe was common for more established bands or bands with members who were more established in the scene. Jolanda points out the importance of connections to the DIY scene, which makes touring across Europe possible. Erik also discusses the worldwide DIY network, and views his own place within it as trying to establish as many network contacts as possible. The process of putting on a gig is a reciprocal one to him; if you organize a gig for an international band in your country they should do the same for you. In this way, networks of connections are built up, maintained, and then passed on. Tom suggests that the aging punk population in Groningen is key to this; those who have remained in the scene have built up bigger and more extensive networks. These are then passed between the generations. This intergenerational transmission of knowledge is enabled by the small size of the scene in which people know each other, as well as the prevalence of intergenerational bands such as Noodweer.

The Groningen scene maintains well-established links with the Americas. Whereas non-Groningen based Andre commented that 'America is really hard to go to for a tour,' Jolanda reports that (for the Groningen bands that she knows) 'there are very many bands who go on tour to America really quickly.'

Connections have been made across large swathes of the Americas, particularly the United States, by Groningen-based bands. In 1992, Jacob and Jaap travelled to America to play at their friends' (Fred and Toody from Dead Moon) twenty-fifth wedding anniversary party. They then toured the US West Coast, including Portland and Seattle. Wim and Bram also discussed American connections stemming from a joint tour undertaken by Fleas and Lice and Boycot in 1998. They started in Canada and travelled down America's East Coast before finishing the tour in Mexico; although only Boycot played New York's ABC No Rio, Fleas and Lice were banned after a member made disparaging comments about Americans in an interview with *Profane Existence*.

Each time a band organizes and goes on tour they strengthen and widen their translocal connections. Their touring mobility becomes a form of rhizomic cultural flow in which Groningen's local punk is shared globally.

The Dead Moon connection is one that originated in Groningen in Café Vera, and with the support of the local government. In order to celebrate the city's 925th anniversary, money had been provided for cultural endeavours. Café Vera, as a 'larger' venue, was relatively well established in the city as the place which attracted better-known touring bands, playing host to the Vibrators, Crass, Joy Division, Nirvana, and At the Drive-In, to name only a few. They were seen by the government as worthy of receiving financial support. This gave those at Café Vera the freedom to indulge themselves with gigs that they would ordinarily not be able to afford.

> We flew in Dead Moon, our most favourite unknown band, from Portland, Oregon [for the release gig]. They came to Europe for one gig only, and that was here. And since then they played about twenty times. They always started their tours in the cellar bar with like a free secret gig, but of course all the people knew about it. It was always packed and sweaty and they would play for two and a half hours. And the last gig of the tour was always in the main hall. They played like thirteen times in the main hall and about maybe nine times in the downstairs. (Jaap)

It was this musical connection that resulted in a transatlantic friendship between members of Dead Moon and Portland, Oregon's 'punk hearted' 'rock and roll' scene (Jaap), and individuals in Groningen such as Jaap and Jacob. It facilitated visits and tours in both directions, and therefore enabled the creation of yet further networks of contacts.

The interest in punk rock and roll in Groningen meant that Café Vera also booked bands such as the Gun Club, who are mentioned by three participants as particularly influential on both their tastes and those in the wider scene (Lotte). Relationships and touring patterns, affected by particularly influential people who are actively engaged in booking many of the bands that come to Groningen, result in the shaping of individuals' tastes within a scene. This heightened interest in rock and roll-influenced punk is something particular to the Groningen scene when compared to the rest of the Netherlands.

The Crowbar occupies a similar position to Café Vera, although within a different international touring network. A small venue, set up to help support the local scene, it still holds a key position for DIY punk internationally. 'We book not only local bands, we book from throughout the world; Venezuela, Brazil, America, South America, England, Europe; bands that are on tour.' At all levels, the venues in Groningen's punk scene reinforce its global connectivity.

Historically and contemporaneously, Groningen has had a sizeable enough local scene to support many gigs. From the earliest days of punk, the 'big' bands would visit Groningen; 'my daddy was a bit of an old beatnik. He actually went, here in Groningen, to see the Sex Pistols and the Ramones' (Bram). The scene has maintained and continued to create new connections at varying levels of the 'music industry' to retain a position within international touring networks. These translocal connections feed into Groningen's understanding of its locality, but Groningen has also had an effect on the global punk scene – an example of a rhizomic process of cultural flow.

One last way in which the Groningen scene maintains high levels of connectivity in spite of its relative isolation is by being a city that people wish to migrate to. Of fourteen participants[20] I spoke to, only five were born in Groningen or the surrounding villages. Three were from nearby Leeuwarden, and five from elsewhere in the Netherlands. One participant was international, however this (as far as ethnographic data can suggest) potentially underrepresents the internationalism of the scene, with other scene participants

---

20 Out of fifteen.

I met during fieldwork having moved to Groningen from France, Scotland, and Ireland. Ruben commented (exaggerating, perhaps) that 'it's mainly non-Dutch people here [in the Groningen punk scene].'

For at least some of those who moved to Groningen, the punk scene was the key reason for their choice. 'When we started to play [punk shows] in Groningen we were amazed how many people were actively busy here and how much people were going to the shows here. I packed my stuff and moved my ass over here' (Ruben).

These migrations highlight individual commitment to the scene – people are willing to make important life decisions based on this. When Groningen University did not offer the course that Lotte wanted to study, she chose to study something else: 'I really came to Groningen for the music scene and the city; twenty years ago there really was a lot happening. I wanted to study Journalism but they didn't have that at Groningen. I really wanted to come to Groningen, so when I came here I studied Dutch Language and Literature.'

This added form of mobility may be the result of connections with the scene, and will always bring new opportunities and fresh connections, both from people who have left scenes elsewhere to come to Groningen and those who leave Groningen to go elsewhere.

The GGI Festival

The GGI Festival is an annual punk festival that was founded in 2004 and alternates between three homes: Groningen (G), Glasgow (G), and Ireland (I).[21] Each year, the popular bands from the Groningen, Glaswegian, and Irish punk scenes are joined by other new bands to form a weekend's entertainment. At the time of the fieldwork for this research, participants were gearing up for GGI Groningen 2011.

The festival was set up as a celebration of the connections that had already been forged between these locations by participants of the scenes. More and more, it can be seen as a yearly 'reunion-festival' (Lotte) in order to rekindle those translocal friendships.

> Basically the festival is a celebration of the links between the punk rock communities of Groningen in the Netherlands, Glasgow in Scotland and Ireland. Over the last ten years bands such as Kidd Blunt from Ireland, Brawl from Wexford, Ex-Cathedra from Glasgow and Link from Groningen have toured in each other's countries and many friendships have been made between people from the three places. This link is still very much alive with Fleas and Lice now having two Glaswegians in the band, Groningen bands Makiladoras, Link and Fleas and Lice touring Ireland on separate occasions and Easpa Measa washing up on the hospitality of Groningen people some summers ago, for example. (GGI 2008)

The GGI Festivals are an example of the way in which both locality and connectivity are celebrated within the Groningen punk scene and those to which it is especially

---

21 All Groningen's events have taken place in Groningen itself, in 2005, 2008, and 2011. Glasgow's' first event took place in Edinburgh(!) in 2006, and the rest have taken place in Glasgow in 2009 and 2012. The first three Irish dates, 2004, 2007, and 2010, took place in Wexford, and the 2013 event took place in Ballina.

Figure 2.2: Poster for GGI Festival Groningen 2008, 5–7 September. Artist Unknown. Source: GGI (2008)

connected. Information on the 2014 event on its Facebook page says that it 'continues to grow and develop, with the firm intention of uniting people from different countries through a shared love of music, and demonstrates a commitment to supporting acts from the three countries' (GGI Fest 2014). The emphasis on making those personal translocal connections whilst supporting the bands that are at the core of the individual local scenes highlights the themes discussed in this chapter.

Figure 2.2 above shows the poster for GGI Groningen 2008.[22] It is notable that all Dutch bands playing are from Groningen. The Scottish bands are centred on (but not limited to) Glasgow. The Irish contingent highlights the number of towns in Ireland with connections to the festival with bands playing from Belfast, Dublin, and Kilcoole. There are also two American bands on the line up, highlighting further connectivity beyond the three nodes of the 'G,' 'G,' and 'I.'

The GGI Facebook page set up for the 2012 event in Glasgow further describes the nature and importance of the connections that are made in terms of how it enables the mobility and continuation of the punk scene;

> GGI was founded back in 2003/4 with the intention of celebrating the links forged between Groningen in the Netherlands, Glasgow in Scotland and various towns and cities in Ireland by the punk and hardcore bands that visited these places on tour over the last 20 odd years. Using the DIY network that has evolved

---

22 The most-recent GGI to have taken place in Groningen at the time of my fieldwork.

through small record labels, promoters and fanzines and the spirit of co-operation and mutual aid, many friendships and allegiances have been struck so this year we hope to recognise the origins of the festival but also bring in new bands that represent the evolution of punk /hardcore and underground metal in these three places. (GGI Glasgow 2012)

A significant proportion of individuals involved in the punk scene in Groningen have played at GGI Festivals, helped to organize them, or travelled to Glasgow or Ireland to attend them. A number of participants talk about the importance of the GGI festival in the social calendar. Whilst Bram talks about being too old to go on tour or play many gigs, travelling to Scotland to play at GGI is an important exception. For Lotte, GGI represents everything she loves about Groningen's punk scene:

That's what's nice about the punk scene here, there's lots of contact with England, Ireland, Scotland; lots of people who know each other … Lots of friends from all over the place, also America and Germany. That's the best thing about the punk scene, if someone comes along and says 'I'm a friend of such and such and I need somewhere to stay.' Yeah, it's a really nice scene.

Conclusion

This chapter presents the Groningen punk scene as distinct from the rest of the Dutch punk scene. Unlike many Dutch punks who do not feel connected to notions of the 'local,' those in the north actively construct a discourse of difference and locality represented in part through their desire to maintain and support the *local* scene. However, this process is intertwined with their negotiations in terms of positioning themselves within national and international scenes, largely absent from the former and highly connected with the latter. Their *locality* is based on a proximity to the German scene, with more positive comments directed in relation to German than to Dutch punks. Moreover, they regularly discuss their position as highly mobile and connected with scenic friends all over the world.

The Groningen punks emphasize their locality whilst simultaneously discussing the importance of their transnational connections; the two are not at odds with each other. The specific manifestations of their locality (e.g. the desire to support their own scene) feed into their position as globally well connected (their strong scene produces high quality touring bands and venues which others wish to visit); the global and the local are inextricably linked. Punk is a rhizomatic cultural form which is produced and reproduced by both local and translocal experiences on the part of those who are involved.

References

Berkers, P. (2012). 'Rock Against Gender Roles: Performing Femininities and Doing Feminism Among Women Punk Performers in the Netherlands, 1976-1982.' *Journal of Popular Music Studies*, 24(2), 155-75.

Cohen, S. (2007). *Decline, Renewal and the City in Popular Music Culture: Beyond the Beatles*. Aldershot: Ashgate.

Deleuze, G. and F. Guattari. (2003). *A Thousand Plateaus: Capitalism and Schizophrenia*. London, New York: Continuum.

GGI (2008). 'GGI Home.' http://www.bacteria.nl/GGI_Mainframe.htm.

GGI Fest (2014). 'GGI Fest 2014.' https://www.facebook.com/pages/GGI-Fest-2014/1431181713795015.

GGI Glasgow (2012). 'GGI Glasgow 2012.' https://www.facebook.com/pages/GGI-Glasgow-2012/319792204743852?sk=info.

Goossens, J. and J. Vedder. (1996). *Het gejuich was massaal: punk in Nederland 1976–1982*. Amsterdam: Jan Mets.

Groningen Pop Archive (n.d.). *Pop archief Groningen*. http://www.poparchiefgroningen.nl/.

Hannerz, U. (1992). Cultural Complexity: Studies in the Social Organization of Meaning. New York: Columbia University Press.

Hodkinson, P. (2002). *Goth: Identity, Style and Subculture*. Oxford and New York: Berg.

Hodkinson, P. (2004). 'Translocal Connections in the Goth Scene.' In A. Bennett and R. Peterson (eds.), *Music Scenes: Local, Translocal and* Virtual, 131–48. Nashville: Vanderbilt University Press.

Kempton, R. (2007). *Provo: Amsterdam's Anarchist Revolt*. Brooklyn: Autonomedia.

Kennedy, P. (2010). *Local Lives and Global Transformations: Towards World Society*. Basingstoke: Palgrave Macmillan.

Lashua, B., K. Spracklen, and S. Wagg (eds.). (2014). *Sounds and the City: Popular Music, Place, and Globalization*. Basingstoke: Palgrave Macmillan.

Lohman, K. (2013). 'Dutch Punk with Eastern Connections: Mapping Cultural Flows between East and West Europe.' *Punk & Post Punk* 2 (2): 147–63.

Lohman, K. (2015). *Punk Lives: Contesting Boundaries in the Dutch Punk Scene*. Unpublished PhD Thesis. University of Warwick.

O'Connor, A. (2002). 'Local Scenes and Dangerous Crossroads: Punk and Theories of Cultural Hybridity.' *Popular Music* 21 (2): 225–36.

Peterson, R. A. and A. Bennett. (2004). 'Introducing Music Scenes.' In A. Bennett and R. A. Peterson (eds.), *Music Scenes: Local, Translocal and Virtual*, 1–15. Nashville: Vanderbilt University Press.

Pilkington, H. (2004). 'Youth Strategies for Glocal Living: Space, Power and Communication in Everyday Cultural Practice.' In A. Bennet and K. Kahn-Harris (eds.), *After Subculture: Critical Studies in Contemporary Youth Culture*, 119–34. Basingstoke and New York: Palgrave Macmillan.

Pilkington, H. (2012). '"Vorkuta is the Capital of the World": People, Place and the Everyday Production of the Local.' *The Sociological Review* 60 (2): 267–91.

Pilkington, H. (2014). 'Sounds of a "Rotting City": Punk in Russia's Arctic Hinterland.' In B. Lashua, K. Spracklen, and S. Wagg (eds.), *Sounds and the City: Popular Music, Place, and Globalization*. Basingstoke: Palgrave Macmillan.

Robertson, R. (1995). 'Glocalization: Time-space and Homogeneity-heterogeneity.' In M. Featherstone, L. Scott, and R. Robertson (eds.), *Global Modernities*, 25–44. London: Sage.

Sabin, R. (1999). 'Introduction.' In R. Sabin (ed.), *Punk Rock: So What?: the Cultural Legacy of Punk*, 1–13. London: Routledge.

Shank, B. (1994). *Dissonant Identities: the Rock'n'roll Scene in Austin, Texas*. Hanover: Wesleyan University Press.

Viadukt. (2011). 'Tribute to Phil Vane.' http://hellpunk666.blogspot.co.uk/2011/04/tribute-to-phil-vane.html.

Appendix: Demographic Notes

Participant (pseudonym)	Age (at interview)	Location
Bram	44	Groningen
Erik	29	Leeuwarden
Henk	50	Groningen
Jaap	55	Groningen
Jacob	c. 41	Groningen
Jasper	23	Groningen
Jolanda	28	Groningen
Kosta	44	Amsterdam
Larry	28	Nijmegen
Lisa	28	Groningen
Lotte	42	Groningen
Maarten	50	Groningen
Ruben	34	Groningen
Suzanne	40	Groningen
Theo	47	Amsterdam
Tom	31	Leeuwarden
Wim	c. 40	Alkmaar

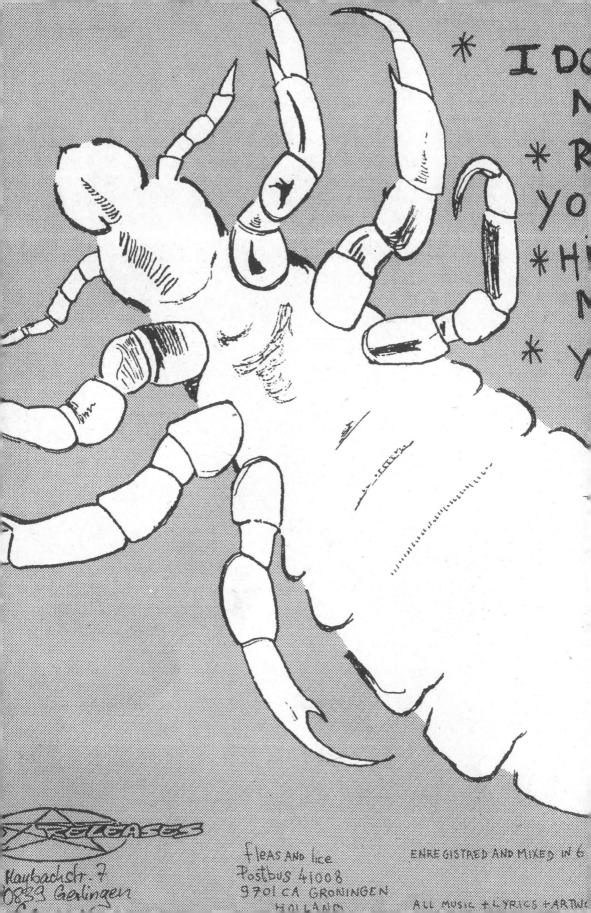

* I DO
N
* R
YO
* HI
N
* Y

RELEASES

Haybachstr. 7
0889 Gerlingen

Fleas AND lice
Postbus 41008
9701 CA GRONINGEN
HOLLAND

ENREGISTRED AND MIXED IN 6

ALL MUSIC + LYRICS + ARTWI

CONCERTO
DIA 8 JANEIRO PELAS
21:00H/PREÇO: 400$

CRUST PUNK CORE

SUBCAOS

FART

GRIND CRUST CORE

SIMBIOSE

KRUX DA PEDRA

FUCK YOU! I'M PUNK!

DESTROY THE SYSTEM OR BE DESTROYED

NO PALCO ORIENTAL /CALÇADA DUQUE DE LAFÕES, 78
BEATO (JUNTO AOS BOMBEIROS VOL. DO BEATO).
APANHAR O AUTOCARRO 39 NO ROSSIO PARA MARVILA ←

3. THE GLOBAL AND LOCAL IN MUSIC SCENES: THE MULTIPLE ANCHORING OF PORTUGUESE PUNK

AUGUSTO SANTOS SILVA & PAULA GUERRA

Abstract

What is punk's geography? How does the global background of the punk scene articulate with its various local manifestations? Is it a real transnational movement or are there as many punk scenes as the national figurations it can assume? This chapter addresses these issues considering the Portuguese punk scene. Our analysis is based on (1) seventy interviews with punk protagonists, (2) a database of bands, records, and songs, and (3) a database of fanzines. We consider, first, the balance between the international influences on the Portuguese scene and its specific characteristics. Then the meaning of global is redefined, taking into account the new information and communication technologies. Correspondingly, the local nature of the Portuguese punk scene is rebalanced through the identification of sub-scenes established in different locations within the country, and by pointing out the general sentiments punk activists express regarding Portuguese society. Finally, we explore the dialectics between the global dimension of punk culture and the sense of community it inspires in its members, concluding that the multiple anchoring of punk – simultaneously national and international, local and global, macro and micro – is a particular driver of its ability to survive and spread.

Keywords: punk scenes, Portugal, globalization, community

Augusto Santos Silva is a sociologist and Full Professor at the Faculty of Economics of the University of Porto (FEP), as well as a researcher in the Institute of Sociology of the University of Porto (IS-UP). As a politician, he participates as researcher in the KISMIF Project and is the author of several publications in the fields of sociology of culture and arts, sociological theories and methodologies, and political theory. Recently, he published (with Paula Guerra), among other works, the book *As palavras do punk* [*The Words of Punk*] (2015). E-mail: asilva@fep.up.pt

Paula Guerra is a sociologist and Assistant Professor of Sociology at the University of Porto (FLUP), a researcher in the Institute of Sociology of the same university (IS-UP), and an invited researcher at the Centre for Geography Studies and Territory Planning (CEGOT). She is also Adjunct Professor at the Griffith Centre for Social and Cultural Research, Australia (GCSCR). She is the founder and coordinator of the KISMIF Project/Conference and coordinates/ participates in several other research projects in the field of youth cultures and the sociology of art and culture, having published numerous works on those themes in the last few years. E-mail: pguerra@letras.up.pt

THE GLOBAL AND LOCAL IN MUSIC SCENES: THE MULTIPLE ANCHORING OF PORTUGUESE PUNK

Punk: Omnipresence and a Different Kind of Tension

'Punk did not start and end in the late '70s.' This statement by Don Letts[23] (quoted by Rodrigues 2012) is an essential starting point for our approach. After its emergence in the media in the late 1970s, punk turned into a global 'mediascape' with either more or less expressive local translations: punk is not only British or American, it is also Portuguese, Spanish, Mexican, or Tailandese. Our perspective refutes the interpretation that punk is a form of cultural imperialism (Sabin 1999, 3), as well as, purely and simply, a British invasion. Instead, it suggests that punk emerged as the outcome of a process of cultural syncretism (see Lentini 2003, 153). In the words of Laura E. Cooper and B. Lee Cooper (quoted in Lentini 2003), 'since the Second World War, some American and British music and subcultures developed through adapting musical forms to local conditions. These accommodations evolved into distinctly new approaches to the music and subcultures. Thereafter, they returned to the reputed country of origin where they were consumed and re-interpreted as further mutations with substantially different attributes to the original version.'

Renato,[24] one of our interviewees who is associated with three bands, says the following about how punk was formed:

> Firstly, punk excels in being something indefinable. As I try to think about punk, I'll consider it as a counterculture of undetermined origins, having been picked up by the 'money-making machine' and having been tightly packaged and given determined boundaries inside the rock culture. Rock culture is of paramount importance, as punk thrives from it, from the visual aspect of it, from concerts and music, although it's arguable it's a bit more than that. Let's see one thing, which is, even in the most acceptable side, the most commonly acceptable part of punk culture – the Ramones, formed by some kids in Queens 1974 that couldn't play shit and really liked the Beach Boys, the Searchers, '60s garage rock bands, playing that much faster, much noisier, and in shorter tracks, as it's the only thing they can do. That single fact, that they hadn't any technical skills, was so important that it shook, culturally speaking, the whole foundation of popular music culture. All popular music owes that debt to the Ramones. (Renato, 43 years old, bachelor degree, teacher, living in Lisbon)

---

23 Don Letts is an important actor in the world punk scene. He started his career participating in the first years of London punk. From there on after, he created more than twenty documentaries about punk, exploring a diversity of protagonists and scenes, among which one can distinguish *Punk: Attitude* and *The Clash: Westway to the World* (See Letts and Nobakht 2008).

24 Throughout this text, we will resort to parts of speeches by our interviewees as a way of exemplifying. All the interviewees hold a fictitious name and the parts used here follow the indications of the Deontological Code of the Portuguese Sociology Association.

Figure 3.1: Concert of the band The Parkinsons, 2014. Source: Photo by Rui Oliveira, KISMIF Project.

The word 'punk' was American slang for certain groups of youngsters at the base of the social structure, such as 'hoboes' and 'black homosexuals' (Laing 1978, 124). However, it only gained recognition upon its application to music. First, it denoted a New York music scene, and then, with the development of the British, predominantly London-based, scene following the Sex Pistols, it acquired global visibility. In the United Kingdom, punk reflected the concerns over matters of social class and showed itself as a form of hybrid music. Its roots are not only in the New York punk scene but also the British subcultures that came before (skinhead, mod, teddy boy, glam rock, reggae, and rockabilly) (Cogan 2010). From London and New York, punk spread to other cities (such as Washington or Los Angeles), countries (such as Mexico), and regions (South America, North Africa, Middle East, and Asia). It gradually grew to constitute a 'popular culture geopolitics' and integrated never-ending variations and specialties (Dunn 2008, 195).

This double movement of globalization and localization heightened punk's nature as an assemblage of popular culture morsels in a chaotic and paradoxical mixture. It combines aesthetics, music, image, text, and landscapes and articulates specificity and hybridism (Adams 2008, 3–4). It represents a new sort of global communication – not just musical, but also cultural, social, political, and economic (the 'Do-it-Yourself' model, henceforth DIY).

According to Moore, the original British punk subculture expressed a 'culture of deconstruction' as a response to the postmodern conditions of the late twentieth century, thus creating a different kind of tension (2004; 2007). 'Punk,' Dunn notes, 'provides the possibility for disalienation, offering means for resisting the multiple forms of alienation prevalent in a late capitalist society' (2008, 198). But the elements of subordination will also become present. Referring to Barthes, Hebdige noted that punk reconverted subcultural signs (pertaining to clothing, music, props, hairstyles, flyers, and so on) into objects that were produced, commercialized, and mass consumed. At the same time, punk legitimated the labelling and redefinition of deviant behaviours by the mainstream groups, thus adding an ideological effect to the mercantile effect (Hebdige 1979). Therefore, it is also instrumental for the social processes that vulgarize and domesticate the Other by denying their autonomous existence, or transforming them in an entity that, according to Dunn (2008, 200–1), is 'meaningless exotica, a pure object, a spectacle, a clown.'

Perhaps the most adequate perspective seems to be the one that refuses to place punk at a position of co-optation *or* counterculture. The most fertile hypothesis might be that it really is the two things at the same time, i.e. a complex cultural arena dashed and filled by contradictions and tensions. This does not necessarily mean ignoring Jameson's (1991; 2002) remarks that point out the potential counter-hegemony of these cultural forms; in fact, many are the means used by punk in a counter-hegemonic orientation. It is enough to note the systematic use of informal social networks, the Internet, and the tours that allow the flux of records, fanzines, bands, ideas, and styles; the use of independent companies and shops; and the DIY ethics and the option of recording and releasing songs with one's own funds. All these means allow for a global and differentiated communication, reaching virtually the whole world. And it is through this that the dialectics between identity and differentiation, globalism and territoriality, and the unbalances that structure the worldwide standard of punk take place, namely in the opposition between centres and peripheries (O'Connor 2002; 2004).

The tensions between counter-culture and integration make punk a very complex reality, internally contradictory and variable (O'Hara 1995). What is punk? Where are the punks? What influences them? What is used to distinguish them from other social groups? And how do such influences endure? These are all questions in the discourse, behaviour, and self-representation of everyone that identifies themselves with the movement. The answers are neither simple nor univocal – in fact, they can be widely diverse and very antagonistic. This plasticity, however, may be the great secret of the punk history. 'Punk faked its own death' (Clark 2003, 229), to be able to survive; it tried to reinvent itself, releasing itself from its own orthodoxies, be it styles or values. Punk might be an identity so wide that one might say, as Clark (2003, 230) suggests, that 'it is called punk, however it has no name.' Or in the words of Renato, punk does not want to enclose itself inside the punk label, for each one is as they are:

I was once coming out the subway at Areeiro [a station in Lisbon], army boots, rolled up trousers, Motorhead t-shirt, chess shirt, leather jacket, and I heard 'Nowadays punks wear Motorhead t-shirts,' to which I turned and simply said 'punk is your cunt of a mother.' Of course I got slapped right there, but that was my reaction. I am myself, an individual, not a punk. Looking behind, I am a product of punk culture, and this sort of fashion is important in the way that it shapes a series of things, it's a bit like that. Saying

Figure 3.2: Concert of the band Dokuga, 2014. Source: Photo by Rui Oliveira, KISMIF Project.

'I am punk,' there is not a single lyric in which that could be said. For example in flyers and so on, we would never do a flyer of a band, by me for our band, saying 'Lisbon punks,' 'Punks as Fuck.' The whole thing of doing a tattoo saying punk and stuff – no, never thought like that.

This chapter explores the constitutive tension of punk culture on a particular dimension: the dialectics of the global and local. It fits into ongoing research[25] examining Portuguese punk from 1977 until now. We shall consider its multiple 'geographies' that ensue from the territorial seeding of bands in relation to Portuguese society and international punk, along with its media and symbolism.

Methodologically speaking, the following analysis uses the statements of seventy punk protagonists (musicians, editors, promoters, fans, critics) that we interviewed, and a database constituting: (a) 539 Portuguese bands, (b) 1,429 phonographic records, (c) the lyrics of 264 songs, and (d) 93 fanzines with a total of 177 editions. This material is already a substantial part of the collection, and the objective of the research to census and archive it for public use.[26]

25 This approach was possible with the funding by FEDER through the COMPETE Operational Program from the FCT, the Foundation for Science and Technology led by The Institute of Sociology of The University of Porto (IS-UP), developed in partnership with the Griffith Centre for Cultural Research (GCCR) and Lleida University (UdL). The following institutions were also participants: the Faculty of Economics of the University of Porto (FEP), the Faculty of Pschicology and Educational Sciences of the University of Porto (FPCEUP), the Faculty of Economics of the University of Coimbra (FEUC), the Centre for Social Studies of the University of Coimbra (CES), and the Lisbon Municipal Libraries (BLX).

26 In addition to the authors of this chapter, the following researchers were part of the project team: Ana Oliveira, Ana Raposo, Andy Bennett, Carles Feixa, Hugo Ferro, João Queirós, Luís Fernandes, Manuel Loff, Paula Abreu, Pedro Quintela, Rui Telmo Gomes, and Tânia Moreira. In the recollection of data, the team had the support of the researchers Filipa César, João Carlos Lima, João Matos, João Pereira, Paulo Lemos, and Pedro Barbosa.

Because of the central role that they play in our analysis, it is necessary to make a particular note about the group of interviews. They encompass topics related to: (1) the international background of the Portuguese punk scene, (2) the use of the Internet and social networks, (3) the perspective regarding the place and trajectory of Portugal in the world system, (4) the justifications related to the use of the Portuguese and English languages in lyrics, and (5) the dissemination of the punk scenes throughout the national territory and the identification of local communities and their models of functioning.

Gender	%
Male	87.14
Female	12.86
Age	
19–24	2.86
25–30	7.14
31–35	18.57
36–40	21.43
41–45	14.29
46–50	27.14
51–55	5.71
56–60	2.86
Academic Degree	
Bachelor Degree (and higher)	47.14
Incomplete Bachelor Degree	10.00
Upper Secondary Education	34.29
Lower Secondary Education	8.57
Place of residence	
Lisbon	41.43
Porto	10.00
Another location in the Metropolitan Area of Lisbon	12.86
Another location	35.71

Table 3.1: Characterization of the interviewees according to gender, age, academic degree, and residence (in %, N=70). Source: KISMIF Project

Global, Local and Translocal Music Scenes

The notion of cultural scene was developed from the concept of field, as was described by Pierre Bourdieu, and art world, as Howard S. Becker proposed it (see Bennett and Peterson 2004, 3). According to several authors, this concept can readily articulate the dimensions of local and global contemporary dynamics. It is born in the context of the theories called 'post-subcultural studies' to determine several sociocultural activities that are clustered by location (normally a neighbourhood, city, or urban area) and/or type of cultural production (for instance, a style of music) (Bennett 2004, 223; Straw 2004, 411). The work of Straw (1991) was seminal in this. He offers a sophisticated analysis of the interaction between music, taste, and identity, exploring the idea of translocalism – that is, how clusters of different agents musically and geographically disperse so as to be involved in collective cultural practices thanks to the ability music has to transcend physical barriers. Since then, the concept has been progressively used in the analysis of the production, performance, and reception of popular music, taking into account time and space coordinates.

Space is truly a critical factor when approaching musical scenes, whose practices and relationships are inscribed in space, and are in constant articulation with other social processes. Cultural scenes have a predominantly urban nature (Blum 2001, 10) but are not circumscribed to cities. Due to new communication technologies and the mobility of physical supports – such as cassettes, CDs, and vinyl – as well as gigs and tours, the limits of each scene have expanded. On the one hand, more people can access recorded music, for instance. On the other, current technology, besides making processes more accessible, warrants a quality similar to the old recording processes. Thus, musicians and bands do not need the support of major labels to get the attention of the public, instead doing all things needed autonomously, from recording to publicizing their music. The development of the Internet has made the communication between bands and fans easier, accelerating the scene dynamism, from its beginning and development through to its disappearance. Scenes can be nurtured in urban as well as rural contexts, and in areas of rural-urban contiguity. They arise in both centres and peripheries. Moreover, the bond between scene and fixed physical location has become more tenuous – today, a scene can be translocal and even virtual (Bennett and Peterson 2004).

With these variations taken into account, we examine the international background of the Portuguese punk scene. Its most obvious aspect is the frequency in the use of the English language in the naming of bands, in song lyrics, and in the names of fanzines and phonographic registries. Table 3.2 below synthesizes the relevant information.

	%	N
Name of the bands	42.30	539
Fanzine titles	26.88	93
Records	38.63	1429
Song lyrics	22.00	264
Fanzine content	2.82	177

Table 3.2: The use of the English language in the naming of bands, records, fanzines, lyrics, and fanzine content (% of the total N of each category). Source: KISMIF Project

There are two key points regarding the language used in the band names. The first is that the percentage of those that choose English (42%) is roughly the same as those that choose Portuguese (41%), with the remainder using symbols and imaginary languages. Secondly, English has gained a particular relevance, with the bands of the 1990s and 2000s

Figure 3.3a: During concerts, 2014. Source: Photo by Rui Oliveira, KISMIF Project.

using it much more frequently than in previous decades. This fact is also observed in what concerns phonographic registries; however, Portuguese is once again the norm from 2008 onwards, in what might be an indication of the consolidation of the Portuguese punk scene across local areas.

At the same time, it is of utmost interest to analyse – in line with what has been done in other studies concerning non-Anglo-Saxon social reality (see Gololobov, Pilkington, and Steinholt 2014) – the ways in which the protagonists interpret the relationship between Portuguese punk and the global punk scene. In this aspect, our interviewees' discourse can be organized into three positions. The first defines this relation as mimetic. The second prefers to describe it as an adaptation and re-appropriation of themes; that is, it stresses the specific dimensions of Portuguese punk. Lastly, the third denies in itself the existence of any autonomous Portuguese punk, and questions the relevance of such a relationship. Each of these positions admits several nuances and variations. Let us then take a closer look at each one.

According to the first position, the Portuguese punk scene is nothing but an imitation, first of the UK scene and then of the US. All we have is the transposition of a pattern of sound, aesthetic, age, and generational bonds. But three important variations are evident within this general view. The first reflects the time lapse in the transposition. In punk as well as in other social expressions, the reproduction of foreign artistic expressions has allegedly taken place one or two decades later. After all, besides being a peripheral country, Portugal suffered from fifty years of political dictatorship, isolating it from various international trends. One of the interviewees states, for instance, that compared to the

English punk scene (strongly associated with a much broader expression, when it comes to both people and venues), the Portuguese punk scene was 'nearly child's play,' coming off as a reproduction and imitation of what took place at the international level: 'Here, it's all much diluted' (Luís, 39 years old, upper secondary education, cameraman, Lisbon, leader of an active punk band).

The second nuance, while stating that the scene is mostly a form of imitation, stresses that it took place in the same historical period. Records, bands, and aesthetics arising in England arrived in Portugal around the same time. The positive side of such a hasty presence of the global trend in the Portuguese punk is actually emphasized by punk being a 'transmitter of other realities,' that is, of other possibilities (Frederico, 49 years old, bachelor degree, translator, presently living in London). For instance, there are several mentions of how the Portuguese punk of the 1970s and 1980s derived directly from the Sex Pistols' attitude and behaviour and from their simple way of playing, which brought hope to the young people who aspired to be musicians yet had no technical knowledge to accomplish any sort of musical endeavours. This would pave the way for several other bands that embraced these ethics, whether they were directly connected to the music genre or not (Robb 2009; Middles 2009). In the words of Pedro (teacher from a small municipality, bachelor degree, 49 years old):

> I think in Portugal we have a similar situation. We have a type of band that really connects with the attitude that was born in England and referred to them [the Sex Pistols]. We had that type of bands, like in Spain, like in the USA. There are two major English icons, on one side you have the sort of model that is [Sid] Vicious, and on the other there are the intellectual issues that, in the majority of the themes, for me, aren't really punk in musical terms, such as the Clash, for example.

The third nuance of the mimetic position of Portuguese punk, compared to the North American and English punk, sees in this a sign of inferiority in terms of aesthetic, musical, and social vitality. This was the price paid for the fragility of our urban and musical culture.

> The punk movement in Portugal was nothing more than a 'cliché' – it was short, fast, restricted to some groups, it had no 'global' national image. The youth of that time got punk, nearly in its final stages, through some record releases which came from the outside. Only later, after a big time-lapse, was there actual material being recorded in Portugal. Punk, in Portugal, was viewed as a fashion, a musical fashion. Its main reason for existing is in the countries where its first embryo was born. (César, 48 years old, bachelor degree, computer programmer, living in Seixal near Lisbon)

Meanwhile, the global influence on the Portuguese punk scene can be interpreted in the light of a second positioning, which points out an attitude of appropriation and assemblage. This logic takes into consideration two main elements – the proximity to what is being done on an international level, and an effort to adapt global influences to the Portuguese reality. Here, too, one can see nuances. The first can be called objectivist. The Portuguese scene would be

Figure 3.3b: During concerts, 2014. Source: Photo by Rui Oliveira, KISMIF Project.

inevitably different due to the size of the country, as well as its political, social, and economic background. Thus, the specificity of the national punk scene doesn't really derive from any deliberate act of appropriation. It is rather a consequence of an objective context, and this fact condemns it to its small size, informality, and inability to attain international status.

In the second variant, the interviewed protagonists began from the same idea of objective specificity. However, they associate this circumstance with a potential for reinvention. The very scarcity of resources, namely regarding fund-raising and production capabilities, ends up stimulating a DIY savoir-faire: doing it oneself. The motto is 'do a lot with little.' Musicians create their own resources, and in some cases even their instruments, which contributes to reinstating the specificity and local roots of the Portuguese punk scene. Luís, the cameraman and musician we have already met, puts it like this:

> Do a lot with little: it was a bit reinvented; it was DIY, with little means to do it, with something to say … There was no support, no actual means, and on the other hand it was a bit of that which led so many people to be pushed or inspired by a punk/hardcore philosophy.

A third component of the local appropriation of global influences is manifested in the adaptation of the message relative to a defence of the Portuguese context. It is therefore more a matter of content than process. There are, for instance, several accounts of the use of pamphlets and flyers of international organizations (namely in defending animal rights), for the spread of the respective messages in Portugal. That can involve the translation, synthesis, or adaptation of the texts and visual supports. The fourth and last nuance of this position, which values the local appropriation of the global, is one of the most significant aspects of our research. Since we are dealing with the intersection of various global influences Portuguese activists had access to, the importance of contact with multiple international bands and subgenres, and cross-mixing them into projects, languages, and products of their own, is of central importance.

Take the case of the Sex Pistols as an example. Despite the many different reactions that might arise when talking about such an iconic band, it is always described as a starting point for several musical projects (Goshert 2000). According to many interviewees, the punk music the Sex Pistols produced was meant to surprise, provoke, and outrage audiences. It was a simple, direct, nihilistic, provocative punk, hoping to break rules, barriers and conventions. The band is held as authentic and genuine, pioneering in its own right and strongly influential, having contributed to the birth of dozens of other bands. In this sense, it was absolutely necessary to examine how such influences were transmitted and shared. The means were several: sharing tapes and discs brought by those who travelled, or who had the means to purchase foreign goods; collective listening of the songs and group debates about them; and, foremost, the access to radio shows which publicized and commented on the newly formed punk music and the associated lifestyle.

In Portugal, the key role was taken by the well-known radio disc jockey António Sérgio,[27] active in the Portuguese radio from the early 1970s until his passing in 2009. Many interviewees report the nearly sacred aspect of listening to programs such as Rotação [Rotation], Rolls Rock, Som da Frente [Sound of the Vanguard], and Rock em Stock [Rock in Stock]. António Sérgio is consensually thought of as the engine that drove Portuguese punk, being the person who brought, publicized, and made accessible the various influences which were then appropriated (Guerra 2014). Without his mediation, the Portuguese punk scene would have undoubtedly been different. In addition, the program titles mentioned above speak for themselves – he did not focus on a single subgenre of underground music, but rather took full account of the vitality and diversity of all music representing the 'sound of the vanguard.'

This is not, however, the sole mediation that transforms and 'locates' punk, and gives localized punk a hybrid cultural potential, combining different sources of inspiration into a new and peculiar composition. Another mediation is the one that takes place in the local areas and social milieux where punk groups and scenes arise. People and contexts are naturally different, and diversity matters. The various local scenes are, most of the time, examples of the appropriation of cultural signs from other places; symbols which were remixed, surely, but symbols from other places nonetheless.

27 António Sérgio (1950–2009) was an important Portuguese radio host, radio producer, DJ, record editor, and specialist who supported leading and innovative rock and pop music artists on his shows. Starting in the late 1970s, António Sergio played the music of many artists at that time unknown in Portugal, putting local audiences in touch with them and their music. In this sense, Sérgio is regarded in some circles as the Portuguese equivalent of the late British Radio DJ John Peel. He was responsible for the release of the first punk record in Portugal, 'Punk Rock '77 New Wave '77' by Pirate Dream Records in 1978.

We have considered, thus, the second of the three positions distinguished by the protagonists interviewed regarding the relationship between the Portuguese and global punk scenes. Unlike the first, which characterized it simply as a copy, this one emphasizes the elements of appropriation and transformation. It is, therefore, the position which connects punk and cultural hybridism – assuming that punk is not uniform but rather appropriated and redefined locally, according to the resources and the social and political needs of each location. Each punk scene thus seems to be a process of combining global and local elements.

Contrasting as they do – one underlining mimesis, the other transformations – both positions assume the existence of a Portuguese punk scene. It is, however, this assumption that the third position questions, as expressed by some of the interviewees. The reasons presented that deny the existence of a Portuguese scene are several, but can be grouped in four main arguments. Firstly, there has not been a 'proper' punk scene in Portugal due to the time lapse from when international punk arrived in the country, thus making punk and post-punk simultaneous phenomena. So there was, and still is, a vibrant and influential underground music scene in Portugal, but it is highly debatable whether it can be brought into a single form of 'punk time.'

The second argument contests the existence of a Portuguese punk *scene*, since its long-term outcomes are scarce in the crucial years of the late 1970s and 1980s. At that time, there are few phonographic recordings by Portuguese punk bands. The bands did exist and gave several concerts, but very few recordings of any kind were made. That lack of materiality, of historical products, in the sense of something that transcends concerts and rehearsals, did not allow for the *structuring* of a recognizable scene as such. It was a movement, but not a scene, says Lucas, 37 years old, living in Lisbon and with secondary education:

> There was a punk movement, but it didn't bring anything to be materialized. That is, there are no records. You know they existed, played here and there, but there aren't any records, not a single disc ... nothing, or very little. Even in demo tapes there's very little, that is, you come to the conclusion that Portuguese punk became stagnant. It existed, but got tied up, I don't know, there was a sort of inertia ...

The third argument appeals directly to the internal stress of punk. 'Real punks' are one thing; 'weekend punks' are another, very different thing. The first were scarce but genuine, thoroughly involved in the sub- and countercultural stance of the global movement. The others were larger in number, but constituted by a superficial relationship to punk; they lived as an aesthetic and occasional evasion of cultural and social norms. On a daily basis, these 'weekend punks' were conformists with no revolutionary spirit; once a week, they wore leather jackets and safety pins and sought a sort of liberation, calling themselves punks. The Sex Pistols, for instance, captivated audiences with their pose and aesthetic, their dyed hair and extravagantly coloured clothes, cut up ties, spikes, pins, and

Dr. Marten's boots. However, was the attitude behind these looks, expressed in the music, equally felt? For most occasional fans, as for the public opinion, punk was reduced to a fad, losing its sense and ideal. That is what Fernando (54 years old, PhD and professor, living in Lisbon) regrets: how can there be a real scene if the people are not genuinely punks?

> In my understanding, punk started degenerating into a certain aestheticization of the movement, and because of that people started dressing like punks; that is, there was a sort of a fad starting, a punk aesthetic and fashion, no? People started to listen to punk music, dress like punks, but inwardly they weren't punks. It was when, shall we say, punk's public started to grow and, as generally happens, when the consumers increase the original essence and quality are lost.

The last argument adds to the previous ideas of indistinctiveness, immateriality, and lack of authenticity germinating from the notion of perceived weakness. According to this position, there was no punk scene, because what did exist – the bands, the venues, the public, and the media – did not gather enough sturdiness. The movement was too vague and unstructured to gather any sort of projection and a singular identity. It was somewhat too weak, and ended up diluting the wider scene. There was a lack of consistence and persistence. Apparently, many ideas and projects existed, but the stamina necessary to realize them did not. Here, some interviewees perceive a demonstration of the allegedly national 'destiny' – 'the ease with which one gives up on one's dreams' – or more realistically the negative effects of the periphery. As Gonçalo (a young web designer with a bachelor's degree, living in a small city on the northern coast) says: 'We don't have the structure which allows the development of a continuous flow of bands, editors and means to sustain punk.'

This assessment converges with O'Connor's point on centre vs. periphery. O'Connor considers that the hegemony of the North American scene is due to the economic resources available there. In this case, European scenes would be semi-peripheral and Third World ones clearly peripheral (2002, 2004).

Live Fast and Be Online: Virtual Scenes
We have strived to understand the beginnings and development of the Portuguese punk scene, and its relations to the international punk scene, dominated by the Anglo-Saxon paradigm of the United Kingdom and the United States. Like several other popular culture youth movements of recent years, punk was quick to globalize. Urban youngsters from all over the world quickly had access to the sounds and languages of punk, as well as the production and diffusion methods, and the worldview and lifestyles associated with punk. Portugal was no exception. A simple way of understanding this global force is to take into account the widespread use of the English language, be it in the names of the bands, in their recordings and fanzines, or in the lyrics of their songs.

However, we cannot end our analysis here if we are to understand the relationship between the locally grown Portugal punk scene and the global one. In that sense, the first exercise we undertook was to overview the proposed interpretations by the actors involved in the Portuguese scene. By taking into account seventy interviews with such protagonists, we identified three main interpretations. Two of those assume the existence of a Portuguese punk scene. This scene is structured as a form of mimesis to the global scene, as holds the first interpretation, or by appropriation and re-creation, as holds the second.

Mimesis can be lived as a radical form of inferiority, a time lapse of international references, since these factors will be transposed directly over yearly intervals. Or, it can be modulated, being a rough copy of foreign products, albeit chronologically contemporaneous. On the other hand, the protagonists who refuse the idea of a plain copy point out a sort of appropriation and thus re-creation of Portuguese punk when compared to the international. In a string of arguments, ordered by their rising intensity, this had to happen, given the objective difference between the national situation compared to, for instance, the British; because the small size of the Portuguese reality forced its actors to reinvent and adapt, in a very realistic application of the DIY principle; because there were efforts to adapt the causes and contents that were central to punk to the Portuguese circumstances; or, finally, because the actors involved were able to access various influences and mix them, creating their own seminally hybrid scene.

As we have seen, the controversy between mimesis and transformation is not suffice to detail the international status of the Portuguese punk scene. A third position is thus possible and expressed in the debate. Its focus is essentially on the *inexistence* of the scene as such: the Portuguese punk scene did not distinguish itself enough from other subgenres, like post-punk; it did not produce material results of a long-lasting nature in sufficient quantity; it was too residual, with most of its members being non-authentic, followers of a fashion rather than adherents to a culture; it never grew, continued to be fragile in nature, and never gained strength and visibility. These arguments – mentioned in turn by several interviewees – deny the autonomy of the Portuguese scene, converging with the first interpretation: either the Portuguese scene is not Portuguese, because it is just a copy of the international scene (the first interpretation), or it is not a scene because it never gained any structure and density (the third interpretation).

The relationship between Portuguese punk and global punk is thus a critical matter that divides the protagonists of this field, which is yet another demonstration of how it is organized by tension, ambiguities, and contradictions. It also demonstrates the extreme pertinence of the relationship between national and international for the actors discussed here. That relationship is vital for the formation of the collective identity of Portuguese musicians, mediators, and audiences who want to refer themselves to the new international underground music of the late 1970s and onwards.

However, the notion of global goes beyond 'international.' Global punk is not limited to the planetary dissemination of groups and sounds which originally gained recognition in the United Kingdom, and then in the United States. The new information and communication technologies, overcoming the barriers of time and space and allowing

Figure 3.3c: During concerts, 2014. Source: Photo by Rui Oliveira, KISMIF Project.

for the instantaneous contact of people worldwide, provide the word global with a whole new meaning. The Internet drives cultural globalization with widely dispersed and horizontal global communication flows (Appadurai 2005). This also frames the tensions between hegemony and counter-hegemony in punk as well as in other cultural arenas. The issue of global vs. local must then be modulated.

Like in various other scenes, Portuguese punk has, from the late 1990s onwards, used the Internet and, in particular, social networks. The quick spread of news, images, sounds, ideas, and connections between actors and groups from all over the world, and the immediate access to multiple data and topics through the use of digital archives and editions, have promoted a sense of global community, of belonging to a global scene, which characterizes the Portuguese punk scene as much as other national scenes. The consequence is obvious – the Portuguese punk scene is a local scene, since it has formed in a specific social, economic, cultural, and political background; but it is *also* part of a global scene, part of the global community of punk culture.

The interviewed protagonists – 90% of whom confirm they have a Facebook page, which they use to gather information and attend events – agree with this conclusion. In a general fashion, they recognize that the Internet and the associated social networks have come to stay, and not having to access to them means being left out of a series of relevant dimensions, not only in terms of musical creation and fruition, but also in what relates to quotidian life in its whole. They defend the new possibilities offered by the Internet contributing to keeping punk alive and active, stopping its stagnation and erosion.

If we look now to our database of bands active in Portugal between 1977 and 2013, we will find equally interesting data. From the total of 539 bands, 43% have a Facebook account, and 54% have a MySpace account. And one should keep in mind that 39% of the bands precede the 2000s, before any of those services were first offered. The global framework which is thus constituted in virtual space certainly does not eliminate the micro and meso levels of social relationships. Using a case study of musical groups from a Portuguese region, Moreira (2013) showed how the bands' Facebook pages host mostly the interactions of those who are physically or socially close to them. But, through the Internet, another scale is added to social interaction (O'Connor 2003; 2008).

When questioned about the added value of the Internet to the development of punk as a global culture, the interviewees identified one or several of the following four advantages. Firstly, the Internet has made a true democratization of information access possible. Not only is there a huge amount of available content, the access to it is quick, easy, and nearly unlimited. It will not come as a surprise then that many of the interviewed mention how file sharing means that the public can access a wide variety of musical projects, even before acquiring their records. The access to digital editions has taken an increasingly important role, frequently being free. Myspace seems to be an efficient platform in this area, but has been surpassed by others with links to Facebook (such as Bandcamp, Soundcloud, Spotify, and podcasts).

The second advantage, very much associated with the first but now concerning the bands, is in the possibility of publicizing their work. Many interviewed musicians state that they use the Internet to publicize their projects and recent works, to sell records and demos, to establish contacts, and to trade records and fanzines. Simultaneously, the Internet and social networks also serve as vehicles for mobilization around messages and social causes which are part of the Portuguese punk scene. The third advantage relates to the conditions for creating and producing music. Many researchers have written about this (Kahn-Harris 2007; Bennett 2008; Dale 2010; Guerra 2013). At its extreme, new resources and tools result in every person being able to play from home, and even record at home. Combined with the accessibility of contents and the possibilities of dissemination, these production facilities broaden the horizons of the underground scene actors immensely. New media and digital social networks democratize the access to products and music makers, making both producers and products more attractive, preventing the stagnation of the musical scene. As said melancholically by Alberto (46-year-old veteran punk promoter, secondary education completed), nowadays 'things' are easier:

> What has changed is the ease with which things now happen. When I started there were one or two concerts a year. Now there are two or three concerts a week in Porto alone. That is, the speed with which things happen is much greater nowadays than it was in my time … However, the positive side is that you have a lot more bands than before, and they play much better.

Last but not least, the Internet allows for the communication between members of the punk community to last beyond the moments of greater involvement in the scene. This aspect is made more relevant as ageing occurs, both at the individual and the musical forms levels (Bennett 2013). It is not surprising, then, that one of the frequent advantages mentioned by the interviewees is precisely this one. Many underline the importance of blogs, which create bridges between the scene and those who had to step away for professional reasons. Others consider Facebook a quintessential tool in reconnecting with old acquaintances. For others, social networks do facilitate the communication between geographically dispersed scenes. By overcoming physical distance, by keeping or recovering contacts, and by building a sense of community beyond time and space, the Internet strengthens bonds and affiliations. It relates to emotion:

> I've come across many people from those days. Due to Facebook I've found people I haven't seen in over 20 years, something not only impressive but almost emotional. (Cristiano, 44 years old, upper secondary education, photojournalist, living in Lisbon)

Of course, the virtual world does not escape the criticism from the interviewees, the protagonists, active or retired, of punk culture. Identifying the perceived flaws is no less important than identifying the virtues. We have found three essential criticisms. The first regards the lack of personal contact caused by impersonal technology. With no need for a physical presence, the Internet can lower the quality of the interaction, making encounters, in the sense of prolonged face-to-face interactions, less usual if not entirely unnecessary. The second criticism deplores the disappearance of physical objects, so important to the punk culture. For some of the interviewees, the progressive substitution of digital files for 'ancient' vinyl, CDs, or demo tapes seems to suck the energy from the countercultural movement. All punk artefacts can now be found online, and all can be diluted, that is lost, on a digital screen. Frederico (49 years old, professional translator with a bachelor's degree, now living abroad) echoes this point: 'The Internet kills rock culture and expression, killing the physical object to replace it with the screen, the copy. It takes all ability to move, to act, because it places it on a screen – and then it takes all the will to act too.'

Perhaps in this light the resilience of the fanzine as a physical object can be better understood (only 30% of the 93 fanzines in our database have an online edition), as perhaps can understood the persistence – and present revivalism – of vinyl in the music scene (Thompson, 2004). The data from our case study is clear: the vinyl edition never reached high numbers (when compared, for instance, with the CD), but today's numbers are relatively similar to thirty years ago, and the curve presents a slight increase in more recent years.

The last criticism, concerning the idea of 'trivialization,' is also relevant. The vastness of the amount of information available, the extreme ease of access, and the haste with which ideas and forms are constructed, eroded, and substituted have all contributed to the vulgarization of punk. They make it trivial, reducing to consumption what should be a multimodal participation, and degrading in fashion what should be an attitude and a choice. As stated by one of the interviewees (Alberto, a veteran promoter from Porto), they 'pollute' the concept of punk. How to distinguish the projects which matter, in the midst of such an immense and banal information? How to build a strong bond to a culture and a way of life when all seems to be circumscribed to, as Boris Vian would put it, 'the froth on the daydream'?

Let us, for the first time in this chapter, listen to a female voice. Isabel (51 years old, a secondary-school teacher living in Lisbon) compares the present times with her youth:

> Access to music is easier, but much has been lost in terms of contacting people, with all the ease in music mediatization. What I'm seeing in the younger generations is that they seem to have lost interest and diluted their interests. Before, for example, it was all divided by scenes … but when I was in school there were the punk guys, the metal guys, it was all in niches. Nowadays, I don't know if they still exist or not, but back then things were divided in visual terms, in posture, everything was taken seriously and defended ardently.

Even Carolina (34 years old, an active punk composer and interpreter with a bachelor's degree, , living in Lisbon) makes this sort of inter-generational comparison:

> Nowadays, I don't know if the younger fellows still defend it as their scene. At least, when I come across youngsters I don't really see it. They listen to what is going on the radio, a lot of MTV culture, the bands they listen to are those that sold at least a million CDs, and they don't go looking for anything more underground.

Rise Up Punk: Local Scenes in Portugal

In considering the influence of the Internet on punk culture, we have identified another kind of tension. The identity of Portuguese punk not only derives from the tension between global and local scenes, as was addressed in the second section of this chapter. In fact, the Internet transforms what we understand by global, adding to the idea of a worldwide physical dissemination of goods and services the new reality of a virtual world where there are no time or space restrictions. This broadens the global community immeasurably – that is, all the people, no matter the place they occupy or their personal stories, can feel connected to that young musical culture and be brought together. However, this questions the very nature of *community* (Duncombe 1997). The Internet, by trivializing punk, can converge with other factors, like the music industry and the media, in transforming punk into a fashion fad or a mass consumption product. In doing so, it can strip it of its genuine underground essence. Here lies other tension that constitutes the geography of punk, when this is analysed in terms of global vs. local and centre vs. periphery.

Meanwhile, if global implies at least two different notions – (a) the international scene polarized in the United Kingdom and the United States, and (b) the virtual world of digital technologies and platforms – what does *local* mean? What is the 'internal' geography of Portuguese punk as a local scene? How does this scene articulate itself across a territory of 92 thousand km^2 and a population of 10.5 million people? The answer seems to be clear. By the end of the 1970s and throughout the 1980s, the punk scene was centred on certain places, with particular emphasis on the Lisbon urban area. Starting from the 1990s until the present, it has spread through the national territory, as shown in Figure 3.4 below. This tendency is, by turn, associated with the growing number of bands (see Table 3.3 below). The bigger the number of bands in action, the bigger its geographical dispersion.

Decade	N
1970–1980	10
1980–1990	41
1990–2000	157
2000–2010	246
Since 2010	85
Total of bands recorded in the database	539

Table 3.3: Creation of bands by decade (number). Source: KISMIF Project

This dispersion is noticed in the interviewees' statements. The idea seems to be of a originally urban culture that has spread everywhere. Carolina, the previously mentioned 34-year-old musician, says:

> I think it's [punk] everywhere. It has to do with concentrations of people. It's normal that, say, in Lisbon and Porto there are more people who like punk, because there are more people per se. From what I gathered, there's punk everywhere, not just here … a lot of times we went to play in the north, in festivals in Trás-os-Montes, to the Beiras, the centre region, to the south, even Alentejo, in Évora and Beja. There were always people, mostly connected to the places where there were students perhaps. But I think they exist everywhere, there aren't 'punk towns' or 'punk villages', we can't think that way. It has to do with the density of the local population.

The idea is clear: where there are people, there are young people; where there are young people, there can be punk. Therefore, Carolina signals several Portuguese regions, and mentions Evora and Beja, two small southern cities. Correspondingly, when asked to identify local punk scenes (that is, different places in the country where there was some punk activity or spirit), the interviewees contributed a relatively vast list. The two main cities, Lisbon and Porto, are always mentioned, as are their respective metropolitan areas (places like Loures, Oeiras, Cascais, Almada, Seixal, Barreiro, and Espinho). Next come the medium-sized towns of the vastly populated coastal areas, like Viana do Castelo, Braga, Aveiro, Coimbra, Leiria, Setúbal, and Faro. After that come small towns of the inland, such as Viseu, Guarda, Covilhã, and Castelo Branco. Then come small coastal towns like Barcelos, Caldas da Rainha, Torres Vedras, Lagos, and

Loulé. There are even mentions of undoubtedly rural areas, such as Celorico da Beira and Sabugal. The list is not exhaustive, but it shows quite efficiently the dispersion of punk over the national territory.

These local scenes present specific overtones about which various interviewees spoke, a theme with which we will deal on another occasion. For the sake of our argument it is only necessary to understand that Portuguese punk is divided by territory, in the sense that it penetrates virtually all corners of the country. Being an urban cultural manifestation, deeply related to youth and the transition to adulthood, it accompanies the processes by which urban culture becomes hegemonic in all areas, be they metropolitan, suburban, or even rural. That is: emerging in Portugal only a few years after the democratic revolution of 1974, which put an end to almost fifty years of political dictatorship, Portuguese punk has witnessed a profound sociocultural change in the country from the second half of the 1970s. Given its countercultural nature and explicit challenge to conventions, habits, and dominant values, punk has never stopped expressing, to this day, the complexity and contradictory nature of that change.

This is actually one of its major interests, in terms of sociological analysis. Looking at the words and attitudes of punk music and punk people, we can understand better the dialectics of social change experienced by the Portuguese society. Punk is a keen observant of that dialectic, from its own, underground, point of view. The way it looks at the recent evolutions and the current state of Portuguese society is influenced by the attitude it takes, its choice of marginality and periphery, the distrust towards any and all things related to the mainstream, be it in music or in life, and the opposition to the power of the music industry and social hierarchies.

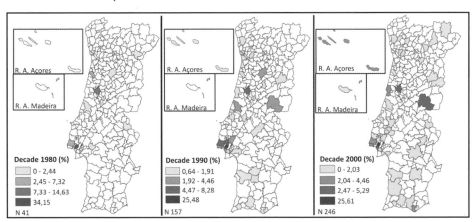

Figure 3.4: Bands by decade of their inception and location (%). Note: For reasons of presentation, R. A. Açores (Azores) and R. A. Madeira appear on the NUTS III level (Nomenclature of Units for Territorial Statistics), while Portugal Continental is on municipality level. Source: KISMIF Project.

It comes as no surprise, then, that song lyrics and the statements of the interviewees carry a deeply felt criticism. Denunciation and protest characterize the attitude conveyed by 42% of the 264 songs whose lyrics we have already analysed. The themes of 60% of those songs are related to social criticism, and one sixth explicitly speak of the current Portuguese situation (Guerra and Silva 2013). As for the statements of the interviewees, the most common topic is a flagging of how conformist and closed the Portuguese society still is after four decades of democracy. The self-presentation of punk people, less shocking than it seemed in the early years, still seems exotic. Their music and aesthetic preferences continue to disturb a society which, in the eyes of the punk, is conservative. Because of that, punk identity, in the Portuguese local scene, implies a regular bond to the 'outside,' that world which is much wider and more cosmopolitan than Portugal. To say it in a single phrase: to be a 'local' punk in Portugal, one needs to be global.

Frederico, the translator interviewee, confesses that his time as a punk in Portugal in the 1980s was, 'an asphyxiating time of wanting to do something and not being able to.' Photojournalist Cristiano recalls those times in equivalent terms:

> Society, despite the 1974 revolution, was very narrow-minded, very closed. That is, going out in different clothes than normal was, even in Lisbon, in the capital, let's say, seen with very suspicious eyes, people looked at us with a mix of fear and hate, it was all very complicated.

Luís, the 39-year-old cameramen, stresses how necessary it is to go out of the country once in a while: 'In Portugal things were always very closed, and I think when you travel you come back with a different energy, a lot more will happen.'

It is not only the fact that it is a country with little resources, without the size or the landmass to develop a strongly felt underground music scene; it is also, and foremost, the social organization which systematically makes difficult and sometimes blocks the integration and the future of young generations. Both characteristics – scarcity of resources and the current crisis which limits the opportunities – harden, on one side, the social insertion and impact of punk, which lacks conditions of production and distribution, media support, and public interest. However, on the other side those characteristics increase the punk's 'raison d'être,' highlighting the meaning of its option for the underground, its specific way of doing things – the Do It Yourself paradigm – and its rebellious voice. In Portugal, as in so many other countries (see Thompson 2004 or Gololobov, Pilkington, and Steinholt 2014), the punk *momentum* – that is, the initial and heroic phase – has passed. Nevertheless, there are still many reasons today, given the size of the crisis and its effects on youth, for punk to continue to live, come back to life, or double its energy.

Multiple Anchoring

The idea of the group is central to punk culture. It accentuates its status of a subculture – in the sense of a specific culture, with a core of specific values, rules, and expressions – and a counterculture – opposing all that is perceived as a socially hegemonic culture. The group is defined in a twofold moment: firstly, it results from sharing common goods and taking up a standard behaviour, creating an internal unity – the punk community;

secondly, it claims a difference and opposition, sometimes being symbolically violent towards those with the power to oppress.

The lyrics of the songs clearly demonstrate these two aspects (see Guerra and Silva 2013). In the majority of cases (145, or 59%) of the 260 lyrics we have in our database, the singers address the interlocutors directly. In 10% of these, there is a perceptible emotional connection between 'transmitter' and 'receiver'; in 28% the bond is one of group solidarity (they are peers, friends, members of the same 'generation'); but the most common case, in 37% of the cases, is a relationship of hostility, regardless of its intensity. The songs oscillate, then, between the celebration of interpersonal relationships and group connections and hostility towards the out-group. The frequent use of 'crass language' (seen in 36%) is an instrumental expression of that hostility.

Several interviewees, namely aged punks, propose a correspondence between the sentiment of community and the early, heroic stages of their activism. Nostalgia tends to improve their memories: it seems as if there was really a community of life; each local scene, first in Lisbon and Porto, then in other towns like Coimbra and Leiria, by the end of the 1970s and throughout the 1980s, was apparently based on an intense and reciprocal bond, almost acting as a 'tribe' or a family. People did the same things, went to the same places, dressed publicly in the same way, and shared the same interests not only in music, clothes, accessories, and texts, but also in values and causes. It was an intensely urban culture, whose decline some of the interviewed attribute, as we have seen earlier in this chapter, to the revolution of the access and production methods caused by the Internet. Albano (39 years old, a translator, living in Asia) describes this way of life as a philosophy:

> There was a whole philosophy revolving around punk, it was something where people with the same interests got together, especially in the streets, listening to music, sharing ideas, and ended up doing their own skate ramps and going to places they didn't know, like going to the pools of abandoned houses, etc.

Groups were defined by their meeting spots (such as the cafés of the renovated areas in Lisbon, as Inácio told us, a 55-year-old bachelor's degree holder, with connections to the world of editing); or by their influences (as explained by Elias, a 37-year-old architect from Coimbra with a master's degree) – some were closer to British Punk, some were closer to American Blues, others more connected to rock, etc.; or by the cities where they built their scenes, the singularities of each making the scenes partially divergent. The group identity can be expressed in names or brands, like LB Punkx (standing for Lisbon Punk) or LVHC (for Linda-a-Velha, a suburban area of Lisbon, and hardcore). In any case, it was the group that defined itself in a way that, for the 'old punks,' is now lost. As Rui (a 33-year-old hotel receptionist, with secondary education, and living in Lisbon) says: 'We actually went around with those initials in our jackets, the LB Punkx, it was a way of identifying ourselves, sort of like a gang. We had that sense of community, which in a way, is lost today. Back then we constituted almost all a single group.'

The punk scene was, and throughout its mutations still is, a scene. That implies: (1) a cultural background, (2) built by several actors, such as musicians, producers, promoters, critics and audiences, (3) which share amongst themselves several roles (some being the audience, or the promoters, or the co-producers of the others), (4) which are connected by the same core values and activities, not only musically but also in terms of public performance, body language, communication, aesthetics, and (5) whose effects combine into the creation of a singular artistic and cultural atmosphere, which borders and separates a given territory, be it a quarter, an urban district, a city, a region – or a virtual world.

The scene defines itself, therefore, in the relationship between culture, society, and territory. Here, different scales and configurations are crossed, including the global and local, central and peripheral, modal and marginal, macro and micro, reproduction and creation, imitation and invention, norm and deviance, integration and transgression. The scene is built with the combination of these and other elements via a double tension, internal and external. The underground scene legitimizes the peripheral, marginal, inventive, and transgressive sides of things (Dines, 2004). This is where it stands, and the reason why scenes sometimes split radically when the impact of audiences or the interest of the recording and concert industry moves from underground towards mainstream. But how does the underground music scene stand regarding the balance between global and local, macro and micro, reproduction and creation?

In this chapter, Portuguese punk has served as a case study for approaching this problem. That balance is itself critical for the definition of a punk identity – that is, to find what brings punk people together and what sets them apart, be it from the social environment or other scenes and ways of life. As we have seen, punk is global: a musical movement which, emerging in the last years of the 1970s in the United Kingdom and the United States, quickly spread throughout the world. It is also global in the sense that it brings together the cultural and social practices of the urban youth of the working and middle classes, and the popular culture associated with them centred on music, the concert, the group and generational bonds, and self-presentation. The vernacular language of this culture is the most global of all – English. Its discourse is urban, modern, and cosmopolitan. The Internet quickly became a relevant technology, network, and communication model, fostering what Castells (1996) called the 'virtual reality culture.'

Thus, punk culture appeals to a sense of global community. To be global – that is, to refer constantly to the structure and centres of the international movement – is a necessary condition to be punk. But it is not a sufficient condition, and nor does it imply a linear process. First, the punk community, aspiring to a common way of life and an active involvement in all stages of the musical process (according to the DIY principle), can only fully achieve its goal in a *local* context. The in-group must be circumscribed and limited by a status and a code – even when the 'space' to which it refers is no longer a physical territory, but rather the virtual world. Then, the relationship between 'local' and 'global' is not a linear but complex issue. Like other global phenomena, punk, by spreading, has 'localized,' assuming different aspects and becoming a cultural hybrid in the different countries and regions where it penetrated – and inside each country, in different towns and areas. Portugal illustrates quite well both dimensions: a local scene with multiple 'internal' local sub-scenes. Additionally, the underground, margins, and peripheries celebrated by punk have a microcosmic dimension: if punk does not necessarily want to change society, at least it wants to propose a separate location and lifestyle, a distinct sub and counterculture, a cosmos of its own. Finally, the self-management of the music process, which DIY epitomizes – that is, the control of production, marketing, communication, concerts, recording and archiving – forces the adoption of a micro scale, not a macro or global one.

The dynamism of punk culture, which currently surprises both its members and scholars, has a lot to do with this potentially multiple anchoring. It benefits from the ability to refer to several scales and cross-mix them in a specific and singular figuration. The punk scene is neither fully local nor fully global. Its geography is complex and dynamic. When there is a need to crystallize, punk makes use of various anchors. That is exactly what it does nowadays, four decades after the beginning of the voyage, and that is why it manages to reach and visit several harbours.

References

Adams, R. (2008). 'The Englishness of English punk: Sex Pistols, Subcultures and Nostalgia.' *Popular Music and Society* 31 (4): 469–88.

Appadurai, A. (2005). *Dimensões Culturais da Globalização.* [*Cultural Dimensions of the Globalization*]. Lisboa: Editorial Teorema.

Bennett, A. and R. A. Peterson (eds.) (2004). *Music Scenes: Local, Translocal and Virtual.* Nashville: Vanderbilt University Press.

Bennett, A. (2004). 'Consolidating the Music Scenes Perspective.' *Poetics* 32 (3–4): 223–34.

Bennett, A. (2006). 'Punk's Not Dead: the Continuing Significance of Punk Rock for an Older Generation of Fans.' *Sociology* 40 (2): 219–35.

Bennett, A. (2008). 'Towards a Cultural Sociology of Popular Music.' *Journal of Sociology* 44 (4): 419–32.

Bennett, A. (2013). *Music, Style and Aging: Growing Old Disgracefully?* Philadelphia: Temple University Press.

Blum, A. (2001). Scenes. *Public* 22/23: 7–35. http://www.publicjournal.ca/.

Castells, M. (1996). *The Rise of the Network Society.* Cambridge: Blackwell.

Clark, D. (2003). 'The Death and Life of Punk, the Last Subculture.' In D. Muggleton and R. Weinzierl (eds.), *The Post-Subcultures Reader*, 223–36. Oxford: Berg.

Cogan, B. (2010). *The Encyclopedia of Punk.* New York: Sterling Publishing.

Dale, P. (2010). 'Anyone Can Do It: Traditions of Punk and the Politics of Empowerment.' Unpublished PhD thesis. Newcastle University.

Dines, M. (2004). 'An Investigation into the Emergence of the Anarcho-punk Scene of the 1980s.' Unpublished PhD thesis. University of Salford.

Duncombe, S. (1997). *Notes from Underground: Zines and the Politics of Alternative Culture.* London and New York: Verso.

Dunn, K. C. (2008). 'Never Mind the Bollocks: the Punk Rock Politics of Global Communication.' *Review of International Studies* 34: 193–210. http://journals.cam.

Gololobov, I., H. Pilkington, and Y. B. Steinholt. (2014). *Punk in Russia. Cultural Mutation from the 'Useless' to the 'Moronic'.* London: Routledge.

Goshert, J. C. (2000). '"Punk" after the Pistols: American music, economics, and politics in the 1980s and 1990s.' *Popular Music and Society* 24 (1): 85–106.

Guerra, P. and A. S. Silva. (2013). 'Music and More than Music: Difference and Identity in Portuguese Punk.' Paper presented at Music, Gender and Difference. Intersectional and Postcolonial Perspectives on Musical Fields. University of Music and Performing Arts: Vienna, Austria.

Guerra, P. (2013). *A instável leveza do rock: génese, dinâmica e consolidação do rock alternativo em Portugal (1980–2010)* [*The Unstable Lightness of Rock: Genesis, Dynamics and Consolidation of Alternative Rock in Portugal (1980–2010)*]. Porto: Afrontamento.

Guerra, P. (2014). 'Punk, Expectations, Breaches and Metamorphoses: Portugal, 1977–2012.' *Critical Arts*, 28 (1): 111–22.

Hebdige, D. (1979). *Subculture: the Meaning of Style.* London: Routledge.

Jameson, F. (1991). *Postmodernism or the Cultural Logic of the Late Capitalism.* London: Verso.

Jameson, F. (2002). *A Singular Modernity: Essay on the Ontology of the Present.* London: Verso.

Kahn-Harris, K. (2007). *Extreme Metal: Music and Culture on the Edge.* New York: Bloomsbury Academic.

Laing, D. (1978). 'Interpreting Punk Rock.' *Marxism Today* (April), 123–132. http://www.amielandmelburn.org.uk/collections/mt/pdf/04_78_123.pdf.

Lentini, P. (2003). 'Punk's Origins: Anglo-American Syncretism.' *Journal of Intercultural Studies* 24 (2): 153–74.

Letts, D. and D. Nobakht. (2008). *Culture Clash: Dread Meets Punk Rockers.* London: SAF Publishing.

McNeil, L. and G. McCain. (2006). *Please Kill Me. L'histoire non censurée du punk racontée par ses acteurs.* Paris: Éditions Allia.

Middles, M. (2009). *Factory: the Story of the Record Label.* London: Virgin Books.

Moore, R. (2004). 'Postmodernism and Punk Subculture: Cultures of Authenticity and Deconstruction.' *The Comunication Review* 7 (3): 305–27. http://www.stevenlaurie.com/wp-content/uploads/2012/01/moore-punkauthenticity.pdf.

Moore, R. (2007). 'Friends Don't Let Friends Listen to Corporate Rock: Punk as a Field of Cultural Production.' *Journal of Contemporary Ethnography* 36 (4): 438–74.

Moreira, T. (2013). 'Sons e lugares: trajeto e retrato da cena rock no Tâmega' ['Sounds and places: path and portrait of the rock scene in Tâmega']. Unpublished MA dissertation. Porto: Faculdade de Letras da Universidade do Porto.

O'Connor, A. (2002). 'Local Scenes and Dangerous Crossroads: Punk and Theories of Cultural Hybridity.' *Popular Music* 21 (2): 225–37.

O'Connor, A. (2003). 'Anarcho-punk: Local Scenes and International Networks.' *Anarchist Studies* 11 (2): 111–21.

O'Connor, A. (2004). 'Punk and Globalization: Spain and Mexico.' *International Journal of Cultural Studies* 7 (2): 175–95.

O'Connor, A. (2008). *Punk Record Labels and the Struggle for Autonomy: the Emergence of DIY*. Lanham: Lexington Books.

O'Hara, C. (1995). *The Philosophy of Punk: More than Noise!!* Edinburgh and San Francisco: AK Press.

Robb, J. (2009). *The North Will Rise Again: Manchester Music City 1976–1996*. London: Aurum Press.

Rodrigues, S. (2012). 'In-Edit 2012 tem como convidado o renomado diretor Don Letts' ['In-Edit 2012 has the Renowned Director Don Letts as a Guest']. *Rolling Stone Brasil* http://rollingstone.uol.com.br/noticia/edicao-de-2012-do-edit-tem-como-convidado-o-renomado-diretor-don-letts/.

Sabin, R. (1999). 'Introduction.' In R. Sabin (ed.), *Punk Rock: So What?: the Cultural Legacy of Punk*. London: Routledge.

Straw, W. (1991). 'Systems of Articulation, Logics of Change: Communities and Scenes in Popular Music.' *Cultural Studies* 368–88. http://strawresearch.mcgill.ca/straw/systemsofarticulation.pdf.

Straw, W. (2004). Scenes and Sensibilities. *E-Compós* 6. http://www.compos.org.br/seer/index.php/e-compos/article/view/83/83.

Thompson, S. (2004). *Punk Productions: Unfinished Business*. New York: State University of New York Press.

VNO V
DE TRIS

nseruíbl

4. 'CRACK IN THE SYSTEM': A BOTTOM-UP ANALYSIS OF THE ANARCHO-PUNK MOVEMENT IN MEXICO

ALICE POMA & TOMMASO GRAVANTE

Abstract

In this chapter we seek to analyse the changes present in the Mexican anarcho-punk movement in Mexico over the past thirty years (1984–2014) through the biographic experiences of some of its protagonists. The analysis is based on the ethnographic work carried out in meeting spots of collectives and in-depth interviews conducted with members of different generations of two of the main scenarios of the Mexican anarcho-punk movement (Guadalajara and Mexico City). In particular, we will show how the interviewees got close to the movement, what their thoughts and feelings were, and how they have appropriated and re-elaborated the anarcho-punk identity. Finally, taking the Mexican anarcho-punk movement as a political subject, we will show how collectives have related to other political and social experiences, such as the Zapatista movement, and what meanings the ethical political practices, such as vegetarianism or the Do It Yourself (DIY) ethos, have for its members.

Keywords: Mexican anarcho-punk, prefigurative politics, self-organization, grassroots movements

Alice Poma is a PhD in Social Science (UPO, Spain) and a postdoctoral fellow at UNAM (Mexico). Alice is a social movement research, and her main research issues are protest and emotion, self-organized environmental conflicts, empowerment, and social change. E-mail: alicepoma@gmail.com

Tommaso Gravante is a PhD in Political Science (UPO, Spain) and a postdoctoral fellow at CEIICH-UNAM (Mexico). Tommaso is a social movement research, and his main research issues are protest and emotion, self-organized grassroots movements, and anarchist movements. E-mail: t.gravante@gmail.com

'CRACK IN THE SYSTEM': A BOTTOM-UP ANALYSIS OF THE ANARCHO-PUNK MOVEMENT IN MEXICO

Introduction

The spread of punk in Mexico was linked from its beginning in the mid-1980s to anti-authoritarian values and practices that, in the 1990s, took the praxis of anarchism to a new level. In fact, what characterizes the Mexican anarcho-punk movement is that it grew, gaining strength and setting itself apart from the mere musical, cultural, and aesthetic dimension of punk, giving birth to a real political subject articulated in the entire country. The hundreds of collectives that constitute the anarcho-punk movement in Mexico represent one of the most important urban laboratories for experimenting with policies and self-management in the country.

In this chapter we seek to analyse the changes present in this anarcho-punk movement in Mexico in the past thirty years (1984–2014) through the biographic experiences of some of its protagonists. The analysis is based on the ethnographic work carried out in meeting spots of collectives (concerts, social spaces, alternative markets, etc.) and in-depth interviews conducted with members of different generations of two of the main scenarios of the Mexican anarcho-punk movement: the city of Guadalajara (Jalisco) and Mexico City.

Through the analysis of the biographic experience of the 'new' and 'old' protagonists of the movement, which includes an emotional aspect, we will seek to show what things have changed and what stayed the same in the movement in the early twenty-first century. In particular, we will show how the interviewees got close to the movement, what their thoughts and feelings were, and how they have appropriated and re-elaborated the anarcho-punk identity. Finally, taking the Mexican anarcho-punk movement as a political subject, we will show how collectives have related to other political and social experiences, such as the Zapatista movement, and what meanings the ethical political practices, such as vegetarianism or the Do It Yourself (DIY) ethos, have for its members.

Methodology

The data was collected through ethnographic observation developed in Guadalajara and Mexico City between September 2012 and June 2013, comprising fifteen in-depth interviews with members of the anarcho-punk collectives in said cities, and the analysis of self-produced material of different anarcho-punk collectives in Mexico over the years.

In order to ensure an analysis that included these different stages the anarcho-punk movement in Mexico has witnessed, we decided to interview members of different collectives from various generations: (1) interviewees whose experience in the anarcho-punk movement started with the movement in the mid-1980s; (2) interviewees who joined the movement after the Zapatista insurrection in 1994; (3) the last-generation members who joined the anarcho-punk movement in the early twenty-first century. All the in-depth interviews were conducted in private households or anarchist social centres. Likewise, and consistent with our bottom-up approach, we chose to investigate places where anarcho-punk became common practice. In particular, we undertook a series of brief random interviews with random anarcho-punks selling or exchanging self-produced materials in the anarcho-punk area of the cultural *tianguis* market *el Chopo*.[28]

Anarcho-punk Movement in Mexico: the Result of a Cultural Hybridity

In order for both the non-Mexican reader and researchers interested in the subject to compare and understand these realities, before looking into the analysis we consider it appropriate to briefly explain what characterizes the Mexican anarcho-punk movement. As it is widely known and as highlighted in several ethnographic papers regarding punk in Mexico (O'Connor 2002b; 2003b; 2004; Sandoval Vargas 2012), the punk subculture does not have its origin in a Latin American country but in cities such as London and New York in the 1970s (Dines 2004; Gordon 2005). Despite this, in both Mexico and other international urban contexts, punk music has represented a crucial aspect in the process of articulation of a determined collective identity (Eyerman and Jamison 1998; Roscigno and Danaher 2004; Dines 2004; Gordon 2005).

Punk music in Mexico and other countries is not only the form through which these groups express their dissatisfaction and discontent, but also a collective discourse by means of which the collectives nourish their own identity. In fact, from the analysis of the interviews conducted, we were able to observe that music continues to be the foremost medium with which to approach Mexican anarcho-punk. The songs, lyrics, and the form in which music is made are the first elements the interviewees of the three generations mention. In spite of the years, and the merchantilization process it has undergone, anarcho-punk in Mexico still expands through underground channels linked to the social environment where youths grow up. To put it in clear terms, the music the brother listens to, the fanzine a friend gives you, or simply the first concert to which your oldest friends take you remain the main channels of contact of youths with anarcho-punk. The music is one of the most evident identitary encounters, both in Mexican collectives and other international experiences. Meanwhile, what makes the Mexican movement different from the scenes in other countries is the political dimension itself.

Although there are evident connections between the punk subculture (such as music, aesthetics, and DIY) and some political phenomena such as the Campaign for Nuclear Disarmament (Dines, 2004) and anti-racism with Rock Against Racism in the United Kingdom or feminism in the United States with Riot Grrrl (Moore and Roberts 2009), it

---

28 The cultural *tianguis* El Chopo takes place every Saturday in Mexico City and is the result of the continual occupation of the sidewalks surrounding the University Museum El Chopo in Santa Maria la Ribera, which began in the 1980s to create a non-commercial exchange of discs, fanzines, and self-produced materials (Ríos Manzano 1999).

is inappropriate, and sometimes superficial, to see the punk scene in a wholly ideological or political light. Despite the often highlighted links between punk and anarchist thought (O'Hara 1995; Dines 2004; Gordon 2005), the punk subculture continues to be a great spectrum within which we can find anything from the Nazi-punk scene, of the likes of Skrewdriver (UK), the Dirty White Punks (USA), Böhse Onkelz (Germany), the Exploited (UK), Legittima Offesa (Italy), Midgårds Söner (Sweden), Nauravat Natsit (Finland), or Ódio Mortal (Brazil), or bands related to authoritarian Communism thought as the experience of CCCP Fedeli alla Linea[29] (Italy). In the same way, it is also not correct to unify the punk scene according to its practices, as in the case of DIY; for example, grassroots extreme rightist groups in Italy are characterized by showing alternative ways of living through developing anti-consumerist and self-reliant projects (Di Nunzio and Toscano 2011), or lifestyles such as the straight edge with the slogan 'No-Drugs, No-Alcohol, No Exceptions,' which could also be appropriated by extreme rightist groups (Kuhn 2010). We can then assert that, on one hand, we have the punk subculture internationally brought together by the musical and aesthetic dimension, while on the other there has been a balkanization of its political dimension.

As we noted in the introduction, contrary to Europe, the spread of punk in Mexico was linked from its roots in the mid-1980s to the anti-authoritarian and anarchist values and practices. Therefore, the punk scene in Mexico is divided into two trends: the anarcho-punk – the largest one, lasting until 2004 – and an apolitical and commercial trend that is exclusively based on the musical and aesthetic aspects.

But what makes the Mexican anarcho-punk movement different? Punk and anarcho-punk in Mexico are the result of a 'cultural hybridity' (Canclini 2001; O'Connor 2002a; 2003a; 2004), that is to say, the outcome of a *mezcla* – melting pot – of indigenous people, and urban and popular cultures. Indeed, the majority of people interviewed come from popular barrios and neighbourhoods, often built by indigenous communities that emigrated from industrial areas. On the contrary, in Italy, as in other European countries, in the 1980s the punks came mainly from local (white) working-class families (Andresen and Van der Steen 2016). These punks could access social services such as education, culture, and health; their homes had water, gas, and electricity; their parents could go on holidays and they could occupy a building without being disappeared or murdered by police. Mexican punks are instead *mestizos* – they have grown up in popular barrios and neighbourhoods excluded from access to education, culture, health, water, electricity, etc. Their culture was a hybrid between the indigenous customs and urban life: a mix of *tortillas*,[30] mohawks, the shadow economy, social marginalization, and a strong feeling of social injustice.

The cultural hybridity that characterizes the Mexican anarcho-punk movement generates a starting point that is totally different from the European scene. As the

---

29 In order to better comprehend the difficulty of contextualizing the punk scene under a single political dimension, it is necessary to recall that founder Giovanni Lindo Ferretti, after CCCP, successively embraced the Italian right-wing racist ideas and the posture of catholic fundamentalism.

30 A thin Mexican pancake made with corn (maize) flour, usually eaten hot and filled with meat and cheese.

interviewees affirmed, most of the youths in the anarcho-punk collectives in Mexico come from the poorest and most marginalized areas of cities, and despite sharing with European punks the same wrath and rage towards ruling classes, they do not share the same social contexts with their contemporaries(Andresen and Van der Steen 2016), such as German punks (Katsiaficas 1997) or Italian punks (Pandini and Giaccone 1997), countries where, leaving the authoritarian state policy aside, people enjoy the welfare state guaranteeing high-quality public services such as education, health, and human rights for the whole population. These differences in the social and economic context affect anarcho-punk projects and activities, which depend on everyday life and experiences. For example, while in Italy the anarchic squat Virus (1982–7) focused on spreading the then-new punk culture in Italy (Francalanci 1984), the first anarcho-punks in Mexico City were confronted daily in the streets of their barrios, among the debris left by the 1985 earthquake, the economic crisis, and the marginalization and repression policies performed by the government. Thus, the emergence of anarcho-punk in the Mexican urban society is more than simply a new youth subculture, since it gives 'continuity to the long stories of solidarity among the victims of all times' (Gaytán Santiago 2001, 96).

Finally, the Mexican anarcho-punk movement, nourished on one hand by the anarchist practices and experiences present in the country, and on the other by the everyday experience of their peripheral *barrios*, has been able to mature and build on a common collective identity that surpasses personal differences, as expressed by one interviewee: 'Even though each of us had our own story, we agreed all of us were repressed … and that repression in this case was something that brought us together and had always been there' (I4).

This way of doing politics on a daily basis takes place with a set of practices that constitute the 'territory of infrapolitics' (Scott 1990), or, in other words, the politics of subordinate groups. Following James Scott's (1990) proposal, infrapolitics is the great variety of discrete forms of resistance, characterized by informal leadership rather than by elites, conversation, and oral speech. Analysing infrapolitics instead of analysing the formal and organized events such as meetings or organized protests, for example, allows us to understand the changes lived by the anarcho-punk movement throughout these years.

Appropriating and Making Use of Anarcho-punk

Over the past thirty years (1984–2014), young people have become interested in anarcho-punk mainly through music. Three activists of different generations highlighted that there has been no change in how and why teenagers get involved in anarcho-punk groups. The first anarcho-punk activist in Mexico City told us that: 'I came close to anarcho-punk in '82 or '83, because of music' (I5). An anarcho-punk from the 1990s generation claims that: 'I started in the anarcho-punk movement in 1997. In my case, I got close to punk music' (I4). Likewise, a 2000s generation activist from Guadalajara expressed: 'Mainly, I got close to anarcho-punk owing to music, the rhythms, the lyrics' (I3).

Although punk music plays important roles in recruitment, the approach to anarcho-punk through music is more than just the result of personal tastes; rather, it involves other elements that belong to the emotional and biographical dimensions. For instance, music and lyrics allow youth to empathize with other punks by sharing both emotions, such as anger, and their claims of inconformity and disobedience. Music allows anarcho-punks to redesign their identities and question the values and practices of the dominant system, for example, such as the need for professionalization to make music:

> [Music], more than a musical piece of work, is a matter of rupture with the standards of how music must be, how things must be, the matter of speed, of silence, of screaming instead of having a good normal voice, the matter of having a simple voice, as common as the others. You don't need to go to school, if you want to sing you can do it and use the voice you have. (I2)

The music our interviewees created is not only characterized by its 'sound and aggressiveness' (I3), but also by not respecting the rules and conventions of a dominant system that decides the form and modalities of making music, as another interviewee stated:

> It was a way of giving voice to those who didn't have one, so it´s a matter of simplicity, though it also has to do with breaking musical structures. I mean, we can do whatever we can and we don't care about standards telling you which is a song and which is not, or how long it must be. (I2)

The questioning of the dominant system of production and spread of music allows the protagonists to make their own individual and collective identities emerge. The melody, the irony in the texts, and performances in the scene turn into a political practice in a way to make and extend the vision of the world of those creating, and are vehicles to reflect themselves and others. While music is a core element of the Mexican anarcho-punk movement, we have been able to suggest that the centrality of the *tocadas* – the concerts – changed over the time: 'the people, now, get closer when they are having fun, as if there was less political engagement' (I6). As another interviewee stated, at the beginning the concerts were the main valued moment:

> In the 1980s we considered that in anarcho-punk our way to attract people was the *tocadas* (the concerts). We made concerts and flyers were handed out; the fanzines and the groups reflected the ideas and it was the way we used to come together. I always saw it like that, it was our way of recruiting people without forcing them but because they simply wanted to join and come. (I5)

Over the years, the concerts have lost some importance because, on one hand, the music has been the first common ground for anarcho-punks to meet and express themselves, and on the other it also represents the first element of merchandising where political values and practices dissolve in favour of the most playful aspect:

> Nowadays you go to the *tocadas* and it's about having fun, sometimes there isn't even any engagement with the bands. There isn't any respect for the scene as it used to be. (I3)

Moreover, as the interviewees demonstrate, the reasons that move youths to make music have changed. Before, music represented an important constituent of their own identity, a way of breaking with the hegemonic culture; they did not seek to appropriate consensus or the audience, as one of the first anarcho-punks in Mexico City recalls:

> When we made songs, when the punk band made songs, they were songs about defying the system. Now it's not like this, songs are made for the public to like them. (I5)

At first, music was a form of making politics and the musical band was a tool through which they spread their own ideas and expressed solidarity with other struggles:

> Before, in a concert, the one who sang stood up and talked about prisoners of a certain place, condemning the repression going on, etc. They were a sort of spokesman of the protests, and today few do it. There are still punk bands and anarchists in Mexico that still do so, but those groups don't talk about that and they have more to do with aesthetics, with playing louder. (I5)

This does not mean that all concerts today are commercial. Rather, the capacity of politicization through musical events seems to have weakened this process. In order to make a concert, more effort is required than before, since, as a young interviewee explains, the collectives now 'make *tocadas* but there is not the same motivation and if there is some, it's even more difficult because you must have the money and all that' (I3). As an interviewee recollects, 'with time the capitalist system is very clever and absorbs everything' (I5), and concerts, next to hairstyles, piercings, tattoos, clothing, make up, etc., have been absorbed and reinterpreted by the market and cultural industries. This has changed the role of aesthetics for participants in the scene:

> Aesthetics is another of the important forms to say, for example, 'No! I don't agree! I don't want to be like you! I want to be as I want!' [Aesthetics] is a way to identify with others like you; it had lots of importance and relevance, it's like non-verbal language saying many things. The way to dress has to do with who you are. (I2)

The words of one of the first anarcho-punks in Guadalajara summarizes the opinion of all the interviewees. The *mohawks*, the clothing – many times self-produced – the jackets, the incorporation on clothes of patches, badges, and daily objects, etc. no doubt represent aspects that have differentiated punk from other cultural phenomena. In punk, the body is transformed into a space of identification, where subjects express their vision of the world, their values, and their tools to relate to one another and identify with others (López Cabello 2013), as the same interviewee from Guadalajara expresses:

> I liked everything because it had a meaning. It had an important meaning like wanting

to scream, you want to tell them you don't agree, that there are different ways of doing things and that's a way of expressing some things you don't agree with. (I2)

In the creation of anarcho-punk identity, the body represents the first re-conquered space from the hegemonic culture, as another interviewee relates:

Aesthetics was very, very important before. I consider it was our way to protest without having a way to do it, just our clothes, our slogans, our own T-shirts. We ourselves drew them, painted them, wrote the slogans, the messages we wished to make. We did it and obviously we faced the rejections of society, and discrimination. (I5)

Although, as an interviewee asserted, aesthetics 'was a priority not only for me but also for the whole anarcho-punk scene' (I3), the process of commodification of the punk scene has made both the 'old' and the youngest anarcho-punks distance themselves from the aesthetical aspect, since 'people now don't get scared anymore: everyone can be punk now. This aesthetics thing makes no difference, what matters is what you have inside, what you think, what you do' (I10).

From the interviewees, we can see a process of individual maturation emerge on the side of the protagonists, a process later shared with others. It is due to this dynamic process that Mexican anarcho-punk has become a political subject capable of transforming its imagery in concrete proposals. Indeed, 'being involved in social issues' (I7) reflects a process of maturing that is perceived by all the interviewees, because they feel that they themselves have changed over the years. From our perspective, the main element that has nourished this process of maturing is the permeability that Mexican anarcho-punk has demonstrated with other experiences of struggle and resistance in the country, as we will analyse in the following section.

Anarcho-Punks – Zapatistas – Co-Operativists: the Game of Labels

Due to the biographical status of the protagonists, anarcho-punk in Mexico never dissociated itself from the social problems that existed in the country and was always present in the social struggles: 'from the earthquake of Mexico City in 1985, the punk band was there, rescuing people, opening wells, etc., in the protests of teachers (1990s), in Atenco (2006), in Oaxaca (2006), the punk band was always present' (I5). However, undoubtedly one of the episodes that most impacted, influenced, and raised doubts in the protagonists of the anarcho-punk movement was the insurrection of indigenous communities in Chiapas in 1994 with the uprising of the National Liberation Zapatista Army (EZLN).

On the morning of January 1, 1994, the Chiapas Rebellion began in Mexico's southernmost state. led by a then-unknown group, the EZLN. Some three thousand poorly armed, mostly Mayan guerrilla soldiers marched out of the jungles and seized half a dozen towns and briefly took the city of San Cristóbal de Las Casas. The EZLN had chosen January 1 because on that day in that year the North American Free Trade Agreement (NAFTA), an international treaty between Canada, Mexico, and the United States, took effect. The EZLN rebels called for the cancellation of NAFTA, the overthrow of the Mexican government, and the convocation of a constituent assembly to write a new Mexican constitution. In part under the influence of indigenous ideas, the EZLN had rejected the old Marxist paradigm of the proletariat struggling for state power, putting on the agenda a new theory and practice of revolution that seemed to have more in common with anarchism: anyone from any social class could begin to make the revolution by asserting their dignity and forming a liberated community where they were (Holloway and Peláez 1998). After more than twenty years, the Zapatistas are building such a communitarian alternative to capitalism in the remote communities in Chiapas.

The Chiapas Rebellion had an enormous impact at the time, not only in Mexico but all around the world. With the experience of the Neozapatismo, the anarcho-punk collectives not only acted in solidarity towards the Zapatista communities and participated into La Otra Campaña and FZLN,[31] but also started a process of elaboration of concepts such as autonomy, community, and communality, which have been introduced in the discussions of collectives and reflected in the fanzines, debates, and slogans, as one interviewee claims:

> I believe that the punk and anarcho-punk movement has been influenced by many social struggles; one of them is the Zapatista, something that we can't deny even though there's confrontation that sometimes is ideological, biased or sometimes because of the symbolization of Marcos. But yes, many fanzines are based on the issue of autonomy and the municipalities, of *Caracoles*, of living in indigenous communities. I mean, this has fuelled the movement a lot. (I4)

Nevertheless, unlike other political subjects in Mexico, like FZLN, and other countries – such as the group ¡Ya Basta! in Italy, which developed total faith towards EZLN and a cult around Subcomandante Marcos' personality – the approach of Mexican anarcho-punk collectives was always critical towards EZLN and showed great respect towards the uses and customs of the indigenous communities, as the interviewee from Guadalajara mentioned earlier, and as highlighted by an interviewee from Mexico City:

> Yes, we support the Zapatista peoples and the Zapatista struggle and we will always do so, let's be clear on this. This doesn't justify the Zapatista Army, nor Marcos, nor the cult of his personality even though many people are involved in that. There are anarchists that had Zapatista people put up in their houses, when they made their tour they supported them. Of course when there's an attack on Zapatista communities we don't doubt going down to the streets to stop everything, this is clear, to us there isn't any other way. (I5)

But the Zapatista struggle is not the only one from which the anarcho-punk movement drew strength: having to survive every day, looking for a minimum income

---

31 The Other Campaign (La Otra Campaña) is a political program by the EZLN, as a new approach in its sixteen year-long struggle for the recognition and protection of indigenous rights and autonomy in Mexico. This tour began in January 2006 and was intended to create connections among the Zapatistas and pre-existing resistance groups throughout Mexico. The Zapatista Front of National Liberation (FZLN) was a political organization linked to EZLN from 1997 until it broke up in 2005.

to have something to eat and helping the weak family economy, meant that many of the interviewees got close 'to unions and co-operatives' (I5), becoming supportive of the struggles of workers and also developing self-managed labour alternatives to sustain or finance social projects. In the words of a youth from Guadalajara: 'We started to sell vegetarian food in the cultural *tianguis*, going to each stall to offer *tostadas de ceviche de soya* (soy fish tostadas) or fried *tacos* with potato or beans inside. We saved part of the earnings and another part was for the rent' (I4).

The outcome of the interviews is that, at the outset, anarcho-punk collectives never rejected other experiences and social struggles surrounding them, since the same protagonists, living in everyday social exclusion in their barrios, always tried to not replicate the dynamics of exclusion they themselves suffered from the hegemonic class.

Do It Together: Practices and Values

Despite the years and changes lived, the fundamental values that sustain the anarcho-punk movement have not changed: anti-militarism, animal liberation, environmentalism, and anti-authoritarianism are still its major values, though they are values that depend on the historical moment or, on many occasions, the biographies of the protagonists. As expressed by an interviewee, 'there have been booms, there are moments in which many people are in favour of animal liberation, vegetarianism or against drugs, for example' (I5). Practices such as vegetarianism or veganism are still a hot topic, and are linked to a 'radical and struggle-based' re-elaboration (I3) of animal liberation and environmentalism. This process of re-elaboration is not only experienced as individual struggle but as a collective learning process, since the debate is shared socially, for example with the family. As a youth from Guadalajara told us in relation to the decision of being vegan:

> I feel that with my decision I influenced the habits of my family. They started to read for curiosity, to know why I didn't want to eat meat. They have greatly reduced the consumption of meat and industrial products by themselves. I believe it's the other way round, I contributed to informing them with my practice rather than being convinced by them to quit. (I3)

While the family can serve as a spectrum for confrontation, ethical political practices such as vegetarianism and veganism surpass the family sphere and are claimed and shared in the fanzines, songs, and other self-produced materials, or located in alternative social projects such as the culmination of 'the co-operative of self-managed work that is the vegetarian diner *La Papa Liberada* – The Liberated Potato' (I4), created in Mexico City.

Unlike the changes we observed in music and aesthetics, the values of the anarcho-punk movement there have not undergone substantial changes. As an interviewee told us:

> The band was always anti-war and will always be, obviously, anti-McDonald's. Abstentionism has always existed, the anti-state struggle, anti-government, they always remain. These are very classic struggles which have always been [there]. (I5)

Despite this, and as we have seen before, the interviewee stated 'perhaps the newest [struggle] was that of the Zapatistas … maybe another struggle is that of women' (I5); he also asserted that the matter of gender and 'the equality of women became newer irrespective of the previous collectives like the CHAP [Chavas Activas Punk – Punk Active Girls, an anarcho-punk feminist group], the Gatas Punks [Punk Female Cats – an anarcho-punk feminist group], and the Brujas [the Witches – an anarcho-punk feminist group). But that's a struggle that still reinvents itself' (I5). Indeed, the first anarcho-punk self-productions – fanzines, music, and videos – of the late 1980s indicated that the matter of gender was always a critical issue, but as highlighted by the interview, the emancipation of women is a struggle that reinvents itself continually in relation to the changes that emerge in society. In recent years, violence and discrimination against women in Mexico has grown with respect to the strength of the process of emancipation that many women are living through. This has led to anarcho-punk collectives re-inventing the struggle of women through the spread of self-managed workshops of self-defence, which are aimed not only at providing women with the physical tools to defend themselves, but also to fight the isolation, fear, resignation, and depression that many female victims suffer after daily violence (Poma and Gravante 2013). In any case, women's equality is still an open fight within the same anarcho-punk collectives, which are not exempt from the discriminatory practices that exist in the rest of society, as claimed by a female anarcho-punk youth in Mexico City: 'Unfortunately, there's a great deal of sexism in the movement, but this is also a test of fighting, trying to change these ways of seeing women as objects when we aren't' (I8). In this respect, anarcho-punk has yet to break with the cultural cages of sexism present in our society; as the same female interviewee asserts, 'there's still a lot to do in this aspect' (I8).

This brief sketch of those values and practices that characterize the anarcho-punk movement in Mexico demonstrate how, throughout the years, different collectives have never been far from the social problems in the country. Poverty, repression, violence, informal work, and lack of social services are all still a reality for many of the interviewees and other people we have encountered during our ethnographic work. This has allowed collectives to continue having a certain permeability with the social context surrounding them, joining struggles such as *zapatismo*. Indeed, the Zapatista experience has allowed anarcho-punk groups to re-think several concepts such as autonomy, which is characterized by the values of community and horizontality. This is very different from the European concept of autonomy, which emerged in the 1970s from autonomous Italian Marxist groups (such as Potere Operaio and Autonomia Operaia), and was characterized by authoritarian values and militarist practices. At the same time, Mexican anarcho-punks do not surpass the limits of the society in which they develop, built with a sexist and chauvinist framework, as occurs in countries like Italy or Spain.

Lastly, we intend to finish our discussion by addressing the DIY practice and how the protagonists of the movement live it. From an analysis of all the interviews and from the ethnographic work, it becomes evident that a core foundation of the anarcho-punk movement is the DIY practice. This practice permeates every aspect, both individual and collective, and has not changed substantially over the years. As we have seen above, the anarcho-punk movement is characterized by the absence of delegation, with the individuals seeking the forms and manners to develop their own learning both in the practical aspect (music, fanzines, etc.) and the political matter, as was the case for many in their approach to anarchism:

> The song 'Anarchy in the UK' was on and I thought, 'if I'm punk and the song talks about anarchy, I want to know what anarchy is.' Then, I got to a library and found a book by Reclus. I started reading it and I liked the ideas, thinking they were appropriate. At that time, the punk band had no anarchists. I started reading and seeing that some had a few ideas. After about one year someone took me to the library of the Spanish exiles (Biblioteca Reconstruir), and it was there I got in touch with the anarchists of the books I'd read. (I5)

If this first excerpt corresponds to an interviewee from the first generation of Mexican anarcho-punks, in this second testimony we can appreciate that the approach to anarchist discourses, values, and practices of the youths of the twenty-first century has not changed:

> I started to ask, my family first, what anarchism is. I looked in the books in our house for something about anarchism and I found a book by Malatesta with the title *Anarchy and the Method of Anarchism.* Then I started going to the cultural *tianguis*, the anarcho-punk area, and talked to the fellows there. (I1)

In the case of DIY we identify a pattern of continuity. For the anarcho-punk movement in Mexico, DIY, despite not being 'easy' (I9), is still a practice that erodes the dependence of participants on professionals and intellectual elites, replacing them with self-learning, informal practices, and collective abilities. Nonetheless, the DIY practice not only involves an individual dimension, as a specific curiosity or interest might be, but also collective abilities and needs where 'you' becomes a 'we,' turning DIY into, as McKay proposed, into 'Do It Ourselves' (1998).

To sum up, our research has proven that there is a line of continuity in the accounts, stories, wishes, and claims articulated by the fanzines, songs, and theatre plays of the different collectives between 1984–2014. The anarcho-punk imagery continues to express itself through both music and transgressive practices such as irony, humour, 'culture jamming,' and provocation, challenging both the dominant forms of organization and the cultural and political practices. In the Mexican anarcho-punk movement, it is the individuals who establish the interpretive frameworks regarding power and creative action because they are not merely consumers of others' reflections, but producers of their own thoughts, aiming to change the forms of building their own lives.

Conclusion: 'The One Who Fights Will Never Die'

In the middle of 2004, the Mexican anarcho-punk movement encountered a strong repression that set it on a downward spiral. From May 24–28 in the city of Guadalajara, the European Union, Latin America and Caribbean Summit was held. This meeting represented one of the many encounters that characterized the first decade of the new millennium with the purpose to strengthen and expand the neoliberal model among the European Union countries and Latin America. Mexico had hosted the WTO meeting in 2003 (in Cancun) and the Summit of the Americas in January 2004. As in Seattle 1999, Genoa 2001, and Cancun 2003, in Guadalajara the repressive apparatus of the Mexican state utilized the same strategies to repress protesters: including police infiltration, condemnation on the part of the mainstream media, and co-option by the institutional left wing. The result for Mexican collectives was that the repression in Guadalajara represented 'the biggest blow they could have given to us, the anarchists' (I5). Following this repression many collectives dissolved, while the ones remaining could only gather strength in the campaigns to release prisoners and collect funds for the legal expenses, and, 'in the end, when the process of struggle against repression and solidarity with the prisoners[32] finished, the collectives dissolved as well, everyone went their different ways and almost no one continued in the anarcho-punk movement' (I1).

In spite of all this, the Mexican anarcho-punk movement still represents a crucial political subject of the imagery of struggle in the face of the dominant system since we consider that the protagonists of the Mexican anarcho-punk movement search for solutions and create alternatives that are ultimately political, as they turn into 'cracks'[33] that undermine the stability of the dominant system. The political practices of anarcho-punk collectives have echoed through a diversity of movements of resistance against plunder, exploitation, and repression. The practices and forms of organization that deny delegation and hierarchy, which question the forms of domination inserted into the everyday lives of people more deeply, have been retaken by other, mostly urban collectives. These are groups which have also proposed to create self-managed relations. The Zapatistas themselves declared their affinity to the practices and the ethical-political horizon when stating that what they seek to construct in southeastern Mexico is libertarian autonomy.[34]

From the wrecks of the 2004 repression, the protagonists were able to reappear, and as *Fallas* del Sistema sing,[35] 'The one who fights will never die.' Therefore, Mexican anarcho-punks are still fighting, and have fought to rebuild, proposing to 'deeply understand things on a personal basis, and continue to seek and do things despite being alone or being a few,

---

32 The last prosecution against those arrested in the 2004 protests took place in 2013.

33 Metaphor used in Holloway (2010).

34 In the first issue of the EZLN´s magazine entitled *Rebeldía Zapatista*, published in February 2014, the Zapatistas decided to confraternize with the anarchists to write statements together and express their solidarity regarding the criminalization of anarchism that the state and media carried out.

35 Fallas del Sistema [Crack in the System] is one of the most important anarcho-punk bands in Mexico. One of our interviewees belongs to the collective.

it doesn't matter' (I2). Rethinking the political practices and where to fight and organize from, Mexican anarcho-punks have rejected the spaces and times imposed by the dominant classes, constructing and affirming their own spaces and times from where they build projects of self-management aimed to favour self-organization and the relation to other struggles and resistances.

If the repression of 2004 essentially generated a quantitative change in the anarcho-punk movement in Mexico, our research highlights that there have not been important changes in terms of values and practices. As our arguments throughout the chapter have stated, even though punk and cultural industries business has absorbed and commodified most of the punk concerts and dimensions, the importance of the musical dimension is still present, being the first meeting place for youths of anarcho-punk collectives. As we have shown, the DIY practice continues to permeate every social and political aspect of the protagonists. The DIY ethic is not strictly limited to being a slogan in songs or fanzines, but instead a practice that can be deployed in everyday experiences of people insomuch as self-management of the different dimensions of life is having a more and more central place among Mexican anarcho-punks; 'the fight is taking a more practical role. It's about taking practice to your personal life, so each individual does so, in order to live and be consistent with what you say' (I10). The DIY practice can be seen in both the concrete projects of alternatives to life, through self-managed work and cooperativism, and the re-definition of the political practices and forms of organization. Thus, we have been able to observe that the political practices dissociate more and more from the commemorative activities and great events, turning into attempts to manage daily life accompanied by processes of self-formation that allow for the insertion of the implications of going against the stream in everyday life from an anarchist and punk perspective that is based on anti-authoritarianism, horizontality, mutual support, and autonomy.

Finally, while punk in Mexico has moved away from its social content and has been –consciously – assimilated by the society of spectacle and money, anarcho-punk in Mexico is after thirty years still linked with that part of the society that, as Jack London wrote in his essay on the East End in London, emerges from the 'abyss' (2005). This has meant that anarcho-punk in Mexico has never moved away from the social problems of the country; instead, it continues incorporating and re-elaborating its ethical-political practices in a radical way, such as vegetarianism and veganism or environmentalism. Likewise, it continuously reinvents the struggle of women both in the society and anarcho-punk collectives. Due to this issue, we assert that the anarcho-punk movement in Mexico continues to be a laboratory for political experimentation, wherein a potentiality of social change is hidden that is more powerful than what it is commonly said to be, since in these experiences, 'social ties are born and grow and germinate and become the mortar of the new world' (Zibechi 2007, 55).

References

Andresen, K. and B. Van der Steen (eds.) (2016). *A European Youth Revolt: European Perspectives on Youth Protest and Social Movements in the 1980s*. Houndmills: Palgrave.

Di Nunzio, D. and E. Toscano. (2011). *Dentro e fuori Casa Pound. Capire il fascismo del terzo millennio*. Rome: Armando Editore.

Dines, M. (2004). 'An Investigation into the Emergence of the Anarcho-punk Scene of the 1980s.' Unpublished PhD dissertation. University of Salford. http://usir.salford.ac.uk/2040/.

Eyerman, R. and A. Jamison. (1998). *Music and Social Movements: Mobilizing Traditions in the Twentieth Century*. Cambridge: Cambridge University Press.

Francalanci, S. (1984). *Virus*. Albedo Productions.

Canclini, N. (2001). *Culturas híbridas*. Buenos Aires: Paidós.

Gaytán Santiago, P. (2001). *Desmadernos. Crónica suburpunk de algunos movimientos culturales en la submetrópoli defeña*. Mexico: Universidad Autónoma del Estado de México.

Gordon, A. R. (2005). 'The Authentic Punk: an Ethnography of DIY, Music, Ethics.' Unpublished PhD dissertation. Loughborough University. https://dspace.lboro.ac.uk/dspace-jspui/handle/2134/7765.

Holloway, J. (2010). *Crack Capitalism*. London: Pluto Press.

Holloway, J. and E. Peláez. (1998). *Zapatista!: Reinventing Revolution in Mexico*. London: Pluto Press.

Katsiaficas, G. (1997). *The Subversion of Politics: European Autonomous Social Movements and the Decolonization of Everyday Life*. Atlantic Highlands, NJ: Humanities Press.

Kuhn, G. (2010). *Sober Living for the Revolution: Hardcore Punk, Straight Edge, and Radical Politics*. Oakland, CA: PM Press.

London, J. (2005 [1903]). *The People of the Abyss*. Project Gutenberg. Ebook#1688.

López Cabello, A. (2013). 'El cuerpo punk como referente indentitario en jóvenes mexicanos.' *Papeles del CEIC* 2 (96). http://www.identidadcolectiva.es/pdf/96.pdf.

McKay, G. (ed.) (1998). *DiY Culture: Party & Protest in Nineties Britain*. London: Verso Books.

Moore, R. and M. Roberts. (2009). 'Do-It-Yourself Mobilization: Punk and Social Movements.' *Mobilization* 14 (3): 273–91.

O'Connor, A. (2002a). 'Local Scenes and Dangerous Crossroads: Punk and Theories of Cultural Hybridity.' *Popular Music* 21 (2): 225–36.

O'Connor, A. (2002b). 'Punk and Globalization: Mexico City and Toronto.' In P. Kennedy and V. Roudometof (eds.), *Communities Across Borders: New Immigrants and Transnational Cultures*, 143–55. London and New York: Routledge.

O'Connor, A. (2003a). 'Anarcho-punk: Local Scenes and International Networks.' *Anarchist Studies* 11 (2): 111–21.

O'Connor, A. (2003b). 'Punk Subculture in Mexico and the Antiglobalization Movement: a Report from the Front.' *New Political Science* 25 (1): 43–53. DOI: 10.1080/0739314032000071226.

O'Connor, A. (2004). 'Punk and Globalization: Spain and Mexico.' *International Journal of Cultural Studies* 7 (2): 175–95.

O'Hara, C. (1995). *The Philosophy of Punk: More than Noise!!*. Edinburgh and San Francisco: AK Press.

Pandini, M. and S. Giaccone. (1997). *Nel cuore della bestia. Culture libertarie: tra controllo sociale e immaginario collettivo*. Milano: Zero in Condotta.

Poma, A. and T. Gravante. (2013). 'Mujeres luchando, el mundo transformando.' Donne e partecipazione politica dal basso in Messico. Paper presented at the XVII Italian Political Science Society Annual Conference. Florence, 12–14 September 2013.

Ríos Manzano, A. (1999). *Tianguis cultural del chopo: una larga jornada*. Mexico: Libraries Australia.

Roscigno, V. and W. F. Danaher. (2004). *The Voice of Southern Labor: Radio Music, and Textile Strikes, 1929–1934*. Minneapolis, MN: University of Minnesota Press.

Sandoval Vargas, M. (2012). 'El movimiento anarcopunk de Guadalajara. Una apuesta por resistir-existir contra y más allá del Estado.' In VV.AA. *Hacer política para un porvenir más allá del capitalism*, 49–60. Guadalajara, Mexico: Grietas Editores.

Scott, J. (1990). *Domination and the Arts of Resistance: Hidden Transcripts*. New Haven, CT: Yale University Press.

Zibechi, R. (2007). *Autonomías y emancipaciones. América Latina en movimiento*. Peru: Universidad Nacional Mayor de San Marcos.

Appendix: List of interviews

Label	Gender/ Age	Anar-cho-punk Generation	Date	Place
I1	M/ about 30	2000s	03/06/2013	Guadalajara
I2	M/ about 45	1980s	04/06/2013	Guadalajara
I3	M/ about 20	2000s	05/06/2013	Guadalajara
I4	M/ about 30	1990s	05/06/2013	Guadalajara
I5	M/ about 50	1980s	27/06/2013	DF
I6	F/ about 50	1980s	29/06/2013	DF
I7	M/ about 18	2000s	29/06/2013	DF
I8	F/ about 20	2000s	29/06/2013	DF
I9	M/ about 30	1990s	29/06/2013	DF
I10	M/ about 35	1990s	29/06/2013	DF

5. ONE STRUGGLE, ONE FIGHT, ALL DAY, ALL NIGHT: PUNK CARTOGRAPHIES IN THE SUBWAY OF SÃO PAULO

PAULA GUERRA & DÉBORA GOMES

Abstract

We are well aware of the importance of (sub)cultures' manifestations and localizations in a territory or context. That is this chapter's focus: to consider the metropolitan rail transport system – the subway system (lines, entry-exit zones, vehicles) – as an appropriation of the punk movement; more specifically, that of in São Paulo between 1975 and 1985, at which time both the formation of the first punk bands and the construction of the first subway lines were beginning. With this, we will resume the exercise of Marc Augé (1986) held in the Paris subway for almost thirty years, in order to rebuild the spaces, borders, belonging, barriers, obstacles, and protections that are included in the lyrics of São Paulo's punk rock bands. It is our objective to understand the representations, directions, ideologies, beliefs, and specific practices that are part of punk through the urban space. This chapter attempts to recover the plasticity of this profoundly image-based music scene through its own music production and the construction of a narrative based on everyday movement space and the preferred vehicle – the subway. It is essential to consider here the illustrative importance of urban space and its transience, fragmentation, and mobility on the emergence of punk scenes where we quintessentially include contemporary punk rock. We intend to reconstruct a historical and ethnographic outlook of the São Paulo subway punks, through an analysis of the songs' lyrics and some documentaries and interviews.

Keywords: punk, subway, urban space, São Paulo, Marc Augé

Paula Guerra is Assistant Professor of Sociology at University of Porto (FLUP), a Researcher in the Institute of Sociology of the same university (IS-UP), and an Invited researcher at the Centre for Geography Studies and Territory Planning (CEGOT). She is also Adjunct Professor at Griffith Centre for Social and Cultural Research, Australia (GCSCR). She is the founder and coordinator of the KISMIF Project/Conference, and coordinates/participates in several other research projects in the field of youth cultures and the sociology of art and culture, having published numerous works in the last few years on those themes. E-mail: pguerra@letras.up.pt

Débora Gomes dos Santos graduated in Architecture and Urbanism at the Campinas State University and has a master's degree from the University of São Paulo. She currently teaches on Universidade São Francisco's undergraduate course of Architecture and Urbanism. Her research interests include the contributions of popular and underground cultures to the investigation of contemporary urban phenomena. E-mail: deborags@gmail.com

ONE STRUGGLE, ONE FIGHT, ALL DAY, ALL NIGHT: PUNK CARTOGRAPHIES IN THE SUBWAY OF SÃO PAULO

How nice it is to be punk, just down the truncheons
And there on the subway you thread the pin
How nice it is to be punk, to eat a whole jackfruit
To enter into a collective, to vomit at the turnstile
How nice it is to be punk, there is only one thing that hurts me
It's to wait for the apocalypse, while having to be an office boy

Como é bom ser punk, descer logo o porrete
E lá no metrô se entuchar de alfinete
Como é bom ser punk, comer toda uma jaca
Entrar no coletivo, vomitar na catraca
Como é bom ser punk, só uma coisa me dói
É esperar o apocalipse tendo que ser office-boy

'How Nice It Is To Be Punk' by Rag Tongue, from the album *How Nice It Is To Be Punk* (1985)[1]

'Como é bom ser punk,' Língua de Trapo, álbum *Como é bom ser punk* (1985)

'How Nice It Is to Be Punk in the City!'

We are well aware of the importance of (sub)cultures' manifestations and localizations in a territory or a context. That issue will form the basis of this chapter: to focus on and consider the metropolitan rail transport system – the subway system (lines, entry-exit zones, vehicles) – as an appropriation of the punk movement, and more specifically that of São Paulo from 1975 to 1985, at which time the formation of the first punk bands mirrored the construction of the first city subway lines. With this focus, we resume the exercise of Marc Augé (1986) held in the Paris subway for almost thirty years in order to rebuild the spaces, borders, belongings, barriers, obstacles, and protections included in the lyrics of São Paulo's punk rock bands. It is our objective to understand the representations, directions, ideologies, beliefs, and specific practices central to the punk scene through such spaces. This chapter attempts to recover the plasticity of this iconic music scene through its own music production and the construction of a narrative based on everyday city movement via the subway. It is essential to consider here the illustrative impact of urban space and its transience, fragmentation, and mobility on the emergence of the São Paulo punk scene where we quintessentially include contemporary punk rock. We intend to reconstruct a historical and ethnographic outlook of the São Paulo subway punks through an analysis of song lyrics, documentaries, and interviews.

Therefore, the present chapter is split into three main sections. Firstly, we intend to introduce the São Paulo city of the 1970s, when its complexity began to increase through the demarcation of spaces between the central and peripheral zones, inevitably becoming a profoundly unequal social space. The emergence of the punk subculture in São Paulo is undoubtedly associated with social inequality, which was a reflection of the deterioration in living conditions and the consolidation of São Paulo as the most important industrial and economic centre of Brazil. It is in this context that the punk scene appears as a response to robust social segmentation and with the intent to shock and impose itself on the world. It arises as a result of urban fragmentation and segregation.

But what impact has this territoriality had on the punk scene in São Paulo? The second section of this chapter addresses this question. Here, we describe the locations and forms of appropriation of this demarcation on the punks in São Paulo city. The subway stands out as the central physical and social space of this analysis; in particular, and in a paradigmatic way, the São Bento subway station. The development of punk style is thus associated – indelibly – with the emergence and development of the subway system in São Paulo; the subway stations and the surrounding areas appear as the scenarios which the young punks use as visual signs of such demarcations. The street and the central areas of the city (which converge in the subway space) became important spaces of the São Paulo punk scene.

The third section is based on the notion of the young punk as a street guy: that is, in colloquial terms, a punk, a boy from the street. The street appears thus as a primordial area not only for the punk subculture but, instead, for youth subcultures in general. It is an indelible space of interaction and a territory of urban social and cultural manifestations.

Punk, Urban Fragmentation and Segregation

In 1977, the year that punk exploded from England across the world, a study[36] in São Paulo revealed the existence of a dispersed, segregated, and unequal city, mainly divided between rich and poor, represented by physical and social distance between the centrality of the rich and the marginality of the poor. Socially heterogeneous and geographically concentrated, the city grew vigorously throughout the twentieth century (see Figure 5.1 below). Indeed, it expanded beyond the district limits in the form of rings that left a rich and well-equipped centre, where the upper and middle classes lived, toward the poor and impoverished urban infrastructural peripheries encompassing the lower classes of the population (see Figure 5.2 below) (Rolnik, Kowarick, and Somekh 1990, 13).

This urban setting was a result of the overlap of numerous urban planning interventions, especially the shifting dynamics within the city space. The Avenues Plan, a road project prepared by engineer and mayor of São Paulo[37] Francisco Prestes Maia in 1930, undertaken between the late 1930s and mid-1940s,[38] was the key spark for this process. The plan – responsible for opening a series of wide expressways that traversed the city to connect the centre to the suburbs – completely and definitively changed the circulation system of São Paulo, as well as connected São Paulo's urban configuration and ultimately the way citizens related to it.

---

36 Study commissioned by the Department of Economy and Planning State of São Paulo (Seplan) in 1977 (Caldeira 2003, 230).

37 On two occasions: 1938–1945 and 1961–1965 (Villaça 2004, 149).

38 The last stage, which was the opening of the current 23 de Maio Avenue, was only made in the early 1960s during the second term of Prestes Maia in São Paulo (Villaça 2004, 149).

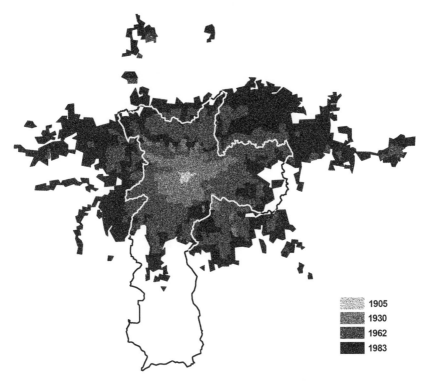

Figure 5.1: Map of the growth of São Paulo's urban fabric between (1905–83). Source: CeSAD.

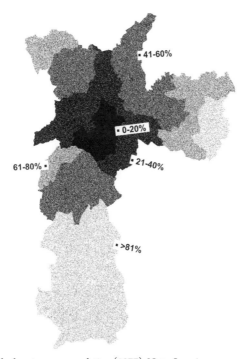

Figure 5.2: Map of the low-income population (1977). Note: Low-income population means, in this case, population that receive up to 5 minimum salaries. Source: Kowarick, Rolnik, and Somekh (1990, 62).

The opening of large avenues led to the deactivation of the old tramway system, whose costly installation works limited its expansion; on the other hand, this encouraged the establishment of road transport – an obvious change stimulated by the development of the suburban automobile industry. Through this flexible and low-cost installation, buses began to circulate throughout the city (even the streets without asphalt of the outer boroughs), stimulating population dispersion and fuelling the disordered growth of São Paulo. Meanwhile, the central regions followed suit with an improved road structure and the intense construction of avenues and viaducts for private cars, which were a status symbol of the upper classes (Villaça 2004, 150).

Confined to the margins of the urban conurbation of São Paulo, the working class were subject to a perverse accumulation of exclusionary factors: the deficiency of urban equipment and services; the precariousness of education, health, and labour; and also lack of control and authority over their own time[39] – 'radically out of places where they circulate the opportunities' (Rolnik 2003, 51) in the 'invisible city' mentioned by Milton Santos (1990, 53):

> The legislation itself guaranteed the exceptional nature of the periphery: while carefully regulated what was defined as an urban area, it left the suburban and rural areas largely unregulated and therefore open to various forms of exploitation. (Caldeira 2003, 220)

The incorporation of the punk subculture by the São Paulo youth at the end of the 1970s is objectively linked to a widespread pessimism about the precarious living conditions of the city that 'has to stop.'[40] They were also affected by the stressful experience of direct repression and control by the Brazilian military dictatorship. This situation occurred as the city and its metropolitan area were consolidating themselves as a major industrial centre to become the most important economic hub of the country (Caldeira 2003, 228). In fact, the relationship between the origin and social experience of young people and the way they organize their identities and lifestyles was the principle focus of cultural studies since the formation of the Birmingham Centre for Contemporary Cultural Studies (CCCS). Its initial research was concerned with two main issues: to what extent the youth musical cultures express their contextual working-class identities in industrial cities and services of the 1950s, 1960s, and 1970s, and to what extent the songs, artefacts, and collective rituals of those cultures were represented as an imaginary resistance to the prevailing social order (Hall and Jefferson 1976).

In the segmented São Paulo mega metropolis, where social interaction was increasingly restricted, elements of youth took punk as an expressive identity form, a style to shock and to suggest their social disenchantment to the world. In this sense, we agree with Clarke's dictum that: 'What makes a style is the activity of stylisation – the active

---

39 Teresa Caldeira points out that in 1977 the residents of the East Zone of São Paulo were 13 hours (average) away from home, spending 4 to 5 hours in shifts by public transport (Caldeira, 2003, p. 221).

40 This sentence belongs to José Carlos de Figueiredo Ferraz, the mayor of São Paulo between 1971 and 1973 (Ferraz, 1976, p. 4); in contrast to the famous jargon of the 1950s 'São Paulo: the city that cannot stop', by Ademar de Barros, Mayor between 1957 and 1961.

organisation of objects with activities and outlooks, which produce an organized group-identity in the form and shape of a coherent and distinctive way of "being-in-the-world"' (Clarke et al. 1997, 108). Thus, a style, to express itself, requires a social arena, a cultural space to negotiate and develop itself.

São Paulo has alleys, it has buildings	*São Paulo tem becos, tem construções*
It has punks Mohicans, Mohicans or not	*Tem punks moicanos, moicanos ou não*
It has crazy people talking for nothing	*Tem gente louca falando à toa*
São Paulo is cold with sun or drizzle	*São Paulo é frio com sol ou garôa*
Walking through the centre the anthill	*Andando pelo centro, pelo formigueiro*
Mohicans protesting the people pass looking	*Moicanos protestando o povo passa olhando*
It has all kinds of visuals	*Tem todo tipo de visual*
But what matters is the general content	*Mas o que importa é o conteúdo geral*
São Paulo is huge,	*São Paulo é gigante,*
It is large the underground	*É grande o underground*
'São Paulo is Gig' by Cholera, from the album *Let the Earth in Peace!* (Devil Discos 2004)	'São Paulo é gig,' Cólera, álbum *Deixe a Terra em paz!* (Devil Discos 2004)

As the city grows, the more it progresses and the more it becomes central. According to Flávio Villaça (2004, 148), the centre is seen by punks as a revealing mediation of contemporary issues, as a space par excellence of otherness, because it 'implies and shows oppositions, the inside and the outside, the centre and the periphery, the integrated in the urban society and the not integrated' according to Henri Lefebvre (1969, 63). The song 'São Paulo is gig' by Cólera,[41] one of the first and most important punk bands of São Paulo, alludes to the city centre as a place where the meeting of the differences that characterize urbanity is enabled. The tingling of the city that is a gig[42] permits the madness, the Mohican, and the protest (Thompson 2004).

Thus, through punk these young people will respond not only to their inability to discern reasonable prospects for the future, but above all to conditions of marginality and social and spatial invisibility. In this sense, they are fighting for the right to share urban opportunities for human development offered in the more centralized areas of the city, while they propose to dignify the marginal origin by showing that the city is a place for other plans, cultures, and realities.

Placed in a context of constant cultural exchanges, the punk scene emerged around the second half of the 1970s simultaneously with the United States and the United Kingdom as an artistic uprising, especially musical, representing contestation and resistance against the cultural situation of the time. With the proposal to break with the musical scene of the moment – the instrumental erudition and thematic distancing from subgenres such as progressive, psychedelic, and folk rock, and the supposed banality of commercial music, especially disco – punk promoted a return to simple musical forms and the appreciation of

41 Cholera, in English.

42 *Gig* is used as a metaphor alluding to the huge size of the city of São Paulo and equally as slang for parties or concerts, a term coined on the jazz circuit of the 1920s and later incorporated into punk vocabulary.

the common reality of everyday life. Thus, punk brought the sonorities of the large cities as narratives of urban daily life to the centre of the composition and transformed the music into a powerful vehicle of absorption and transmission, reflecting the difficulties of city living. So we can say that punk was a landmark break with and repositioning against the existing social structure, with its own soundtrack, aesthetics, and attitudes. Punk has always been more than a simple t-shirt or a song: in our case, it was an unyielding attitude challenging the status quo and offered stark visibility to a dissatisfied and incredulous youth. Punk sees itself as the impetus of return, resurrection, and renewal, but it also has the impulse of the change, the inversion of sound and aesthetics (Guerra 2013; 2014).

In the Brazilian peripheral context of incomplete, multipurpose, and chaotic modernization, punk became more radical and developed critical political contours. Brazilian punk music has its own accent, marked by super acceleration and the maximum incorporation of noise and distortion, short song duration and the general use of a darker tone. The lyrics focus politically around contextual issues such as oppression, lack of freedom, exploitation, unemployment, poverty, and the boredom of life in the peripheral zones.

Open up your eyes	*Abra bem seus olhos*
But be careful not to spot them with blood	*Mas cuidado para não manchá-los de sangue*
You will see what you don't want to see	*Você vai ver o que não quer ver*
So do not be surprised	*Por isso não se espante*
You will see a blind crowd	*Você vai ver uma multidão cega*
Creeping to the city	*Pela cidade a se arrastar*
So oppressed, so massacred	*Tão oprimida, tão massacrada*
That it can't even think	*Que não consegue nem pensar*
No strength to fight, having to shut	*Sem forças pra lutar, tendo que se calar*
And submit, having to accept	*E se submeter, tendo que aceitar*
This submissive life, this submissive life	*Essa vida submissa, essa vida submissa*
This submissive life which destroys us	*Essa vida submissa, que nos destrói*
They walk without fate	*Andam sem destino*
Weakly disorientated	*Debilmente desorientados*
Unaware that for life	*Sem saber que pela vida*
They were badly marked	*Foram duramente marcados*
In their homes their children	*Nos seus lares os seus filhos*
Will not know ever	*Não saberão jamais*
If not now change	*Que se não mudarem agora*
They are doomed to be like their parents	*Estão condenados a serem como seus pais*

'Submissive Life' by Innocents, from the *Poverty and Hunger* album (Devil Drives 1988). This was a reissue of the 1983 EP including previously censored tracks	'Vida Submissa,' Inocentes, álbum *Miséria e Fome* (Devil Discos, 1988)

All the punk action forms are structured around what Abramo calls 'appearance,' as the public display of shock and provocation, the intention of which is to state, by their own presence, the existence and need for attention to certain social issues: they are 'spectacular groups [that] produce a critical intervention in the public space. They put together an act, they articulate a speech, with its filled figures of signs, with their movement through the city streets, with their songs' (1994, xv). Thus, through the 'appearance' strategy, punk draws attention and forces society to realize and recognize issues that would otherwise be submerged. Through exposure in social spaces, movements, crowds, and agglomerations – like the centre and the subway – the peripheral youth intends to escape from the invisibility of its liminal status. Here, it is important to introduce the concept of 'bricolage.' Relying on Levi-Strauss, where the concept was used to explain how different elements can be 'used in a variety of improvised combinations to generate new meanings' (Hebdige 1997, 135), Hebdige advocates that it is possible to understand punk – although it means chaos at all levels, it is organized into a coherent, signifying whole. Thus, to analyse punk style as a practice to which a meaning is assigned, the author notes the traditional semiotic failure to provide a deeper ideological analysis. Thus, he supports the idea of polysemy, by which every text creates an infinite potential of meanings.

Thus, it is worth mentioning that all signifying objects used in punk have served to achieve unity at the level of relationships and experiences. This factor has been particularly important for visibility on the Brazilian punk scene. The occupation of the streets and the subway was notorious through its concern with aesthetic and stylistic elements now signified as political problems. However, 'the key to punk style remains elusive. Instead of arriving at the point where we can begin to make sense of the style, we have reached the very space where meaning itself evaporates' (Hebdige 1997, 139).

Standing on the Station

The access to city circulation and transport has been a long-standing problem on the São Paulo City Hall agenda because of the unsustainability of increased traffic. The wide valorization of the car and bus as means of transportation and the authorities' omission control, together, with the road system failure resulted in traffic chaos. This is still a residual problem in São Paulo. However, from the mid-1950s onwards the subway installation proposal began to be discussed seriously, resulting in a decision in the late 1960s to make it a viable transport system, beginning in earnest in the mid-1970s (Lagonegro 2004).

Thus, São Paulo was the first Brazilian city to receive a subway railroad transport system. Its first stretch was operational in 1974, seventy-four years after the Paris Metropolitan opening and almost a decade before the publication of *Un Ethnologue dans le métro*[43] by French anthropologist Marc Augé. Launched in 1986, the book was the result of over fifty years of Augé's daily life on the subway. In this book we can find the author's personal memories, which are marked sensorial and spatially in terms of stations, transfers, corridors, and wagons:

> Certain subway stations are so associated with exact moments of my life, nonetheless,
> that thinking about or meeting the name prompts me to page through my memories as

---

43 *In the Metro* is the title in the English-language version used in this article.

if they were a photo album: in a certain order, with more or less serenity, complacency, or boredom, sometimes even with heartfelt emotion – the secret of these variations belonging as much to the moment of consultation as to its object. (Augé 2002, 4)

In the mid-1970s, however, spaces on the single subway line in São Paulo were too new to forge prominent memories in the population. However, for the youth of that time the subway would become a nostalgic feature: nostalgia for something that is not lived directly, but indirectly through music, movies, and photos – those products of an internationalized cultural industry, whose topics were relatively different from the national production, which was still strongly based on the 'Rio-Bahia model of *Brazilianness*' (Abramo 2004, 192). Brazil, before the military coup, heralded a nostalgic mood reflected in Brazilian popular culture which was largely absent in the memory of the new generation of young people who were looking for other languages which were closer to their immediate urban reality marked by a certain 'quality narcotic' – a language sedimented by the advent of the subway (Conley 2002, 81).

Since the 1920s, when the city experienced its first industrial boom, the concern of São Paulo's cultural elite was to build its identity based on the ideas of modernity and urbanity, such as the Modern Art Week of 1922.[44] This imaginary vision consolidated itself in the 1950s, transforming a once understood aesthetic into an exceptional perspective and henceforth an undeniable reality (Bassani 2003, 84). São Paulo gradually entered the arts and world culture route, with consecutive biennial exhibitions and displays in the city. Examples of this are the São Paulo International Biennial of Art in 1951, the São Paulo International Book Biennial in 1970, the São Paulo International Architecture Biennial in 1975, and the International Film Festival in 1977.

Jorge Bassani stated that, 'the media, like any urban phenomenon, establishes as the next reality everything that is international. São Paulo has been internationalised – while the internal migratory flows have to be recognised as one part of the nation – and the city has intended to catch up with other centres and create its own social project' (2003, 85). From this moment on, a specific São Paulo culture was established in a broad sense (artistic, architectural, media, industrial) and is distinct from any other Brazilian regionality, yet equally close to an international language on account of its reflection of the urban, metropolitan, and industrial modernist aesthetic.

At first, the introduction of the subway did not significantly alter the population's movement dynamics, which continued to cling to buses, cars, and pedestrianism. The strike held by the Collective Transport Movement in 1979 undermined the popularity of the bus in the public mind on account of the associated city deadlock arising from the industrial action. This event illustrated how fragile and insufficient São Paulo's predominant circulation system was in comparison to an incipient subway system at the time when there was only one line (see Figure 5.3 below), which was built, in the first place, with regards to economic interests rather than the real needs of population mobility (Gohn 2004, 161).

---

44 This event intended to promote the modernist movement in the Brazilian art scene.

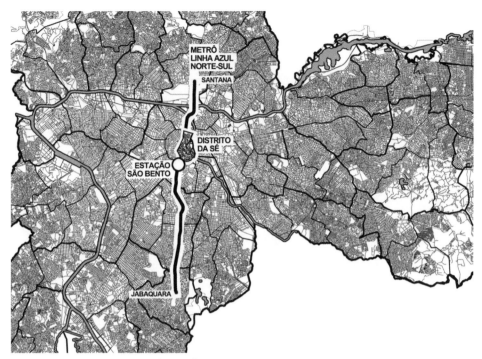

Figure 5.3: São Paulo subway map (1974–5)

The introduction of the subway, however, had the symbolic effect of rapidly propelling the city into a new technological era of efficiency in Brazil. It reinforced a specific São Paulo lifestyle: effectively modern and reflexively equivalent to those in the largest and most important urban centres of the world. The adoption of aesthetics and punk culture in part, especially for the needy and poor among the city's youth, arose from a desire to discover and invent links between the urban reality of São Paulo and these major world cities. Therefore, São Paulo punks reflected on and embraced what they understood to be the style of punk life. For example, New York poet Ed Sanders commented that punk encompassed, 'brave, threatening, the Final Judgement drums; only you do not know whether it is Final Judgement drums or someone's music. But the drums are always in the background, drumming' (in McCain and McNeil 2007, 44). Such a description is a token of the incipient subway's immersion into a symbolic form of punks mapping their own underground worlds. Such São Paulo underground mapping, however, was not necessarily built in the subway, but *coupled* with it:

> The subway was expensive at the time; we didn't use the subway so much; we used to use the bus. The Subway was more expensive than the bus. But sometimes we used it. They [punks] use to meet down there, I remember. (ex-punk, in an interview[45])

> We didn't use the subway very much, but as soon as the blue line was inaugurated we did like entering there and staying there all day and we used to go from one end to the other, more for fun. (ex-punk, in an interview)

45 Interviews with the first-generation São Paulo punks were undertaken in April 2014.

Figures 5.4 & 5.5: Punks in the São Paulo subway areas. Source: *Punks* (1983).

Our interviews with active punks during the first years of the movement in São Paulo indicated that subway travel was not an everyday occurrence. Instead, such journeys were used as an occasional weekend adventure or as some kind an exploratory tool of the city pegged to a connection and discovery of new stops, places, and different realities. Within a daily context, the closeness and the permanence of the punks around the new stations became more important than the train journeys:

> 'Will you go to São Bento [subway station]?' 'Tomorrow I will be there at São Bento!' The people who worked in the city centre — as office boy or similar — usually meet each other at the São Bento station by the lunch time and then go to the Punk Rock [store]. (Dead, *Botinada* documentary, 2006)

A number of São Paulo punks retained minor occupations in the tertiary sector. They were office boys and assistants, clerks and receptionists in banks, offices, firms, and shops located in the city's central regions. Therefore, aside from formal working spaces, there was a functional link which it become a meeting and leisure space for punks. During lunch breaks or after work, punks would meet on the access staircase at São Bento subway station; this became a traditional space to show up and hang out, because of the large amounts of people passing through the station.

The São Bento station was inaugurated in September 1975 and was the most central station of the city. The Cathedral station – the largest and most central of the city to this day – was only added to the system three years later. This central location allowed for the development of unprecedented, numerous public spaces, meeting points and an agglomeration of event areas. Thus, through the dissolution of the immediate territorialities that were created by displacement and access to multiple places there arose new possibilities for action making the city more permeable and accessible.

From this moment, peripheral youth were no longer confined to their home districts. Instead, they preferred the variety of crowds where they could simultaneously feel camouflaged while also standing out. In the surroundings of the stations, the young punks acted out roles of 'regular subway travellers,' yet liked the elegance and naturalness that Augé considered qualities of the passenger in the dynamics and flows of the subway-railroad system (2002, 6). Contrasting groups of punks thrived on the discomfort and violence of their appearance juxtaposed with the stark concreteness of the station's modernist aesthetic. Their performance was at once an invasion and conquest of these agglomeration areas in order to demand and tease attention from passers-by, 'using the body as the environment mirror' (Abramo 1994, 107):

> If you are an office boy, you're fucked. Then, if you turn punk you are someone, everyone will identify you. If someone looks at you, he knows what you think of society; you do not need to say anything more. You find an identity – you are proud: I am punk. It was cool; people were frightened. (Former punk Abramo 1994, 103)

Thus, the punk relied heavily on the visual signification of modern urban life, whose strength is particularly felt in the new spatiality designed city to assist the functional movement of people. This is an issue that sociologist Georg Simmel previously observed in the early twentieth century: 'Before the development of buses, railroads, and trams in the nineteenth century, people had never been in a position of having to look at one another for long minutes or even hours without speaking to one another' (2009, 573). However, it is precisely this exchange of glances that 'moves away after sometimes settle for a moment' (Augé 2002, 6). This 'look' was what punk's actively sought by adopting a public subway station as a meeting point.

International comparisons can also be drawn from this example. In Portugal, punk began in Lisbon contemporarily with the post-revolutionary Carnation society of accelerated urbanization (Silva and Guerra 2015; Guerra and Bennett 2015). In Spain, punk was a contemporary of the post-Franco democratization and the emergence of Madrid (Fouce 2006; 2004). In France, punk's genesis was led by young people mostly from Paris or Lyon (Humeau 2011). In today's Russia, the spread of punk extended from Moscow and Leningrad (Pilkington 2014). Punk is both urban and suburban: it is located in territories marked by the diversity and the density of people, by the relationships and the exchanges, and it takes place in the context of late modernity and cosmopolitanism.

Another day in vain leaning against the corner	*Mais um outro dia em vão encostado na esquina*
Watching people pass, a cigarette to smoke …	*Vendo gente passar, um cigarro pra fumar...*
In a very cold night, the sirens screaming	*Numa noite muito fria, as sirenes a gritar*
Violence on street corners and noise everywhere …	*Violências nas esquinas e barulho em todo*
Ooh ! Ooh ! Ooh ! City! Ooh ! Ooh ! Ooh ! City!	*lugar...*
Another day in vain leaning against the station	*Ooh! Ooh! Ooh! Cidade!*
Seeing the hatred of the people, every time they fight	*Ooh! Ooh! Ooh! Cidade!*
for nothing …	*Mais um outro dia em vão encostado na estação*
Police violence, bitch; what a shame	*Vendo o ódio das pessoas, toda hora brigam à*
When will this change? Holy shit place …	*toa...*
Ooh ! Ooh ! Ooh ! City! Ooh ! Ooh ! Ooh ! City!	*A violência da polícia, puta-merda que vergonha*
When will this change? Holy shit place …	*Quando isso vai mudar? Puta merda de lugar...*
	Ooh! Ooh! Ooh! Cidade!
'São Paulo,' by Cholera, from *Try to Change To-*	*Ooh! Ooh! Ooh! Cidade!*
morrow album (Front Attack 1984)	*Quando isso vai mudar? Puta merda de lugar...*
	'São Paulo,' Cólera, álbum *Tente mudar o amanhã* (Ataque Frontal 1984)

Through their public visibility on the subway, punk kids would soon draw the attention of newspaper articles, magazines, documentaries, and television and cinema in addition to being featured in degree shows in the most prestigious São Paulo colleges. They were becoming a recurring theme in all media channels. In the early years of the 1980s,

Figures 5.6 & 5.7: Punks in São Bento station areas. Source: *Punks* (1983) and *Pânico em S.P.* (1983).

many documentaries were made such as *Panic in S. P.*[46] by Claudio Morelli (1982), *Boys of Suburbia*[47] by Fernando Meirelles (1983), and *Punks* by Sarah Yakhni and Alberto Gieco (1984). These documentaries captured the São Paulo punks' daily city lives while reinforcing the aesthetic ritual of sartorial and aesthetic punk style. They also highlighted the working routines in the city centre and the meeting with colleagues to chat, rehearse, and have fun. All these activities were enhanced by the punk movement's actions, either on foot or by train, but mostly by bus. Indeed, there are countless scenes where you can watch the young getting on and getting off the vehicles (see Figure 5.6). However, all records ever show are the punks gathered together at São Bento station and its surroundings, such as the Santa Efigénia viaduct and the Great Galleries record store – a commercial building nicknamed the Rock Gallery, such was the concentration of punk and rock lovers there. In these places the punks are pictured in their leisure time between a typically teenage aesthetic rebellion entwined with more serious discussions about their own and their country's future.

The subway, the route underneath the city into the earth, is the absolute space of artifice and the complete negation of the natural, and the product par excellence of the metropolis. In addition to a means of transport, it is equally of symbolic importance offering a new sensibility due to its underground status and independence from of any other traffic structures. The subway hence becomes a metaphor for the punks' 'power to come out of nowhere, or from a darkness so deep that' it is difficult to distinguish them of 'the contours of the alleys. In the shadows, from the distance of the most obvious negotiations, punks' appearance shines, therefore, from a much more intense light' (Caiafa 1985, 9).

Therefore, the subway images link with the notion of the underground imagery. On the one hand there exists identification with the decay of the scenarios that live in the imaginary punk: debris, wreckage, and failure. 'An underground place is also a place apart, is opposed to the normal plane of the city, and by adopting it, these young people want to proclaim their difference' (Abramo 1994, 146). On the other hand, the adoption of the condition of being 'under' does not mean a gap or an alternative society, but instead is an outstanding and evidential strategy of punk reality. Thus, the underground is at the same time in the city centre, in the centre of the events, of the opportunities and the attention. So, the underground imagery has taken the subway spaces as the ideal scenic environment, as in the image that covers the *Descanse em Paz*[48] album by *Ratos de Porão*[49] (see Figure 5.8). The back cover image of the *Pior que Antes*[50] album by *Garotos Podres*[51] is even more emphatic and literal: not only are the band members located beyond the reach of the sight underground, but are the rats of sewage who observe the city from manholes (see Figure 5.9).

---

46 'Pânico em S.P.' in the original Portuguese version.
47 'Garotos do Subúrbio' in the original Portuguese version.
48 *Rest In Peace* in English.
49 In a free translation, we can call this band *Basement Rats*.
50 *Worse than Before* in English.
51 *Bad Kids* in a free translation to English.

Figure 5.8: Inside cover of *Rest In Piece* album by Basement Rats (Baratos Afins 1986) (photo by Rui Mendes).

Figure 5.9: Back cover of *Worse Than Before* album by Bad Kids (Continental 1988).

Urban Animal	Animal urbano
Crises, violence	Crises, violência
Sad existence	Triste existência
We performed the decay	Realizamos a decadência
Urban Animal	Animal urbano
Underground dweller	Habitante subterrâneo
Among the rubble and ruins	Entre escombros e ruínas
His soul is hungry	Sua alma está faminta
It howls for you	Ela uiva por você
'Urban Animal,' by Innocents, from *Innocents* album (Warner 1989)	'Animal Urbano,' Inocentes, álbum *Inocentes* (Warner 1989)

At that time, in the 80s, we had a craze linked to architecture that was knowing the city more intimately and deeper. We used to go through the tunnels, to the underground, into the rainwater sewer. We used to know how to escape and also how to create problems when we wanted to. (former punk, in an interview in April 2014)

'I'm a Kid From the Street'

> And the punks are going, in pairs, trios, bands, like warriors after the battle, all in black uniform, walking from the PUC, in the Partridges, to the São Bento square, through the Francisco Matarazzo and Saint John avenues. 200 punks is an impressive stage show. And the punk march continues. It's five o'clock on Saturday morning to Sunday. The punks are now going through the corner of Ipiranga with the St John. A little more and they pass through the Paysandu square, and they turn, they cross the Santa Ifigenia viaduct and they gain the São Bento square. They are exhausted but alive. Some fall in banks and sleep, others fall to their girls, embraced; one will sleep at the school door. And while they're waiting for the first subway, they're talking, they're commenting on the show and about what happened. Dawn, it is Sunday. One by one, they're all taking the course to their homes. All are still a little more than children and, though they're already working, they're still living in the parental home. But, as is Sunday, after lunch the punks will back to the square. (Bivar 2001, 112–14)

Augé's statement that 'all the people I meet there [in the subway] are the *other*, in the full sense of the word' is appropriate (2002, 13). In life, passing hurried through the corridors, the interconnections, and the subway stairs, we meet with thousands of people whose stories we do not know and we ignore in the isolation of our own issues and concerns. However, the 'invasion of the *under* bands,' in Caiafa's words, figured by young punks is harder to ignore: the image of skinny, pale, and angular boys and their occasionally rude, loud, and violent behaviour simultaneously diverges from and draws public attention.

However, the subway used by the punks is parasitic, as they use the inherent clusters of space to stage their shows. They rarely contribute to subway life in practical terms because they do not use it for their personal travel. The act of moving is still necessary: the route is undertaken not only as a daily necessity tied to work and leisure activities, but equally as a speculative and subjective experience of the city. Their excursions and involvement within city meanderings integrate their spectacular strategy within the canvas of subway life; there is an eagerness to know new places and overcome barriers. When exposed, the punk gains aesthetic territory and control over their adopted environment. As punk rock discourse frames the inconsistent and contradictory definitions of the term itself they are rapidly communicated in all directions, punk presence in space is total – it has a holistic character (Laing 2015). Thus, the 'punk show' is complete.

Wandering the streets they try to forget	*Vagando pelas ruas tentam esquecer*
All that oppresses them and prevents them from living	*Tudo que os oprime e os impedem de viver*
Wonder if forgetting would be the solution	*Será que esquecer seria a solução*
To dissolve the hatred that they have the heart	*Pra dissolver o ódio que eles tem no coração*
Will to scream suffocated in the air	*Vontade de gritar sufocada no ar*
The fear caused by repression	*O medo causado pela repressão*
All this tries to prevent the kids from the suburbs to exist	*Tudo isso tenta impedir os garotos do subúrbio de existir*
Suburban boys, suburban boys	*Garotos do subúrbio, Garotos do subúrbio*
You cannot give up living	*Vocês não podem desistir de viver*

'Boys of Suburbia,' by Innocents, *Scream Suburban* compilation (Punk Rock Records 1986) — 'Garotos do Subúrbio,' Inocentes, compilação *Grito Suburbano* (Punk Rock Discos 1986)

The city and its metamorphoses have been significant in the research corpus of the Chicago School and described as an incessant subcultural appropriation; the street, the city, the space of (un)appropriation, the place of possible existences. As noted elsewhere, the Portuguese punk and the life from and on the street and the city consitute a matrix and central scene of existence in post-war youth culture. This is captured in the song by Opinião Pública[52] 'Puto da Rua[53]': 'I'm a kid from the street, in the city sewer/ Searching for the faces behind the masks' (Silva and Guerra 2015, 230). We can take the verses of this song as a poetic synthesis of the punks and their relationship and interdependence with the urban revolution, with the birth of a fragmented city and the emergence of the subway:

> I'm a kid from the street, in the city sewer, searching the faces behind the masks. I'm a kid from the street in the city sewer searching the faces behind the masks, I was a kid of the street in the city sewer searching the faces behind the masks, I think I was a kid from the street in the city sewer searching the faces behind the masks, I dreamt I was a kid from the street in the city sewer searching the faces behind the masks, we were kids from the street in the city sewer searching the faces behind the masks, will we still be in the city sewer kids from the street searching the faces behind masks? I will still be a kid from the street in the city sewer searching the faces behind the masks, I still have with me a kid from the street, searching my face behind the mask, we are masks that only the kids from the street can see as faces, I left from being a kid from the street

52 Public Opinion (free translation).
53 'Boy From the Street' (free translation).

in the city sewer to stay as a mask in the city as sewage, we returned to the city sewer needed to return to be kids from the street to preserve the faces behind masks, I am while I was a kid from the street the city sewer searching the faces behind the masks, I am, hear me, see me, I am, I force you to hear me because I speak loud, I force you to see me because I shock you, I am, I am! Am I? A kid from the street in the city and metro sewer searching the faces behind the masks. (Silva and Guerra 2015, 230–31)

References

Abramo, B. (2004). 'Música em trânsito: a circulação do pop.' In C. M. Campos, L. H. Gama, and V. Sacchetta (eds.), *São Paulo: metrópole em trânsito. Percursos urbanos e culturais.* São Paulo: Senac.

Abramo, H. W. (1994). *Cenas juvenis: punks e darks no espetáculo urbano.* São Paulo: Editora Página Aberta.

Augé, M. (2002). *In the Metro.* Minneapolis: University of Minnesota Press.

Bassani, J. (2003). *As linguagens artísticas e a cidade: cultura urbana do século XX.* São Paulo: FormArte.

Bivar, A. (2001). *O que é punk?* Coleção primeiros passos. São Paulo: Editora Brasiliense.

Caiafa, J. (1985). O movimento punk na cidade: invasão de bandos Sub. Rio de Janeiro: Zahar.

Caldeira, T. P. R. (2003). *Cidade de muros: crime, segregação e cidadania em São Paulo.* São Paulo: Editora 34.

Clarke, J. *et al.* (1997). 'Subcultures, Cultures and Class.' In K. Gelder and S. Thornton (eds.), *The Subculture Reader*, 100–11. London: Routledge.

Conley, T. (2002). 'Afterword.' In M. Augé (ed.), *In the Metro.* Minneapolis: University of Minnesota Press.

Ferraz, J. C. F. (1976). São Paulo e seu futuro: antes que seja tarde demais. Rio de Janeiro: IBAM.

Fouce, H. (2004). 'El punk en el ojo del huracán: de la Nueva Ola a la Movida.' *Revista de Estudios de Juventud* 64: 57–65.

Fouce, H. (2006). *El futuro ya está aquí.* Madrid: Velecíoeditores.

Gohn, M. G. (2004). 'Movimentos e lutas sociais.' In C. M. Campos, L. H. Gama, and V. Sacchetta (eds.), *São Paulo: metrópole em trânsito. Percursos urbanos e culturais.* São Paulo: Senac.

Guerra, P. (2013). 'Punk, ação e contradição em Portugal. Uma aproximação às culturas juvenis contemporâneas.' *Revista Crítica de Ciências Sociais* 102/103: 111–34.

Guerra, P. (2014). 'Punk, Expectations, Breaches and Metamorphoses: Portugal, 1977–2012.' *Critical Arts* 28 (1): 111–22.

Guerra, P. and A. Bennett. (2015). 'Never Mind the Pistols? The Legacy and Authenticity of the Sex Pistols in Portugal.' *Popular Music and Society* 38 (4): 500–21.

Hall, S. and T. Jefferson. (1976). *Resistance Through Rituals: Youth Subcultures in Post-war Britain.* New York: Holmes & Meier.

Hebdige, D. (1979). *Subculture: the Meaning of Style.* London: Methuen.

Hebdige, D. (1997). 'Subculture: the Meaning of Style.' In K. Gelder and S. Thornton (eds.), *The Subculture Reader*, 130–42. London: Routledge.

Humeau, P. (2011). 'Sociologie de l'espace punk indépendant français: Apprentissages, trajectoires et vieillissement politico-artistique.' Unpublished PhD thesis. Nantes, l'Université Picardie Jules Verne.

Kowarick, L., R. Rolnik, and N. Somekh (eds.). (1990). *São Paulo: crise e mudança.* São Paulo: Brasiliense.

Lagonegro, M. A. (2004). 'Metrópole sem metro.' Unpublished PhD thesis. São Paulo, Faculdade de Arquitetura e Urbanismo da Universidade de São Paulo.

Laing, D. (2015). *One Chord Wonders: Power and Meaning in Punk Rock.* Oakland: PM Press.

Lefebvre, H. (1969). *O direito à cidade.* São Paulo: Documentos.

McCain, G. and L. McNeil. (2007). *Mate-me por favour,* vol. II. São Paulo: L&PM Pocket.

Pilkington, H. (2014). 'Punk, But Not As We Know It: Rethinking Punk from a Post-socialist Perspective.' In I. Gololobov, H. Pilkington, and Y. B. Steinholt (eds.), *Punk in Russia. Cultural Mutation from the 'Useless' to the 'Moronic',* 1–21. London: Routledge.

Rolnik, R. (2003). *São Paulo.* São Paulo: Publifolha.

Santos, M. (1990). *Metrópole corporativa fragmentada: o caso de São Paulo.* São Paulo: Nobel, Secretaria de Estado da Cultura.

Silva, A. S. and P. Guerra. (2015). *As palavras do punk.* Lisbon: Alêtheia.

Simmel, G. (2009). *Sociology: Inquiries into the Construction of Social Forms.* Leiden: Koninklijke Brill NV.

Thompson, S. (2004). *Punk Productions: Unfinished State.* New York: University of New York Press.

Villaça, F. (2004). 'Elites, desigualdade e poder municipal.' In C. M. Campos, L. H. Gama, and V. Sacchetta (eds.), *São Paulo: metrópole em trânsito. Percursos urbanos e culturais.* São Paulo: Senac.

Videos

Morelli, C. (dirs.) (1982). *Pânico em S.P.* Brasil: ECA-USP. Escola de Comunicações e Artes da Universidade de São Paulo. 9 min.

Meirelles, F. (dirs.) (1983). *Garotos do subúrbio.* Brasil: Produtora Olhar Eletrônico. 42 min.

Yakhni, S. and A. Gieco. (dirs.) (1984). *Punks.* 35 min.

Moreira, G. (dirs.) (2006). *Botinada: A história do punk no Brasil.* Brasil.

Albums

Cólera. (1984). *Tente mudar o amanhã.* Ataque Frontal.

Cólera. (2004). *Deixe a Terra em paz!* Devil Discos.

Garotos Podres.(1988). *Pior que antes.* Continental.

Grito Suburbano. (1986). *Compilação.* Punk Rock Discos.

Inocentes. (1988). *Miséria e fome.* Devil Discos.

Inocentes. (1989). *Inocentes.* Warner.

Língua de Trapo. (1984). *Como é bom ser punk.*

Ratos de Porão. (1986). *Descanse em paz.* Baratos Afins.

Cabo Villano
Armiz
S. Pelayo
Baquio
Bermeo
Izaro
Laida
Barrica
Plencia
Andracas
Alto del Sollube
Mundaca
Pedemales
340
Busturia
Canala
Guecho
Sopelana
Icasta
Arrieta
cero
Algorta
Gatica
Munguía
Murueta
turce
Las Arenas
Lejona
R. Plencia
Rigoitia
Gue
alete
Sestao
racaldo
Asúa
Basabilotra
Fica
Lezama
Larrabezúa
Garaitondo
Ajuria
Retuerto
narán
BILBAO
Alonsotegui
Galdácano
Usánsolo
üeñes
Sódupe 996
Rio Arratia 10
(69)
Echano
Amorebieta
Ganecogorta
Zollo
Arrigorriaga
Miravelles
Yurre
63
A8
Yurreta
uela
Oquendo
Llodio
Areta
Castillo
Elejabeiti
Bernagoitia
Peña Oba
Durango
(102)
Luyando
Orozco
(Zubia)
Sa de Mendiguisa
Galiartu
Villaro
Ceánuri
718
Mañaria
liza
roño
Iberra
Urigoiti
Amurrio
Bergana
Unduraga
1037
Alto de
Barazar
688
64 240
Ochandi
ada
Orduña
(293)
Lezama
Ciórroga
Peo d. Gorbea
Uzquiano
Ubidea
Tertanga
Sa d. G
Echagüen
S. Engr

6. GOLFOS, PUNKIS, ALTERNATIVOS, INDIGNADOS: SUBTERRANEAN TRADITION OF YOUTH IN SPAIN (1960–2015)

CARLES FEIXA & PAULA GUERRA

This text is based on an article published in Feixa and Porzio (2005). It is an attempt to update this article, including the evolution from 2005 to date.

Abstract

This text is an attempt to review academic work on youth cultures carried out in Spain since the transition to democracy (although some earlier work related to the subject, stemming from the late Franco period, is also discussed). Approximately two hundred contributions were analysed (books, papers, theses, unpublished reports, and journal texts) and grouped into different academic areas such as criminology, sociology, psychology, communication, or anthropology, and theoretical trends ranging from 'edifying' ecclesiastic post-war literature to the Birmingham school and post-subcultural studies. The works are classified into five major periods marked by different youth styles which act as distorting mirrors of social and cultural changes that are taking place: the late Franco times (*golfos* and *jipis*), the transition to democracy (*punkis* and *progres*), the post-transition (*pijos* and *makineros*), the 1990s (*okupas* and *pelaos*), the beginning of the twenty-first century (*fiesteros* and *alternativos*), the *Latin kings* and *ñetas* (2005–10) and finally, in the present, the *ninis* and *indignados*.[54] The social context, the academic framework, and the main research lines for these periods are analysed, and we also touch upon what we consider as representative of the emerging ideological, theoretical, and methodological tendencies.

Keywords: youth cultures, urban tribes, punks, youth (sub)cultures, Spain

Carles Feixa is Professor of Social Anthropology at the University of Lleida (Catalonia, Spain). He has investigated youth cultures and has conducted fieldwork in Spain and Latin America. He is the author of several books like *De jovenes, bandas y tribus* (1998), *Jovens na America Latina* (2004), and *Global Youth?* (2006). He has been an advisor for youth policies of the United Nations and Vice President of the International Sociological Association Research Committee 'Sociology of Youth.' E-mail: feixa@geosoc.udl.cat

Paula Guerra is Assistant Professor of Sociology at the University of Porto (FLUP), a Researcher in the Institute of Sociology of the same university (IS-UP), and an Invited Researcher at the Centre for Geography Studies and Territory Planning (CEGOT). She is also Adjunct Professor at Griffith Centre for Social and Cultural Research, Australia (GCSCR). The founder and coordinator of the KISMIF Project/Conference, she coordinates/participates in several other research projects in the field of youth cultures and sociology of art and culture, having published numerous works on those themes in the last few years. E-mail: pguerra@letras.up.pt

---

54 In this paper we use some Spanish terms that correspond to different local and global youth lifestyles. See the Glossary.

GOLFOS, PUNKIS, ALTERNATIVOS, INDIGNADOS: SUBTERRANEAN TRADITION OF YOUTH IN SPAIN (1960–2015)

Introduction

In his article 'Subterranean Traditions of Youth,' David Matza (1973) proposed a model for exploring the evolution of youth lifestyles in the twentieth century. It takes into consideration several rebellious 'youth traditions' at the crossroad of class and lifestyle, such as the 'delinquent' proletarian tradition, the 'radical' student tradition, and the 'bohemian' middle class tradition. The Birmingham School updated this model in order to analyse the emergence of British subcultures in the 1960s and 1970s (Hall and Jefferson 1983). The emergence of punk was a kind of hybrid synthesis of the history of the 'subterranean traditions of youth' in post-war Britain, mixing middle-class countercultural and subcultural working-class traditions (Hebdige 1981). From this point of view, the globalization of punk in the second half of the 1970s and the 1980s could be interpreted as a third wave in the process of the hybridization of these traditions, mixing countercultures and subcultures, middle and working class, Anglo-Saxon and other local and cross-national traditions. This is the case of Spain in the Francoist and post-Franco eras.

In 1975, when General Franco died, the presence of youth subcultures was something 'unnatural' in the Spanish political scenario. Indeed, the same was happening in Portugal and Italy. This fact allows us to verify a very interesting 'analytical unit' in the southern Europe countries in contrast to the Anglo-Saxon reality (Guerra 2010). The outcome of the Spanish Civil War (1936–9), with the victory of the fascists over the legal republican government, led to an attempt to impose the logic of monolithic Youth Fronts inspired by the German *Hitler-Jugend* and Italian *Barilla*, as adapted by the so-called National Catholicism. For decades, the *Frente de Juventudes* (Youth Front) and *Sección Femenina* (Female Section) [along with *Acción Católica* (Catholic Action)] were the sole and compulsory forms of youth citizen participation. Only after 1960, with economic development and the opening of Spain, could youth lifestyles gain visibility. The tourist boom and new media (both commercial and countercultural) introduced new youth movements (mostly hippies and rockers), albeit with some particularities. They arrived some years after their European counterparts and settled only in metropolitan areas (like Barcelona or Madrid) and some enclaves (like Ibiza). The normalization of the Spanish youth scene came about through the process of transition into democracy (1975–81). All the youth styles that had been created in Europe and America during the post-war period mixed and burst upon the public scene at the same time and were christened by the media with a very popular local term – *tribus urbanas* [urban tribes] (something similar happened in Russia in 1989 during the *perestroika*, with the so-called *neformalniye grupirovnik* – [informal groups]). Nevertheless, only after the integration into the European Union (1986) were Spanish 'urban tribes' definitively included in the global youth scene. The way in which these urban tribes developed across the country was, however, greatly influenced by the multicultural and multilingual diversity of the Spanish state (for example, the more dynamic territories for subcultures, besides Madrid, were those of Catalonia, the Basque Country, and Galicia).

This text is an attempt to review academic work on youth cultures carried out in Spain since the transition to democracy (although some earlier work related to the subject stemming from the late Franco period is also discussed). The nearly two-hundred contributions analysed (books, papers, theses, unpublished reports, and journal texts) were grouped into different academic areas such as criminology, sociology, psychology, or anthropology, and theoretical trends ranging from edifying post-war literature to the Birmingham school. The works are classified in five periods marked by different youth styles that act as distorting mirrors of social and cultural changes: the late Franco period (1960–76), the transition to democracy (1977–85), the post-transition (1986–94), the late 1990s (1995–9), the new century (2000–4), pre-crisis (2005–9) and post-crisis (2010–14). The social context, the academic framework, and the main lines of research for these periods are analysed, and we also touch upon what we consider as representative of the emerging ideological, theoretical, and methodological tendencies.[55]

The Time of Gangs: *Golfos* and *Jipis* (1960–76)

> *Find yourself a girl, a girl ye-yé*
> *Who has much rhythm*
> *And could sing in English*
> *Tousled hair*
> *And coloured stockings*
> *A girl ye-ye, A girl ye-ye*
> *Who could understand you as I do.*
>
> (Concha Velasco, 'Una chica ye-yé,' 1966)[56]

Why do you see more and more young men with long hair? This is something we have all wondered about sometime, but ... do we ever find an answer? No, we don't, because we can't understand that some men don't appreciate one of the qualities that we most value in them: a manly aspect. This is why it astonishes us also that they'd rather exhibit a different sweater every moment of the day. And to push their bad taste even further, they'd even hang a little chain on their arm. It wouldn't be surprising to see them one day full of jewellery like

---

55 This study is part of a larger project commissioned by the Spanish Youth Institute (Injuve) under the title *Youth Cultures in Spain. Urban Tribes* (Feixa, Porzio, and Bordonada 2004). We have focused on two hundred books, anthologies, articles, papers from specialized magazines, and academic works (PhD theses), although unpublished papers and journal reports have also been used.

56 'Búscate una chica, una chica ye-yé/ Que tenga mucho ritmo/ Y que cante en inglés/ El pelo alborotado/ Y las medias de color/ Una chica ye-yé, Una chica ye-yé/ Que te comprenda como yo' ('Una chica ye-yé,' Concha Velasco, 1966).

an Indian chief. What will so many years of civilisation serve if there's still someone into stupid showing off? (Ros 1964)

Los Golfos, one of the first films by Carlos Saura (1959), shows the adventures of a youth gang in a Spanish suburb in the middle of the post-war period on the threshold of modernization under the auspices of the 'plans for development' which were being drawn up that year. The film is the story of four young people in a Madrid suburb progressively inclined towards a more engaged offensiveness. Inspired by Luis Buñuel's *Los Olvidados* [*The Forgotten*], Saura shows with a reportage-like style (converging with *cinema-verité*) the frustrations of youth at the beginnings of this development. *La lenta agonía de los peces* [*The Slow Agony of the Fish*] (1974) portrays the doubts of a young Catalan man who falls in love with a Swedish girl in the Costa Brava, and discovers the countercultural movements across the Pyrenees. Each of these films shows opposed youth cultures (the proletarian *golfos* and upper class *jipis*) that become symbols and emblems of the process of accelerated cultural modernization taking place in the country.

Youth cultures in Spain appeared in the middle of Franco's regime at a stage which some people called *dictablanda* [soft dictatorship] (as opposed to *dictadura*, the hardest times and also the Spanish for 'dictatorship'), a period of about two decades from the time of the development plans (1959) to the first democratic elections (1977). From the institutional point of view, the *Frente de Juventudes* became *Organización Juvenil Española*, changing authoritarian schemes into more democratic models of service to youth (Sáez Marín 1988). Academically, the social sciences were still suspected of sympathizing with democratic movements, although within the *Instituto de la Juventud* (Youth Institute) a modernizing tendency cropped up that eventually used the techniques of empirical sociology to promote the first youth reviews (Martín Criado 1998; De Miguel 1979; 2000). However, youth culture hardly appeared in these reviews, which offered only a very general understanding of the attitudes and values.

In order to find references to the youth styles long existing in Europe and the United States during this time we have to focus on other types of work. Most are translations or adapted texts from international publications, although they are often commented upon or even censored, as happened with the Spanish version of a work about the hippies (Cartier and Naslednikov 1974). However, other studies from Spanish researchers start to appear. First are essays linked to edifying literature or criminology, usually by ecclesiastic authors interested in the negative influence of the new trends on young people's morality, seen through the double lens of vandalism and political and cultural dissidence (Trías Mercant 1967; López Riocerezo 1970). Second are works by writers or journalists, urban chronicles of the birth of a consumption culture on the outskirts of cities (Gomis 1965; Huertas 1969), or travel books about journeys to Europe and North America, describing the author's impressions of countercultures in a half-documentary, half-testimonial way (Mellizo 1972; Carandell 1972). Third are more-academic essays, especially by authors writing about the university protests which took place in retaliation to Franco`s regime (Tierno Galván 1972; López Aranguren 1973), and some studies by young researchers carried out as a first step in theories based on field data (Gil Muñoz 1973; Salcedo 1974).

In 1970, Father José María López Riocerezo, author of many 'edifying' works for young people, published a study entitled *The Worldwide Problem of Vandalism and its Possible Solutions*, in which he shows interest in a series of demonstrations of nonconformist, offensive youth trends: *gamberros*, *blousons noirs*, teddy boys, *vitelloni*, *raggare*, rockers, beatniks, *macarras*, hippies, *halbstakers*, *provos*, *ye-yes*, *rocanroleros*, and *pavitos*, for instance, were variants of the same 'species': the 'rebel without a cause.' Although he considers Spain safe from this dangerous trend ('maybe because of historical constants, the weight of centuries and family tradition'), he considers whether these trends have something to do with the transformation of a rural or agricultural society into an industrial or post-industrial society: 'When this step is taken quickly, there is a cultural and sociological crisis, like an obstruction of the channels of the individual's integration into the regulations of society' (López Riocerezo 1970, 244). For the author, a *gamberro* is nothing but the Spanish variant of the foreign model being imported. He discusses the etymology, as the word is not included in the dictionary of the Royal Academy of the Spanish Language. He searches in Basque-French (*gamburu*: joke, somersault, open air diversion) and Greek (*gambrias*: with the same meaning as the Spanish word). This second meaning not only justifies the declaration of dangerousness 'against those who cynically and insolently attack the rules of social coexistence by attacking people or damaging things, without a cause or a reason' in the *Ley de Vagos y Maleantes* (Tramps and Malefactors Act), but also 'explains its origin or objective.'

Discussing the Spanish case, López Riocerezo insists that the phenomenon is still not overly apparent. According to 1963 statistics, there were only 161 offenders per 100,000 inhabitants in Spain (the figures overseas were 852 in England, 455 in the USA, 378 in Germany, and 216 in Italy).

> The rate in Spain ... is still below that of other countries with the same degree of civilisation, maybe due to the historical constants, the weight of centuries and the family tradition that, as we know, constitute a baggage difficult to get rid of ... (also) due to the Spanish woman, who still has a very deep sense of maternity and accomplishes her duties with real diligence, even with sacrifice. (López Riocerezo 1970, 9, 14)

The Time of Tribes: *Punkis* and *Progres* (1977–85)

> *And I fell*
> *In love with young fashion*
> *With the prices and the sales that I saw*
> *I fell in love with you*
> *And I fell*
> *In love with young fashion*
> *With the boys, with the girls, with the mannequins*
> *I fell in love with you.*
> ('In Love with Young Fashion,' Radio Futura, 1980)[57]

---

57 'Y yo caí/ enamorado de la moda juvenil/ de los precios y rebajas que yo vi/ enamorado de ti/ Sí, yo caí/ enamorado de la moda juvenil/ de los chicos, de las chicas, de los maniquís/ enamorado de ti' ('Enamorado de la moda juvenile,'

They grew up surrounded by the big city's cement. They are the shipwrecked of the asphalt. Loud sounding names – punks, heavies, mods, rockers – keep themselves inside the warm security of their tribe. Sometimes, the battle commences to dye with blood a world full of music … Dominions, areas of transit, territories under dispute, the other map of an unknown but everyday city, where other laws other values, take over. ('Tribus '85: morir en la chupa puesta' 1984, 31)

Pepi, Luci, Bom y otras chicas del montón, the first of Almodovar's films (1980), shows the beginning of the *movida madrileña*, the more or less spontaneous youth movement that reflected in an anarchic way the effects of Spain's transition to democracy: the explosion of urban tribes. Three women of different ages and social circumstances (Alaska, well inside the punk wave, the postmodern Cecilia Roth who lives life madly, and Carmen Maura, the housewife in her forties married to a policeman) share nights in cool and exciting Madrid that is becoming a hub of modernity thanks to the mayor, Tierno Galvan. Almodovar shows the subculture of *la movida* in a more elaborate (but just as acerbic) way in his later work, *Laberinto de pasiones* (1982).

By the end of the 1970s, along with the transition to democracy, a new social subject appeared in the Spanish scenario labelled very significantly *tribus urbanas* [urban tribes]. The communication media would soon devote great attention to the phenomenon, inciting campaigns of moral panic (like when a young mod was killed by a rocker) in tandem with commercial appropriation (like the reports advertising where to buy each tribe's outfit). A teddy boy from Zaragoza wrote a letter to the director to remind him that 'the only tribes in the world are the blacks of Africa.' But a disabled punk (el Cojo) became famous thanks to television for breaking a street light with his crutch during the huge student demonstrations in 1987, which prompted this comment from a columnist: 'Sociologists should give an explanation for this African and underdeveloped phenomenon' (in Feixa 1988, 5). The institutional context of the time was characterized by the democratization of the Youth Institute and the transfer of competence from youths to local councils and autonomous communities. In nearly all fields, one of the first initiatives of the organizations was to promote youth studies, nearly always through opinion reviews, brilliantly analysed and criticized by Cardús and Estruch (1984) for the Catalan case. Paradoxically, during the peak of *la movida*, qualitative and testimonial studies that could explain the emerging youth cultures disappeared. Only at the end of the period do some studies show a shift in interest towards young people's cultural consumption.

We can group the studies issued during this period into three fields: first, those focusing on youth countercultures in the 1970s, be it for theoretical balance (De Miguel 1979; Moya 1983) or historical reconstruction (Racionero 1977; Vázquez Montalbán 1985). In this sense, Romaní's (1982) contributions about hashish subcultures and Funes' (1984; 1985) work on youth delinquency and the emerging cultures may be included. Second, studies based on quantitative methodologies start to highlight young

Radio Futura, 1980).

people's cultural consumption (Gil Calvo 1985; Gil Calvo and Menéndez 1985). The third field encompasses some proto-ethnographic studies about the phenomenon of night *movidas* and the emergence of urban tribes, like a pioneering article about the disco Rock-Ola, one of the wellsprings of Madrid's *movida* (Muñoz 1985), and a bachelor's thesis about youth subcultures in an average size city, which introduced the postulates of the Birmingham School (Feixa 1985).

In 1982 Isaías Díez del Río, director of a college in Madrid, published an article in the *Revista de Estudios de Juventud* under the title 'La contracultura' (The Counterculture), although it is really about a new type of youth movement, appearing in Spain immediately after the transition to democracy, which was commonly called *pasotismo*. In the 1980s, the most widespread vision of youth – nearly always analysed as a homogeneous social sector, using a quantitative methodology, or described in opinion essays – pictured a generalized lack of interest in social problems and the loss of any form of revolutionary spirit which, according to analysts, had marked the preceding generations. The central thesis of the study is that *pasotismo* is one of the many youth movements appearing in the West as a product of, and in response to, the breakdown of a society in crisis. Díez del Río takes the loss of interest in political militancy and social battles on the part of the majority of the youth culture at the time as a contradiction embedded in society itself. *Pasotismo* is a lifestyle that symbolically protests through new means of fighting against the values that institutions and the dominant culture are trying to impose.

In 1985, sociologists Enrique Gil Calvo and Elena Menéndez published *Ocio y prácticas culturales de los jóvenes* [*Youth Leisure and Cultural Practices of Young People*], which is part of the Youth Report in Spain, promoted by the Youth Institute on the occasion of the International Year of Youth. The authors suggested the following definition of youth culture:

> The problem is not that young people are more closely related among themselves than with others: the problem is that their relationships are closed to the outside, sealed off, totally enclosed; and such a closure traps each young person into the group, not letting them out, establishing unsurpassable borders that separate the comfortable inside of the centripetal group from the outside chaos and darkness, where the young person is horrified to venture into. This could be called youth subculture or something like it: what's important however, is not the name, but the facts … (Gil Calvo and Menéndez 1985, 238)

Something similar would appear in Madrid in 1978 and would last until 1983: *la Movida*. By analysing the composition of the music bands that identified with *la Movida*, Gil Calvo and Menéndez tried to demonstrate their definition of a youth movement. For this purpose, they used an organization chart showing the relationship between the musicians of different groups, which was supposed to demonstrate that youth cultures were closed, impermeable groups.

Figure 6.1: Punks during a concert, Barcelona, 2000s. Source: Photo by Mireia Bordonada (Feixa, 2004).

> Such a movement had an exclusively musical public expression (politics, 'culture' or ideology were absent): it was started, composed, promoted, developed and made to succeed by a bunch of young musicians and FM DJs … only 30 young people, under the age of 25, composed the twenty different groups – simply the same people, friends among themselves … flowed from one group to another … The world of the Madrid 'modern' 'new wave' in 1978–1983 were 30 people: totally closed to the outside, even declared enemies of other 'musical/youth groups' as closed as themselves (and these other enemy worlds of the modern world, were also perfectly visible due to their own closedness: rockers, heavies, punks, hippies). (Gil Calvo and Menéndez 1985, 238)

After a considerable amount of data, figures, and graphics, the whole of Calvo and Menendez's conclusions can be summarized as follows: young people in the 1980s devoted more time and money to leisure activities. Young people's wealth and social class ensured that their leisure behaviour was not homogeneous. Social structure determines an unequal leisure culture; in the end, economy determines differences in young people's cultural behaviour. The most interesting part of Calvo and Menendez's work shows the importance of the young people's purchasing power for their leisure opportunities. From a methodological point of view, the subject of cultural consumption can be envisaged by macro approximations from the class perspective. The image the authors project of youth cultures is largely from the outside, although the search for objectivity through figures and percentages coexists with ironic comments about certain youth cultural experiences:

It is not that young people close off their groups of equals like musical groups do: musical groups close up because they imitate real groups of real young people; the social structure of music groups is only a reproduction of the social structure of young people, and young people socially structure themselves in closed groups. (Gil Calvo and Menéndez 1985, 240)

The Time of Styles: *Pijos* and *Makineros* (1986–94)

We will meet in Ibiza, Mallorca, San Luís and Mahon
We will dance in Valencia, Alicante, Gandía and Benidorm
From La Escala to Playa San Juan
In Cadaques, Sitges, Playa Libertad
We will be the chosen in the temple of the Sea God.

('Mediterraneum,' Los Rebeldes, 1990)[58]

I like Madrid … everyone's got their own business. Every *movida* has its own area. If you want the craic of *pijos*, you've got it, if you like a particular sort of music, or gays, or whatever, you've got the place and the people for everything. (Carlos, *Historias del Kronen*, J. A. Mañas 1994, 95)

Historias del Kronen (Kronen Stories), the film by Montxo Armendáriz (1994) based on the novel by José Ángel Mañas (1994), shows the lives of a group of upper class young people (*pijos*), their night-time adventures, their fresh styles, and their uneasy feelings about life. Other films of the same time picture the birth of other forms of youth sociability: *El angel de la guarda* (1995) presents the life of a young mod from a family that sympathizes with Franco's regime, and who is in conflict with rockers. It is the time of the socialist government in Spain, when the generations that had led the fight against Franco are settling into power and view with suspicion the apathetical and apolitical young people, and see their aesthetics and ways of living as purely commercial and consumerist. From the point of view of youth cultures, this period is characterized by three different processes: the segmentation of youth cultures into many styles that appear like a shopping catalogue; the revival of the *pijo* (a way to openly recover a higher-class identity); and spearheading the nightlife with the generation of a new style, the *makinero* (between the proliferation of new clubs, the explosion of electronic commercial music and the results of synthetic drugs). The International Year of Youth (1985) was a milestone in studies about youth in Spain. The hegemony of opinion surveys was in crisis for internal (a methodological criticism of the gaps and excesses) as well as external reasons (changes in youth policies brought about by integral planning). A certain myth about youth of the past arose: old *progres* [progressives], now in places of power, idealize their rebel past and criticize the young people's lack of argument and for living under the

58 Nos veremos en Ibiza, en Mallorca, San Luis y Mahón/ Bailaremos en Valencia, en Alicante, en Gandía y Benidorm/ Desde la Escala hasta Playa San Juan/ En Cadaqués, en Sitges, Playa Libertad/ seremos los elegidos en el templo del Dios del Mar/ ('Mediterráneo,' Los Rebeldes, 1990).

rules of consumerism – the hegemony of the *pijo*. A sociologist even suggested that the term 'urban tribes' be replaced by 'shopping tribes':

> Those rebel tribes, inorganically organized, who invented cries like songs, who knew how to make a great to-do to create social uniforms. They invented a way of drinking, a way of eating, a way of sitting down, a way of walking, a way of talking or cheering, and dressing. They don't have sense any more … Hippies were buried long ago … *Pijos*, on the contrary, are unconditional kings of big shopping areas, and they are certainly the hegemonic tribe in the 1990s. (Ruiz 1994, 192–6)

Among the studies about youth cultures published during this period, three groups can be discerned: first, different essays based on theoretical formulations and historical contributions (Ucelay da Cal 1987; Feixa 1993); second, a series of local and police examinations of football hooligans and skinheads (Barruti 1990; Dirección General de Policía 1993). The third group contains some ethnographic studies that question the categories in use and suggest new methodologies based mostly on life stories. Some of the theses here are outstanding (Gamella 1989; Feixa 1989; Adán 1992), or international studies about punks and rastas (Sansone 1988). Outside of the academic arena, some journalist texts that contributed to the popular use of the term 'urban tribes' were published. For instance, the most popular Spanish newspaper (*El País*) devoted several reports to the subject, like an illustrated feature called 'Y tú, ¿de qué vas?' (And you, what's the matter?) (*El Pais Semanal* 5/10, 1994).

In 1989 the linguist Francisco Rodríguez edited *Comunicación y lenguaje juvenil* [*Communication and Juvenile Language*], an anthology that gathered together some of the main contributions to youth cultures by Spanish researchers. The aim of all the essays, each one from a different perspective and academic area, was to describe and analyse the pattern of young people's linguistic behaviour as a means of understanding their cultural expressions in general. The authors include anthropologists, sociologists, linguists, and experts in communications. The theoretical, methodological, and thematic perspectives are diverse, although the thread running through all the studies is the analysis of language as a system of symbols in relationship to significant and symbolic elements of youth cultures (music, clothes, cultural practice, etc.) and other channels of communication such as fanzines, comics, and graffiti. Among all the articles, we want to highlight the analysis of fashion as a communication system amongst youth in the 1980s (Rivière 1989). The article's author is a journalist who analyses the transformation process that fashion followed from the beginning of the twentieth century and its appropriation by young people who would radically transform its significance. First, they broke the old pattern of fashion as a tool for identifying social class; second, they de-sexualized it, and boys' and girls' styles were intertwined. Another interesting element was the rejuvenating power that fashion had – and still has:

> In the '80s everyone wants to look (be) young to the point that social marginalisation occurs in all cases, to the those who, for their age, cannot look young any more. The

outfit is the main vehicle for eternal youth. Although a juvenile outfit does not hide certain effects of old age, the young people's trends (for our mass and communication culture's adults) are imperatively categorical in their most generic features, both formal and mental: the compulsory physical rejuvenation brings along a certain cultural infantility. (Rivière 1989, 73)

The Time of Scenes: *Okupas* and *Pelaos* (1995–9)

> *You can see, my age is so difficult to bear*
> *Mixture of passion and naïveté, difficult to control …*
> *I am just an adolescent, but will get into your death*
> *Stepping on it, stepping on it.*
> ('Stepping on it,' Alejandro Sanz, 1994)[59]

The *okupa* movement is worrying Spain's security forces, who are convinced that the disturbances in Barcelona on the 12th are closely linked with the Basque street fight or 'kale borroka' … Police reports indicate that these groups make decisions in an assembly that very few attend, and then the orders are passed to the rest of *okupas* orally … In Catalonia, *okupas* and radical nationalists add up to about 2200 young people, while skins and the extreme right number about 200. ('Los miedos que se desataron en Sants', 1999)

Taxi, one of the latest films by Carlos Saura (1999), depicts the life of a group of young *pelaos* who are manipulated by an extreme right-wing taxi driver. They attack immigrants and homosexuals, and they get as far as murder. *Pelaos* are the Spanish version of *naziskins*, young neo-Nazis getting into the skinhead movement and carrying out some dramatic actions (somehow linked to the football hooligans) according to the Spanish press in the late 1980s (although the *pelaos* didn't really become socially well known until the mid-1990s because of the greater social concern about the arrival of new waves of immigrants). They coincided with the explosion of *okupas*, the Spanish version of the squatters who appeared after 1968, linked to the occupation of empty houses and experimenting with alternative and countercultural ways of living together. October 12th, the festival of El Pilar, is the day to celebrate hispanity (Adell and Martínez 2004). During the last decade, extreme right-wing groups have used this date to make their notorious presence felt in public. The Països Catalans square is the meeting place of extremists, although those who are nostalgic about Franco have been giving way to the new waves of skinheads. Every year there's *movida* (trouble), but in 1999 it involved not just the skins. In the nearby neighbourhood of Sants, some anti-fascist groups organized an alternative demonstration as a protest against recent attacks by skinheads. The press mentioned 'about 600 extreme young people … communists, *okupas* and radical independents' (*El País* 14 October 1999).

The presence of about 250 riot police (who officially appeared to prevent any contact between demonstrators from both sides) could not stop an 'explosion of rage' from some

---

59 Ya ves, mi edad es tan difícil de llevar/ mezcla de pasión e ingenuidad, difícil controlar … / Yo soy sólo un adolescente, pero entraré en tu muerte/ pisando fuerte, pisando fuerte ('Pisando fuerte', Alejandro Sanz, 1994).

alternative young people, expressed in the form of damage to public facilities, bank offices, real estate, and recruiting agencies. During the following days, the media reproduced the police reports about serious material damage, vandalism, organized violent groups, and urban guerrilla tactics. All reports underlined the participation of the *okupa* movement, who had called for mobilization and, according to the police, had led the battle from their two emblematic 'social centres.' These facts described the peak of the confrontations between two of the present-day youth subcultures on the urban scene: squatters (known in Spain as *okupas*) and skinheads (known in Spain as *pelaos*).

From the societal perspective, certain structural problems, such as the new immigration, limited access to housing for youth, and the nocturnization of youth leisure, opened spaces for renewed youth culture activities. From the media point of view this phenomenon was shown by newspapers and campaigns reflecting moral panic nearly always following the same pattern: news event – media amplification – creation of a social problem – feedback in youth cultures – fresh news event (Cohen 1980). As regards social control, the different police bodies (state, autonomous, and local) organized specific brigades, and sometimes issued reports that reach the press. In universities, 'urban tribes' as a subject attained a certain status and started to be the subject of numerous publications (a decade after the advent of the actual phenomenon). Publications varied a great deal in quality and were based on studies done previously, often with an outdated theoretical methodological approach. In spite of this, they make up a corpus of publications, theories, and empirical data that contribute to consolidating an 'object.' Thematically, these studies have three prominent features: a non-critical concept of 'urban tribes' and a stereotyped catalogue of different styles, a denial of political conflict (presented as a set of aesthetic conflicts), and a removal of differences (i.e. 'all skins are the same').

Among the many publications of this period, three tendencies are discernible: general essays, applied reports, and ethnographic studies. Some publications try to show a general view of the different urban tribes, although they are nearly always based on very limited research in terms of time and space. By chronological order of edition, we can mention the contents of the review *Cuaderno de realidades sociales*, devoted to urban tribes, which includes monographs, general papers and others based on local studies (VV.AA. 1995; Adán 1995; Delgado 1995; Donald 1995); a journalist essay based on an amusing musical description (Colubi 1997); an original sociological monograph about youth taste according to Bourdieu's theories (Martínez and Pérez 1997); a pseudo-ethnographic book about several urban tribes (Aguirre and Rodríguez 1998); and a book based on the life stories of two punks from Catalonia and Mexico, which argued in favour of replacing the model of urban tribes with that of youth cultures (Feixa 1998).

Public institutions and forces of order have commissioned applied studies concerning three problems caused by urban tribes and perceived as more serious: urban violence (*pelaos*), urban moods (*okupas*), and synthetic drugs (*makineros*). Regarding violence, there have been a few unpublished reports (Ministerio de Justicia e Interior 1995; Injuve 1998) and some attempts to understand it (Martín Serrano 1996). Most of these publications arise from conferences about ideology, violence, and youth organized by the Youth Institute (Dirección General de la Guardia Civil 1998a; 1998b). Regarding *okupas*, some studies reproduce an institutional or in-group point of view (Heruzzo and Grenzner 1998; Navarrete 1999). Regarding dance cultures, Gamella and Alvarez (1999) published a book about synthetic drugs, commissioned by the Plan Nacional sobre Drogas. The first qualitative ethnographic research results, the fruit of serious fieldwork and direct knowledge of the international literature about the question, began to be published. We must also mention some studies about extremists and skinheads (Adán 1995; 2004; Casals 1995), punks (Feixa 1998; Porrah 1999), *makineros* (Feixa and Pallarés, 1998), *okupas* (Costa 1998; VV.AA. 1999/2000), and heavies (Martínez 1999; 2004). Other research does not focus on groups but an aspect of youth culture, like language (Pujolar 1997) or lifestyle (Ruiz 1998).

In 1996, Pere-Oriol Costa, José Manuel Pérez, and Fabio Tropea published *Tribus Urbanas [Urban Tribes]*, a book that would become a bestseller. The text is defined by its authors as an essay. In other words, it is the fruit of research, the results of which are not presented as such, but used to construct a narrative text addressed to a broader public, with the aim of spreading knowledge of the phenomenon called 'urban tribes.' The three authors come from the Faculty of Communication Sciences of the Universitat Autònoma of Barcelona, where the theoretical perspective of this research stems from. Although the authors' main aim is said to be disseminating knowledge about the phenomenon of urban tribes, when they list the theoretical approaches from different disciplines used to examine youth cultures, the subject of the work was defined as urban violence and tribes as a phenomenon. This places them within the tendency to see youth styles from a stigmatizing perspective; for example, they quote relevant key concepts in neuro-psychiatry (syndromes, paranoids, and schizoids) and criminology (deviant behaviours).

The Time of Cybercultures: *Fiesteros* and *Alternativos* (2000–4)

> They call me the disappeared
> The one who arrives and is gone
> I fly back and forth
> Fast in a lost track
> They never find me when I'm sought
> When they find me I'm not any more
> The one in front
> 'cause I left quickly far beyond.
>
> ('Underground,' Manu Chao, 2001)[60]

Mixture and union, this could be seen in el Sot on Saturday night, and the most flabbergasting proof of it was from ... *los perros*. If bogus street tramps with scarfs

---

60 Me llaman el desaparecido/ Que cuando llega ya se ha ido/ volando vengo volando voy/ deprisa deprisa a rumbo perdido/ Cundo me buscan nunca estoy/ cuando me encuentran ya no soy/ el que está enfrente porque ya/ me fui corriendo más allá. (Manu Chao 'Clandestino', 2001, Original).

on their necks and fleas on their back monopolise the canine contribution to the argument, the antiglobalisation verbena of el Sot you could also see small pet dogs, little woolly ones without any fleas on, with shiny belts. Whoever wanted to limit argument to neohippies or neopunks had only to look on the floor to state such a canine variety, although it suggested just as big a human variety that would have ended with any a priorities … ('La fiesta de la contestación' 2002)

With the new millennium, Spanish youth cultures' characteristics may be generalized by three major tendencies. First, a certain activism in the public sphere is revived and reflected in the anti-globalization movement and its cultural effects (from the singer Manu Chao's hybrid music to a neo-hippie trend). Second, the *dance* culture becomes symbolized in the different expressions of the *fiestero* movement (most intellectualized around festivals like Sonar, digital publications, and the techno style, most ludic around new clubs and fashion styles, and most clandestine around rave parties). Third, the Internet opens a space to the generation of room cultures and virtual communities that express different styles (like cyberpunks and hackers), although the use of virtual space affects all groups. The impact of the various cultures' distinctive elements is projected onto different age groups. But what is most representative of this period is the fading of boundaries between the different subcultures, and the processes of social and symbolic syncretism ('mixture and union,' to use the journalistic term).

The number of studies published in Spain about youth cultures have increased over the last three years at a greater rate than over the preceding three decades. Different factors have contributed to this. First, the processes of cultural and media globalization (including the broadening of young Spanish people's access to Internet) have consolidated the internationalization of youth culture: the Spanish scene, together with the scenes of other peak places, is very heterogeneous, with a diversity of juvenile expressions (nearly all the tendencies on the planet are present in a contemporary big city). Second, a new generation of young researchers, often trained abroad, are publishing studies about youth cultures they have lived in themselves. Their research is comparable to the latest work on the international level (for instance, cultural studies are consolidated). Third, research on youths is being institutionalized thanks to the creation of research observatories and centres of third cycle university programs, and thanks to the consolidation of editorial collections about this subject. *De Juventud*, the academic journal of the Instituto de la Juventud [Youth Institute], has been reissued and some articles have appeared in international magazines, and some specialized collections like *Estudios sobre Juventud* have been published (with several books including the re-editing of classic books and anthologies of studies by Spanish authors: Rodríguez 2002; 2003; Feixa, Costa, and Pallarés 2002; Feixa, Costa, and Saura 2002). The translation and re-editing of some representative international works about youth cultures (Willis, 1990; Monod, 1968/2002) are important here, although the Spanish versions of a number of classic books still remain to be realized, e.g. *The Gang* (Thrasher 1926), *Resistance Through Rituals* (Hall & Jefferson 1983) and *Subculture* (Hebdige 1981).[61]

---

61 When this paper was in press, Hebdige (1979) *Subculture: The Meaning of Style* was translated into Spanish

We can isolate five significant tendencies in the studies published during this period. First, monographs about the two main youth groups of the previous decade (skinheads and *okupas*), in the form of journalist chronicles (Salas 2002; Batista 2002), militant denunciations (Ibarra 2003), applied sociological analysis (González et al. 2003) and ethnographic comparisons (Feixa, Costa, and Pallarés 2002). Second, ethnographic studies about dance cultures (and their variants – *makinera*, techno, raver and fashion) in the form of surveys on the routes of ecstasy (Gamella and Alvarez, 1999); theoretical reflections about the process of globalization (Lasén and Martínez 2001); anthologies about trends in electronic music (Blánquez and Morera 2002); or journalist features about the cathedral of the techno world – the disco Florida 135 (Gistain 2001). Third, studies about the brand new social movements that characterize the emergence of alternative styles and *antiglobos* (Romaní and Feixa 2002). Fourth, studies on specific groups focusing on some relevant thematic aspects like music (Viñas 2001; Feixa, Saura, and De Castro 2003), gender (Martínez 2002), communication (Tinat 2002; 2004), tattoos (Porzio 2002; 2004), media (Delgado 2002), graffiti (Reyes and Vigara 2002) or the history of youth cultures in the past (Cerdà and Rodríguez 1999). Fifth, in-depth studies on the impact of youth cultures on young people's daily lives or, in Willis' terms, their 'common culture' (Lasén 2000; Rodríguez, Megías, and Sánchez 2002).

In 2001, Núria Romo published *Mujeres y drogas de síntesis. Género y riesgo en la cultura del baile* [*Women and Synthetic Drugs: Gender and Culture in the Dance Culture*]. Romo is an anthropologist and this publication is part of a wide analytical and descriptive effort. The research is located in the second half of the 1990s, when the dance culture related to drugs and car accidents became an omnipresent paradigm in institutional and media speech. Her primary aim was to analyse the drug consumption in the *fiesta* and electronic music contexts for both men and women, and later focussed on the interpretation of women's specificity from a comparative perspective: in other words, whether there were any differences in drug consumption between boys and girls. Examining the state-of-the art reveals that there is no research about female roles within youth cultures in relation to electronic music and synthetic drugs. This research was done to contrast a different hypothesis under the form of an open question to which the author tries to find an answer: what is the role of women within the youth culture associated to the consumption of ecstasy and other synthetic drugs; are there any gender differences in their perception or the limiting strategies; what are the 'style' features of the female consumers; what are the differences in the strategies of obtaining substances; and what is the role of women within the illegal synthetic drug market.

Romo's most interesting contribution is her description of intersubjective relationships from inside the group. The author describes elements of cultural consumption (the body, music, focal activities) through the concept of style, emphasizing not only material and immaterial elements in themselves, but in the ways they are used. The gender perspective must be evidenced too. The whole work is based on female specificities in

---

(25 years after its original publication).

relation to synthetic drugs and parties. The author claims that all the literature devoted to female drug consumption describes them as doubly deviant: 'Their experience is usually analysed as a deviation from the rule, an altered version of what would be considered as a "normal woman" or "normal femininity." Most of the specific research about women and use of drugs focuses on heroin or cocaine consumers' (2001, 282). The popularization and vulgarization of the youth movement allow it to get to other sectors than the first *fiesteros*. A series of elements get into youth culture, affecting relationships between the sexes and the role of women in youth culture. The increase of violence or the change into a more sexual environment makes women refrain from participating in these festive elements and establish new strategies of control to minimize risk situations (Romo 2001, 283).

The Time of Latino Gangs: *Latin Kings* and Ñetas (2005–10)

> Young Mill:
> We are family united as one. United by the Flow specialising
> In locating talent and growing upcoming youth
> They found me, groomed me up from grass to grace
> Queen Melody:
> No horizons or borders that separate us
> No differences of belief or messages
> United by the same dream in a song.
> (United by the Flow, 2008)[62]

They came for a better future to escape the ghosts they left behind. (Case for the prosecution during the trial of Ronny Tapias — Efe Agencia 2005).

In Search of Respect, a documentary film by José González Morandi (2012), shows the stories of a group of young migrant boys and girls, members of different Latino gangs in Barcelona but with roots in the United States, Ecuador, Central America, and the Caribbean: Latin Kings and Queens, Ñetas, Mara Salvatrucha, and Black Panthers. The film, produced by Luca Queirolo Palmas and Carles Feixa in the context of the European project YOUGANG, mixed reality and fiction: the story of an imaginary gang conceived by themselves is mixed with the process of producing this film in a workshop, discussing the script and the scenarios. The title of the film, proposed by the protagonists, evokes not only the classical book by Philipe Bourgois about the drug subcultures in New York (1995), but a concept explained by the American leader of ALKQN (Almighty Latin King and Queens Nation), King Tone, in an interview conducted in Stockolm (Queirolo Palmas 2012; Feixa 2009; 2014): for marginalized youth, deprived of a political and material point of view, discriminated in daily life, searching for respect in and through the gang is one of the only ways to became an adult in transnational settings.

---

62 No hay horizontes ni fronteras que nos separen/ No hay diferencias de creencias ni de mensajes/ Unidos por el mismo sueño en una canción (Unidos por el Flow, 2008).

The second half of the first decade of the century was dominated by a revival of the first youth prototype studied in the 1960s: the bands. But in this case, it was not a local actor linked to internal migration processes, but a transnational actor linked to international migrations, particularly from America. We are referring to the so-called 'Latino bands' (although in fact their origin is North America), which we will look at in more detail below. Significantly, the term 'band' becomes a paradigm of a new form of youth socialization, which is applied from now on only to young migrants' origins and limited in most cases to the criminal side, while the term 'urban tribes' identifies itself with native young people only, becoming linked to fashion or disappearing. The academic research is behind the media interest and often reproduces the same stereotypes, which in 2010 were transferred to the penal code in which the figures of 'criminal association' and 'criminal groups' were introduced, with less probative guarantees than 'illicit association.' Besides the books based on police sources (Asociación de Jefes y Mandos de la Policía Local-Comunidad Valenciana 2010; Botello and Moya 2005), we can cite several studies resulting from the orders of the local or regional governments, some closer to the criminal perspective and others more focused on the cultural and sociability dimension (Aparicio & Tornos 2009; Feixa, Porzio, and Recio 2006; Martínez and Cerdá 2009; Scandroglio 2009).[63]

On 2 February 2013, a 16-year-old teenager was killed leaving a park in Puente Vallecas, a suburb in Madrid. According to the subsequent police investigation, the murder was an act of revenge in the ongoing violence between the two major Latino gangs in Spain (Latin Kings and Ñetas). Two days later, another fight in Hospitalet de Llobregat, a suburb in Barcelona, resulted in four adolescents wounded and many arrested. These cases take us back to another assassination from ten years earlier, on 28 October 2003, when the Colombian adolescent Ronny Tapias was killed by a group of young people while leaving school. According to the police investigation at the time, the murder was an act of revenge by gang members (the Ñetas) who allegedly confused Ronny with a member of another gang (the Latin Kings), with whom they had fought a few days before in a disco. After a month, nine young people of Dominican and Ecuadorian nationality were arrested. Three juveniles were tried and convicted (including the perpetrator of the crime). Following this event, and similar incidences, that took place later in Madrid and Barcelona, the Spanish Ministry of Home Affairs and the media alarms resulted in an increasingly stigmatized image of Latin American youth, and aroused a wave of 'moral panic' that has not eased since (Cohen 1980).

The *Webster Dictionary* defines 'flow' as 'a smooth uninterrupted movement.' Another meaning given is 'a continuous transfer of energy.' In hip hop culture the word is used to express movements and blending in a musical and bodily sense and, by extension,

---

63 In this period, it is also published an issue of the journal *Revista de Estudios de Juventud* [Journal of Youth Studies] on 'Youth cultures and languages' with an emphasys on the social communication (Bernete 2007). It is published also a rigorous doctoral thesis on the Madrid's movement (Fouce 2006); a complete dissection of the violent world of football (Viñas 2004; 2005); essays on the educational and consumer dimension of youth culture (Lozano 2007; Montesinos 2007); and journalistic chronicles on the new tribes of cyberspace (Barbolla, Seco, and Moreno 2010).

a social and cultural sense. This is why the young Latin Kings and Ñetas, two immigrant collectives in Barcelona who were considered dangerous 'Latin gangs' until a few years ago, chose this term for their project of conflict resolution through music. The project was presented in January 2009 after two years' hard work in a youth centre in Nou Barris (a working-class Barcelona neighbourhood with a long tradition of hosting immigrants). The presentation took place in the Centre for Contemporary Culture of Barcelona (CCCB), the city's laboratory for cultural creativity. About a hundred Latin Kings, Ñetas, and other youngsters participated in the project, with the aim of producing a hip hop, rap, and reggaeton music CD, a documentary about the experience, a book about their lives and their vision for the program, and a theatre play. In the words of Xaime López (known as Chispón), the promoter of this initiative: 'We've got to keep on creating life, but life from the life, 'cause otherwise it's starting over and over. It's an urban art project. The whole idea is that all young people participate, not just Latins and Ñetas, but there's other ones: gipsies, Nigerians ... Other people in the neighbourhood who fancy singing with them' (VVAA 2008).

The story started in the same place, the CCCB, in November 2005 when our study about young Latin groups was presented under the auspices of Barcelona City Hall (Feixa et al. 2008). The study revealed that although only a minority of Latin American youngsters belonged to gangs, the social imaginary had established a strong identification between Latin youngsters, gangs, and hip hop culture (the rapper look – 'baggy clothing'– started to be mistaken for 'being in a gang'). The study also revealed the capacity of cultural creativity among these transnational young people who were rediscovering 'Latinness' in Europe. The study presentation allowed the Ñetas and Latin Kings to become exposed and to meet each other. This gave a place for what was known as the 'peace process.' As a result of the study, Barcelona City Hall and the Catalan Institute for Human Rights fostered a process of dialogue between the two main groups which gave rise to two new youth associations recognized by the Catalan Government: the Cultural Organisation of Latin Kings and Queens of Catalonia (established in August 2006) and the Ñetas Sociocultural, Sports, and Music Association (established in March 2007). Once legalized, the associations wanted to show that, beyond the violence problems that had stigmatized them before, they were able to generate social and cultural projects for the whole of the city. The most successful one was Unidos por el Flow [United for the Flow]. In the words of King Manaba, one of the participants in the project:

> Now we're together, not as enemies, but as if we'd known each other for ever, y'know? You just don't walk around as a Latin King, and a Ñeta just doesn't walk around as a Ñeta, we're all together with the flow, we're all for what I really like. I joined this project 'cause I'm also creatin' and I also have my own group, so, I like music and I'm into music production. It's the project from the base point, from creating a track to the artists' actually singing and rhyming the lyrics.

And in words of Julio Bravo, a Ñetas representative:

> The important thing for me is that the message gets through. I want the message to get through for the whole world. I want everyone to see that we're together, that it's not all about war and fighting. All immigrants fight for the same purpose. The message is that there isn't any difference between us.

The project was based on the principles of participative research including a group therapy technique called 'refleaction,' which approaches conflict resolution through music (in the favelas in Brazil around intercultural hip hop). The process matured with the interaction of the educators who believed in it and who drove it at first – the young people in the Ñetas and Latin Kings associations, some organizations that gave their material and moral support to it, and other people that cooperated at given times, such as some academics, artists, and political militants. The turning point was a massive concert that took place in June 2006, in which about five hundred Latin Kings and Ñetas participated and ended up dancing together and rapping 'peace, peace,' which happened with no incidents. This showed that a group project involving both supposedly rival groups was possible. The project took shape by the end of 2006, but paradoxically didn't get any institutional funding so the leaders had to seek private funding from a record label (K Industria Cultural), and well-known alternative artists like Manu Chao and la Mala Rodriguez cooperated. The record label took charge of the trainers (audio technicians, musicians, dancing and drama teachers) and the technical process of producing the record and all the products. The songs were created through a complex process of interaction between the young participants' imagination in the different workshops (they're the authors of all the lyrics), along with the technical resources from the trainers and the production and mastering carried out by the record label. Some professional musicians participated in some of the songs. The young people found it hard to understand that accomplishing an objective involved hard work, with weekly classes and rehearsals, and many of them gave up. But many others continued, and new enthusiastic young men and women from different origins joined in.

In recent years, coinciding with the dramatic effects of the financial crisis, which dramatically impacted young people and migrants (and doubly young migrants), the so-called Latino gangs have become the protagonists of the crime news, although the magnitude of police interventions has spread, the names of the groups involved have increased, and social rejection has become chronic. The Spanish media has extensively reported lurid details and images of a dozen massive police raids on major gangs performed by different police forces, with hundreds of arrested, many of them teenagers or young, appearing always as 'decommissioning,' 'beheading,' 'eradicating,' and 'dismantling' such groups (although they are quick to reunite and the news almost never realizes how many detainees are eventually tried and convicted). Another collateral effect of the crisis has been the increase of conflicts within the so-called 'Latin Gangs,' the reduction of most social programs aimed at their members, and a change of the political-police discourse, going back to 'zero tolerance,' considering these groups as 'criminal organizations,' the end of mediation and the reinforcement of the 'penal state.' In 2009 we gathered biographic narratives of migrant young people within the framework of the project Eumargins, about inclusion and exclusion in seven different European cities. In 2011 we started the project Yougang, which had the aim of evaluating public policies on gangs in Barcelona and Madrid. The first results revealed the stagnation of big groups that had participated in the constitution of the associations (Latin Kings and Ñetas); the emergence of smaller groups, some of which presented higher amounts of conflict or were linked to organized crime groups; the increase of arrests, fights, murders and convictions; and the increase of the prison population linked to these groups (Bourgois 2003; Queirolo Palmas 2012).

The Time of Social Movements: *Ninis* and *Indignados* (2011–15)

> (We advocate) a revolt of young people against youth ... We had underestimated the desire of young people to enter adulthood against an entire social, political and cultural structure that wants to keep them in childhood ... Capitalism deprives them of their own home and work, two things that children do not need and that, moreover, should not have. (Juventud sin Futuro [Youth Without Future] 2011, 10)

On 15 May 2011, Basilio Martín Patino, a veteran Spanish filmmaker with relevant works on the Franco regime, both as fiction (*Nueve cartas a Berta* 1966), and as documentary (*Canciones para después de una guerra* 1976), returned to Madrid from his native Salamanca and from his home listened to the protesters who had just occupied the central Madrid square of Puerta del Sol. Without thinking twice, he came down to the square, where he met the photographer Alfonso Parra, a regular contributor. Martin Patino talked to his team of technicians and they began filming what was happening before his eyes, without being aware of what impact the movement and images would have. He remained there for two months of the occupation until the popular indignation march that closed it, and has been documenting the daily life of the suggestive and fleeting utopia founded in Sol. The result is *Libre te quiero* [*I Want You Free*], an emotional film over the #acampadasol.

After the occupation of the plazas by the 15M movement, the studies on youth cultures have experienced a triple transformation. First, they became politicized by reconnecting the lifestyles with the forms of participation in public life, which in theory involves connecting British cultural studies with the theories about the new social movements. Second, they focus on cyberspace by exploring the use of ICT by new generations and the emerging form of activism networks (Feixa 2014). Third, they have expanded themselves to areas of daily life away from visibility and showmanship by addressing the study of lifestyles, which are no longer strictly youth and have become intergenerational. The ethnographies of the indignant squares that we see below have replaced the Latin bands as dominant study subjects. Significantly, the *REJ* does not devote any number during this period to

157

Figures 6.2: Indignados during the #àcampadaBarcelona, 2011. Source: Photos by Carles Feixa.

youth culture, but it included several articles on the subject in the numerous case studies about young people in the network (Espín 1986; 2011; Galán and Garlito 2011) and on the screens (Muela and Baladrón 2012; Chicharro 2014).[64] At the end of 2008 the international financial crisis exploded. Spain was one of the worst affected countries, with some social categories such as young people and immigrants were being hit with special intensity (young immigrants were affected twofold).

This can be summarized in two media archetypes that became research objects: on the one hand the *ni-nis*: young people that are supposedly not in education, employment, or training (NEET), a metaphor for the dramatic consequences of unemployment. On the other hand, the *indignados* [indignant], young activists of the 15M movement who in May 2011 occupied the squares of most Spanish cities protesting against the political class, opposing the image of the 'neet' to that of 'yeeep': the young person who is not only getting an education and is working in some sort of job – a precarious one – but who also finds the time to engage in a solidarity endeavour to find a way out of this social unrest. Before the crisis exploded, some voices raised concerns about the vulnerability of large groups of young people regarding employment, education, housing, and reproduction. In spite of Spain being one of the European countries with the highest rates of economic growth, the booming housing market and the high immigration rates experienced since the mid-1990s

64 Several studies have been published on cybercultures, among which we can highlight one coordinated by Néstor García Canclini comparing the forms of digital youth creativity in the cities of Mexico and Madrid with innovative case studies on trendies, musician networks, coolhunters, VJs, hackers, and autophotographers (García Canclini, Cruces and Urteaga 2012).

caused deterioration of the educational and employment conditions for young people, as well as lowest access to housing and falling birth-rates. This gave rise to a generational stereotype called the *mileurista* (the well prepared young person who earns less than 1,000 euros per month and therefore has difficulties being independent from their parents) (Soler, Planas, and Feixa 2014).

Following the initial surprise, the Indignados became a media image which, by contrast with the Ni-Nis, gained strong popular support, as some of their claims (such as foreclosure on mortgaged homes and criticism of the banking system, political corruption, and welfare cuts) were shared by large segments of the population. As with the Ni-Nis, the nickname came to refer to an entire generation, which was recognisable to those who camped out in the squares from May 15 to the end of July 2011. On the first anniversary of the movement, 15 May 2012, which had gone back to local neighbourhoods and initiatives, various studies began to appear, often conducted by young activists or participants in the protests, addressing issues such as the role of social networks and communication technologies, new forms of political participation, and cyber-activism and its connections with similar other movements, such as the Greek protests, the Arab spring, and Occupy Wall Street (Feixa, Sanchez García, and Nofre 2014; Fernandez-Planells, Figueras, and Feixa 2014). Last but not least, a further effect of the crisis has been the sharp decline in publicly-funded youth research. At a time when it is more necessary than ever to have real data on youth development, the institutes and observatories dedicated to promoting such research have suffered well above-average cuts, affecting the number of studies commissioned and publications produced.

Final Remarks

Since the 1960s, the emergence of youth cultures in Spain is one of the signs of the intense transition processes within the country: the economic transition from scarcity to wealth; the social transition from a monolithic to a plural model; the political transition from dictatorship to democracy; and the cultural transition from puritanism to consumerism. Matza (1973) proposed a model for exploring the evolution of youth lifestyles in the twentieth century, taking into consideration several rebellious 'youth traditions' at the crossroad of class and lifestyle: the 'delinquent' proletarian tradition, the 'radical' student tradition, the 'bohemian' middle-class tradition, and so on. The Birmingham School updated this model in order to analyse the emergence of British subcultures in the 1960s and 1970s (Hall and Jefferson 1983). The emergence of punk was a kind of hybrid synthesis of the history of the 'subterranean traditions of youth' in post-war Britain, mixing-up middle-class countercultural traditions and subcultural working-class traditions (Hebdige 1981). Post-subcultural studies came into this arena in the late twentieth century, claiming the need for greater plasticity in the term 'subculture.' So the question becomes: how did youth cultures emerge and develop in contexts outside the English-speaking world? In a somewhat different yet similar way, this is the case in Spain due to specific socio-histories.

This text is an attempt to review academic work on youth cultures carried out in Spain since the transition to democracy (although some earlier work related to the subject stemming from the late Franco period is also brought up). The nearly two hundred contributions analysed (books, papers, theses, unpublished reports, and journal texts) were grouped into different academic areas such as criminology, sociology, psychology, and anthropology and theoretical trends ranging from edifying post-war literature to the Birmingham School. The works are classified in five periods marked by different youth styles that act as distorting mirrors of social and cultural changes: the late Franco period (1960–76), the transition to democracy (1977–85), the post-transition (1986–94), the late 1990s (1995–9), the new century (2000–4), pre-crisis (2005–9), and post-crisis (2010–14).

Thus, our historic document analysis develops these works over the last 50 years, portraying the evolution of Spanish youth. In this timeframe, we also take into account the artistic manifestations of cinema and music, seeing them as key moments of the spirit of the age in terms of youth (sub)cultures. In the approach of 'The Time of Gangs: *Golfos* and *Jipis* (1960–1976),' the focus on the Spanish case stems from news, papers issued in church magazines, or magazines from the regime (conflating data about delinquent gangs with information about trends and student movements). We stand in front of rebellions against the dictatorship and absolute power in a Spain, yet remain distant from mass consumption society. Following this, between 1977 and 1985, in 'The Time of Tribes: *Punkis* and *Progres*,' in a time of transition to democracy, a new social subject appeared in the Spanish scenario, significantly named, 'tribus urbanas' [urban tribes]. The communication media would soon dedicate focussed attention on such phenomena, inciting campaigns of moral panic (like when a young mod was killed by a rocker) in tandem with commercial appropriation (like the reports advertising where to buy each tribe's outfit). We can group the studies issued during this period into three fields: first, those focusing on youth countercultures in the 1970s, be it for theoretical balance or historical reconstruction. Second, studies based on quantitative methodologies starting to highlight young people's cultural sensibilities. Third, proto-ethnographic studies about the phenomenon of night *movidas* and the emergence of urban tribes (Feixa 1985).

Following this path, the next stop is 'The Time of Styles: *Pijos* and *Makineros* (1986–94).' This was a time of the socialist government in Spain, when the generations that had led the fight against Franco were settling into power and viewed the apathetical and apolitical young people with suspicion, seeing their aesthetics and ways of living as purely commercial and consumerist. From the point of view of youth cultures, this period is characterized by three different processes: the segmentation of youth cultures into many styles that appear like a shopping catalogue; the revival of the *pijo* (a way to openly recover a higher class identity); and spearheading the night life with the generation of a new style, the *makinero* (between the proliferation of new clubs, the explosion of electronic commercial music, and the results of synthetic drugs). Among the studies about youth cultures published during this period, three groups can be discerned: first, different essays based on theoretical and historical contributions; second, a series of local and police examinations of football hooligans and skinheads; third, select ethnographic studies questioning the categories deployed, suggesting new methodologies based mostly on life history approaches.

The second half of the 1990s was dominated by the 'Time of Scenes: *Okupas* and *Pelaos* (1995–99).' *Pelaos* are the Spanish version of Nazi skinheads (somehow akin to football hooligans) according to the Spanish press in the late 1980s (although the *pelaos* did not really become socially well known until the mid-1990s, because of the greater social concern about the arrival of new waves of immigrants). They coincided with the explosion of *okupas*, the Spanish version of the squatters who appeared post-1968, linking the occupation of empty houses to experimenting with new alternative and countercultural ways of living together. From the social point of view, certain structural problems such as the new immigration, limited access to housing for youth, and the nocturnization of youth leisure open spaces for renewed youth culture activities. From a media perspective, this phenomenon is represented in newspapers and campaigns as reflecting moral panic following the same pattern with minimal variation: news event – media amplification – creation of a social problem – feedback in youth cultures – new news event (Cohen 1980). As regards social control, the different police bodies (state, autonomous, and local) organized specific brigades, and sometimes issued reports that reached the press. In universities, 'urban tribes' as a subject attained an important status and began to be the subject of numerous publications (a decade after the advent of the actual phenomenon).

The twenty-first century brought forth the 'Time of Cybercultures: *fiesteros* and *alternativos* (2000–4).' With the new millennium, Spanish youth cultures' characteristics may be generalized by three major tendencies. First, a certain activism in the public sphere is revived and reflected in the anti-globalization movement and its cultural effects. Second, dance cultures became symbolic of the different expressions of the *fiestero* movement. Third, the Internet opened a space for generational interaction in chatroom cultures and virtual communities that express different styles (like cyberpunks and hackers), although the use of virtual space affects all groups. We can isolate five significant tendencies in the studies published during this period: monographs about the two main youth groups of the previous decade (skinheads and *okupas*), in the form of journalist chronicles, militant denunciations with applied sociological analysis, and ethnographic comparisons; ethnographic studies about dance cultures in the form of surveys on the routes of ecstasy; theoretical reflections about the process of globalization; studies about the brand new social movements that characterize the emergence of alternative styles; studies on specific groups focusing on some relevant thematic aspect like music, gender, communication, tattoos, media, graffiti, or the history of youth cultures in the past; and in-depth studies on the impact of youth cultures on daily life, or in Willis' terms of their 'common culture.'

The second half of the first decade of the century was dominated by a revival of the first youth prototype studied in the 1960s: the bands. But in this case what we deal with is not a local actor linked to internal migration processes, but a transnational actor linked to international migrations, particularly from America. These are the so-called 'Latino bands' (although in fact their origins lie in North America) which will be looked at in more detail below. Significantly, the term 'band' becomes a paradigm of a new form of youth socialization, which is presently applied to young migrant origins and limited in most cases to the criminal side, while the term 'urban tribes' identifies itself only with native young people, becoming linked to fashion or disappearing. In recent years, coinciding with the dramatic effects of the financial crisis, more strongly felt by young people and migrants (and young migrants doubly), the so-called Latino gangs have become the protagonists of the crime news, although the magnitude of police interventions have spread, the names of the groups involved have increased, and social rejection has become chronic. The Spanish media has extensively reported lurid details and images of a dozen massive police raids on major gangs, performed by different police forces, with hundreds of arrests, many of them teenagers or young people, appearing always as 'decommissioning,' 'beheading,' 'eradicating,' and 'dismantling' such groups (although they are quick to reunite and the news almost never realizes how many detainees are eventually tried and convicted).

Besides focusing on the occupations of the 15M movement, the studies on youth cultures have suffered a triple transformation. First of all, they have grown in their political aspect, reconnecting the sort of lifestyle expression of previous movements to the public life – which in theoretical terms means connecting the classical cultural studies approach with new social movements. Secondly, they take their roots to cyberspace, exploring the use of ICT through younger generations in network-activism. Thirdly, they have extended their interest towards aspects of daily life not directly contained in the visible and spectacular aspects of these phenomena: these studies approach the lifestyles associated with the cultures, which slowly become intergenerational rather than youth-centred. It is the 'time of the social movements: *Ninis* and *Indignados*' – the present time.

References

'La fiesta de la contestación.' (10 March 1999). *El País*.

'Los miedos que se desataron en Sants.' (10 October 1999). *La Vanguardia*.

'Tribus '85: morir en la chupa puesta.' (April 1984). *Triunfo* 31.

Adán, T. (1992). 'Pautas y rituales de los grupos ultras del fútbol español. Análisis del caso Ultras Sur.' Unpublished BA thesis. Universidad de Salamanca.

Adán, T. (1995). *Ultras y skinheads: la juventud visible*. Oviedo: Nobel.

Adán, T. (2004). 'Ultras. Culturas de fútbol' ['Football cultures']. *Revista de Estudios de Juventud* 64: 87–100.

Adell, R. and M. Martínez (eds.). (2004). ¿Donde están las llaves? El movimiento okupa: prácticas y contextos sociales. Madrid: Catarata.

Aguirre. A. and M. Rodríguez. (1998). *Skins, punkis, okupas y otras tribus urbanas*. Barcelona: Bárdenas.

Aparicio, R. and A. Tornos. (2009). *Aproximación al estudio de las Bandas Latinas de Madrid*. Madrid: Gobierno de España: Ministerio de Trabajo e Inmigración.

Asociación de Jefes y Mandos de la Policía Local-Comunidad Valenciana. (2010). *Grafitis y Bandas Latinas*. Valencia: Mad.

Barbolla, D., J. Seco, and J. Moreno. (2010). *Las nuevas juventudes en la aldea global. Hikikomoris, friquis y otras identidades*. Badajoz: Abecedario.

Barruti, M. et al. (1990). *El món dels joves a Barcelona. Imatges i estils juvenils*. Barcelona: Ajuntament de Barcelona.

Batista, A. (2002). *Okupes. La mobilització sorprenent* [*Squatters. The surprising mobilization*]. Barcelona: Rosa dels Vents.

Bernete, F. (ed.) (2007). 'Culturas y lenguajes juveniles. Monográfico.' *Revista de Estudios de Juvetud* 78.

Blánquez, J. and O. Morera (eds.) (2002). *Loops. Una historia de la música electrónica* [*A History of Electronic Music*]. Barcelona: Reservoir Books.

Botello, S. and A. Moya. (2005). *Reyes latinos: Los códigos secretos de los Latin Kings en España*. Madrid: Ediciones Temas de Hoy.

Bourgois, P. (2003). *In Search of Respect: Selling Crack in El Barrio*. London: Cambridge University Press.

Carandell, J. M. (1972). *La protesta juvenil* [*The Youth Protest*]. Barcelona: Salvat.

Cardús, S. and J. Estruch. (1984). *Les enquestes a la joventut de Catalunya*. Barcelona: Generalitat de Catalunya.

Cartier, J. P. and M. Naslednikov. (1974). *El mundo de los hippies*. Bilbao: Desclée de Brouwer.

Casals, X. (1995). *Neonazis en España. De las audiencias wagnerianas a los skinheads (1966–1995)*. Barcelona: Grijalbo.

Cerdà, J. and R. Rodriguez. (1999). *La repressio franquista del moviment hippy a Formentera (1968–1970)* [*Franco's Repression of the Hippy Movement in Formentera*]. Eivissa: Res Pública.

Chicharro, M. (ed.). (2014). 'La Juventud en la pantalla.' *Revista de Estudios de Juventud* 106.

Cohen, S. (1980). *Folk Devils and Moral Panics: The Creation of the Mods and Rockers*. Martin Robertson & Co: Oxford.

Colubi, P. (1997). *El ritmo de las tribus*. Barcelona: Alba Zoom.

Costa, C. (1998). 'La dimensión afectiva en los movimientos sociales. El caso del movimiento okupa' ['The Sensitive Dimension of Social Movements. The Case of Squatters']. Unpublished MA thesis. Bellaterra, Universitat Autònoma de Barcelona.

Costa, P-O., J. M. Pérez, and F. Tropea. (1996). *Tribus urbanas* [*Urban Tribes*]. Barcelona: Paidós.

De Miguel, A. (1979). *Los narcisos. El radicalismo cultural de los jóvenes*. Barcelona: Kairós.

De Miguel, A. (2000). *Dos generaciones de jóvenes 1960–1998*. Madrid: Injuve.

Delgado, M. (1995). 'Cultura y parodia. Las microculturas juveniles en Cataluña' ['Culture and parody. Youth micro-cultures in Catalonia']. *Cuaderno de Realidades Sociales* 45/46: 77–87.

Delgado, M. (2002). 'Estética e infamia. De la distinción al estigma en los marcajes culturales de los jóvenes.' In C. Feixa, C. Costa, and J. Pallarés (eds.), *Movimientos juveniles. Grafitis, grifotas, okupas*, 115–44. Barcelona: Ariel.

Díez del Río, I. (1982). 'La contracultura.' *Revista de Estudios de Juventud* 6: 101–32.

Dirección General de la Guardia Civil. (1998a). *Jornadas sobre Ideología, Violencia y Juventud* [*Seminar on Ideology, Violence and Youth*]. Madrid: Instituto de la Juventud.

Dirección General de la Guardia Civil. (1998b). *Jornadas sobre Ideología, Violencia y Juventud. Dossier de prensa.* Madrid: Injuve.

Dirección General de la Policía. (1993). *Análisis policial del racismo y xenofobia: Tribu Skinhead* [*Police Analysis of Racism and Xenophobia: The Skinhead Tribe*]. Madrid: Ministerio del Interior.

Donald, M. (1995). Tribus urbanas: Los hijos de la cultura postindustrial [Urban Tribes. The Children of Postindustrial Culture]. *Cuadernos de Realidades Sociales* 45/46: 25–44.

Espín, M. (1986). 'La falsa imagen de los jóvenes en los medios de comunicación social: un factor de marginación.' *Revista de estudios de Juventud* 21: 57–65.

Espín, M. (Coord.) (2011). 'Adolescentes digitales.' *Revista de Estudios de Juventud* 92.

Feixa, C. (1985). 'Joventut i identitat: una etnologia de la joventut a Lleida.' Unpublished BA thesis. Lleida, Universitat de Barcelona.

Feixa, C. (1988). *La tribu juvenil. Una aproximación transcultural a la juventud.* Torino: l'Occhiello.

Feixa, C. (1989). 'Pijos, progres y punks. Hacia el estudio antropológico de la juventud urbana.' *Revista de Estudios de Juventud* 34: 69–78.

Feixa, C. (1993). *La joventut com a metàfora. Sobre les cultures juvenils.* Barcelona: Secretaria General de Joventut.

Feixa, C. (1998). *De jóvenes, bandas y tribus. Antropología de la juventud.* Barcelona: Ariel.

Feixa, C. (2009). 'Vida Real. Reyes y reinas latinos de Cataluña (y más allá).' *Documentación Social* 155: 229–60.

Feixa, C. (2014). *De la Generación@ a la #Generación. La juventud en la era digital.* Barcelona: NED Ediciones.

Feixa, C. (ed.). (2004). *Culturas juveniles en España (1960–2004).* Madrid: Ministerio Trabajo y Asuntos Sociales.

Feixa, C. et al. (2008). 'Latin Kings in Barcelona.' In F. van Gemert, D. Peterson & I.-L. Lien (eds.), *Street Gangs, Migration and Ethnicity*, 63–78. Cullompton: Willan Publishing.

Feixa, C., and J. Pallarés. (1998). 'Boîtes, raves, clubs. Metamorfosis de la festa juvenil.' *Revista dEtnologia de Catalunya* 13: 88–103.

Feixa, C., and L. Porzio. (2005). 'Jipis, Pijos, Fiesteros. Studies on Youth Cultures in Spain 1960–2004.' *Young* 13 (1): 89–114.

Feixa, C., C. Costa, and J. Pallarés (eds.). (2002). *Movimientos juveniles. Grafitis, grifotas, okupas.* Barcelona: Ariel.

Feixa, C., C. Costa, and J. R. Saura (eds.). (2002). *Movimientos juveniles. De la globalización a la antiglobalización.* Barcelona: Ariel.

Feixa, C., J. Sanchez García, and J. Nofre. (2014). 'Del altermundismo a la indignación. Cronotopos del activismo político juvenil en Barcelona.' *Revista Nueva Sociedad* 251.

Feixa, C., J. Saura, and X. De Castro (eds.). (2003). *Música i ideologies* [*Music and Ideologies*]. Barcelona: Secretaria General de Joventut.

Feixa, C., L. Porzio, and C. Recio (eds.). (2006). *Jóvenes latinos en Barcelona. Espacio público y cultura urbana*. Barcelona: Anthropos.

Fernández-Planells, A., M. Figueras, and C. Feixa. (2014). 'Communication among young people in the #spanishrevolution.' *New Media y Society* 16 (8): 1287–1308.

Fouce, H. (2006). *El futuro ya está aquí. Música pop y cambio cultural*. Madrid: Velecío Editores.

Funes, J. (1984). *La nueva delincuencia infantil y juvenil*. Barcelona: Paidós.

Funes, J. (1985). *Cultura juvenil urbana* [*Urban Youth Culture*]. Projecte jove, Barcelona: Ajuntament de Barcelona.

Galán, C. and L. Garlito (eds.). (2011). 'Jóvenes en(red)ados.' *Revista de Estudios de Juventud*, 93.

Gamella, J. F. (1989). 'La peña de la Vaguada. Análisis etnográfico de un proceso de marginación juvenile.' Unpublished PhD thesis. Madrid, UAM.

Gamella, J. F. and A. Álvarez. (1999). *Las rutas del éxtasis: Drogas de síntesis y nuevas culturas juveniles*. Barcelona: Ariel.

García Canclini, N., F. Cruces, and M. Urteaga. (2012). *Jóvenes, Culturas Urbanas y Redes Digitales*. Madrid: Ariel-Fundación Telefónica.

Gil Calvo, E. (1985). *Los depredadores audiovisuales. Juventud urbana y cultura de masas*. Madrid: Tecnos.

Gil Calvo, E. and E. Menéndez. (1985). *Ocio y prácticas culturales de los jóvenes*. Madrid: Instituto de la Juventud.

Gil Muñoz, C. (1973) *Juventud marginada. Los hippies a su paso por Formentera* [*Marginalized Youth: The Hippies in Their Passage through Formentera*]. Madrid: Dopesa.

Gistain, M. (2001). *Florida 135: Cultura de clubs*. Zaragoza: Ibercaja-Biblioteca Aragonesa de Cultura.

Gomis, J. (1965). *Cartes a set joves Juke-Box per al final de l'adolescència* [*Letters to seven young juke-box people in late adolescence*]. Barcelona: Edicions 62.

González, R. et al. (2003). *Joventut, okupació i polítiques públiques a Catalunya* [*Youth, Squatterism and Public Policies in Catalonia*]. Barcelona: Secretaria General de la Joventut.

Guerra, P. (2010). 'A instável leveza do rock: génese, dinâmica e consolidação do rock alternativo em Portugal (1980–2010)' ['The Unstable Lightness of Rock: Genesis, Dynamics and Consolidation of Alternative Rock in Portugal (1980–2010)'] Unpublished PhD thesis. Porto, Faculdade de Letras da Universidade do Porto.

Hall, S., and T. Jefferson (eds.). (1983 [1975]). *Resistance through Rituals. Youth Subcultures in Post-war Britain*. London: Hutchinson.

Hebdige, D. (1981[1979]). *Subculture. The Meaning of Style*. London, New York: Routledge.

Heruzzo, M. and J. Grenzner. (1998). 'Desokupadas.' *Ajoblanco* 110: 28–31.

Huertas, J. M. (1969). *Chicos de la gran ciudad*. Barcelona: Nova Terra.

Ibarra, E. (2003). *Los crímenes del odio. Violencia skin y neonazi en España*. Madrid: Temas de Hoy.

Injuve (1998). *Violencia, juventud y movimientos sociales marginales*. Madrid: Injuve. Informe.

Juventud sin Futuro [Youth Without Future] (2011). *Juventud sin futuro. Sin casa, sin curro, sin pensión, sin miedo* [Youth without future. Without a house, without a job, without a pension, without fear]. Barcelona: Icaria.

Lasén. A. (2000). *A contratiempo. Un estudio de las temporalidades juveniles*. Madrid: CIS.

Lasén. A. and I. Martínez. (2001). 'El tecno: variaciones sobre la globalización.' *Política y Sociedad* 36, 129–49.

López Aranguren, J. L. (1973). 'La subcultura juvenil.' In *El futuro de la universidad y otras polémicas*. Madrid: Taurus.

López Riocerezo, J. M. (1970). *Problemática mundial del gamberrismo y sus posibles soluciones*. Madrid: Studium.

Lozano, J. O. (2007). *Jóvenes educadores. Tribus educadoras entre los lugares y las redes*. Barcelona: Graó.

Mañas, J. Á. (1994). *Historias del Kronen*. Barcelona: Ediciones Destino.

Martín Criado, E. (1998). *Producir la juventud* [*Producing Youth*]. Madrid: Istmo.

Martín Serrano, M. (1996). *Los jóvenes ante la violencia urbana*. Madrid: Injuve.

Martínez, E. and P. Cerdá. (2009). *Bandas juveniles. Inmigración y ciudad: España y México*. San Vicente, Alicante: Editorial Club Universitario.

Martínez, R. (2002). *Cultura juvenil i gènere* [*Youth Culture and Gender*]. Barcelona: Observatori Català de la Joventut.

Martínez, R. and J. D. Pérez. (1997). *El gust juvenil en joc*. Barcelona: Diputació de Barcelona.

Martínez, S. (1999). *Enganxats al heavy. Cultura, música i transgressió*. Lleida: Pagès.

Martínez, S. (2004). 'Heavies, ¿una cultura de transgresión?' *Revista de Estudios de Juventud* 64, 75–86.

Matza, D. (1973[1961]). 'Subterranean Traditions of Youth.' In H. Silverstein (ed.), *The Sociology of Youth: Evolution and Revolution*, 252–71. New York: McMillan.

Mellizo, F. (1972). 'En torno a los hippies.' *Revista del Instituto de la Juventud* 39: 103–19.

Ministerio de Justicia e Interior. (1995). *Violencia y tribus urbanas. Informe*. Madrid: Ministerio de Justicia e Interior.

Monod, J. (2002[1968]). *Los barjots. Etnología de bandas juveniles* [*The Barjots. Ethnology of Juvenile Gangs*]. Barcelona: Ariel (Paris: Juliard).

Montesinos, D. P. (2007). *La juventud domesticada. Cómo la cultura juvenil se convirtió en simulacro*. Madrid: Editorial Popular.

Moya, C. (1983). 'Informe sobre la juventud contemporánea.' *Revista de Estudios de Juventud* 9: 17–51.

Muela, M. and A. J. Baladrón (eds.). (2012). 'Jóvenes: Ídolos mediáticos y nuevos valores.' *Revista de Estudios de Juventud*, 96.

Muñoz. A. (1985). 'El ceremonial comunicativo y la expulsión de la palabra.' *Los Cuadernos del Norte* 29: 32–8.

Navarrete, L. (1999). *La autopercepción de los jóvenes okupas en España*. Madrid: Instituto de la Juventud.

Porrah, Huan. (1999). 'La juventud rupturista en el enriquecimiento de la cultura vasca' ['The Breaking Youth in the Enrichment of Basque Culture']. In *VIII Congreso de Antropología*. Santiago de Compostela: FAAEE-AGA.

Porzio, L. (2002). 'Tatuaje, género e identidad. Un estudio sobre la subcultura skinhead en Cataluña' ['Tatoo, Gender and Identity. A Study of Skinhead Subculture in Catalonia']. Unpublished MA thesis. Barcelona, Universitat de Barcelona.

Porzio, L. (2004). 'Skinheads. Tatuaje, género y cultura juvenil.' *Revista de Estudios de Juventud* 64: 101–10.

Pujolar, J. (1997). *De què vas, tio?* [*What's the Matter, Guy?*]. Barcelona: Empúries.

Queirolo Palmas, L. (2012). *Intervenir sobre las bandas. Etnografía de un campo burocrático del estado*. Marie Curie Intermediate Report. Lleida: Universitat de Lleida-European Union.

Racionero, L. (1977). *Filosofías del underground*. Barcelona: Anagrama.

Reyes, F. and I. M. Vigara. (2002). 'Graffiti, pintadas y hip-hop en España.' In E. Rodríguez (ed.), *El lenguaje de los jóvenes*, 169–226. Barcelona: Ariel.

Rivière, M. (1989). 'Moda de los jóvenes: un lenguaje adulterado' ['The Fashion of Young People: The Adulterated Language']. In F. Rodríguez (ed.), *Comunicación y lenguaje juvenil* [*Communication and Juvenile Language*]. Madrid: Fundamentos.

Rodríguez, E. and I. Megías. (2003). *Jóvenes entre sonido. Hábitos, gustos y referentes musicales*. Madrid: Injuve-Fad.

Rodríguez, E., I. Megías, and E. Sánchez. (2002). *Jóvenes y relaciones grupales. Dinámica relacional para los tiempos de trabajo y de ocio*. Madrid: Injuve -Fad.

Rodríguez, F. (ed.) (1989). *Comunicación y lenguaje juvenil*. Madrid: Fundamentos.

Romaní, O. (1982). 'Droga i subcultura. Una història cultural del haix a Barcelona (1960–1980).' Unpublished PhD thesis. Barcelona, Universitat de Barcelona.

Romaní, O. and C. Feixa. (2002). 'De Seattle 1999 a Barcelona 2002. Moviments socials, resistències globals.' *Revista dEtnologia de Catalunya* 21: 72–95.

Romo, N. (2001). *Mujeres y drogas de síntesis. Género y riesgo en la cultura del baile* [*Women and Synthetic Drugs. Gender and Risk in Dance Cultures*]. Donostia: Hirugarren Prentsa.

Ros, N. (1964) 'Nueva ola.' Magazine *Relevo* 42–3. Lleida.

Ruiz, J. I. (1994). 'Ni rebeldes ni narcisos (estilos de vida y juventud).' *Aguruak. Revista Vasca de Sociología y Ciencia Política* 10: 190–6.

Ruiz, J. I. (ed.) (1998). *La juventud liberta: Género y estilos de vida de la juventud urbana española*. Madrid: Fundación BBV.

Sáez Marín, J. (1988). *El Frente de Juventudes, 1937–1960*. Madrid: Siglo XXI.

Salas, I. (2002). *Diario de un skin*. Barcelona: Temas de Hoy.

Salcedo, E. (1974). *Integrats, rebels i marginats. Subcultures jovenívoles al País Valencià.* València: L'Estel.

Sansone, L. (1988). 'Tendencias en blanco y negro: punk y rastafarismo' [Black and White Trends: Punk and Rastafarians]. *Revista de Estudios de Juventud* 30: 73–86.

Scandroglio, B. (2009). *Jóvenes, grupos y violencia. De las tribus urbanas a las bandas latinas.* Barcelona: Icaria.

Soler, P., A. Planas, and C. Feixa. (2014). 'Youth and Youth Policies in Spain in Times of Austerity: of Juggling to Trapeze.' *International Journal of Adolescence and Youth* 18 (3).

Thrasher, F. M. (1963[1926]). *The Gang.* Chicago: University of Chicago Press.

Tierno Galván, E. (1972). *La rebelión juvenil y el problema universitario.* Madrid: Seminarios y Ediciones.

Tinat, K. (2002). 'Identité et culture d'un groupe juvenile urbain: les pijos de Madrid.' Unpublished PhD thesis. Bourgogne, Université de Bourgogne.

Tinat, K. (2004). 'Pijos/as. Una cultura juvenil de identidad fluctuante.' *Revista de Estudios de Juventud* 64: 67–74.

Trías Mercant, S. (1967). 'Apuntes para una clasificación de grupos juveniles.' *Revista del Instituto de la Juventud* 13: 61–95.

Ucelay da Cal, E. (ed.) (1987). *La joventut a Catalunya al segle XX.* Barcelona: Diputació de Barcelona.

Vázquez Montalbán, M. (1985). 'Casi treinta años después.' In VV.AA., *Crónicas de juventud.* Madrid: Ministerio de Cultura.

Viñas, C. (2001). *Música i skinheads a Catalunya,* Barcelona: Diputació de Barcelona.

Viñas, C. (2004). *Skinheads a Catalunya.* Barcelona: Columna.

Viñas, C. (2005). *El mundo ultra. Los radicales del fútbol español.* Madrid: Temas de Hoy.

VV.AA. (1995). 'Las tribus urbanas.' *Cuaderno de Realidades Sociales* 45–6 (special issue).

VV.AA. (1999/2000). *Okupación, represión y movimientos sociales.* Barcelona: Diatriba.

VV.AA. (2008). *Latin kings, ñetas y otros jóvenes de Barcelona … Unidos por el Flow.* Barcelona: K. Industria Cultural.

Willis, P. (1990). *Moving Culture. An Inquiry into the Cultural Activities of Young People.* Lisbon: Galouste Gulbenkian Foundation.

Research Projects

Eumargins. (2008–11). 'On the Margins of the European Community. Young Adult Immigrants in Seven European Countries.' European Union. FP7 [FP7-SSH-2007-1.217524]. http://www.sv.uio.no/iss/english/research/projects/eumargins.

Genind. (2013–16). 'La Generación Indignada. Espacio, poder y cultura en los movimientos juveniles de 2011: una perspectiva transnacional.' Ministerio de Economía y Competividad. VI Programa Nacional de Investigación Científica, Desarrollo e Innovación Tecnológica. [CSO2012-34415]. http://genindyoungpower.blogspot.com.es.

Jovlat. (2005–8). '¿Reyes y reinas latinos? Identidades culturales de los jóvenes de origen latinoamericano en España.' Mininisterio de Educación y Ciencia. Plan Nacional I+D+I, Programa Nacional de Ciencias Sociales, Económicas y Jurídicas (SEJ). [SEJ2005-09333-C02-02/SOCI].

Tresegy. (2006–8). 'Toward a Social Construction of an European Youth-ness: Experience of Inclusion and Exclusion in the Public Sphere among Second Generation Migrated Teenagers.' European Union. FP6 [FP6-2004-CITIZENS-5.029105]. http://ec.europa. eu/research/social-sciences/projects/278_en.html.

Yougang. (2011–13). 'Gang Policies: Youth and Migration in Local Contexts.' European Union. Marie Curie FP7-PEOPLE [PIEF-GA-2010-272200]. http://www. yougangproject.com.

KISMIF. (2012–15). 'Keep it Simple, Make it fast! Prolegomenon and Punk Scenes, a Road to the Portuguese Contemporaneity (1977–2012).' Portuguese Foundation for Science and Technology [PTDC/CS-SOC/118830/2010]. http://www.punk.pt/ projeto-2.

Webgraphy

Burke, J. (2006). 'Row Erupts in Spain over Treatment of Latin Kings.' *The Guardian* (October 6). http://www.guardian.co.uk/world/2006/oct/05/spain.gilestremlett.

EPA. (2012). 'Encuesta a la población activa.' Madrid. Instituto Nacional de Estadística. http://www.ine.es/prensa/epa_prensa.htm.

Idescat. (2012). 'Evolució de la població total i estrangera. 2000–2010.'http://www. idescat.cat/poblacioestrangera/?b=0&nac=a&res=a.

Efe Agencia (2005). 'Empieza el juicio contra seis pandilleros por el asesinato del colombiano Ronny Tapias.' http://www.libertaddigital.com/sociedad/empieza-el-juicio-contra-seis-pandilleros-por-el-asesinato-del-colombiano-ronny-tapias-1276248136.

Torres, G. (2006). 'Latin kings: del mito a la realidad.' *BBC World* (September 27) http:// news.bbc.co.uk/hi/spanish/misc/newsid_5384000/5384426.stm.

Visión Sociológica de España. (2011). 'Extranjeros en países europeos.' http:// visionsociologica.es/Contexto%20internacional/extranjeros_paises_europeos.php._

Warden, R. (2006). 'Hard Cases Show Soft Side.' *Times Higher Education* (October 15). http://www.timeshighereducation.co.uk/story.asp?storyCode=205826&sectioncode=26.

Filmography

Casals A. and J. C. Martinez (dir.) X, X. (2006). *Vida real: latin kings en Barcelona*. http:// www.jolinesproduccions.com/vidareal/index.htm.

González, J. (dir.) Queirolo, L. X, X. (2013). *Buscando Respeto*. Spain: UdL, Unige, European Union. Yougang FP7 Marie Curie Project. https://www.youtube.com/ watch?v=kSMHicXO7F0.

Unidos por el Flow. (2008). *Unidos por el Flow*. Latin Kings, Ñetas y Jóvenes de Barcelona. KL Industria. http://www.youtube.com/watch?v=SocJJT2sV4E.

Glossary

Alternativos: Mixture of grunge style and anti-globalization movements

Fiesteros: Young people that like dance music and attend discotheques, clubs, and raves

Golfos: Hooligans, Spanish version of working-class gangs

Jipis: Hippies, Spanish version of countercultures

Makineros: Young people from working-class origins who like electronic music

Movida: Night routes through leisure spaces in Spanish cities

Okupas: Spanish version of squatters

Pasotas: Young people disenchanted with politics and moral values

Pelaos: Spanish version of Nazi-skinheads

Pijos: Upper-class, conservative, who celebrate *materialis*, the consumer culture

Progres: Middle-class, leftist, politically engaged, and culturally dissident young people

Punkis: Spanish version of punks

Estoy tan contento !

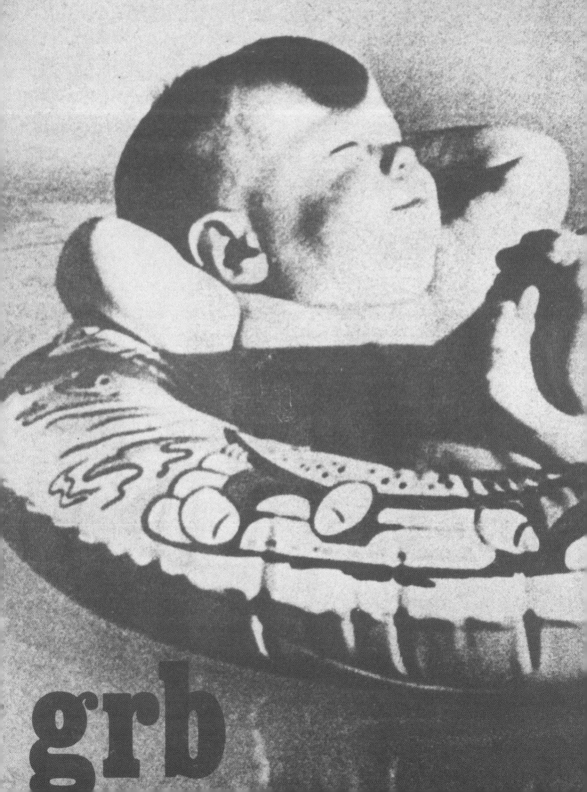

grb

7. NARRATIVES OF TRANSITION WITHIN A SUBCULTURE: A CASE STUDY OF NOMADIC PUNKS

EDWARD AVERY-NATALE

Abstract

Throughout their lives, individuals are continually in some sort of identitarian flux, and yet work to make it seem as if this is not the case. This chapter will focus on a particular element of this fluidity. Specifically, I will show how those who go through changes in their life story related to a particular lifestyle also work to maintain a sense of continued identification. In the case of the interviewees here, being a 'traveller' punk at an earlier point in their life was an important identification that also related to their larger punk and/or anarchist (anarcho-punk) identification. At some point they gave up this practice; they rejected a particular character that had played a role in their narrative(s). However, this did *not* correspond to rejecting punk or anarcho-punk. This leaves us with a question: how does one maintain an identification and its corresponding identity-label ('punk' or 'anarcho-punk') while rejecting an important character with particular behavioural traits that had been related to the still-existing identification?

Keywords: Punk, subculture, travelling, identification, life histories

Edward Avery-Natale is a sociologist who studies identification, popular culture, punk rock, and social movements. His most recent publication, *Ethics, Politics, and Anarcho-Punk Identifications* (2016) explores the ways in which individuals who are both punks and anarchists in Philadelphia, Pennsylvania navigate the complexities of combining these identities. His current project is an attempt to apply affect and assemblage theories to the study of identity. E-mail: ednatale@gmail.com

NARRATIVES OF TRANSITION WITHIN A SUBCULTURE: A CASE STUDY OF NOMADIC PUNKS

Introduction

Throughout their lives, individuals are continually in some sort of identitarian flux, and yet work to make it seem as if this is not the case. This chapter will focus on a particular element of this fluidity. Specifically, I will show how those who go through changes in their life story, related to a particular lifestyle, also work to maintain a sense of continued identification. While there is a great deal of literature on the ways in which people switch identifications, less work has been done on the ways in which people *maintain* one or more existing identifications while experiencing changes in certain signifying practices and behaviours associated with that identification. In other words, there is less work on how people might reject a particular identification while maintaining other existing identifications, narratives, and characters. It is my position that narrative identification theories are essential to explaining this process.[65]

In the case of the interviewees here, at some earlier point in their life being a 'traveller' punk was an important identification that also related to their larger punk and/ or anarchist (anarcho-punk) identification. At some point they gave up this practice; they rejected a particular character that had played a role in their narrative(s). However, this did *not* correspond to rejecting punk or anarcho-punk. This leaves us with a question: how does one maintain an identification and its corresponding identity-label ('punk' or 'anarcho-punk') while rejecting an important character with particular behavioural traits that had been related to the still-existing identification?

Only a small amount of literature has focused on this unique process. Instead, most focuses on the outright rejection of a previous identity and the creation of a new one, which is sometimes referred to as 'becoming an ex' (Wacquant 1990). The analysis here is different because the individuals have not become 'ex's.' Instead, they have remained anarcho-punks and have even maintained their train-hopping character in a way by creating new alliances between characters in their narratives. Unlike the work about becoming an ex, there is no contention here that a previously existing stable identity has somehow been eliminated in exchange for a new identity. Instead, the focus is on how individuals, when going through a change in their narratives and corresponding characters, maintain their

---

65   Throughout this chapter, I use terms from narrative identification theories, such as 'identifications,' 'characters,' 'plot,' and so on. These describe the process by which individuals use stories to construct a coherent identification from their multiple subjectivities. For my purposes, an individual is seen as having a particular plot through which they see their lives progressing. It is this plot that makes particular narratives useful and that calls forth particular characters for use in the stories. Furthermore, I choose the term 'identification' over 'identity,' as the latter, a noun, implies a stable and permanent self, while the former, a verb, implies an active process by which identifications are constructed.

plot and identifications even while shifting the narratological location of characters that exist in their stories. I will argue that this kind of change process can be best understood through a narratological analysis of identification processes. I will follow this with examples from my research on anarcho-punks in Philadelphia, and I will conclude with reflections on the potential radical nature of choosing this kind of 'drop out' lifestyle.

Literature Review

There are two primary topics to be reviewed here: the first is previous work concerned with the way in which individuals change their identifications from being one thing and then another. The second, though not unrelated to the first, is on the ageing process specifically, and the effect that ageing has on identification, especially among subcultural members. Each of these is important to this chapter because the narrators will discuss the ways in which a particular character with particular behavioural signifiers associated with their punk or anarcho-punk identification went through a change, but without giving up their already-existing identification(s). In short, each participant at some point in their life participated in nomadism, which can be understood as a subsection of the larger punk culture that chooses – at least temporarily, and in some cases permanently – a kind of homeless lifestyle that often involves hitchhiking, hopping freight trains, and other non-traditional but romanticized forms of travel. However, at the time of the interview, each participant was *not* actively nomadic.

Life change processes

In post-subcultural work it has been recognized that the belief in a stable subject is a mythological construct of the Enlightenment (Bennett 1999). Rather than taking on a single position in society, their position depends on conditions and power struggles, relationships, connections, and associations with other individuals and structures. In music-based subcultures such as punk rock, this has also been recognized by theorists who have rejected the traditional homological analysis of subculture (Vila 2015), in which is it presumed that a particular identity, usually class, directly corresponds to the value of the subculture: 'This way of understanding the relationship between music and identity has many difficulties in explaining changes in the musical tastes of social actors who neither have changed their structural position in society, nor have modified the basic characteristics of their subculture' (Vila, forthcoming, 5–6). In other words, the traditional approach to subculture, often grounded in the Birmingham Centre for Contemporary Cultural Studies (CCCS), presumed a definite relationship between one's structural location (often class) and subcultural identity. The CCCS therefore struggled to explain changes in identities, shifts between subjectivities, or an individual's or group's sense of multiplicity and fluidity. This left the CCCS further unable to explain how those who did not fit the social stereotype (e.g. those who were not working class) came to participate in what were supposed to be working-class subcultures, such as English punk in the 1970s (Hebdige 1979).

For the CCCS, identitarian changes should presumably correspond to structural changes. In practice, though, this is not the case, and changes to one's identifications are far more complex and heterogeneous. For Degher and Hughes (1991), using an interactionist perspective, 'the "identity change" process must be viewed on two levels: a public (external) and a private (internal) level … In order to fully understand the identity change process, it is necessary to explain the interaction between outer and inner processes' (391–2). The 'life course' perspective also emphasizes this double nature of change, reflecting on 'the intersection of social and historical factors with personal biography,' and claiming that, 'Transitions refer to changes in status that are discrete and bounded in duration although their consequences may be long term' (George 1993, 358). However, the life course perspective is also flawed as it fails to recognize the heterogeneous ways that transitions take place, and overstates structural control on individuals and processes (365).

'Role Theory' sought to do a good deal more in dealing with the changes that people go through in their lives: 'The link between role theory and life transitions is straightforward: role entry and exit are, by definition, transitions' (354–5). Role theory also attempted to pay more attention to the heterogeneous ways in which people enter and exit various 'roles.' This is especially true of Ebaugh's (1988) work on 'becoming an ex,' based on interviews with a number of 'exes,' ranging from ex-nuns to 'transsexuals.' Furthermore, Ebaugh rightly recognizes that previously held identifications (or previous 'roles') need not be entirely abandoned in the change process. In fact, 'Her model suggests that former roles are never abandoned but, instead, carry over into new roles' (Brown 1991, 220), a finding that has been replicated in more-recent studies (Menzies and Sheeshka 2012) and plays a role in the findings presented here as well. Often used to study 'deviance,' role theory offers suggestive reasons for why an individual who has apparently 'exited' a given role (taken on a new identification) may still maintain elements of their 'ex' self, whether these be variations on a behaviour (Sharp and Hope 2001) or turning one's previous 'deviant' role into a 'professional' variation that relies upon the earlier role (Brown 1991). Similar results have been found with those entering into new identifications such as parenthood and 'oldness' (Logan, Ward, and Spitze 1992), a finding that is relevant here as many of the participants are entering similar life stages.

Role theory, though, ultimately falls short of its aim. Ebaugh's model of 'becoming an ex,' rather than properly embracing heterogeneity, focuses on discovering objective truths that span the different changes. Beginning with four 'natural stages' of role exit, progressing through five 'turning points' in the process, and concluding with eleven 'salient properties' that affect the way in which one exits, the text, while laudable in its goals, ultimately falls back on positivistic and objectivist notions, reducing heterogeneity to ideal types (Wacquant 1990). Furthermore, Ebaugh fails to recognize that while some 'role exits' may be enormous moments in a given life, we are, in fact, constantly exiting and entering roles 'as we shift audiences, locales, scenes, and temporal frames' (Wacquant 1990, x). Her model has no way to deal with this reality. In this sense, even Goffman's *Presentation of Self in Everyday*

Life (1959) is ahead of Ebaugh on this account. If Ebaugh was perhaps outdated as early as 1990 her model is archaic today as it implies a permanence to identification processes and a singularity to the self. Therefore, I will argue below that narrative identification theories, influenced by post-structuralism and psychoanalysis and yet moving beyond both, offer us a better path to understand life changes and the processes of identification.

Ageing

The literature discussed here attempts to deal with the way in which individuals confront the social reality of ageing, 'a construct having social content and personal meaning' (Logan, Ward and Spitze 1992, 451) in a society that treats age as a significant marker. Much of this literature emerges out of post-subcultural studies. Rejecting the approach of the CCCS, these theorists emphasize the ways in which subcultural members do not necessarily stay the same, while also rejecting the homological thesis of a direct connection between structural location and (sub)cultural identification.

While it was traditionally believed that subcultural participation was the bastion of youth (roughly, teenagers to age 20–5), we now know that some individuals choose to continue participation beyond this seemingly arbitrary marker. This was even true of those subcultures studied by the CCCS: 'Many of those who follow punk today were first attracted to punk music during the late 1970s and have remained fans ever since' (Bennett 2006, 219). Such a finding contradicts early studies of punk, such as Hebdige (1979). So, while a static character and rigid definition of authenticity would mean that 'members have no choice *but* to age out, particularly as they begin to participate in the mainstream world and its institutions (careers, family, marriage)' (Davis 2006, 64), current findings indicate that those who feel a strong identitarian connection to a given subculture will find a way to maintain that relationship later in life.

Additionally, showing a postmodern influence, authors in this tradition often recognize that some individuals come and go regarding particular identifications. Therefore, while they may at times reject elements of an identification or drift away from a scene, they may come back to it or include that previous subjectivity in another part of their life. Aspects of this research will be particularly salient for the study at hand, as many of the participants quoted below eventually made the choice to no longer participate in the nomadic lifestyle – in part because of significant life moments that some may understand as a 'signposts' of ageing, such as having a child (Logan, Ward and Spitze 1992). However, such processes of change do not necessarily mean a rejection of the existing identification. Instead, those with a deep commitment to a subculture find ways to make sense of their continued subcultural identification even after rejecting a previously important personal signifier of it.

Changes to one's identification during the ageing process can take a seemingly infinite number of nuanced paths. In Nicola Smith's (2009) study of ageing in England's Northern Soul subculture, she finds that 'the self of youth constructed in relation to scene affiliation need not diminish with age' (428). Instead, individuals find different ways of negotiating their ageing status. Smith, taking a neo-tribal approach, focuses on the ways in which some ageing participants 'can freely move between neo-tribes as, when and – importantly – *if* desired' (431). The 'if' here is particularly significant as it tells us of the fact that participants *may* have the kind of neo-tribal fluidity that Bennett (1999) describes, but that they do not necessarily *have* to. In short, Bennett's work shows us one possible way in which contemporary cultural members may behave, but not all do so, and some may, in Smith's words, participate in 'post-subcultural subcultural play.' For Smith, this turn of phrase is meant to indicate that some subcultural members, even those who are aware of the lack of a 'Truth' to any identification, will still behave as if traditional subcultural models were an accurate reflection of subcultural behaviour.

However, even with the contingency that Smith builds into her work, there are several flaws. Most significantly, she does not fully recognize the social nature of identification processes. She claims, in line with Bennett, that as individuals age they may choose to take an identification on and off and come back to the old identification (return to the neo-tribe) as they please. However, this may not always be possible. If we recognize that the creation of an authentic identification is not only individualized but also social, in relation to others who identify similarly, then we must recognize that exiting, even temporarily, from the identification may mean that other participants may reject one's later attempts at regaining authentic status. As Hodkinson (2002, 2011) has indicated, this may be particularly true for subcultures that require a high level of commitment to obtain authenticity, such as goth and punk. Other research has also indicated that the level of commitment is an important part of the process: 'When people are loosely connected to a lifestyle built around an identity, exiting is easier and has less impact on their new identity than it does when people are strongly enmeshed' (Menzies and Sheeshka 2012, 164). Therefore, the strength of one's attachment and the level of commitment necessary for authenticity in the eyes of others will play a significant role in determining whether or not one can enter and exit at their leisure.

Smith does recognize that continued participation in a scene can require shifts in one's behaviours that do not necessarily mean the loss of identifications. For older participants in the Northern Soul scene, 'There is the internal conflict between the identity of the participant in youth and of that participant, still in the scene, having to rectify the contradictions inherent in an *aged* youth identity' (2009, 441). Smith invokes the idea of nostalgia here to tell us that participants reflect upon the scene 'as it used to be' and compare it to the scene 'that is,' producing in them a unique perspective. However, Smith's analysis offers limited information about how people maintain a particular identification through these changes. Nostalgia may be a useful emotional tool, but this tells us less about the actual change process, especially in cases that might not always involve ageing. Furthermore, the very notion of nostalgia is limited when applied to other cultural groupings. Bennett (2006) finds this regarding older punks in England whose previous experiences in punk remain important to them, but it is not nostalgia that they experience; instead, these individuals celebrate 'punk's longevity … and [the] stylistic innovations of new punk generations' (230).

Hodkinson's (2002; 2011) work on the goth subculture is one of the best examples of subcultural work that focuses on the processes of change and ageing while maintaining an identification without suffering from some of the pitfalls mentioned above. His work shows, first and foremost, that individuals do not necessarily need to 'age out' of subcultural participation, as was previously noted. However, he also shows that we do not need to fall back on the myth of a stable self in order for the subject to remain identified with a given culture. Instead, both the subject and the culture, or the subject's experience of the culture, can shift to accommodate the ageing individual(s): 'As its participants have grown up together, the collective values, norms and infrastructure of the subculture have adapted to their shifting lives. Continuing participation, then, seemed often to have more to do with the collective negotiation of adulthood than with the individual quests to cling onto youth' (2011, 263). Thus, for Hodkinson's participants, continued participation into one's thirties, forties, and beyond coexisted with more stereotypically 'adult' roles in the workforce, education, and family. Therefore, 'continuing participation … might be better conceived not as an alternative to the development of adulthood, but rather as a fully fledged part of the process' (264).

Particularly important to this process of identification maintenance rather than rejection is the subjective feeling of attachment to the identification in question. A variety of works on subculture(s) (Hodkinson 2002; Vila 2012) have shown that for many participants, identifying as a subcultural member is of great personal consequence, and not likely to be given up lightly in spite of ageing or major life events. Instead, the identification is so important to the individual's sense of self that they will find ways to incorporate it into a changing life narrative. As I will show below, this is not surprising if we understand narrative identification theory.

While there is certainly a postmodern element to all of these works, emphasizing change, fluidity, and so on, they also challenge some of the post-subcultural approaches such as Bennett's (1999) work on 'neo-tribes.' Contrary to that approach, these works indicate that individuals in some cultural groupings cling strongly to their identification. Rather than opting in and out from moment to moment, they maintain their identification but with alterations that accommodate new statuses. Thus, for Hodkinson, 'goth as a community remained of great importance to participants. Not only did they continue to feel strongly attached to it in subjective terms but most had continued to understand goth as a specific set of collectively experienced tastes and practices' (2011, 277). Hodkinson claims that this is in part because of the strength of commitment that is necessary to maintain an authentically 'goth' self at a younger age. This necessity results in a level of commitment that is harder to walk away from than Bennett and other post-subculturalists found in their work.[66] In noting this, though, we must also recognize certain changes to one's behaviours

---

66 This is not to indicate that Bennett's work is inaccurate, but instead that it is contextual. It is certainly the case that some cultural groupings do behave in the way that Bennett describes, and thus can be accurately described as 'neo-tribes.' However, for some groups, such as the goths that Hodkinson interviewed and many punks, this is not the case due to the high level of commitment necessary to become an 'authentic' participant.

and signifiers, even if there is not a change to one's identification (meaning that one may change the *way* in which one is punk, goth, etc. and yet still claim to *be* these things, and that there is no *necessary* identitarian conflict in doing this). It is through narrative that we can best understand how this takes place.

Narrativity and the continuation of a life story

It is through a narrative approach to identification, coupled with Althusserian theories, that we can best understand the ways in which people engage with changes that have taken place in their lives. The narratological approach tells us that individuals organize their lives in storied formats; that people have 'plots' to their lives. A plot is a large, overarching direction in which people see their lives progressing. The other elements of our life story are always organized in relation to our plot. Furthermore, the various narratives that we recount about who we are will be told because of their contribution to the plot. Similarly, we will also leave certain stories *un*told at times because they do not fit our plot. In each of these stories, our identifications are characters (for example, those who were interviewed for this chapter worked from the hyphenation of at least two characters: the punk and the anarchist, creating the unification of the anarcho-punk character). However, while we will often be the protagonists of these stories, there will also be antagonistic characters, 'Others' that serve particular purposes in the progression of the narrative.

Such theories allow us to better understand how people both change and stay the same. While post-subcultural theorists have stressed the points of change and transition (and are not wrong to do this), it is important to remember that, in organizing their discourse, people will commonly articulate their sense of self as having been the same as in the past. The reason for this is easily explained with narrativity and Althusserian theory. Althusser tells us that individuals' identifications come into existence through an interpellative process, and in this process the individual 'turns toward' the hailing; it is in this 'turning toward' that the power of a particular discourse can produce subjectivity. From a narratological perspective, it is a particular character that is subjectivated in this process. However, a given character is necessarily part of the evaluative process of the hailing. Contrary to some of Althusser's work that implies a lack of agency on behalf of the subject doing the turning, narrative theories tell us that there is a back and forth between the potential subject and the discursive hailing. If an individual then chooses to invest identitarian meaning in the identification, this is because the new subjectivity somehow fits better with the existing plot; or perhaps the new hailing is so powerful or intriguing that an entire plot shift takes place, producing new characters, new narrative events, and so on. Regardless, the fact that the existing character had to invest in the identification indicates that the subject who existed at the moment immediately prior to the hailing was a part of the construction of the new subject that emerges. And, if we accept that people construct their lives in story, the future narratological process will allow for the previous self to be included in stories about the current or future self. The process allows us to understand continuity *and* change, similarity *and* fluidity.

To put it another way:

> In this sense, it is precisely the plots of my narrative identities (i.e., the narrative plots that sustain my imaginary and situational identifications) that help in the process of selectivity toward the 'real' that is concomitant to every identity construction. And this is done both retrospectively (when telling a story, for example), and prospectively, at the time of designing and performing an action. This is so because such projection and action are always done (at least initially, before the concrete social interactions modify the initial plan of action) from the point of view of what a character did in relation to such an action in the past, a character who is remembered for the person in question. That what the character does is 'habitual' or 'daring' does not change the fact that the action is done from a known character. (Vila, forthcoming, 54–5)

The given action could just as readily reference the 'turning toward' of Althusserian theory. Therefore, we see here that the existing characters are a part of the interpellative process. In regards to the process of a change to one's identification, the effect of this will be that the previous self will in some way be a part of the new self, even if that previous self goes 'unstated' in the new narrative. Thus, 'Following Derrida, we can say that all of them have the traces of many of the other possible identifications as the condition of the possibility of their own existence' (Vila, forthcoming, 60).

We should thus expect, following Hodkinson, that if a previously existing identification involved a particularly strong pull on the subject, as is the case with some subcultures, and if continued identification and participation are significant markers of authenticity, then the subject will find a way to continue with the existing identification, even through moments of change in their characters, behaviours, and signifiers. Following Vila, Seman, and Martin (2011), we can understand that this is because music is a particularly powerful performative sense (Butler 1990), and that this unique power results, for some, in an identification that 'sticks' quite strongly throughout life, meaning that the plot and character remain even through times of change. I will return to the importance of narrative later. For now, I wish to show how narrators approach these kinds of transitions.

From 'No Future' to 'Future': Travellers in the Punk Scene

It is not uncommon for participants in the nomadic elements of punk culture(s) to narrate their commitment to 'dropping out' of mainstream life as a form of opposition to capitalism, the state, or even civilization, and many will see this as a lifelong commitment. However, those discussed here have moved away from nomadism. It is important to recognize, though, that these individuals did not reject homelessness and nomadism as a part of rejecting punk or anarchism, but instead have produced a new part of their punk or anarcho-punk story that accommodates these characters. If one's plot determines the characters that exist within the narrative stories that form our identifications, then we have to understand that here the characters have not changed, and thus one of two things has happened: either their plot has not changed in the transition from traveller to 'house punk,' but new characters and narratives have been worked into the existing plot; or their plot changed to another that is capable of accommodating the punk or anarcho-punk character in new forms.

For many, their transition took place when they realized that some sort of future did exist for them. Narratologically, this is not coincidental. Narrative identification theories indicate that stories are constructed in the present but with an eye on the past and the future. Therefore, what we find is that the narrator's *particular* image of the future changed and expanded to either include a greater period of time in their life or new events that were not a part of their past futures.[67]

> Nate: It wasn't immediate, but I stopped hitchhiking. She [his daughter] was alive when I was still hitchhiking. I was going down to see her, but [seeing her] meant that I had to be places at certain times; it meant that I'd need a certain amount of money for things. And train hopping, I wasn't gonna do, due to safety: there's no sense in messing myself up when I've got my daughter. And hitchhiking … I would still hitchhike but timing wise it doesn't really work out now usually, and mostly I can't go hitchhike with my daughter.

Nate is one of two participants with a child who referenced parenthood as one of the reasons that they were no longer participating in nomadism. Specifically, we see here a narratological shift that takes place in relation to a dramatic event in one's life story: reproduction. Furthermore, we see here the way in which diverse identifications come together to produce a particular self. It is not just that these individuals are punks and anarchists, but they are punks and anarchists *who now have children*; each of these characters comes together. In this way, they feel that their identification had to change due to the life-changing event of parenthood. As Hodkinson (2011) pointed out regarding the goth subculture, 'such concerns meant that the onset of children often prompted a fairly significant decline in goth participation. Interestingly, though, continued subjective attachment to the scene and to social networks connected to it sometimes prompted parents to eventually find ways to overcome the obstacles' (Hodkinson, 2011, 270). In this case, it is less significant whether or not the participant still goes out to shows and other subcultural events (all do, though some less frequently than others) than that their subjective attachment remained a part of their narrative regardless of their current behaviours. While they once saw traveling nomadically as important, they were able to negotiate remaining subjectively attached to a punk identification throughout the transition into parenthood.

However, it is not only parenthood that allows for this kind of transition to take place. Other narratological changes can also produce shifts in behaviour.

> Jack: It's very exhausting, and it's a dangerous way to be. You know, everyday is a new sort of struggle, and that's fun, but it gets tiresome. You want to put some kind of foundation in your life so that you don't wake up every morning and think, 'All right, how am I going to make it today?' You do actually recognize the existence of a long term. I personally

---

67 I use the term 'past futures' to indicate previously existing narrative futures, meaning how the narrator had, in their past, imagined that their future might turn out.

have realized that I am going to be alive for many more decades, you know? And I need to start thinking with those decades in mind as opposed to the present day now. Years and years I spent not thinking about the future at all. And certainly there's relationships to punk rock with that … but, it's a terrible way to think about things … It's very romantic, but it's also really, I don't know, it's rough, it wears on you. There is something nice about saying, 'I'm going to be alive for a while' … Even stupid things like going to the dentist, or saving money, or anything like that … I almost had to consciously say, 'Look, cut some of the tumult out of your life, because it's wearing on you.'

Jack has no intentions of having children, and yet we again see a significant shift in his narrative that produced a more stable life. For him, train hopping and travelling were very romantic ways of being in the world. However, this romance also brought with it a level of struggle that 'wore on him.' Eventually, Jack came to realize that he was actually going to remain alive for a long time, and with this shift in the future of his narrative his behaviours also had to shift. In this realization, we should understand all the weight of his choice of the word 'romantic' to describe train hopping. We have to remember that nineteenth-century romanticism stressed 'authentic' aesthetic experience, as might be found by travelling freely and experiencing the country and world without the confines of normal 'tourist' experiences. However, this same philosophical school stressed awe in the face of sublime horror and terror, as when one might be confronted with the reality of death (Byrne 2006; Radley 1999; Wellek 1949). Therefore, the combined risk, beauty, and freedom of nomadism represent a romantic experience in the grandest meaning of the term.

There is also something deeper going on with Jack's narrative. Train hopping is potentially dangerous, and it is not uncommon to hear about people dying doing it. Therefore, it is not just that Jack 'realized' that he was going to be alive for a long time (though this may have happened), but that there was some sort of shift that produced this knowledge and resulted in Jack making choices that would further elongate his life. In other words, coming to believe that he would live a longer life itself produced actions that are likely to result in this being true. Presumably, he could have chosen to continue train hopping, perhaps even choosing to participate in even more dangerous activities and this would have resulted in his death being more likely. Thus, in Jack's case what we see is a narrative shift that resulted in a change in behaviour that reinforced the new narrative.

Paul's story, though different from the two above, shows a similar process by which the individual's narrative changes, and how this results in changes to behaviour:

Paul: It's almost experimental. I never really was into just traveling without a goal. I always liked to go somewhere and stay for a while, have a job and work there. Even when I was living in squats I was squatting and working … When you're traveling you can travel and that's fun. But when you're traveling that's all you can do. And you're experiencing something that's great, but you don't build skills. When you're stable somewhere it gives you a chance to really study something … I like carpentry, I like history. You can't really travel somewhere and get books from the library. It's really hard to get jobs or maintain any kind of real continuation of learning. And I guess this latest manifestation is sort of almost to see if I can do it, if I can get a house, if I can maintain having a truck and everything. I do have urges to get back on the road. I always feel like I want to hit the train. I hear the trains in the distance and totally want to do that again. But it's always there, it's not going away.

In Paul's case we can specifically see that while his behaviours have changed, his sense of self has not. He narrates himself as someone who always preferred to have a version of the travelling life that involved reading, working, and so forth. According to his narrative, he did not embrace what some other participants described as the 'nihilistic' side of the traveller lifestyle. Instead, he developed a positively oriented relationship to the lifestyle, while others did not. Again, though, it is this narrative that controls his behaviours. His narrative includes characters who like reading, working, and taking things seriously, resulting in a desire to have a lifestyle that allows for these things more easily than nomadism. Therefore, he had to change his behaviours for this part of his self – not the punk, but the dedicated person with desires that are not easily met on the road – to blossom.

In Paul, though, we also see something that was true of the other narrators, but less obvious. In rejecting their behaviours as a traveller, they did not reject the importance of that past self to their current self. As I said above, this previous character was a part of the interpellative process, and as such is also a part of the existing narrative(s). In Paul we see that he, at least at the time, felt that train hopping and travelling might be a part of his life again someday. For others, even if this is not going to be the case, the character of the train hopper is still a part of their stories, and remains one of several possible futures. They reflect upon this period of their life positively, they still interact with those who do travel in this way, and having participated in these activities is still an important part of their narrative. We thus see very clearly that these individuals have not 'become an ex' because they are maintaining the same identity labels that are of greatest importance. Instead, they have made a transition within an identification.

The possibility for this kind of maintenance of a previous self has been reflected in the narratives of other travellers as well. For example, in *One More Train To Ride* (2009), Cliff Williams quotes 'The Texas Madman' who says, 'When my mama [who was also a hobo] got pregnant with me, she settled down, but that didn't make her any the less of a hobo. She still had that spirit in her from when she was traveling and working like she was' (1). This spirit is what we see reflected in Paul and the other narrators above. Like the hobos in Williams' work, those here never lose their wanderlust and spirit of freedom. Instead, that spirit simply manifests itself differently. In fact, it may be easier for this to happen to punks than other nomads. If 'Hoboes feel shackled when they are living in normal society. Rules and regulations make them feel imprisoned' (1) and 'The hobo's yearning to rove is symptomatic of a larger spiritual yearning' (30), we might find that punk is a more comfortable place to 'settle' than a community trapped in the confines of mainstream society. The punk culture allows for the transgression of rules and boundaries, rejects authority, and works to exist outside of 'normal society.' Therefore, it may be easier to rest in punk even while maintaining the traveller self as a part of one's narrative.

This is a particular manifestation of the interpellative process. Ultimately, it is likely that the process of getting to this point in life went something like this: the individuals, at some point, were hailed by the discourse(s) of 'punk.' There are many different reasons that people narrate why they entered into this subculture that there is not space to account for here (see Avery-Natale [2016] for a full explanation of this), but regardless, they invested identitarian meaning in this discourse and created the character of the 'punk.' At some point, the punk character was exposed to the possibility of nomadism as a part of the punk character, possibly, though not necessarily, as a discourse of punk authenticity.[68] In doing so, they were interpellated as a traveller, a train hopper, etc., and this latter interpellation coincided with the 'punk' character and became one of the multiple characters that contributed to their narrative. Moving forward, a new interpellation took place – the responsible parent, the person with a future, etc. – producing a change in their narrative, or an already existing identification became more salient – the character who wishes to engage in carpentry and read history. However, this new character or narrative was, for any number of reasons, at odds with the character of the train hopper. Obviously, here we see that the train hopper character is a necessary part of the interpellative evaluation: this character evaluated the responsible parent, the person with a future, the worker, and found that they could not coexist within the same present. Therefore, one had to change. It is at this point that the future of the narrative takes a shift; effectively, the train hopper character 'loses' and becomes a part of the narratological past, but not a part of the present other than as a character that helped to create the present narrative and as a possible future character. In other words, when people tell stories about their present self and their present future, the train hopper is still present as a past self who engaged in the interpellative processes that create the present self and the new future. The train hopper is not gone – the character is present in the past and imagined into the future.

However, a crucial question remains: did their plot shift? I believe that, ultimately, it did not. Instead, new narrative identifications and new stories emerged within the confines of the already-existing plot. To understand why, we have to look again at Vila (forthcoming, 35):

> In this sense I think that we evaluate, provisionally and situationally, what the musical practice has to offer us in terms of interpellations in relation to the basic plots that are always behind the different narrative identities we construct to understand the diverse subject positions we end up accepting (through a complicated negotiating process) in our everyday life. Thus the narrative plots of our diverse narratives, provisionally and situationally, are responsible for the actual establishment of the different alliances we establish between our diverse, imaginary narrative identities and the imaginary essential identities different musical practices try to materialize.

---

68 Some may choose nomadism for a variety of reasons unrelated to punk as well, such as poverty coupled with a desire for travelling, a hobby all too often relegated to those with wealth.

The last sentence in the above is crucial: if it is our plots that are responsible for the linkages that exist between our various identifications, then the plot for these particular individuals has not changed. Instead, new alliances have been established between previously existing and newly existing characters. The most important of these previously existing characters was the punk or the anarcho-punk, and as we have seen this did not change. Instead, another character (the train hopper) worked alongside the punk character to evaluate the interpellative potential of a hailing. Through this evaluative process, a new alliance emerged between characters, and the train hopper was banished to the past and, maybe, the future, allowing a new character to materialize in the narrative, but still under the same plot. We know that this is the case because none of the characters have left the story entirely – they have simply changed their practices.

Conclusion

Post-subcultural studies, such as the 'neo-tribal' approach of Andy Bennett (1999), have emphasized that in the postmodern age there is a level of constant change to the identitarian commitments of cultural memberships. Undoubtedly, Bennett is right about this in some cases. However, as Hodkinson (2002; 2011) has shown, and as I have shown elsewhere (Avery-Natale 2016), this is not true for all groups. Instead, some groups demand a high level of commitment in order for a member to be perceived of as 'authentic.' What has been shown here is that there are various ways in which this commitment might play out. Commitment does not necessarily mean that the individual does not change. On the contrary, significant changes can occur. These changes, though, do not necessarily correspond to the loss of an identification or even to the wholesale exiting of a culture, nor do they correspond to the 'comings and goings' from cultural attachments that Bennett finds. Instead, narrators often find a way to maintain allegiance to the existing subculture, though in new and creative ways. These methods, however, are developed out of a limited number of resources afforded by the subculture. To maintain one's punk identification after a major shift, one still has to work with the existing discourses of authenticity that have been developed in punk scenes. Therefore, there is a level of relative consistency to the possibilities of identitarian attachment that limit the choices that an individual may make should they wish to maintain their authenticity as a subcultural member. How people navigate such shifts has been shown here.

References

Bennett, A. (1999). 'Subcultures or Neo-Tribes? Rethinking the Relationship between Youth, Style and Musical Taste.' *Sociology* 33 (3): 599–617.

Bennett, A. (2006). 'Punk's Not Dead: The Continuing Significance of Punk Rock for an Older Generation of Fans.' *Sociology* 40 (2): 219–35.

Brown, J. D. (1991). 'The Professional ex-: An Alternative for Exiting the Deviant Career.' *The Sociological Quarterly* 32 (2): 219–30.

Byrne, W. F. (2006). 'Burke's Higher Romanticism: Politics and the Sublime.' *Humanitas* 19 (1–2): 14–34.

Davis, J. R. (2006). 'Growing Up Punk: Negotiating Ageing Identity in a Local Music Scene.' *Symbolic Interaction* 29 (1): 63–9.

Degher, D. and H. Gerald. (1991). 'The Identity Change Process: A Field Study of Obesity.' *Deviant Behavior: And Interdisciplinary Journal* 12: 385–401.

Ebaugh, H. (1988). *Becoming an Ex: The Process of Role Exit.* Chicago: University of Chicago Press.

George, L. K. (1993). 'Sociological Perspectives on Life Transitions.' *Annual Review of Sociology* 19: 353–73.

Hodkinson, P. (2002). *Goth: Identity, Style, and subculture.* Oxford: Berg Publishers.

Hodkinson, P. (2011). 'Ageing in a Spectacular 'Youth Culture': Continuity, Change and Communist amongst Older Goths.' *The British Journal of Sociology* 62 (2): 262–82.

Logan, J. R., R. Ward, and G. Spitze. (1992). 'As Old as You Feel: Age Identity in Middle and Later Life.' *Social Forces* 71: 451–67.

Menzies, K. and J. Sheeska. (2012). 'The Process of Exiting Vegetarianism: an Exploratory Study.' *Canadian Journal of Dietetic Practice and Research* 73 (4): 163-168.

Radley, A. (1999). 'The Aesthetics of Illness: Narrative, Horror, and the Sublime.' *Sociology of Health & Illness* 21 (6): 778–96.

Sharp, S. F. and T. L. Hope. (2001). 'The Professional Ex-revisited.' *Journal of Contemporary Ethnography* 30 (6): 678–703.

Smith, N. (2009). 'Beyond the Master Narrative of Youth: Researching Ageing Popular Music Scenes.' In D. B. Scott (ed.), *The Ashgate Companion to Popular Musicology.* London: Ashgate Press.

Vila, P. (forthcoming). 'Introduction.' In P. Vila (ed.), *Music and Youth Culture in Latin America: Identity Construction Processes from New York to Buenos Aires.* Oxford: Oxford University Press.

Vila, P., P. Seman, and E. Martin. (2011). *Troubling Gender: Youth and Cumbia in Argentina's Music Scene.* Philadelphia: Temple University Press.

Wacquant, L. (1990). 'Exiting Roles or Exiting Role Theory? Critical Notes on Ebaugh's "Becoming an Ex".' *Acts Sociologica* 33 (4): 397–404.

Wellek, R. (1949). 'The Concept of "Romanticism" in Literary History. I. The Term "Romantic" and its Derivatives.' *Comparative Literature* 1 (1): 1–23.

Williams, C. (O). (2009). *One More Train to Ride: The Underground World of Modern American Hoboes.* Bloomington: Indiana University Press.

8. POWERVIOLENCE, OR HOW TO PLAY PUNK WITH A 'HAMMER'

BENJAMIN VAN LOON

Abstract

As a subgenre of rock 'n' roll, punk rock has itself spawned various sub-generic musical and subcultural followings – or cults, of a sort. While many of these sub-generic reinterpretations of punk rock – Oi!, crust punk, skate punk – can be connected to a single musical group or geographically collectivized group of musicians with an associated coterie of cult adherents, the way in which these sub-generic movements impact or affect the greater punk rock 'scene' is far more difficult to quantify. It is with this prolegomenon in mind that this essay will investigate the phenomenon of 'powerviolence' (Man is the Bastard, Infest, Mind Eraser, Iron Lung, etc.) by first tracing the musical and social provenance of the subgenre and then analysing it in its present form, which is both sub-subcultural (and localized as such) and internationalized (Yacøpsæ, Fuck on the Beach, Merda, etc.) in its sub-subculturalism. There is little documentation and no accessible scholarship on powerviolence, either as a musical and cultural genre or as an instantiation of punk rock. As such, this essay will compile and analyse the current documentation available regarding powerviolence, and perhaps not surprisingly, most of this documentation is available almost exclusively online. Varied in both form and articulation, that this material is primarily accessible through online avenues is also telling of the way powerviolence has not only survived as a genre but also how it has grown in its reception and realization.

Keywords: technology, powerviolence, Jacques Ellul, Guy Debord, Internet, Iron Lung, DIY culture

Benjamin van Loon is a writer and researcher from Chicago, IL. He is the co-founder and former managing editor of Anobium (www.anobiumlit.com), and his work can be viewed online at www.benvanloon.com. He holds a master's degree in communication, media and theater from Northeastern Illinois University.

POWERVIOLENCE, OR HOW TO PLAY PUNK WITH A 'HAMMER'

Context

The year is 1986 and we're in Los Angeles, California. It's the second year of Ronald Reagan's second term in the White House. The first test-tube baby, Robert Anthony Brewer, who was born in an LA hospital, is celebrating his first birthday. The Space Shuttle *Challenger* explodes on live television. The Tax Reform Act of 1986 bursts the American savings and loan bubble, leading to a nationwide economic crisis. A meltdown at the Chernobyl Nuclear Power Plant in the Soviet Union leads to the worst nuclear accident in world history. The first MS-DOS based computer virus, Brain, begins infecting personal computers. The Soviet Union launches the Mir Space Station. A DC-9 charter jet carrying sixty-seven people and a single-engine Piper carrying three collide over Cerritos, a southern LA neighbourhood, killing all aboard the planes as well as fifteen people on the ground. Whitney Houston, Heart, and Madonna are topping the pop charts. *Top Gun*, *Crocodile Dundee*, and *Platoon* are dominating the box office. TVs are tuned into *Cheers*, *The Cosby Show*, and *Magnum, P.I.* People are watching movies on VHS or LaserDisc, and listening to music on CD or cassette tape.

And, at least in the eyes of popular culture – having been thoroughly caricaturized, vilified, and sanitized through Hollywood films and other mainstream media – punk is dead.[69] At least, that's how it looked. But Los Angeles – a major cultural hub for punk rock from the mid-1970s and into the early 1980s – has long been a city suspended between its appearance and its 'reality.' These 'spectacular oppositions,' as Debord says, provide an overarching 'unity of misery' (2010, 63), which is to say that requisite with the tension of being suspended between these two supposed polarities – appearance and reality – a deeper psychic anxiety lurked in the bowels of the City of Angels. Even with punk rock *apparently* fading out in the mid-1980s, its relevance lingered, and congealed. It was no surprise, then, that the city that produced such volatile, precedent-setting bands like the Germs, FEAR, and Black Flag *also* produced punk rock's most twisted and bizarre subterranean spawn: powerviolence.

The powerviolence sound – championed by early genre innovators such as Neanderthal, Man is the Bastard, Despise You, and others – strips punk rock down to its basic song structure and time signature, but then speeds it up (when it wants) to counts over 400 bpm, with sudden stops and tempo changes, with guitar or bass drones; screamed or growled vocals; and an overarching lo-fi sound quality which is as confrontational as it is polarizing – much to the pleasure of the powerviolence crowd, themselves baptized in punk rock's contrarian waters. But as much as powerviolence is aggressive, confrontational, and depressive, it is itself the end product of a creative process; or what philosopher Jacques Ellul would call a product of 'technique,' which tends 'not only to create new environment[s], but alters man's very essence' (Ellul 1964, 325). It is thus no surprise that now, three decades

---

69 PUNK: Chaos to Couture (9 May to 14 August, 2013), http://www.metmuseum.org/exhibitions/listings/2013/punk.

later – even as punk rock has gone through various mutations, transformations, and manifestations on an international scale – powerviolence continues to persist (or subsist) in the same sorts of conflicted, chthonic spaces that hatched it in 1986.

In this chapter, I establish powerviolence not only as a type of spectacle as withdrawn from contemporaneity's 'unity of misery,' but also as a type of ambivalent technical production whose relevance continues to be as timely as it is superfluous. It's a musical scene, a punk rock subgenre, but there's much more to powerviolence than what we see on its surface (even if it is buried underground). But in order to understand what powerviolence was, and what it now is, we first need to explore the chain of events that led to its unofficial inception in 1986 (the key term here being 'unofficial'). And almost all accounts of the history of punk in LA go back to the early 1970s and core group of eccentric, artistic, and relatively well-connected anglophiles in Hollywood splitting their affinities between image-obsessed LA culture and the records, gossip, and appropriately image-obsessed media associated with Britain's newest export – glam rock (T. Rex, David Bowie, Roxy Music, etc.). The new genre – sassy, flamboyant, and confrontationally androgynous – was exciting to American ears and injected much-needed 'freshness' into what archivist and rock historian Greg Shaw called the 'lull in pop culture' in early 1970s LA (Spitz and Brendan 2001, 6).

What woke the city up was a small, intimate coterie of dedicated aesthetes looking to recreate the magic of UK glam rock for LA's fecund social scene, which saw moderate success by re-appropriating the genre as 'glitter rock.' This trend was largely led by LA-based music promoter Rodney Bingenheimer, along with friend and record producer Tom Ayres, who opened up the E Club in Hollywood in 1972, which later turned into the infamous Rodney's English Disco, attracting scene elites like David Bowie, Led Zeppelin, and many other central rock figures. Toby Mamis, PR giant, said, 'Rodney's was an epicenter. From the rock stars and would-be rock stars to the industry-ites to the teen girls and boys, it was the place to see and be seen' (Spitz and Brendan 2001, 15). Thus, aside from having created an LA cornerstone to double as a port district for British pop-culture products, Rodney's English Disco – with its requisite drug abuses and 'aberrant' sexual proclivities – also set an inviting precedent for the particular strains of punk rock music that would soon call LA home. As Shaw says, 'If New York punk was about art, and London punk about politics, LA punk was about pop culture ...' (Spitz and Brendan 2001, 72).

And pop culture, as Debord says, is about the spectacle (Debord 2010, 1). In the way the nascent scene of punk rock – at least in LA – was as much about the image of punk as it was about how the image moderated the relation between people, the LA punk scene became its own spectacle among spectacles. For the scene's early progenitors, as for this current retrospective, it is quite literally true that the spectacle 'is the historical movement in which we are caught' (Debord 2010, 11). And, for a while, it was Rodney's English Disco that had everyone buzzing.

After a few years in the early 1970s the novelty of glitter rock wore off, as did patronage at Bingenheimer's club, which was officially shuttered in 1975 – a casualty of what Debord calls 'banalization' (2010, 59). But it was during the club's death throes that LA's upcoming punk rock set began to get pulled into the gravity of the underground's changing tides, with Iggy Pop's drug-addled anthems on *Raw Power* and the Ramones brain-dead simplicity fully articulating rock's next sensationalist waves. Bingenheimer began DJing on LA's long-running KROQ radio station in 1976, where he continued to spin new, boundary-pushing music. 'As soon as I went on the air, from the first show on … I went right into punk. The first thing I played was the Ramones,' (Spitz and Brendan 2001, 58). And it wasn't too long thereafter, in the years between 1977 and 1979, that punk rock officially arrived in LA, with bands like the Screamers, the Zeros, and the Germs articulating their own West Coast take on punk's burgeoning iconoclasm. Though even in LA's punk rock infancy, an acute sense of media savvy dominated how these various bands formed and built an audience (Spitz and Brendan 2001, 67), suggesting that punk rock was not totally divorced from the mechanisms of the commercial system it so vehemently protested. Musician Kim Fowley sums it up nicely when he says:

> So [punk rock] went from the garage, through the radio, onto the stage, and into the *LA Times* and *Time* magazine. And of course, LA being a media center, everybody else soon picked up on it, and soon the rest of America was told about punk rock. Californian punk rockers, these throwing-up, open-sore, suburban callow youths, were suddenly the new cock-swaggering shit-asses after one gig apiece … (Spitz and Brendan 2001, 112)

Punk Rock in LA

Punk rock flavours of the week – each with their own legacy and mythos – came and went during the 1970s and into the early 1980s, but much like glam rock before it, punk rock in LA fizzled fast. This was due in part to the self-destructive mechanisms championed by LA's punk rock leaders, but also to the 'new wave' category concoction as dreamt up by the major record labels, like Warner Brothers and Columbia, which sanitized punk rock and thereby made it appealing to a wider audience (sanitization = revenue). 'When culture becomes nothing more than a commodity, it must also become the star commodity of the spectacular society,' Debord wrote (2010, 193) X, Devo (originally an Ohio band that moved to LA in the 1970s), the Go-Go's, and other bands that originally came into being in LA's underground had caught the ear of the majors and effectively gone 'mainstream.' Phenomena like Mercury Records' *Chipmunk Punk* or the Germs popping up on the 1980 Al Pacino vehicle *Cruising* soundtrack (or *Quincy*, 'Next Stop, Nowhere' [1982], *ChiPs*, 'Battle of the Bands' [1982], *Repo Man* [1983], *The Return of the Living Dead* [1985], etc.) further served to normalize punk rock by drawing it out from the underground and exposing it to a wider audience. It is in this vein that in a 1981 *Penthouse* article writer Robert Palmer criticized the LA punk scene, calling it 'derivative and doctrinaire,' but admirably championed by 'a handful of kamikaze bands' (1981, 47–8). But despite whatever bands made it out of the underground and into the Top 40, LA's street-level punk scene was one of recklessness, danger, and violence, even as the decade turned over, and it was precisely this dark seediness – and shades of resentment – that set a precedent for what would be the shape of punk to come as LA moved into the 1980s.

Leading LA punk bands like Middle Class, FEAR, and the Germs (and the ill-fated Germs front man, Darby Crash) would be the entities carrying punk into its sophomore years, framing the 1980s as the decade of hardcore (Blush 2010, 16). The spirit of nihilistic abandon and danger established, for example, at the Germs infamous shows between 1977 and 1980 (when Crash infamously died of a drug overdose) and FEAR's notoriously violent performances – some ending with police helicopters and SWAT vans – attracted a new type of audience that wasn't as interested in the artistic pretence of LA punk as it was in the cultural aspects of a music not yet commoditized; an impulse fuelled as much by grassroots artistic abandon as it was by the media hype surrounding hardcore's originations and ethos (Blush 2010, 211–12). Hardcore was angrier, louder, and more bitter than its punk rock older brother. It is with this new turn in mind that Palmer also wrote: 'Most of the punk groups play anarchic, sociopathic rock-'n'-roll noise for an anarchic, sociopathic youth subculture. In context, the music is chillingly specific. The decline of Western civilization? Could be, could be' (1981, 47–8).

It's no surprise, then, that if punk rock was bred on the streets of LA, hardcore came from the suburban communities in places like Hermosa Beach (Black Flag) and Long Beach (Vicious Circle). Early punk rockers entertained the idea of stardom, but hardcore had no such aspirations, citing the blue-collar, working-class presentation of bands like Sham 69 and the inane musical simplicity of bands like the Ramones as the would-be ethos of the movement (Blush 2010, 15–16). Stylistically, hardcore would be far faster and more contentious than its first-wave forebears, eschewing artiness and eccentricity for all-out aggression, which, as Blush theorizes, was informed partly by the alienation of its early innovators not only from the ageing Hollywood punk rock scene but also from their families and suburban communities – themselves developed by the massive mid-century utopian exurban effort that, by the 1980s, had shown itself to be fallacious and trapped in a downward materialist spiral. Blush puts it more bluntly when he says of the creators of hardcore music: '[They] lived as close to the American Dream as one could get' (2010, 16).

But proximity only partly serves to explain the new kind of aggressiveness encouraged and articulated by this hardcore sound. In a 1982 *Penthouse* article, journalist Robert Keating wrote: 'While punks in the original scene in London playacted a lot of bizarre and deadly games, punks in the LA scene accepted them as real' (1982). Rather than merely being 'close' to the so-called American Dream, these early hardcore innovators in and around LA – most of whom were teenagers or young adult men – lived close to the idealized *image* of the American Dream, with LA serving as the media centre for continued formations and formulations of this ideation. Debord speaks of the obliterative power of the spectacle – in our case, the spectacle of suburban American decorum as one spectacle among many – and how it drives all 'lived truth below the real presence of fraud ensured by the organization of appearance' (2010, 219). In the case of the hardcore culture confronting the materialistic utopian ideology of exurban LA juxtaposed against the harsh realities of early and mid-1980s urban life, the scene, with its anger and aggression, became an obvious cathartic outlet for the regional youths wittingly and unwittingly building on the pre-spectacular counter-cultural legacy established by the punk rock scene in the 1970s. This is a tendency meticulously depicted in Penelope Spheeris' iconic 1981 documentary *The Decline of Western Civilization*. Serving as both a document of the LA punk and hardcore scene at the beginning of the 1980s as well as a social snapshot of the disenfranchised culture surrounding it, Spheeris dedicated a significant portion of the film to some its young patrons, such as the bitter, shaved-headed Eugene who, in his own way, also speaks to this greater conflict between LA as it seems and LA as it is. Spheeris asks him why people fight at hardcore shows:

> Like, when you see a fight, all these people will rush over to the fight. They don't care who it is. … Just to get aggression out. That's why I do it. Just to get aggression out. All this fucking pent-up shit, you know? With me, this [pent up aggression] comes from living in the city, seeing everything – seeing all of the ugly old people, the fucking buses, the dirt. That's what I see all the time, and I'm just fucking bummed thinking about that. If I go [to a show] I can get out some aggression by beating up some asshole, you know? (Keating 1982)

'And We Goes to Hardcore'

Originating in California, but spawning similar scenes in cities like Washington DC, New York, and Boston, hardcore made waves across America throughout the 1980s. Though infectious, the rampant violence, tribalism, and general anti-social ethos – at least in the eyes of the pop media – supposedly traversed the path already cut through the thickets of pop culture by punk rock. Thus, without the mirror of pop media fuelling or informing the social role of hardcore, the development and dramaturgy of 1980s punk rock culture evolved outside of the mainstream spotlight, often being treated merely as nuisance and not an affective or notable cultural force (Blush 2010, 41). This in turn led hardcore's early leaders to eschew the rock star attitude touted by punk rock's earlier progenitors for a more independent, do-it-yourself approach to music-making and scene-building (56). Blush calls the hardcore economy that subsequently arose one of 'tribal syndicalism,' and explains that, 'Unlike money-oriented economies, [hardcore] arose as an objective-oriented, community-based culture, like a commune or an armed fortress' (319).

Bands like Black Flag (California), Minor Threat (DC), and Bad Brains (Washington DC, New York) led the hardcore movement, spawning countless imitators, scene factions, and territorial tiffs. And much like punk, hardcore was hardwired to fizzle out. Blush, whose work is easily the most authoritative in documenting the rise and fall of US hardcore in the 1980s, pinpoints 1986 as the year of hardcore's demise and the subsequent waning of punk rock's second major wave (348). Additionally, hardcore's self-destruction was augmented by the increased banalization of punk rock – the 'smug acceptance' of what exists merging with 'purely spectacular rebellion' (59). Milo Aukerman of the Descendents said, '[Hardcore] went from being incredibly obscure and dangerous in 1980, to 1986, where there was a more popular scene of very safe characters' (Blush 2010, 348). Black Flag, Dead Kennedys, and the Misfits all broke up in 1986; Hüsker Dü signed to Warner Brothers in 1986; Fugazi formed from the ashes of Minor Threat in 1986; bands like the Circle Jerks and TSOL crossed over into 'metal' – hardcore was growing up, shedding its youthful exuberance for prison, paying jobs, and pay-per-view.

Many of the original innovators of hardcore 'died, failed, lost interest, moved on, OD'ed, got girlfriends pregnant, whatever' (Blush 2010, 348), though the nihilisms, antagonisms, and disparities that powered its impact on the sub and counter-cultural music scene were still a social reality, thus demanding to be interpreted through a new lens. Hardcore was, by virtue of itself, short-lived (half of a decade is barely a blip in the greater timeline of modern music evolution), but it was around just long enough to leave an indelible mark on the next generation while simultaneously setting yet another precedent for the continued evolution of punk rock. The 'end' of hardcore at the close of the 1980s begged a new question: where does punk go next? In some ways, grunge picked up the punk rock flag at the end of the decade, but the new genre's tendency to fetishize apathy and ennui effectively sterilized the aggression and pathos that originally defined hardcore and punk rock in general. So in 1986 – especially in LA, a city that always took punk rock at face value – hardcore went deeper underground.

As the second-largest city in the US in 1986 after New York, LA functioned – and continues to function – as a major cultural and social centre both nationally and internationally. The years between 1980 and 1990 marked an especially volatile time for the city's growth, with its population growing 17.5 percent from 2.9 million to nearly 3.5 million over ten years. It was LA's largest population boom since the 1950s, but with that growth came the requisite pangs. In 1986 alone, LA had 820 homicides (Baca 2012), and though most of these were drug-related (Wilkerson 1987), the citywide violence reflected a more latent unease, manifesting economically, racially, and politically throughout LA. The violence continued to escalate into the 1990s, peaking in 1992, one of Los Angeles County's most violent years (Tita and Abrahamse 2010). And with punk rock ever caught in dialectical turmoil with the greater social (or ideological) condition, the negative tides of the city led to even more inventive and dynamic forms of catharsis and expression, first through hardcore in the early 1980s, and later with more clever spectacles. In 1986, emerging from the LA punk rock class, with their heroes disbanded and the LA streets literally awash with blood, a group of four LA natives – Joe Denunzio, Matt Domino, Dave Ring, and Chris Clift – answered the question of what would be next for hardcore. The four of them comprised Infest, the band that would soon open the door for a new faster, angrier, and more aurally confrontational style of hardcore – powerviolence.

Figure 8.1: Infest (1988) *Self-titled* 7" ep: California: not on label.

Origins of Powerviolence

The term 'powerviolence' was coined well after the formation of Infest, but it was the new musical precedent set by them that would officiate the sound and scope of the genre. A powerviolence retrospective from *Decibel Magazine* in 1997 summarizes Infest's sound as fusing, 'the youth crew-styled hardcore of the time (1986) and the proto-grind fastcore of Siege, Impact Unit … Holland's Pandemonium and Vancouver's Neos into short, undeniably violent-sounding bursts' (Bartkewicz 2007). The 19 songs from Infest's 1987 demo range in length from 35 seconds to three minutes and 43 seconds, with a total album time of 25 minutes, and the average song length at the end of Infest's eight-item discography would eventually hover around the 40-second mark. Each song is packed with short, fast, intense bursts, sudden tempo changes, sludgy breakdowns, and sound bites or noise, demanding a high degree of energy and precision as inspired by its metal/grindcore influences, but lax in production and delivery like its punk and hardcore forebears. Eric Wood, frontman of Man is the Bastard and a leading name in the powerviolence world, said of Infest, 'They were fucking blitzing power. Their first demo was a primitive recording but you could feel that everything was there, the emotion and the speed' (Bartkewicz 2007).

Matt Domino, Infest's vocalist, teamed up with Eric Wood, then of the band Pissed Happy Children, to form another group, Neanderthal, in 1989. According to Wood, the scene at the time was tight-knit and compact, so this kind of group crossbreeding was regular practice (Knight 2008). Drawing inspiration for Domino and Wood's attempts to forge new sounds, Neanderthal played music at grindcore's fast pace (the song 'Built for Brutality' on Neanderthal's *Fighting Music* 7" clocks in at 16 seconds), but did so in the spirit of hardcore, with lyrical content inspired more by politics and the DIY ethos than psychic angst. It was thus at a Neanderthal practice session at a place called the Kubby Hole in Pomona, California, that the term 'powerviolence' was coined. Wood explains, 'We wanted to come up with our own description of our sound, and out of the blue [Matt Domino] just said "fuckin' *powerviolence*." Then it was "West Coast Powerviolence." We were trying to give it a sense of humor, like "our geographical location is better than yours," and give it a serious brutality' (Bartkewicz 2007, italics mine).

Aided by the creation of Slap-a-Ham Records, a small record label set up by Chris Dodge – former member of No Use For a Name and a well-connected DIY guru – powerviolence found an official home. Dodge was interested in the bands not getting the level of attention he felt like they were due (Kautsch 1997), and in addition to releasing records by Infest, Neanderthal, Crossed Out, and other late-'80s/early-'90s up-and-comers, Dodge also released early records by bands like the Melvins and Fu Manchu, who would later gain tremendous notoriety in their own respective genres. 'My primary focus became what turned into the powerviolence scene. I loved the music and the people in the bands, but again, there wasn't really anyone else interested in working with them at the time,' Dodge says (Bartkewicz 2007).

Thematically and aesthetically, the advent of 'West Coast powerviolence' unfolded along similar lines to those of punk in the 1970s and hardcore in the 1980s, save that the counter-cultural punk rock path had already been blazed and well-trodden. By the beginning of the 1990s, punk rock – formerly a public nuisance – was less public and thus less of a nuisance. But as the genre *en masse* had unfixed its narcissistic gaze on media feedback – or as these aspects of punk rock culture had lost interest in gaining antagonistic mainstream media attention – the new punk rock Zeitgeist was thus allowed to mature (or stew) in its own subcultural, out-of-the-way, underground context. 'Separated from his product, man himself produces all the details of his world with ever increasing power ...' Debord commented, with coincidentally complementary vocabulary (2010, 33). Unconstrained by the artifice of outside expectations or manufactured pre-conceptions (such as those informed by the mainstream media feedback of punk and hardcore's earlier years) – and bolstered by continued disenfranchisement – the new genres of hardcore, especially powerviolence, more naturally lent themselves to experimentation. This tendency was soon crystallized in Eric Wood's group/collective Man is the Bastard.

In addition to standard hardcore tropes, MITB also incorporated more explicit elements of noise, loops, and DIY instrumentation into the hardcore canvas. Unlike Infest, Spazz, or No Comment – bands more simple and straightforward in their respective technical and musical approaches – Man is the Bastard eschewed the loud electrical guitars for louder bass scales and chords, field recordings, and power electronics jerry-rigged through amateur, built-from-scratch amps, speakers, and instruments. It's a musical approach that today earns certain musicians PhDs and MoMA exhibits, but during MITB's career from 1990 to 1997 it was experimentation for experimentation's sake (Knight 2008) – an approach itself reflective of the greater genre's tendency to play violent music, rather than to simply commit acts of violence. As Wood says, 'Powerviolence is kind of a weird moniker. I believe there was power in the documents that we recorded, and we did kind of get off on the violent hypothetical-ness of it. Power with hypothetically violent subjects' (Bartkewicz 2007).

The powerviolence records that came out in the 1990s are still considered definitive for the genre. The *Downsided EP* by No Comment, released as a 7" in 1992 by Slap-a-Ham, is serious and intense with its depressive aggression. The *Dwarf Jester Rising* album by Spazz, released by Clearview Records in 1994, while still 'dark' as a record, also incorporated humour in the more traditional 'hardcore' elements in the musical fabric. Lack of Interest and Slave State released a split EP in 1993 on Slap-a-Ham that established a reputation of musical brutality yet unmatched, and bands like Plutocracy, Stapled Shut, Bludgeon, and others have since faded into performative oblivion, but are nonetheless canonized for their contributions to West Coast powerviolence and their sonic diversity. Powerviolence had 'rules,' but they were (and are) treated more like loose boundary lines; a refreshing constancy when otherwise faced with the strictures of normal, day-to-day life.

Despite being unconstrained, powerviolence still functioned as the inheritor of the LA punk legacy, socially and economically. Though its message was more direct than punk – communicating social and political disenfranchisement through its art and its lyricism – it nonetheless functioned on the same economics of tribal syndicalism that, despite the aspirations of its primary producers, was and is less a regression towards an 'authentic' or humanistic form of production and exchange and more a pragmatic response to maintaining a sustainable economic system under the authoritarian umbrella of globalized commerce. In other words, if early LA punk was about pop culture, powerviolence was a contrarian response to pop culture and still 'about' pop culture as such. This tension is evinced most strongly in MITB's iconography, which, aside from the trademark skull logo – which Wood found 'in an archeological manuel [*sic*] in the reference section of the CLAREMONT LIBRARY one afternoon in ... early 1991' (Kautsch 1998) – also incorporated instances of Hello Kitty artwork, subverting it, desexing it, and rendering it absurd by juxtaposing it against MITB's bleak, black-and-white, cut-and-paste aesthetic landscapes. This is de rigueur pop culture lambasting.

Figure 8.2: Charred Remains AKA Man Is The Bastard (1992) *Backwards Species*, Germany: Ecocentric Records.

The Challenges of Powerviolence

Aside from some of the so-called 'great' powerviolence records from the 1990s, the decade was also replete with imitators and one-off experiments. This was due largely to increased accessibility to viable recording and communications technologies as afforded by the fast pace of technological evolution over the previous two decades – and here we breach the double entendre of *power*violence. In an interview Dodge explains: 'In the '80s, all of the bands recorded demos well before they released anything on vinyl. So, by the time they had a record out, they usually worked out the kinks, and were able to come out with a solid debut record. That all changed in the '90s' (Kautsch 1998). Technology, in other words, has always been in the background of the punk rock movement – itself the inheritor of the rock 'n' roll ingenuity of plugging a guitar into an amplifier (and rock 'n' roll the inheritor of the guitar, and so on, until Kubrick's man-apes went wild throwing the bone in the air) – but the rapidity of technological changes towards the close of the century lent themselves to easier production access, more affordable forms of reproduction, and essential changes in the propagation of punk rock culture (and perhaps underground music culture in general).

These changes thus framed the arbitrary conclusion of the first 'wave' of powerviolence, which many focus around MITB's disbanding on December 7, 1997 (a date significant for marking the fifty-sixth anniversary of the attack on Pearl Harbor, and a coincidence only worth mentioning for the fact that Wood himself draws attention to it) (Kautsch 1997). Though there are various early powerviolence aficionados who would argue or insist otherwise, powerviolence did not end when the SoCal scene died. The subcultural dominance of the genre ceded by the end of the 1990s, though there were newer bands from more disparate American geographies – like Charles Bronson from DeKalb, Illinois, Endless Blockade from Toronto, Canada, and Apartment 213 from Cleveland, Ohio – who carried the ethos of powerviolence into the end of the decade and a more proliferate technological age

A look at how powerviolence transitioned into the twenty-first century is telling about the fundamental nature of punk rock in general as a technological production/ phenomena. Punk is a culture that originated in modern media, and the artefacts of punk culture – the 7", 10", or 12" inch record; a CD or tape; a live performance; a recording of a live performance; merchandise; publications; websites; and other related physical and digital ephemera – are upheld as totemic or perhaps mystical by the punk rock laypeople (when you page through any punk rock zine or website, it's difficult to ignore the overarching theme of merch fetishisms). It is these products that bear the true history of punk rock, which, in support of its material media obsession, prefers to talk less and make more, as evinced by the oral narrative structures of contemporaneity's most authoritative punk rock chronicles, like those cited in this essay. In its own way, powerviolence and punk rock in general (and the rest of modernity, at that), are indebted to the auspices of technological production. It is here that, in characteristically Marxist mode, Debord locates the history of the struggle of society – the struggle for survival – on production, or more appropriately the development of productive forces (2010, 40). Technology, in other words.

In the little-known work by philosopher Jacques Ellul, *The Technological Society*, technology is cast less as an endless cessation of nifty artefacts and more as a deliberate *force*. Ellul calls it *technique*, which, over the course of history, ceaselessly tends towards ever-maximized efficiency at the cost of human freedom (1964, xxxiii). Both Ellul and Debord agree that as we have given ourselves over to these productive forces, we have gained a type of safety, but in the process have become enslaved to these forces supposedly guaranteeing our safety from the struggle for survival. 'Culture must conform to technique and encourage productivity' Ellul noted (353). In this way, we can begin to understand the scepticism and negativity of the powerviolence genre. Fundamentally, powerviolence is a creative expression, and much like the poetry of the depressive, the very act of creative expression – even if that expression wills destruction – is itself a form of confidence. Additionally, powerviolence, as the inheritor of the punk rock legacy, is duty bound to the auspices of technology for the mode of its creative expression. Technology as productive force is a necessary evil for powerviolence; hence the cynical tension of the genre. The confidence of powerviolence is conflicted, though it is also an adequate expression of our collective enslavement. As we have been cast into this *milieu* – a term Ellul often uses to describe what we would normally call 'the modern world' – we have found ourselves the inheritors of this slavish legacy.[70]

The technological mechanisms and extensions of those abstract productive forces that allowed the genre's growth and development throughout the 1990s are ultimately what led to the genre's preservation and wider geographical reception, which actually comes as a surprise to many of the genre's early innovators. When asked how he feels about newer bands being categorized as powerviolence, Eric Wood – ever volatile in his opinion – says categorically that, 'It is a joke and I am sure [Matt Domino of Infest] would agree. Start your own motherfucking genre!! That's where it's at!' (Kautsch 1997). Countering this opinion, Andy Stick wrote in issue 15 of *Short Fast & Loud*, 'Power Violence was always West Coast Power Violence in the past, [but] now it comes from everywhere' (Stick 1993). The appeal of powerviolence is in the wide range of ways its generic rules are interpreted and translated, though after 2000 these interpretations were filtered almost exclusively through the Internet.

A genealogy of powerviolence from the early 2000s to the time of this writing is difficult, partly because we are still in the midst of its unfolding narrative, and partly because the polyphonic tenor of our 'Information Age' precludes simple, linear narrative summarization. And yet, this latter element is similarly telling about the current so-called 'state' of powerviolence, as it is boiled down almost exclusively through various social media outlets, websites, and other Internet-based resources. Ellul writes that, 'The machine tends not only to create a new human environment, but also to modify man's very essence' (1964, 325). The same can be said of culture (or subculture). Andy Stick summarized this thought more succinctly when he wrote, 'I'm not going to talk about the Internet and how everything is so much different these days and blah blah blah kids in 2006 just don't have the same ideals we had in the 70s/80s/90s/post-WWII baby boom etc. etc. I don't want to be that guy … things change, old people should be pushed out of the way and younger and more enthusiastic people should take over and direct wherever hardcore's going' (Stick 1993).

In a 2013 conversation with Nicholas Pell, music journalist, founder of the I Heart Powerviolence website, and self-proclaimed powerviolence expert, Pell mentioned the lull in the powerviolence scene from 2000 to 2006, and attributes the subsequent revival solely to MySpace.[71] MySpace is now out of favour (in 2013, anyway), but the Internet fervour continues, and though some web-based communities are supplemental to thriving, localized powerviolence/fast hardcore scenes, most seem to function as the primary cultural onus, supposedly describing the same sort of experience one might have had in the past at record-listening parties or concert venues. This is the essential change Ellul means when he says, 'the machine has enriched man as it has changed him' (1964, 325). This

70 The blind irony of 'No Man's Slave' by Infest – that we are indeed no man's slave, but slaves all the same.
71 From an e-mail conversation.

shift to the virtual also explains the strange Internet phenomena where the propagation of powerviolence culture is contained almost exclusively in the material productions of that culture, rather than the 'real' physical experiences and encounters with that culture; a byproduct of the commodification of culture (Debord 2010, 193). Often, it seems that the only difference between a powerviolence aficionado and a record collector is the choice of t-shirt. Alternately, the Internet allows for new individuals and new cultures to be exposed to (and thereby partake in) new ideas, worldviews, and lifestyles that, in the past, would have been entirely inaccessible or unknowable – like West Coast Powerviolence in the early 1990s. What we have now, over two decades from the origination of the genre, is the instance of 'powerviolence' situated within an evolved political, economic, and social milieu, such that powerviolence – while sometimes having the same sounds and signatures as its forebears – claims a type of relevance for its creators and appreciators that was not originally comprehensible in its genesis.

In his essay 'A Bastard Noise: Power Violence Lives on in a New Generation,' writer Andrew Childers argues that. 'Powerviolence was predicated on the notion of self-reliance and, for better or for worse, being DIY in the digital age is as simple as registering a Bandcamp account. Lowering the barrier for participation has democratized punk ever further, allowing an even wider variety of voices to be heard' (2013). This digital age, in other words, has altered the basic nature of DIY, and ease of access into the otherwise cloistered scene requires little more than a few digital sound files and the right meta keywords. The 'democratization' of punk via the wider democratization of information has served to spur the growth of powerviolence across the globe. Childers notes that, 'Holland boasts Jesus Crost and F.U.B.A.R. while Canada birthed bands like The Endless Blockade, Detroit and Greber. Power violence has found a particular toe hold in South America where Beatriz Carnicero represents Uruguay while bands like Chulo find the style perfectly represents the political and cultural ethos of modern Colombia' (2013).

Thus, locating themselves in different cultural contexts, the powerviolence groups – though tapping into a more unified punk rock history – are likewise responding to their own cultural conditions. Sebastián Barragán, vocalist and guitarist of Chulo, says, 'We try to put everything about [Chulo] in Spanish (words and phrases we normally use in our daily basis), from the samples we use for some tracks to the lyrics and titles. We also try to blend different components from other genres into our song structures so that it may result as an appealing sound to anyone, even if that person has been listening to hardcore punk and/or PV since a long time [sic]' (Childers 2013). Reliance on the nuances of idiomatic expressionism has long been a troupe of punk rock, but as it adapts to a particular culture the more universal relevancy of punk rock is further boiled down or made to fit a particular context. And, as it is often used as a creative outlet, this condensation has a far from negative impact for the greater punk rock tradition. That powerviolence was able to grow beyond Los Angeles County is a testament as much to the music as it is to the passion and foresight of the people who comprised the early West Coast Powerviolence scene.

Today, bands like Weekend Nachos from DeKalb, Illinois and Iron Lung from Seattle, Washington DC are leading the powerviolence charge in America, though Iron Lung – the two-member band that also operates a record label, Iron Lung Records – sets a high bar for the 'business' of powerviolence in the twenty-first century. The label and its bands tour extensively and internationally, have an incredibly interactive online presence, and sign bands that aren't 'powerviolence' per se but simply play music in the same confrontational punk rock vein. In the United Kingdom in 2012 the No Clean Singing record label released a massive, forty-six-track powerviolence comp called *The Only Good Tory*, showcasing some of the UK's current powerviolence and fast hardcore leaders, like Incest Funfare, Black Monolith, Botched Copy, and others. In Japan, powerviolence (and punk rock in general) has had a longstanding stakehold, with bands like Fuck on the Beach, Slight Slappers and G.I.S.M. functioning as the country's main powerviolence/hardcore exports, and bands like Tokyo's Vivisick and Nagoya's Unholy Grave carrying grindcore influences into the genre. South America is producing bands like Brazil's Leptospirose, Arquivo Morto, and Pode Pá (who all play in the spirit of early Brazil punk innovators Fogo Cruzado), Chile's Fuga and Antitrust, Argentina's Federico Luppi, and many others throughout South and Central America. Though it's a small subculture – internationally claiming only a few thousand fans and participants – its reach is widespread and its networks intimate, bound by a common interest and a common force. Childers writes, 'The times and tools may change but there's a commonality of intention, a disdain for compromise that links today's neoviolence bands with their musical ancestors. There's a similar drive to play the most destructive hardcore that they can hammer out, standing out in defiance of fashions, trends and shifting public tastes' (2013).

Even after over forty years, punk rock continues to be a relevant force in the world, and though the message of punk is perhaps not perfected in powerviolence it is effectively exposited. Powerviolence was lifted out of the media-saturated culture of Los Angeles and through the ambivalent forces of technology and production – themselves determinants of LA culture – introduced and evangelized to the remote corners of the globe. The dark pessimism of the genre is the result of both creative expression and a useless protestation against the governing dictates of 'technique.' 'The human race is beginning confusedly to understand at last that it is living in a new and unfamiliar universe' (Ellul 1964, 429).

> *Can you feel my pain*
> *Reaching boiling point*
> *Gonna take you all out*
> *Make you all pay*
> *In my world*
> *My fucking world*
> *My way*
> ('The World My Way,' Infest, from the LP *No Man's Slave*.
> Deep Six Records, Draw Blank Records, 2002)

References

Baca, L. D. (2012). *Los Angeles County Sheriff's Department—Department Crime Statistics 1920–2012* (report). Los Angeles: Los Angeles County Sheriff's Department. http://file. lacounty.gov/lasd/cms1_189076.pdf.

Bartkewicz, A. (2007). 'Screwdriver in the Urethra of Hardcore.' *Decibel Magazine* 33.

Blush, S. (2010). *American Hardcore: a Tribal History*, 2nd ed. Port Townsend, Washington: Feral House.

Childers, A. (2013). 'A Bastard Noise: Power Violence Lives on in a New Generation.' *Grind and Punishment* (July 22). http://grindandpunishment.blogspot.pt/2013/07/a-bastard-noise-power-violence-lives-on.html.

Debord, G. (2010). *Society of the Spectacle*. Detroit: Black & Red.

Ellul, J. (1964). *The Technological Society*. New York: Vintage Books.

Kautsch, A. (1997). 'Chris Dodge Interview.' *Short, Fast & Loud* 24: 10–11.

Kautsch, A. (1998). 'Bastard Noise: Electrifying Precision Skull Madness.' *Short, Fast & Loud* 24: 8–9.

Keating, R. (1982). 'Slamdancing in a Fast City.' *Penthouse* 77–8, 149, 156–8.

Knight, J. (2008). 'Eric Wood from Man Is The Bastard.' *Vice* (October 1, 2008). http://www.vice.com/read/eric-wood-158-v15n10.

Mullen, B., D. Bolles, and A. Parfrey. (2002). *Lexicon Devil: the Fast Times and Short Life of Darby Crash and The Germs*. Los Angeles: Feral House.

Palmer, R. (1981). 'End of the World.' *Penthouse*, 47–8.

Spitz, M. and B. Mullen. (2001). *We got the Neutron Bomb: the Untold Story of L.A. Punk*. New York: Three River Press.

Stick, A. (1993). 'Kick Ass, Let's Fucking Go; I Was a Teenage Fuck Up; (Don't) Voice Your Opinion.' *Short, Fast & Loud* 15: 5–7.

Tita, G. and A. Abrahamse. (2010). *Homicide in California, 1981–2008: Measuring the Impact of Los Angeles and Gangs on Overall Homicide Patterns* (report). Sacramento: State of Califorina, Governor's Office of Gang and Youth Violence Policy. http://www.calgrip. ca.gov/documents/Homicide_CA_1981_2008_Tita.pdf.

Wilkerson, I. (1987). 'Urban Homicide Rates in U.S. Up Sharply in 1986.' *New York Times* (January 15). http://www.nytimes.com/1987/01/15/us/urban-homicide-rates-in-us-up-sharply-in-1986.html.

9. MAKING DO IN 'WEIRD' VANCOUVER: DIY, UNDERGROUND VENUES, AND DOCUMENTING A SCENE

BRIAN FAUTEUX

Abstract

Largely due to Vancouver, Canada's growth and the city's 'urban renewal,' municipal restrictions and regulations concerning the sale of alcohol at venues and the emission of noise have created an environment in which live music venues are often forced out of business. However, the city's weird punk scene – marked by an aesthetic that blends garage punk and noise music – has enabled bands to make use of tactical spaces, illegal and otherwise, that do not require a certain standard of acoustics, such as warehouses, basements, and parking garages. Using examples such as the *Emergency Room Vol. 1* compilation album, this paper argues that collaboration between individuals and different cultural institutions enables a vibrant music scene to be built through the DIY recording of musical moments. By exploring the scene's creative output, its coverage in the media, and municipal live music policies in Vancouver, this chapter argues that the city's weird punk scene has been formed in response to, and has effectively challenged, restrictive municipal policies that favour middle and upper-class residential and commercial development.

Keywords: punk scene, Vancouver, DIY, weird punk, live music policy

Brian Fauteux is Assistant Professor of Popular Music and Media Studies at the University of Alberta. He researches the circulation of music, often through music scenes and/or by radio. He holds a PhD in Communication from Concordia University and his recent book, *Music in Range: The Culture of Canadian Campus Radio* (2015), explores the history of Canadian campus radio, highlighting the factors that have shaped its relationship with local music. E-mail: brian.fauteux@gmail.com

MAKING DO IN 'WEIRD' VANCOUVER: DIY, UNDERGROUND VENUES, AND DOCUMENTING A SCENE

Introduction

Largely due to Vancouver, Canada's growth and the city's 'urban renewal,' municipal restrictions and regulations concerning the sale of alcohol at venues and the emission of noise have created an environment in which live music venues are often forced out of business. The September 2008 edition of Canada's *Exclaim!* magazine profiled the Vancouver 'weird punk' scene and the ongoing struggle to keep venues operating in the city's Downtown Eastside. The article explained how 'greedy promoters and over-zealous cops' have shut down venues as fast as they were created (Hughes 2008). Artists and fans are thus continually forced to renegotiate the spaces and places central to live music performance and social interaction. However, the weird punk scene, marked by an aesthetic that blends garage punk and noise music, has enabled bands to make use of tactical spaces, illegal and otherwise, that do not require a certain standard of acoustics, such as warehouses, basements, and parking garages. A DIY ethos, which has been a consistent marker of punk and its subgenres, is likewise integral to Vancouver's weird punk scene.

Vancouver's weird punk scene was built and reinforced in the mid to late 2000s. The growth of the scene was aided by processes of documentation, namely a compilation album that recorded the musical activity that took place at a short-lived illegal venue called the Emergency Room (the ER). *Emergency Room Vol. 1* (2008) is an inspiring document that demonstrates the effectiveness of establishing the means to create culture and defy larger bureaucratic frameworks and systems of power. Moreover, since the demise of the Emergency Room, other bands and cultural producers have made use of underground and alternative performance spaces in the city. By exploring the scene's creative output, its coverage in the media, and Vancouver's municipal policies pertaining to live music, along with drawing on two interviews with individuals who have been involved with punk music in Vancouver, this chapter argues that the city's weird punk scene was formed in response to, and has effectively challenged, restrictive municipal policies that favour middle to upper-class residential and commercial development. Likewise, I argue that the coverage the weird punk scene has received points to the accomplishments of the individuals who have organized illegal and underground live shows, even if the attention has not always been well received by the community.

The scene communicates specific local characteristics, as this chapter will further detail, but weird punk has also figured in online discussions about a larger shift to the *weird* in punk music, often in the context of bands experimenting with their sound. This demarcates the scene as both local and virtual and situates it within both local and translocal scene studies (see O'Connor 2002 and Hodkinson 2004, respectively), as well as those that highlight the relationship between the local and the global (Guerra 2015). Studies of music scenes privilege geography, institutions, technology, and social situations over the focus on style, youth, and class that defined earlier subcultural studies (Hebdige 1979). That said, the ways in which participants in weird punk win space for the performance of music, particularly against a trajectory of 'creative class' urban development, also reflects a subcultural framework (Downes 2012). As with other scenes and musical moments from punk's popular history, Vancouver's weird punk has entered into systems of popular reception that attempt to define and make sense of its parameters and output. The publicity surrounding the scene proves that it executed an effective challenge to Vancouver's city policies concerning the performance of live music and serves as an inspiring example for future advocates of *weird* culture and music.

'Weird Punk'

Vancouver is home to a punk scene that dates back to the late 1970s when bands such as D.O.A. and the Subhumans were first active. In a review of *Bloodied But Unbowed*, a documentary on Vancouver's early punk scene, Marsha Lederman highlighted a defining dichotomy in Vancouver: 'a sleepy West Coast town with a thriving punk scene' (2012). This dichotomy persists in discourse surrounding the city's weird punk scene. Music journalist Josiah Hughes drew upon it in his description of the subgenre's sound, highlighting the ways that it straddles 'the line between harsh noise experimentation and pre-punk dirty rock 'n' roll. This is reactionary music, railing against the endless boredom of the city, the ignorance of genre restraints, and the rain-filled dreariness of everyday lives' (Hughes 2008). Bands and artists operating within this scene have harnessed this sound by employing a DIY ethos. According to Hughes, Vancouver's weird punk bands 'have inspired a counter-cultural renaissance by putting on their own shows (often inventing new venues in the process), recording their own demos, and releasing limited, often handmade pressings of their music.' A subgenre of punk by its very name, weird punk reflects the fluid, elusive, and hybrid nature of musical classifications (Magaldi 1999, 309; Toynbee 2000, 103–4), incorporating the sounds and styles of noise, garage punk, and grunge.

Throughout 2007 and 2008 the descriptive label 'weird punk' circulated in a number of posts on the *Terminal Boredom* community forums.[72] Users attempted to make sense of the term's migration from being used in jest by a select few to appearing in popular publications. In 2007, one forum member shared an article that was written for Concordia University's student newspaper *The Link*. The article promoted a new weird punk DJ night called Time's Up that was hosted on Thursdays in a Montreal bar called Black Jack. Some users found it funny that the term had achieved a notable level of recognition. A user named Eric Cecil claimed to have been 'there for the genesis of the phrase,' adding that 'WEIRD

---

72 *Terminal Boredom* is an online webzine that features and reviews underground music see http://terminal-boredom.com.

PUNK was a far bigger laffnahaff when [he and his friends] would laugh about it in [his] matchbox living room on Hoyne' (*Terminal Boredom* 2007). Now that 'weird punk' had been legitimized 'to the extent that [it was] appearing in music-related columns,' he was not sure he could 'get behind it anymore.' However, a number of users emphasized the positive results of having a term like 'weird punk' catch on. Responding to the Time's Up post, a user named Clint said, 'Sure it's all funny and stupid (not to mention non-descriptive), but the 'weird punk' tag has definitely helped Rapid Adapter get shows' (*Terminal Boredom* 2007). In early 2008, DJ Rick took to the forums to proclaim that, 'For so long, it was the WRONG thing to be on the border between garage and "art" or "experimental," and now look! You can make this music and actually find fans' (*Terminal Boredom* 2008).

For better or worse, weird punk caught on. Its use suggests that the term was a fresh and novel take on the broader punk genre. In 2008, the annual Pop Montreal festival included a weird punk showcase. Writing for the now-defunct alternative weekly *Hour*, Steve Guimond explained that, 'One of the most innovative and, simply put, awesome series taking place during the mass of Pop Montreal 2008 is the weird punk showcase featuring a ton of killer, on-the-edge bands from here and abroad (i.e., the USA)' (Guimond 2008). André Guerette of the Montreal-based band AIDS Wolf and concert promoter Blue Skies Turn Black said, 'The idea was to put something together that would cater to people like us who like this kind of music, and also to give props to a young, emerging scene of really, really interesting new punk bands ... that don't sound like the archetypical punk rock' (Guimond 2008).

As the decade neared its end, the attention that the subgenre was receiving began to wane. A *Terminal Boredom* forum post in March 2009 joked, 'now that weird punk is dead ... what is the next new wave of hyped shit? post-grunge? weird funk? riot grrl drone-wave?' (*Terminal Boredom* 2009). The post's tone paralleled a 2009 interview with *Terminal Boredom* editor Rich Kroneiss in the *Village Voice*. Kroneiss commented on the site's beginnings as a 'small webzine where garage rock aficionados critiqued new (preferably vinyl) releases,' and a message board that 'soon attracted a wider arena of amateur opinionators who vented on everything from haircuts to shitty days jobs' (Krinsley 2009). This nostalgic description of the site's origins is contrasted with a more-recent moment, when *Terminal Boredom*'s focus on lo-fi and garage music was 'crossing wires' with the tastes of larger music blogs and websites such as *Pitchfork*. Kroneiss explained that exposure 'isn't necessarily bad, but it can mean you get a lot of lame people hanging around trying to stick their noses in who didn't [originally] care. People not in line with the original vision of the community' (Krinsley 2009). Kroneiss' wariness of *Pitchfork* reflects a tendency in independent music cultures in which insider participants feel threatened when marginal music crosses over to the mainstream (Kruse 2003, 6). However, as Sarah Thornton's work on dance clubs and subculture emphasized, 'Niche media like the music press construct subcultures as much as they document them' (1996, 117). Discussion forums and the music press helped solidify the actions and work of a number of cultural producers, musicians, and artists in Vancouver and elsewhere, highlighting the effectiveness of this musical moment, especially in relation to oppressive municipal policies and developmental trends that suppress live music.

'No Fun City'

The first time Vancouver was publicly described as 'No Fun City' was in 2002 (McCormick and Antrim 2013). It is a title that reflects the city's poor reputation for supporting live music. In fact, *No Fun City* (James and Kroll 2010) was a documentary that showcased and profiled a number of venues, promoters, and bands that struggled with city policies in their efforts to put on live music. Hughes' *Exclaim!* article situated the scene within the larger problematic state of live music in Vancouver. He explained that Vancouver's Downtown Eastside 'has an oppressive, negative mystique that can drown inhabitants completely if they aren't careful ... It doesn't help that the bars are going through a cultural gentrification,' using the example of the Astoria, a 'once seedy punk club' that 'has built a new stage and switched its focus to DJ nights.' Mish Way, the vocalist for 'messy punk combo White Lung,' also commented on the transformation of the Astoria, noting that, 'they cleaned it all up and now, no more bands. They'll spend the next few months cleaning coke and lipstick off the toilet stands' (Hughes 2008).

Vancouver reflects a wider trend in municipal and cultural planning initiatives that were implemented alongside a rise in the perceived importance of fostering a city's 'creative capital.' For instance, Toronto, Canada's largest city, developed plans and invested money to rebrand the city 'as a cultural hub in an effort to attract highly educated, young professionals ... sparking what officials referred to as a 'Cultural Renaissance'' (Finch 2014, 2). Critics remarked that what surfaces from conceptions of 'an ideal citizenry (the 'creative class')' and an ideal city ('the creative city') are 'cities that are marketed as creative through the promotion of recently developed, high-end cultural institutions, but lacking infrastructural substance and a vision of what economically productive creative work actually looks like' (Finch 2014, 8).

A 'living first' ethos promoted by the City of Vancouver fits within this trend, one that has been described as part of 'a commitment to making the city a liveable place for its residents and reinvigorating its central areas' (Pickersgill 2006, 4). It is an approach to urban planning that advocated for population density in the city and for catering to residential life (as opposed to, say, entertainment or nightlife). Through Local Area Planning (between 1973 and 1985) the City has 'recognized the right for communities to live in amenable and attractive neighbourhoods' (Pickersgill 2006, 78), but an outcome of this adjustment of land use 'was a rationalization that allowed the exclusion of nighttime urban activity and vitality in neighbourhoods' (Pickersgill 2006, 79). Tensions have arisen as the city's growing population moves into areas that regularly feature late night live music. As a result, large entertainment spaces have been strategically concentrated on Granville Street in Vancouver's downtown core. Brian King, the singer and guitarist in Japandroids, criticizes this concentrated entertainment district in *No Fun City*, pointing out that, 'A lot of people don't want to go to Granville Street on a Friday night to get drunk and listen to a bunch of shitty music. Some people just want to go in their regular clothes and drink cheap beer and hang out with their friends and listen to … the Stooges or something. And there aren't a lot of legit places to do that in Vancouver' (James and Kroll 2009).

Critical attention has focused on the preferential treatment that residential and daytime commercial establishments have been given over live music and late night spaces. An article published on two Canadian web magazines, rabble.ca and *The Mainlander*, argued that noise pollution resulting from the 'rapid development of condominiums dominates Vancouver's soundscape, while relatively minor sound intrusions of live music – in the streets, in public venues, or private spaces – are regularly restricted by city officials' (Young 2014). The article explains that this discrepancy is a result of the city's Noise Control Bylaw (City of Vancouver 2014), which favours developers 'and shrouds musical/cultural sound policy in a cloud of ambiguity, hyper regulation and selective enforcement' (Young 2014). The noise control bylaw points to the potential for radio sounds, musical instruments, and voice amplification equipment to cause 'an unreasonable disturbance,' a phrase that is vague and open to interpretation.

These vague and confusing municipal policies, and the means by which they are enforced, extend beyond the city's noise control bylaw. For instance, there is no separate business licensing system for live music. The city has worked to broaden the variety of entertainment allowed in restaurants through amending its bylaws, but these changes have not made things more clear-cut for live music spaces (Pickersgill 2006, 112). A major result of not having a licensing system that 'articulates and separates live music as an activity' is a 'decidedly complex, difficult, and often expensive set of procedures for facilities and venues that wish to provide live music or entertainment, and particularly if they wish to serve alcohol' (Pickersgill 2006, 112). Due to a lack of clear and fair guidelines for live music venues to sell alcohol – an essential means for a venue to sustain its operations and meet its financial obligations – smaller performance spaces have suffered.

The city's frequent and numbered venue closures have been attributed to these poor city planning and municipal policies. A 2013 article published by Straight.com listed all the venues that faced evictions and closures since the beginning of the year. This list included the Waldorf, the Junction, Rhizome, John, the Mansion, the Nines, ROYGBIV, and Nowhere (McCormick and Antrim 2013). Many of these venues 'were small community spaces created out of nothing by passionate, independent artists in the most expensive city in North America, and without any support or legal recognition from the City' (McCormick and Antrim 2013). The article explained why the Zoo Zhop, a Downtown Eastside record store and music venue that held live concerts since 2009, was the city's latest 'cultural causality.' A surprise inspection by the Vancouver fire and rescue services resulted in a list of extensive repairs that would need to be completed in order to stay open. An odd move since the list was preceded by a demand to cease holding live performances entirely.

Interestingly, the city is aware of its need to update policies that shape live music performance. The City of Vancouver's Live Performance Venue Regulatory Review was initiated after the Culture Plan for Vancouver 2008–2018 and the Cultural Facilities Priorities Plan 2008–2023 'found Vancouver's regulatory system (by-laws and processes) to be one of the major impediments to the sustainable creation and operation of cultural spaces' (City of Vancouver 2011). The Live Performance Venue review was launched in 2009; the first of two reviews, the second focused on Artist Studios (launched in 2010). Community roundtables took place under the review, identifying nine key issues with the city's regulatory system that are impeding the operation of live music spaces, including: contradictory and outdated policies, restrictive requirements and permitted uses, complex processes, noise complaints, and inconsistent and costly fees for permits and licenses. More specific issues pulled from the review included the fact that when alcohol is served the existing bylaws make it difficult to hold events, especially for licensed events for more than sixty people. Venues that host more than sixty people and serve alcohol are required to either double their exit capacity or reduce the number of guests by fifty percent. The review recommended reducing the need to always mandate this requirement for both temporary and permanent event spaces.

A second major issue identified by the review is that costly upgrades are required to use a non-assembly space for an event. These upgrades are often tedious and do not adequately take into account the temporary nature of the event (as was the case with the Zoo Zhop). Likewise, there are numerous city approval processes for each event, which means that organizers must obtain separate permissions from a number of city departments. The review suggested streamlining and centralizing this process.

While the city's venue review did initiate *some* changes in the bylaws – namely given that more people are now able to attend a performance venue at a given time there is greater ease in selling alcohol, and a centralized process for approving temporary indoor events was introduced – concerns over the closure of venues have persisted. Ryan McCormick, the director of the Safe Amplification Site Society, an organization advocating for all-ages venues in the city, expressed concern over the fact that venues were shut down even as the review was conducted. McCormick also noted that 'there [were] no underground music voices represented on the city's cultural facilities implementation team' (Cole 2011). However, despite the ongoing closure of venues that host smaller events and independent artists, a number of performance spaces have been created or located by motivated groups and individuals, especially in the city's Downtown Eastside. These spaces have hosted bands and artists grouped under Vancouver's weird punk scene.

DIY and Documentation: the Emergency Room
In a 'Scene Report' for *CMJ*, the Vancouver-based band Tough Age informs readers about the city's notable venues. Tough Age is of the opinion that it takes a little more work to find inspiration in Vancouver. The band says, 'The thing about Vancouver is that Vancouver is oppressive, and anyone who has a different answer probably either has a trust fund or is a liar.' (Tough Age,

Figure 9.1: *Emergency Room Vol.1* album cover reprinted with permission of the artist, Justin Gradin.

2013). This quote emphasizes the class discrepancy in the city, between the musicians and many of the people who are able to afford to live comfortably in Vancouver, but the band also claimed that oppression is inspiring, 'and it creates a kind of quality control … the people here are the most inspiring group of artists you could meet … So I guess there's something going for it, somewhere underneath the condos.' The members of Tough Age are not alone in feeling inspired to take action and create something in Vancouver. The city's weird punk scene and the media attention it attracted can largely be attributed to underground and illegal performance spaces that welcome bands that fall outside of the city's perception of 'legitimate culture.' These spaces and bands have attracted a community of likeminded individuals who have collaborated to document and circulate local punk music both in Vancouver and beyond the city's borders.

Cameron Reed is a former programmer of local music festivals Music Waste and the Victory Square Block Party.[73] He discusses the state of live music in the city and reiterates

---

73 Reed began promoting shows in 2004 while playing in a punk band based in Vancouver. He has been involved with promoting Music Waste and the Victory Square Block Party. His current musical project, Babe Rainbow, is represented by prominent electronic music label, Warp Records.

Figure 9.2: *Emergency Room Vol.1* inside booklet cover reprinted with permission of the artist, Justin Gradin.

the fact that venues have a tendency to close or change locations due to legalities pertaining to noise and the sale of alcohol, in addition to the fact that the city is quite 'young' and currently expanding. 'I would say an obstacle, like right off the top of my mind, is having a venue that lasts a while,' Reed says. If a venue is around for a while a 'shitty booker' will come in and stop putting on the same sort of shows and will eventually 'have a stranglehold over that spot.' Reed is careful to state that he does not feel as though there is a lack of venues in the city, but that 'a lot of community building has to do with familiarity, and if you don't have a single spot or hub to rally around it can be difficult to build that sense of community' (2011). One space that did have a sense of community within the music scene for a period, according to Reed, was the Emergency Room.

The Emergency Room (ER) occupied two locations: first a parking garage and then a warehouse. In *No Fun City*, two of the individuals who helped start the ER, Keith Wecker and Justin Gradin, talk about the origins of the space. Wecker was walking through the parking garage at Emily Carr University of Art and Design and found that its lower floors had power outlets. He figured it would only require an extension cord and a power bar to host spontaneous shows in the space. In this sense, the space can be understood within the larger DIY ethos of the scene. In the film, Wecker and Gradin express their dissatisfaction with claims that there was nothing fun to do in the city. Wecker responds, 'You're either not looking hard enough or not trying,' while Gradin adds, 'Fun city is here. Underground. With all the rats.' By making do with what *was* available to them, as opposed to fixating on what was not, Wecker and Gradin helped to create a performance space that, in turn, contributed prominently to Vancouver's weird punk scene. The ER and spaces like it operate as temporary yet effective solutions: as 'tactics.' Michel de Certeau (1988) characterizes tactics as a contrast to strategy, or, more appropriately, to organized systems of power. Within the organized space of power are tactics that pose challenges to the dominant. A tactic 'takes advantage of 'opportunities' and depends on them, being without any base where it could stockpile its winnings, build up its own position, and plan raids' (37). As with spaces like the Emergency Room, there is a sense of mobility and limited temporality to a tactic, which utilizes a given situation to pose a challenge. Temporary underground performance venues serve as a necessary and effective tactic for participants in Vancouver's weird punk scene, who are able to 'make do' with their situation and circumvent oppressive city plans and policies in order to circulate live and recorded music.

Repurposed and temporary spaces are certainly not built or used with too much consideration for quality acoustics or live performance. Rather, they sprout up as they are needed and as appropriate spaces are located. The live sound at these venues is far from exceptional. Considering the style of the bands and artists performing in these spaces, a pristine listening environment is, likewise, far from needed. This foregoing of acoustic standards allows for punk bands and those from related genres to take advantage of performance spaces that welcome live music, even if they only exist for a short time. A DIY ethos is evidently a driving force in Vancouver's weird punk scene, as it has been for a number of underground and independent music scenes in the past. Anthony Kwame Harrison, for instance, locates DIY practices in the East Bay underground hip hop movement that emerged as a 'response to the commercial rap music industry's unwavering commitment to gangsta rap imagery and themes' (Harrison 2006, 285). He uses Janine Lopiano-Misdom and Joanne De Luca's definition of DIY as 'an independently driven entrepreneurial creed that prioritizes direct action and coalition building over traditional models of career development' (284–5). A DIY approach inspired not only the ER but also its resulting compilation album.

As previously mentioned, much of the space's fame is owed to the *Emergency Room Vol. 1* compilation (2008). Punk artefacts and commodities, argues Stacy Thompson, 'can be interpreted for clues to the desires' that form scenes (2004, 9). Thus, a more detailed account of the compilation's relationship to the venue and the larger scene is warranted. In the album's liner notes, Gradin colourfully describes the venue as being 'located in Vancouver's rat and drug infested downtown eastside. A literal underground, this basement warehouse is an indestructible fortress of creation, destruction and repair with a philosophy of DANCE or DIE' (Gradin 2011). He briefly outlined the history of the venue as beginning as a 'free, D.I.Y. all-ages noise/performance art gathering in the basement of' the Emily Carr Institute of Art and Design parkade. It then moved to a former fish processing factory and continued to 'consistently put on some of the weirdest, most elaborate, entertaining and ridiculous art and music shows in Vancouver's recent underground history.' The compilation documents 'a year of spray-painted walls, bizarre installations and art works, blood, fights, broken glass, punk rock, noise, art, make-outs and more' (Gradin 2011).

The album had an original pressing of 924 copies and included a twenty-page booklet of art, text, and photographs profiling the performance space. A total of eight bands feature on the compilation, including White Lung, Defektors, Mutators, and Nü Sensae. Reviews elaborated on the sound and style of these bands and recall the ways in which weird punk has been defined as blending garage rock and noise. Vancouver weird punk calls attention to the grittiness of the city's underground spaces that showcase this music, something that the ER has been integral in communicating, both through the space itself and the compilation album. Janelle Hollyrock's first review of the album for her own *Mongrel Zine* explained that the ER is a '24-track studio in Strathcona by day, an all night dance or die space by night,' and most importantly, 'an essential after-hours venue in a city that all but shuts down at 1 a.m.' (2008). The compilation consists of 'local art punk bands (mostly young with a lot of female members),' and its noisiness can be heard on Sick Buildings' 'The Commuter,' 'which begins with what sounds like the destruction of a stereo needle and spirals into a blitz of chaotic feedback and distortion' (Hollyrock 2008). Her 2013 review of the album for *Weird Canada* teased out the garage and punk components of these songs, describing the compilation's opening tracks as 'two straight ahead garage-punk tracks from Defektors.' Connecting the sound of the compilation to the feeling of the venue, she added, 'Listening to Twin Crystals and Nü Sensae I can almost taste the cigarette smoke and smell the stale beer and vomit that epitomized shows at the ER' (Hollyrock 2013). The ER lives on through memories and stories connected to the music played there and documented by the compilation album. Hollyrock claims that the vinyl compilation is:

> as important as 1979's *Vancouver Compilation* LP featuring DOA, Subhumans, U-J3RK5 and other seminal Vancouver punk bands. The compilation not only captured Vancouver's weird punk scene at its pinnacle, it was a jumping off point for a lot of these bands. It's a testament to them that, except for the two sadly defunct noise bands Mutators and Sick Buildings, all are not only still performing but deservedly getting reviewed and approved outside Vancouver.

The DIY ethos located in the origins of the ER, as described above, also shaped the compilation album and the way in which it documented this vibrant musical moment. In Hughes' *Exclaim!* article, Gradin explained the impetus behind the compilation, noting that, 'there are so many good bands right now, and people don't want to wait around for something to happen … The whole "Fuck it, let's just do this" thing is pretty strong here.' The head of Nominal Records, Sean Elliott, also contributed to Hughes' article, stating that, 'after years of near total disinterest in Vancouver, I saw some bands and, in the case of the Emergency Room, a spot that needed to be documented, so Nominal was created' (Hughes 2008). DIY practices and aesthetics also influenced the album's production and sound. Jordan Koop was the recording engineer at the ER and a member of Twin Crystals, one of the groups featured on the compilation. Koop said that he is 'so focused on documenting these bands' and added that everyone in the scene 'is so resourceful, they record and put out records or CD-Rs themselves all the time.' Koop offers a, 'lower price for "mid-fi" quality recordings,' and is, 'plugged into the priorities of the bands, where creative output comes first.' These bands, 'trust Koop because he is at their shows and at home listening to their tapes and CDs' (Hughes 2008).

The Emergency Room was a re-appropriated place that offered a space for performance, a recording studio, and a platform for social connection for members of Vancouver's weird punk scene. The individuals involved in this scene were active in documenting the musical and cultural activity taking place around the Emergency Room. In turn, the compilation helped build a scene through circulating recorded music, images, and text. Hughes contextualized his weird punk profile, explaining that, 'If anything, the story of Vancouver's weird punk renaissance should serve as an inspiration, not a hype-piece. In the face of extreme boredom and stifling conditions, the bands in their desperation built a small but sustainable infrastructure that includes everything from recording and releasing music to putting on shows' (2008). At the end of *No Fun City*, Gradin sounds dissatisfied with the fact that more people have not created something similar to the Emergency Room. 'There should be ten of these,' he says. 'So many kids could have just gone out and [done] it.' However, in the years since the end of the ER a number of inspiring examples demonstrate that other individuals and organizations are working to ensure there is a home for live and local music in Vancouver, both weird and otherwise. This legacy of the DIY spirit behind the ER and its influence on subsequent bands and artists in Vancouver is detailed below.

Temporary Alternative Performance Spaces and Sustaining a Music Scene
The blend of live music performances in illegal venues, DIY labels and albums, and attention from the music press illustrated a vibrant weird punk scene in Vancouver especially active in the mid-to-late 2000s. Holly Kruse defined a music scene as a cultural space that can be both social and geographic. They are 'best understood as being constituted through the practices and relationships that are enacted within the social and geographical spaces they occupy' (Kruse 2003, 1). Alan O'Connor used the concept of a scene in relation to punk music, arguing that, 'when punks use the term "scene" they mean the active creation of infrastructure to support punk bands and other forms of creative activity.' A scene, 'requires local bands that need places to live, practice spaces and venues to play' (O'Connor 2002,

233, 226). This conceptualization of a scene as a social urban space that works to sustain itself and ensure there are resources and places to perform is very much in line with the practices and processes of Vancouver's weird punk scene.

The tactics that aided in the formation of Vancouver's weird punk scene have been used by other non-mainstream music makers and concert promoters in the city who have continued to 'make do,' relying on illegal, underground, and alternative performance spaces. A review of 2014's Music Waste festival provided an overview of the various alternative venues in the Downtown Eastside that were used to host live shows. On the festival's Friday night, the Surrey-based She Dreams in Colour played a 6 pm set in the middle of the Kingsgate Mall. Reporting on the performance, Gregory Adams (2014) wrote that:

> the young group's shopping centre performance drew in curious on-lookers and one wildly air guitaring toddler. The act politely noted up front that they'd stripped down their alt-rock crunch for the night, leaving regular drummer Emma Star to slap rhythms out of a mahogany cajón, which was occasionally accompanied by the berry-obliterating blur of the blender at the Sugar Cane juice bar.

The review takes on the site-specific characteristics of this nonconventional performance space. Adams' description includes the sounds and scenes of the mall as though the uniqueness of repurposed performance spaces is becoming commonplace for smaller live music events in the city.

Music Waste, like the Emergency Room, was born out of frustration with the lack of available options for independent, DIY, and punk bands and artists. Music Waste began in the mid-1990s. Its origins lie in a '"fuck you" [to] Music West, a corporate rock festival where bands paid to apply, and the venues were often filled with more networkers ... than music patrons' (Colero 2014). Dustin Bromley, one of the organizers for Music Waste 2014, explained, 'We're curmudgeons who truly love local music ... We want to provide a stage and an audience for those acts, as we feel they deserve to be heard ... and it's important to have a good sense of humour, especially in a city which at times seems to hate all culture-creators' (Colero 2014). The festival began before the start of the ER, but its continual and recent use of alternative venues in the city's Eastside distinguishes the festival from larger, corporate cultural events and reflects the spirit of the ER.

Cameron Reed reflected on his experience programming Music Waste. He explained that there is a disjuncture between bands at different stages in their careers, or with different philosophies and approaches to music making. The more inclusive or independent cultural institutions are, the more important to independent bands and artists they become. Reed added that everything he programmed was Vancouver-centric: 'I'm not involved with putting on big out-of-town acts. I'm all about shows that are all local bands, all local artists, and all local comedians. No corporate sponsorship or anything like that. The idea is to make it easy for people to experience the independent local culture' (2011). Reed illustrated the importance of independent and inclusive cultural institutions and festivals, which are often the irregular and alternative venues and performance spaces in the city. These institutions are discussed in opposition to larger venues or cultural sponsors, which appear to favour bands that have proven their ability to garner national attention and sponsorship and would fit within a policy framework that tries to balance economic growth and residential development within a 'creative city' framework. As detailed above, much of Vancouver's municipal policies have hindered the sustainability of smaller performance venues and non-mainstream culture.

Nardwuar the Human Serviette is known for his work on Canada's music television channel MuchMusic and his interviews with prominent popular music artists. He has hosted a radio show at the University of British Columbia's campus station CiTR since 1987 and plays in two Vancouver-based bands.[74] He offered some poignant comments on performance spaces and places in the city, speaking from experience with his band The Evaporators. Nardwuar's experience suggests that Vancouver bands have been able to use temporary spaces to maintain and sustain music making in the city. He claimed that it is hard get a show at 'one of the bigger established places like the Commodore Ballroom' in Vancouver's entertainment district. He said that it used to be possible to headline the Commodore Ballroom if you were a 'really established local band,' and that there are a lot of places to play if you are 'a bit creative,' arguing that this is 'probably what makes bands even better in Vancouver. Because it's hard to find a place to play, when you do play, you make it really worthwhile' (Nardwuar 2011). Nardwuar believes that it is unfortunate that venues close, but on the positive side these closures force people to find other venues and this process of discovering new performance spaces can be exciting and rewarding.

Conclusion

Alternative, underground, repurposed, and illegal venues help live music circulate in Vancouver, especially music described as independent, underground, alternative, punk, and in this case, weird punk. The Emergency Room provided a space for live performances, recording music, and social connection in Vancouver. The individuals involved in this scene were inspired to document the musical and cultural activity taking place around the Emergency Room and this resulted in the creation of a record label and compilation record that in turn built a scene through circulating recorded music, images, and text. The precarious circumstances surrounding live music in Vancouver make a strong case for the importance of places and spaces and their related cultural productions as well as the knowledge and skill sharing that takes place therein – especially as cities grow and increase their downtown populations.

---

74 Nardwuar's radio show is also broadcast on WFMU in New Jersey. A native of Vancouver, Nardwuar plays in the bands the Evaporators and Thee Goblins. He also puts out records on Nardwuar Records about once a year. He began doing interviews in the early 1990s and is now well-known internationally for this after being involved with MuchMusic for a while. He now hosts his interviews on YouTube and his personal website http://nardwuar.com.

The documentation and DIY production practices in Vancouver's weird punk scene were certainly effective. This is clear from the fact that the scene has been discussed and described in the popular press, on community forums, and in music reviews. Furthermore, many of the bands that came up through the Emergency Room and weird punk scene towards the end of the 2000s have progressed significantly in their musical work. A 2012 *Pitchfork* feature on White Lung and other Vancouver punk bands like Nü Sensae and Defektors claims that, 'From a distance, at least, it seems issues of space have not halted this punk community's creative output' (Pelly 2012). Similarly, a *Rolling Stone* feature titled 'Vancouver's Punk Scene Blows Up' stated that, 'a tight-knit music scene has managed to form in the city, with many bands playing shows in abandoned warehouses, illegal spaces and parking lots. And several local acts have begun attracting serious attention outside Vancouver' (Mertens 2013).

Punk scenes have historically attracted attention from music journalists, record labels, and even academics, especially when their output offers an effective challenge to dominant systems of power or stale and repetitive cultural production. The Sex Pistols rejected the dominant characteristics of rock in the 1970s (Kinsella 2005, 17), American hardcore punk in the 1980s responded to the corporate domination of popular culture (Taylor 2003, 15), riot grrrl incorporated feminism and separated from aggressively masculine punk and grunge scenes in the Pacific Northwest (Kearney 1997), and Sweden's Refused crafted manifestos to usher in an aesthetic transformation of punk before the turn of the twenty-first century (Fauteux 2012). This is why punk and punk-related movements remain worthy of study. The genre is always evolving, offering temporary and necessary responses to a certain problematic of a given time and place. In Vancouver, weird punk rose to challenge oppressive city policies and a stifled creative landscape, and its output serves as an inspiration for future scenes that will do the same.

References

Adams, G. (2014). 'Music Waste Hits its Stride while Showing Some East Van Pride.' *Straight* (7 June). http://www.straight.com/music/661091/music-waste-hits-its-stride-while-showing-some-east-van-pride.

Certeau, M. (1988). *The Practice of Everyday Life*. Translated by Steven Rendall. Berkeley: University of California Press

City of Vancouver. (2011). 'Live Performance Venue Regulatory Review.' http://vancouver.ca/files/cov/LivePerformanceVenueRegulatoryReviewOverview_-2011.pdf.

City of Vancouver. (2014). *Noise Control By-law no. 6555*. http://former.vancouver.ca/bylaws/6555c.PDF.

Cole, Y. (2011). 'City of Vancouver Votes to Reduce Red Tape for Live Performance Venues.' *Straight* (3 February). http://www.straight.com/music/city-vancouver-votes-reduce-red-tape-live-performance-venues.

Colero, J. (2014). 'Vancouver's Waste-makers.' *Discorder* (2 June) http://www.discorder.

ca/discorder-magazine/index.php/2014/06/02/vancouvers-waste-makers.

Downes, J. (2012). 'The Expansion of Punk Rock: Riot Grrrl Challenges to Gender Power Relations in British Indie Music Subcultures.' *Women's Studies* 41 (2): 204–37.

Fauteux, B. (2012). '"New Noise" Versus the Old Sound: Manifestos and the Shape of Punk to Come.' *Popular Music and Society* 35 (4): 465–82.

Finch, M. (2014). '"Toronto is the Best!": Cultural Scenes, Independent Music, and Competing Urban Visions.' *Popular Music and Society* 38 (3): 299–317.

Gradin, J. (2011). 'Releases.' *Nominal Records* (20 September). http://www.recordsnominal.com/er.php.

Guerra, P. (2015). 'Keep It Rocking: the Social Space of Portuguese Alternative Rock (1980–2010).' *Journal of Sociology.* http://jos.sagepub.com/content/early/2015/02/16/1440783315569557.

Guimond, S. (2008). 'Pop Montreal: Weird Punk – Web Exclusive!: If You Think Punk's Dead.' *Hour* (October 2). http://hour.ca/2008/10/02/if-you-think-punks-dead.

Harrison, A. K. (2006). '"Cheaper than a CD, Plus We Really Mean It": Bay Area Underground Hip Hop Tapes As Subcultural Artefacts.' *Popular Music* 25 (2): 283–301.

Hebdige, D. (1979). *Subculture: the Meaning of Style*. London: Methuen & Co. Ltd.

Hodkinson, P. (2004). 'Translocal Connections in the Goth Scene.' In A. Bennett and R. A. Peterson (eds.), *Music Scenes: Local, Translocal and Virtual*, 131–48. Nashville: Vanderbilt University Press.

Hollyrock, J. (2008). 'Emergency Room vol. 1, LP.' *Mongrel Zine* (2 August). http://www.mongrelzine.ca/blog/tag/emergency-room.

Hollyrock, J. (2013). 'Cameo: Janelle Hollyrock on Various Artists – Emergency Room vol. 1.' *Weird Canada* (9 August). http://weirdcanada.com/2013/08/cameo-janelle-hollyrock-on-various-artists-emergency-room-vol-1.

Hughes, J. (2008). 'Strange Brew: Vancouver's Weird Punk Scene Invents Itself.' *Exclaim!* (September). http://exclaim.ca/Features/Research/strange_brew-vancouver.

Hughes, J. (2009). 'Nü Sensae: Nü Sensae.' *Exclaim!* (May 5). http://exclaim.ca/Reviews/PopAndRock/nu_sensae-nu_sensae.

James, M., and K. Kroll. (2010). *No Fun City* (documentary). Make Believe Media.

Kearney, M. C. (1997). 'The Missing Links: Riot Grrrl – Feminism – Lesbian Culture.' In S. Whiteley (ed.), *Sexing the Groove: Popular Music and Gender*, 207–29. New York: Routledge.

Kinsella, W. (2005). *Fury's Hour: a (Sort-of) Punk Manifesto*. Toronto: Random House.

Krinsley, J. (2009). 'Talk to the Blog: Terminal Boredom's Rick Kroneiss on Haterism, Psychedelic Horseshit, and the "Indie Establishment" Oxymoron.' *Village Voice* (August 14). http://blogs.villagevoice.com/music/2009/08/terminal_boredo.php.

Kruse, H. (2003). *Site and Sound: Understanding Independent Music Scenes*. New York: Peter Lang.

Lederman, M. (2010). 'Vancouver's Punk Scene, Then and Now.' *The Globe and Mail* (May 6). http://www.theglobeandmail.com/arts/music/vancouvers-punk-scene-then-and-now/article4317983.

Magaldi, C. (1999). 'Adopting Imports: New Images and Alliances in Brazilian Popular Music of the 1990s.' *Popular Music* 18 (3): 309–29.

McCormick, R. and S. Antrim. (2013). 'Zoo Zhop is Vancouver's Latest Cultural Casualty.' *Straight* (June 4). http://www.straight.com/news/388076/zoo-zhop-vancouvers-latest-cultural-casualty.

Mertens, M. (2013). 'Vancouver's Punk Scene Blows Up.' *Rolling Stone* (January 10). http://www.rollingstone.com/music/news/vancouvers-punk-scene-blows-up-20130110.

Nardwuar the Human Serviette. (2011). Personal interview (8 July).

O'Connor, A. (2002). 'Local Scenes and Dangerous Crossroads: Punk and Theories of Cultural Hybridity.' *Popular Music* 21 (2): 225–36.

Pelly, J. (2012). 'White Lung: A Vancouver Act that Filters Feminism and Anger through Brash Melodic Punk.' *Pitchfork* (August 22). http://pitchfork.com/features/rising/8922-white-lung.

Pickersgill, M. (2006). 'From Nuisance to Amenity: Exploring Planning Policy Alternatives for Live Music Venues in Vancouver.' Unpublished MA dissertation. University of British Columbia.

Reed, C. (2011). Personal interview (11 July).

Taylor, S. (2003). *False Prophet: Fieldnotes from the Punk Underground*. Middletown: Wesleyan University Press.

Terminal Boredom. (2007). *WEIRD PUNK* (October 25). http://terminal-boredom.com/forums/index.php?PHPSESSID=64c5325aa00ab50fd0099e0834054f98&topic=7702.0.

Terminal Boredom. (2008). *Everything Weird=Good* (14 January). http://terminal-boredom.com/forums/index.php?PHPSESSID=64c5325aa00ab50fd0099e0834054f98&topic=8644.0.

Terminal Boredom. (2009). 'ITT: We Try to Predict the Next Big Musical Trend' (3 March). http://terminal-boredom.com/forums/index.php?PHPSESSID=64c5325aa00ab50fd0099e0834054f98&topic=16625.0.

Thompson, S. (2004). *Punk Productions: Unfinished Business*. Albany: State University of New York Press.

Thornton, S. (1995). *Club Cultures: Music, Media and Subcultural Capital*. Cambridge: Polity.

Tough Age. (2013). 'Scene report: tough age on Vancouver, BC.' *CMJ* (14 November). http://www.cmj.com/column/scene-report/tough-age-vancouver-bc.

Toynbee, J. (2000). *Making Popular Music: Musicians, Creativity and Institutions*. New York: Oxford University Press.

Young, B. (2014). 'Live Music and Development: A Double Standard of Noise Pollution in Vancouver.' *Rabble* (2 August). http://rabble.ca/blogs/bloggers/mainlander/2013/08/live-music-and-development-double-standard-noise-pollution-vancouv.

FEARLESS IRANIANS
FROM HELL

DIE FOR ALLAH

10. 'WE JUST MAKE MUSIC': DECONSTRUCTING NOTIONS OF AUTHENTICITY IN THE IRANIAN DIY UNDERGROUND

THERESA STEWARD

Abstract

Following the 1979 Iranian Revolution, the decline and temporary fall of an established music industry necessitated the creation of a new underground DIY culture to help redevelop music culture in Iran. This culture referenced the DIY movements that emerged in mid-twentieth-century Britain and America through the dissemination of cassette tapes, underground shows, word of mouth promotion, and symbolic stencilling and graffiti. Now, with the use of twenty-first-century technology, the DIY movement continues to evolve through online underground networks where music can be easily recorded, uploaded, and downloaded. Bands such as 127, Kiosk, and Hypernova emerged from the Tehrani underground through DIY means while simultaneously channelling the musical influences of Western punk and indie-rock. This chapter explores how the concepts of DIY culture and the underground have been transformed in an Iranian context as young Iranian musicians find themselves trying to navigate dual identities: between the cultural influences of East and West, the mainstream and the underground, and the traditional and the popular. In the process, many contradictions have emerged surrounding notions of authenticity and autonomy. Post-2000 exposure in Western and diaspora publications continues to play a large role in the perception of the Iranian underground, shaping how Iranian popular musicians are perceived globally, while reinforcing images of authenticity. By comparing representations of illegal Iranian popular music in the Western media with personal accounts from underground musicians in Iran, it also becomes clear that the myths surrounding the Iranian underground are actively negotiated by both the Western media and Iranian youth.

Keywords: DIY culture, underground subculture, popular music, youth identity, Iran

Theresa Steward is an independent scholar who currently teaches musicology at the University of Mary Washington in Fredericksburg, VA. She completed her Doctorate in Musicology at The University of Edinburgh. Her research focuses primarily upon contemporary issues of popular music and youth identity in Iran and the Iranian diaspora. Previous research and teaching projects have included investigations into the role of female singers during early to mid-twentieth-century Iran, topics in Western art music, particularly nineteenth-century Romanticism and Western popular music studies, including a study on female punk voices in 1970s Britain. E-mail: tpsteward@gmail.com

'WE JUST MAKE MUSIC': DECONSTRUCTING NOTIONS OF AUTHENTICITY IN THE IRANIAN DIY UNDERGROUND

Figure 10.1: Satrapi, Marjane and Vincent Paronnaud. (2008). *Persepolis*. DVD. Sony Pictures Home Entertainment. 2008.

Since its birth in the 1970s, punk has laid the foundations of DIY culture and amateur rock productions by offering an alternative to the mainstream and an opposition to dominant culture. Emergent subcultures exploit the surroundings to express and change their own condition and, as George McKay points out, offer alternative views of the future, whether through political or social change (2005). Similarly, the post-2000 development of underground culture in Iran provides a place where oppositional ideas can be expressed and shared, and subversion can be easily spread. In Tehran, Iranian youth participate in a vibrant underground music community, creating music from modest means in home studios, basements, and other private spaces. These amateur musicians often have no musical training; they are mostly self-taught and have learned rock and its many subgenres from Internet downloads and bootleg recordings of Western popular music. This self-education in rock, combined with an exposure to a rich tradition of Iranian folk and classical music produced and distributed in the country under limited conditions, generates a unique case of music making that inherently embodies DIY principles. The result is a multi-faceted music-making culture that embraces diverse cultural and musical influences while speaking specifically about the current Iranian youth generation.

While looking forward to an alternative future, Iranian youth participants of contemporary DIY culture simultaneously project a sensibility that is met with a constant need to negotiate with their cultural and social environment but also with their portrayals in the Western news media. Through the interactions between the media and young underground rock musicians, a number of representations of authenticity are promoted. This chapter will explore such notions of authenticity through multiple avenues in order to distinguish and deconstruct what is publicized in the media and discover how musicians are responding to and negotiating with these images. More importantly, the aim is to better understand the Iranian rock underground, beyond its homogeneous media image, as a multi-faceted collection of complex subcultures where Iranian modern youth identity is continually evolving.

Music Practice in Post-2000 Iran

Following the 1979 Iranian Revolution, the Ayatollah Ruhollah Khomeini's aptly dubbed 'Cultural Revolution' changed the future of the arts by severely limiting expression and artistic production. Music endured by far the most suppression, as it was deemed incompatible with Islam and thus inappropriate for the citizens of an Islamic Republic. Initially, all music was banned, but within the following three years traditional and religious music gradually began to re-enter the public domain. Popular music, however, would remain under close authoritarian scrutiny and restriction, as it continues to be today.

Since 2000, and in particular since the presidency of the moderate reformist Mohammad Khatami, the fluctuating laws surrounding music have sometimes offered limited room for popular musicians and their audiences (Siddiqi 2005). In the early 2000s, home-grown pop music began to gain some official acceptance, being seen as a way to counteract the rising influence of Western popular culture. But other genres, including heavy metal, rap, and rock, would primarily remain confined to a budding illegal underground scene. Musicians are required to undergo an arduous and costly process of attaining permits for production and performance – and more often than not for popular musicians their efforts are in vain. Official acceptance of popular music has continued to oscillate between rulings of *halal* [permitted] or *haram* [forbidden], with some musicians having been successful in the unpredictable approval process for seemingly inexplicable reasons, while the majority have struggled, given up, or become disillusioned, having not even attempted to gain government permission.

As Michel Foucault (1976), Michel de Certeau (1984), and others have noted, 'where there is power, there is resistance.' Shifts in power often prompt a collective response as youth form new collectives and new methods of resistance (Hebdige 1983). The lack of consistency and the unpredictability of censorship practice in Iran frequently contribute to the current disregard of laws and lack of concern about new or re-implemented rulings. In many cases, this has inspired Iranian artists to pursue the forbidden and discover new ways of being heard.

The decline and temporary fall of the official music industry led to the creation of a new underground culture over the next three decades. Iranian youth developed a rich underground culture, based strongly on notions of DIY. Just as the beginnings of punk were entirely encompassed by a DIY initiative – a total control over music by amateurs that challenged the output of mainstream professionals – this has also been the path of DIY in Iran, using what little resources are available. In the 1980s and 1990s, the black market flourished, as illegally imported and home-grown cassette tapes were circulated, unofficial basement shows were promoted via word of mouth, and rituals of stencilling and graffiti were carried out at night away from the watchful eyes of the *basij* – Iran's notorious moral police (Reshad 2008).

Iranian DIY's possibilities of refusal and resistance of mainstream culture and political authority have been taken to new grounds with the help of the Internet. Underground networks have spread rapidly online as music can be easily recorded and uploaded by amateur musicians, and downloaded by audiences all over the world. Many bands have emerged from the Tehrani underground, gaining enough recognition through the Internet to attract international media attention, particularly in the British and American media. As a result, they have started to move out of the country in order to fully pursue musical careers.

As youth formulate individual and collective expressions in relation to the Western mainstream media's perception of them, youth culture, as Simon Frith writes, becomes a contradictory mix of the authentic and the manufactured (1978). While the authentic usually represents a search for the truth, for the 'natural,' unadulterated essence of something, differing definitions and interpretations of what constitutes authentic culture often complicate its existence. Most commonly, authenticity manifests itself in various forms of resistance. This resistance can pit itself against the mainstream, the mass-produced, and the mass-consumed, or political authority (Thornton 1996). In the case of the Iranian underground, the notion of authenticity thrives upon its resistance to all of these factors. In order to better understand the diverse and complex nature of Iranian underground identity, this essay will begin to explore the notion of authenticity as a series of constructs that emerge chiefly from a continually shifting symbiotic relationship between Iranian musicians and the Western media.

The View through the Lens of the Western Media

The Western media dominates in the global world.[75] It shapes not only the predominant images of the self, but also those of the 'Other,' or in this case the non-Western subject. Mass media, as both a recipient and distributor of culture, becomes the location of cultural struggle for youth groups that are seeking a new medium to articulate individual experience collectively (Brake 1985). In most instances, the media has contributed to the tendency to position popular global music subcultures within a framework of political resistance.

---

75 'The Western media' to which we will allude in this essay refers primarily to the British and American media industries.

In terms of the Iranian underground, while musicians may be neglected by their own state media due to the illegal nature of their music practices, they receive much publicity in Western and diaspora publications abroad. The Iranian youths have become a symbol of resistance, especially through media-reported student activism and electoral demonstrations in Tehran since the 1990s, and most notably since the recent 2009 presidential election (Memarian and Nesvaderani 2010). Iranian youth culture is easily politicized and romanticized through the process of a self-projection of Western objectives. The portrayals of repressed youth struggling to rise up against an authoritarian regime offer a compelling canvas on which to project the fight for Western-style freedom and democracy. This self-projection through politicization often involves the highly connotative usage of Western subcultural labels.

Generally, subcultural labels, as a creation of convenience by the media, can be highly problematic. Punk is, of course, no exception, as it has become far too easy to stereotype it as a subculture of loud and angry anti-establishment youth, while in the process ignoring all of its nuances and diverse musical practices. To use an example, those familiar with Marjane Satrapi's (2007) popular animated film *Persepolis*, based on her autobiographical graphic novel of the same name, might remember a comical montage of Marjane as a young girl in the 1980s developing a taste for 'punk rock' (2008). Much to the disapproval of her elders, she wears a self-adorned jacket with the words 'Punk is not ded' and rocks out on her tennis racket 'guitar' to a cassette featuring the 50 Toumans' track 'Master of the Monsters.' Later, Marjane attends a 'punk' show, and although initially shocked by the angry screams of the overbearing, mohawked men on stage, soon finds herself pounding the air with her fists like everyone else. The band she is fist-pumping to, however, is not actually 'punk' as many would classify it, but the Norwegian death metal band Blood Red Throne.

This is just one example that illustrates that while subcultural labels are globally influential, they can also transform and evolve depending on their surroundings, with local specificities (Frith 1996). For young Marjane, punk could have simply symbolized angry white males screaming threateningly into microphones – which although can be found in punk rock, can also be found in other genres. Alternatively, her punk experience could simply signify, as the moment in the film implies, a rebellion of youth against an older generation; of youth trying to find its own voice. Or, in the broader context of the film, it could symbolize a young girl's resistance against the changes in her environment brought on by a new authoritarian regime and its severely enforced laws.

The term 'punk' takes on new meanings in Iranian popular music. Rather than a recreation or an imitation of well-known notions or aesthetics of American or British punk, musicians redefine the genre on their own terms relevant to their own surroundings. Often, it is used in a hybridized form combined with local influences, as in the case of the gypsy-punk band 127. On the surface, it could appear that the band has merely adopted a fusion genre that has become fashionable over the last decade or so, one that references the rebellious message of punk combined with an exoticism of the unknown (Silverman 2012).

But upon closer listening, one can hear not only Western instrumentation and English lyrics but also Persian rhythms and percussion, along with a message that is uniquely of the young Iranian generation. 127's choice to take on the descriptive label of 'gypsy-punk' is also significant in how it links their music with the nomadic struggle of the Romani, whose continually shifting diasporic communities are widely spread across the globe. This is not unlike the multitude of Iranians, especially musicians and artists, who chose or were forced to emigrate since 1979, many of them unable to return to their homeland. They continue to find themselves caught in a cultural intersection between East and West.

Due to a lack of institutionalized and formal channels for youth, Iranian youth subcultures are not always synonymous with their Western counterparts either. Iranian popular music practice has become a symbol of a quest for a modern cultural identity, with political resistance being one aspect of this journey. Much of the post-2000 discourse in the West, however, portrays the Iranian underground as a solely political symbol rather than a forum for entertainment – which, it will be argued, is its definition for the social actors. The very label 'underground' thus becomes problematic in its assumptions.

The Western definition of underground music implies a subversive music scene that attempts to defy the norms of society, whether politically, culturally, or aesthetically. The Iranian underground, however, has a much more encompassing meaning than its Western counterpart. Culture critic and founder of the Tehran-based Hermes Records Ramin Sadighi states that the Iranian underground is defined as: 'Anything that does not receive an issuing permit, no matter what the genre.'[76] Cultural studies professor Mehdi Semati explains, 'Since many of the musical acts in Iran do not have the legal permission, the content becomes "underground" automatically, no matter how mundane the subject matter is' (Mowlaei 2007). That is, the underground is defined by the governmental restrictions and censorship placed on the music, rather than the musical content or message. Any musician or band that is not able to gain legal government approval automatically becomes 'underground,' or unofficial. There is, in fact, no word in Farsi for 'underground' as a subcultural construct. Rather, underground music is most commonly known as *musiqi-ye zirzamini*, or 'basement music,' literally referencing the physical location where much of this music takes place. The underground in Iran is entirely a way of life for unofficial musicians, rather than a term or a style for those who choose to produce and record away from the mainstream as they convey messages of resistance. It is not composed of one, growing subculture but rather a highly diverse mix of subcultures typically distinguished by genres, the most prominent being pop, rock, techno, heavy metal, and rap.

By latching onto the anti-authoritarian aspect of Iranian popular music, the Western media creates an image of a united, burgeoning underground mass while aiding

---

76 The other definitions Sadighi (2009) presents are more like subcategories of this first definition: '2) Cover bands who are limited in performance since they are not officially distributed; 3) Bands covering social subject matter, life in Tehran; 4) Amateur musicians who perform in garage shows, street festivals; 5) Those who actually play underground music.' The final definition implies that Sadighi believes in the existence of an underground aesthetic, but this is never fully explained in the article.

in the somewhat mythic claim of 'authenticity.' The sentimentalized image of Iranian musicians united in a struggle to be heard publicly is compelling, particularly with the factor of rebellion in a dangerous political climate. The various sensationalist headlines and even eyewitness accounts from journalists representing the Western media indicate an overwhelming emphasis on the political culture surrounding these musicians, rather than an interest in their musical output.

A reoccurring example of such politicization can be found in the publicity surrounding the rock band Hypernova. Formed in the late 1990s under President Khatami, Hypernova went to the United States in 2007 when popular music was suffering severe crackdowns under the conservative President Mahmoud Ahmadinejad. The band quickly gained popularity in America as media coverage was steeped with references to Hypernova's illegal status in Iran. Hypernova made headlines as an 'Immigrant Rock Band' in America, in a November 2008 *Payvand News* article, despite the fact that lead singer Raam is actually a US citizen – he was born in Oregon and moved back to Iran later in his childhood (Nasri 2008). An April 2007 MTV broadcast on the band used the Beastie Boys' 'You Gotta Fight, For Your Right, To Party' to draw viewers into Hypernova's story, which solely focused on issues of censorship and the dangers of playing music in the Islamic Republic, ignoring the actual music the band was creating in the United States at the time (MTV 2007). In a corresponding article, MTV reporter Gil Kaufman asked, 'what if the very act of stepping to the mic means taking your life in your hands?' (Kaufman 2007). In an April 2010 NPR broadcast, Shereen Meraji admitted, 'I profiled the band … because what's better than a rock band from the Islamic Republic of Iran, where it is illegal to rock?' (2010).

The music combined with the images of illegality and subversive political activity 'sounds amazing' to audiences; without the attached meaning it sometimes becomes ordinary. Critic Peter Holslin, writing for the *San Diego CityBeat*, claims that, musically, much of the Iranian rock that is featured in mainstream Western media is not any different than other current Western bands. He comments on Hypernova: '[They are] catchy, but they're not groundbreaking or unique' (2010). Holslin is among the few to suggest how eager listeners and critics forgive the content of the music simply because of its illegal status. Despite the multitude of Iranian bands and styles of music that are presented to Western audiences through the mass media, ultimately, the music, no matter how interesting or mundane, remains subservient to the perceived political and revolutionary message.

This romanticized politicization may indicate a nostalgic desire for a revival of countercultural movements in the West. After all, popular music throughout the twentieth century has often been depicted as being at the forefront of youth rebellion in the West. Folk musicians Woody Guthrie and Pete Seeger sang pro-union and anti-war songs in 1940s and 1950s America. In the 1960s and 1970s, they were joined by Joan Baez and Bob Dylan, as well as rock bands Jefferson Airplane and Creedance Clearwater Revival, in civil rights and anti-war protest movements. In Britain this sentiment evolved into punk, which flourished as a dissident movement challenging not only political and parental authority but also the status quo of its everyday environment. The Sex Pistols, the Clash, and Sham 69 rallied youth in political and social protest. The Cold War fostered 'Deutschpunk' groups, such as Slime in the GDR, and rock bands such as the Primitives, the Golden Kids, and Plastic People of the Universe in the Eastern and Soviet Bloc countries (Pecakz 1994). Deena Weinstein is one of many critics who write that youth counterculture, and its accompanying protest music, no longer exists in the same way as it did for much of the second half of the twentieth century. She explains that throughout the 1960s 'Golden Age of Rock Activism' in North America, 'Youth involvement in these protests, and simultaneously their interest in rock music, created the conditions for a proliferation of protest songs' (Weinstein 2006). But in the West today the mass protest movement is rare, as is its parallel subversive musical underground. As Western political goals are projected onto non-Western cultures, so is a sense of longing for the West's 'lost' countercultural or underground movements. This perhaps gives rise to a desire to portray the 'new' non-Western undergrounds as embodying the ideals of their lost Western counterpart.

Western accounts produce an image of a vibrant Iranian music scene, but often one that relies heavily on its love of Western rock legends, neglecting any other cultural or musical elements at play. Brian Glass, in a soundtrack review of Bahman Ghobadi's 2009 docu-drama film *No One Knows About Persian Cats*, compares half of the Iranian tracks to their Western 'equivalents.' Take It Easy Hospital is reminiscent of indie-pop bands Vampire Weekend and OK Go; Mirza evokes Iron and Wine and Calexico; Iranian metal band Free Keys mix Metallica, Led Zeppelin, and Stone Temple Pilots; Hichkas's 'Ektelaf' is described as 'a hip-hop single that would be at home on American radio' (Glass 2010). Another critic for *Time Out New York*, David Fear, declares that the film includes 'Pitchfork-approved indie rock' (Fear 2010). He writes about the Iranian 'struggling Springsteens and Strokes fanatics,' and calls Iranian rapper Hichkas a 'Jay-Z wanna-be,' despite his lyrics being solely in Farsi addressing themes specific to his urban Tehrani environment, and his unique use of Iranian percussive and rhythmic elements. In other accounts, Rana Farhan's rich vocals, which integrate Persian vocal tradition and melodies, have been called the voice of an 'Iranian Amy Winehouse' (Burr 2010), and singer-songwriter Mohsen Namjoo has been dubbed 'Iran's Bob Dylan,' despite the fact that the former claims to have long abandoned the politically motivated music from his early career.[77] Although Namjoo admires Dylan's dedication and sacrifice, he says, 'From a musical standpoint, our worries are quite different,' as he chooses to focus on the integration of his music with Persian rhythmic and instrumental traditions (Hochman 2010).

As Raymond Williams stated, 'There are in fact no masses; only ways of seeing people as masses' (Williams 1963). Iranian popular musicians, as with musicians anywhere, do not exist as a homogenous mass, consciously practising dissidence against an overbearing regime. Neither are they unified under their dependence upon the influence of Western popular music. In many cases, musicians are united more by a shared attitude of experimentation and expression, and yet the music emerging from the Iranian underground

---

77 This comparison was first used by the *New York Times* and repeatedly in other news sources since. See Fathi (2007).

continues to be assessed on a Western scale of popular taste and style. The portrayal of relatable, 'revolutionary' music allows for the opportunity for Western audiences to live vicariously through what are often portrayed as the dangerous but 'exciting' lives of Iranian underground musicians, fighting for 'Western freedom.' But if Iranian popular musicians are continually compared to Western artists or depicted only as political symbols, their individuality and cultural distinctiveness are lost.

At the other end of the spectrum, music emanating from a distinct place or peoples can all-too-easily become a symbol of a pure, unadulterated cultural artefact. But as John Connell and Chris Gibson succinctly write, 'self-contained, authentic meaning-making communities' do not exist (Connell and Gibson 2003, 191). Instead, there are mutually entangled, complex relationships where all cultures are involved with one another – popular music is a reflection of these relationships, as it acts as the 'site of symbolic struggle in the cultural sphere' (Shuker 2012, 258).

In non-Western music subcultures, authenticity is sometimes represented as an opposition to Western influence in the attempt to preserve a cultural form or tradition. Iranian popular music, however, has questioned the meaning of an 'authentic' cultural practice, following a highly hybridized route over the course of its development. Influenced by traditions of *avaz* [art song] and classical Iranian music in the nineteenth century, popular music making in Iran reached its zenith in the 1960s and 1970s when the global influence was at a high in the country (Miller 1999). Pop stars such as Googoosh, Ramesh, Dariush, and Sima Bina were pop culture icons, and their music a reflection of Iranian as well as Western influences, such as jazz, blues, psychedelic rock, and Latin music. All the same, Western artists such as Pink Floyd, Queen, and Elton John were equally popular. Iranian culture, as with most non-Western cultures, continues to integrate the influence of outside music and traditions, as they have become inextricably linked to their own cultural traditions. Much of current popular culture in Iran reflects the access that many young urban Iranians have to the West through satellite television and radio, and the Internet. Journalist Roxana Saberi further explains:

> they [the younger generation] never saw the revolution – more and more young Iranians are in touch with the outside world. Because of technology – and many of them are tech savvy ... they travel abroad, they study abroad, they have family abroad, relatives overseas. (Magee 2010)

Western popular music culture has become just as much an influence and a part of Iranian youth culture as Persian musical and poetic traditions. Despite the government's attempts to control popular music and its global influences, new forms of modern technology have ensured that Iran's cultural borders cannot be closed off but rather continue to exchange cultural ideas, underground or not. The search for the 'authentic' fails in the sense that globalization is a continual process.

Negotiating New Identities in a New Host Environment

In the mid-2000s, 127 migrated to Portland, Oregon in order to advance their musical careers and freely tour the West. Rather than completely departing from or immerging themselves in Persian tradition, their music is a redefinition of Iranian popular music. The 2009 album *Khal Punk* features tracks that combine Persian percussive and rhythmic elements with Western influences from pop, rock, jazz, and funk. The album's title literally translates as 'flaw' or 'imperfection,' which 127 translates in terms of their brand of popular music. Lead singer Sohrab Mohebbi claims, 'It's really just this bunch of motley kids, playing a motley style they've created from motley surroundings' (Reverbnation 2008). This fittingly describes the start of so many DIY bands, but more importantly demonstrates how 127 and other Iranian bands are transforming the impetus and original message of punk as they embrace their diverse influences and hybridized style. As Iranian musicians explore language and musical influences outside of Iranian mainstream pop, they are broadening and creating their own musical styles through cross-cultural collaboration.

In addition to the integration of Western and Persian musical elements, the choice of language plays an important role in Iranian DIY. Increasingly, English lyrics have been used by Iranian musicians to spread their music globally as they seek new audiences. The Iranian rock band Kiosk uses a combination of Farsi and English, as the band believes that reaching beyond Iranian communities is important to the band's music (Siletz 2010). Lead singer Arash Sobhani states, 'We do not want to make music to get the attention of a particular group of people …' (Karami 2011).

127's Mohebbi also states the importance of using a globally recognized language: 'It's the world's second language, like [eating] hamburgers.' He explains the band's use of English:

> We have to become universal. In our opinion, even if we want to defend our native and regional spirit in any kind of music itself and not the language of the lyrics … Using Persian lyrics on Western music does not necessarily bring about the Iranianization of that music … (Nooshin 2008)

Mohebbi's claim that language alone does not convey the 'Iranianization' of popular music raises an important issue in the practice of contemporary Iranian popular music – the constant search for the balance between 'authentic' and 'borrowed,' tradition and innovation, and, in this case, home and homeland. 127 do not see the need to rely solely on their native tongue when they have been living in a new home, adapting to new elements of their host culture. Rather than reject the term *khal* as its literal meaning of 'imperfection,' 127 have embraced it as a result of hybridity within diaspora music. 127 offers just one example of how many Iranian musicians are subtly drawing attention to their roots, referencing not only Iranian tradition, but also diaspora and Western pop, all the while, progressively developing their own musical voice.

Popular music subcultures often attempt to resist media assumptions and stereotypes regarding their music or lifestyle (Widdicombe and Wooffitt 1995). Many

Iranian musicians, for instance, insist that they are apolitical and oppose media-enforced labels. British-Iranian rapper Reveal acknowledges the tendency to politicize Iranian music, maintaining that, 'We just make music, but people push things on us rather than discussing the quality of the music and expression' (Lashkari, Golestan, and Kooshanejad 2011). Rock singer Maral Afsharian remarks, 'I know it's really interesting to be an electro/rock female musician from a country that forbids any form of western music and being a female singer! However, I prefer to attract people to my music rather than my story' (Gothic Goddess Media 2010).

Rather than being passive consumers, however, Iran's underground musicians are active participants in a growing music culture. Like all subcultures and resistance cultures, they may rely on the media whether it produces positive or negative publicity, but they also actively negotiate their own identities through the complex relationships of resistance and mediation with their local and global environments. Popular musicians equally participate in the myth of authenticity, perpetuating a variety of complex contradictions. For instance, Ashkan Kooshanejad, of the indie rock band Take It Easy Hospital, admits that his music has inherently political roots, but does not agree with the overtly politicized construct of the underground created by the media. He claims, '[our] work is obviously being politicised … I am not underground; I just play music' (Lashkari, Golestan, and Kooshanejad 2011). All the while, despite his vigorous opposition to the marketing of the Iranian underground as being entirely about political resistance, Ashkan played the vital role of the protagonist in Bahman Ghobadi's (2010) *No One Knows About Persian Cats*, a film that heavily relies on its portrayal of a politically subversive music underground in Iran, with its official poster advertisements announcing: 'The film that sings, howls, and chants freedom!' and its official trailer proclaiming, 'In a country on the edge of revolution, come the new voices of protest …' (*No One Knows about Persian Cats* 2010).

Participation in a music underground restricted by law alone can imply inherent subversive activity and anti-authoritarian action regardless of musical or lyrical content. Frontman Raam of Hypernova stated that, in this way, Iranian musicians are united by defiance: 'every underground musician is subconsciously defying the authorities. Because they are in all reality breaking a stupid law, and even though it's not enforced at all times, it's still a law' (Raam 2007). In several interviews, Raam glamorized the image of rebellion, catering to the media stereotype. In a 2007 interview with Freya Petersen of the *New York Times* he claimed, 'We're jeopardizing our lives every show we play' (Petersen 2007). In a 2008 interview with *Iran Times*, Raam romanticized this sentiment even further: 'The underground scene in Iran is pretty intense. There are many amazing musicians driven by a burning passion who are literally putting their lives on the line for their music, just like we did. There's nothing more beautiful than raw and sincere music' (Nasri 2008). In the very same interview, however, he conflictingly stated, 'I think a lot of people over here [in the United States] are unfortunately misinformed about the realities that exist in Iran. Not to be an apologist for the current regime there, but Iran really is not as bad as they make it out to be in the media.'

As Tehrani youth gain widespread popularity through Internet channels, reaching the diaspora and beyond, they also learn to a certain degree about how to control their image in the international media. Fereidoun Tafreshi, editor of *Zirzamin*, a prominent online Iranian music magazine, criticizes some Iranian musicians for using the 'underground' label to attract publicity to their situation:

> The pathetic aspect is that these so called underground bands and the so called *Zirzamini* [basement] bands are becoming a fashionable label [that] bands or artists give themselves. Everybody wants to profile themselves as [an] underground band nowadays. But in fact they would loooooove to be heard and talked about and [p]lay live and everything else that comes with being 'on-the-ground' [*sic*]. The moment one band label[s] themselves as underground, they get media attention.[78]

Tafreshi's observation of musicians striving for media attention reinforces the contradictory behaviour of youth subcultures. Underground musicians resist certain stereotypes perpetuated by the media, but they also embrace media publicity which establishes them as prominent groups in society (Widdicombe and Wooffitt 1995).

Supporting the myth that mass culture and media indicate a loss of artistic or intellectual value, situating 'authentic' sounds and styles against the mainstream, symbolically opposing the 'general public,' the underground lives in a constant dichotomy (Thornton 1996). Mass media continues to be the major location for cultural struggle, as its projection of mass culture continues to be viewed as a source of 'corruption' for art, lacking in creativity and individuality. Most Iranian rock musicians are perhaps more concerned with a rebellion against mainstream culture than political subversion. Many musicians and critics express their belief that the underground represents musical creativity that cannot be found anywhere else. Shahram Sharbaf, founder of pioneering Iranian underground rock band O-Hum, contends, 'Maybe it's good that the best music is all underground. It keeps us on the edge. It keeps us fresh' (Levine 2008). To continue struggling in the underground towards a seemingly unattainable goal achieves a certain authenticity, and in the eyes of young musicians and their audiences is often seen as better than succeeding in the mainstream.

Music countercultures and underground subcultures are often split between the desire to be released commercially and the determination to resist a mainstream label. In such cases, those – usually pop musicians – who reach 'above ground' status, achieving mainstream appeal and commercial success, are accused by underground musicians of selling out to the 'masses.' Commercial music gains the stigma of artistic compromise. Thomas Solomon writes that the Turkish underground was split between musicians who wanted mainstream success and those who took pride in their underground status, creating tension (2005). British-Asian hip hop and French undergrounds also illustrated a similar division between achieving commercial success and retaining a sense of authenticity in the underground (Huq 2006a; 2006b). In Iran, this issue is complicated by the fact that

---

78 Fereidoun Tafreshi, interview by author, email correspondence (12 June, 2011).

there is a very limited commercial music industry. Morad Mansouri, reporting for PBS's *Tehran Bureau* in October 2010, explained that the underground is, 'not a protest against market norms imposed by a constructive and domineering music industry, but rather a *samizdat* art form in a country whose rulers abhor music altogether and have consigned most expressions of it to the realm of the forbidden until roughly eight years ago ...' (Mansouri 2011). It becomes difficult to 'sell out' to the mainstream when mainstream status is almost impossible to attain, at least nationally. Musicians can be self-conflicted as well, trying to balance their underground identity with the longing for acknowledgement. While Maral Afsharian revels in an 'exciting' underground, she still desires for music restrictions to be lifted in Iran so she can release records and perform without restraint. Until then, she continues to use social networking sites to build relationships with fans across the world. She is not alone, as most Iranian rock musicians, despite their defence of the underground, seek recognition in the public domain and want to spread their music in Iran and beyond. There can be a stigma attached to musicians who decide to leave, as they are presumed to have sold out to not only the mainstream but also the West. The label of authenticity is then attributed to musicians who remain in their country of origin, and even more to those who continue to make music unofficially.

The 'Voice of the Dispossessed'

Commonly, DIY subcultures are known for their roots in class or economic difference. However, these practices can differ greatly depending on the surrounding social climate. Whereas in the United Kingdom the punk movement stemmed from issues of class and economic background, in the United States it challenged the state of music at the time, taking on a narcissistic and even elitist tone (Irving 1988). British punk turned towards a collective political radicalism while American punk became a more individualistic expression of dissatisfaction.

Many Iranian musicians pride themselves on what they consider to be their humble origins as notions of DIY and elements of the punk rock tradition live on through a type of collective resistance that could be rooted in both its British and American counterparts. Typically, underground musicians claim to have no mainstream aspirations since too much popularity is seen as detrimental to their underground reputation. Retaining control over the creative process is of foremost concern as it signifies authenticity in the music-making process. In addition, the appearance of DIY's low-budget approach projects a sense of an honest vision, an authentic musical truth that is at once individual and communal as it is shared by others in the underground. Underground music gains authenticity as a pure, innocent sound, or, as Michael Newman states, the true 'voice of the dispossessed' (Newman 2009).

However, there are elements of this discussion of authenticity that are often ignored in media reports and even academic discourse. In Tehran, the participants of underground rock usually come from a large burgeoning middle-class urban population where, to quote the political theorist Ernesto Laclau's post-Marxist theory of populism, 'Identity as a people plays a much more important role than the identity as a class' (Irving 1988). The main focus of the underground subculture continues to be the expression of Iranian youth as a whole. There are other reasons that could be relevant here, such as the much-explored notion of Western society as individualist vs. non-Western society as collectivist, but in this case class plays an important role. When the vast majority of participants of rock belong to the middle and upper classes, the issue of class seems to be forgotten as music becomes a collective, community-based activity. One could even say it is ignored, as it seems to exclude lower or working-class youth who do not have the same access to the Internet and musical equipment to participate in the music DIY underground. Thus, Newman's 'voice of the dispossessed' takes on a more singular meaning, becoming a characterization of those who seemingly have a limited voice against authority, rather than those who are economically or socially disadvantaged.

Iranian middle and upper-class youth are increasingly being heard above the authoritative mantle of the conservative Iranian government, using the Internet and media portals to express their concerns and creative output to the rest of the world. They are participating in mass movements, such as the 2009 Green Movement where they demanded change after a disappointing election result shrouded in controversy. They are strengthening relationships with diaspora communities and developing their international media image as one of 'the Iranian youth.' But nonetheless, these voices are a fraction of Iran's emergent youth population as the country's poverty line hovers around 50%, with a climbing unemployment rate.[79] Many included in this percentage reside in remote rural areas with little access to the Internet or the music produced in the Tehrani underground.

Again, there is another element to this discussion. Far from being concealed in the underground, many Iranian popular musicians are becoming progressively well known. The underground's virtual existence combined with its popularization in the Western media has encouraged its growth as unofficial music continues to gain global popularity. In Tehran, illegal transactions of popular music far outnumber legal exchanges of government-approved music, since Internet technology allows easier accessibility as the latest underground tracks are usually available to download for free (Lutfi 2007). Self-produced, homemade music videos, uploaded to the Internet, have also become increasingly common. Tafreshi reiterates:

> Underground is a misleading terminology ... The so called underground musicians are in fact ... very visible and an integrated part of artistic society of Iran ... people tend to think that these artists are trying to hide from people ... And as such they refer [to] them as underground. But the main problem is that the official channels do not allow them to release their work and [they] are not recognized [by the government] ...[80]

Underground culture, like many precedent countercultures throughout the twentieth century, could be on the road to becoming mainstream despite its unofficial nature.

---

79 This statistic includes both absolute and relative poverty figures. See *Iran: Rising Poverty, Declining Labour Rights* (League for the Defence of Human Rights in Iran, 2013).
80 Tafreshi, interview by author.

Conclusion

Although subcultures rely on notions of authenticity to assert their identities, authenticity is defined by romantic expectation rather than reality. Thus, the pursuit of authenticity is rarely wholly fulfilled. Authenticity may never be achieved, but that misses the point. The danger of focusing on the idea of an authentic practice, as often seen in the media, or even by musicians themselves, is that only one element of music making is emphasized. Musicians come together, defining music culture as a supposedly authentic, coherent product, ignoring all of the cross-cultural interactions and negotiations as well as individual experiences that occurred to produce such unique musical encounters. A study of the various ways the search for authenticity takes shape begins to illustrate the complexities of a developing subculture. The idealized images of underground culture may perpetuate various myths of authenticity, but upon closer observation they also draw attention to how musicians navigate and cultivate their own images in the media and the global world.

At the heart of this discussion is how young Iranian musicians are traversing traditional notions of DIY culture and readapting them, fundamentally and aesthetically. Using the impetus and original ideas from Western punk and DIY movements, musicians are crossing musical boundaries as they combine these influences with local and traditional rhythms and sounds. New Iranian rock bands express not only themselves individually, but also the cultural in-between-space they collectively find themselves in, as Iranian popular music culture has become a bricolage of global cultural influence. As young Iranian musicians persistently re-invent and re-adapt as they respond to their surrounding cultural climates, they continue to shape their evolving musical identities while providing new models of expression for youth generations around the world.

References

Appadurai, A. (1996). *Modernity at Large: the Cultural Dimensions of Globalization.* Minneapolis: Public Works Publications.

Brake, M. (1985). *Comparative Youth Culture: the Sociology of Youth Cultures and Youth Subcultures in America, Britain, and Canada.* London: Routledge.

Burr, T. (2010). 'No One Knows about Persian Cats' Movie Review.' *The Boston Globe* (14 May). http://www.boston.com/ae/movies/articles/2010/05/14/in_no_one_knows_about_persian_cats_iranian_kids_play_rock_in_a_hard_place.

Clarke, J. et al. (1981). 'Subcultures, Cultures and Class.' In T. Bennett et al. (eds.), *Culture, Ideology and Social Process*, 53–80. London: The Open University Press.

Cloonan, M. (1999). 'Pop and the Nation-state: Towards a Theorisation.' *Popular Music* 18(2): 193–207.

Connell, J., and C. Gibson. (2003). *Sound Tracks: Popular Music, Identity, and Place.* London: Routledge.

Fathi, N. (2007). 'Iran's Dylan on the Lute, With Songs of Sly Protest.' *New York Times* (September 1). http://www.nytimes.com/2007/09/01/world/middleeast/01namjoo.html?pagewanted=all.

Fear, D. (2010). 'No One Knows about Persian Cats – Film Review.' *Time Out New York* (14 April). http://newyork.timeout.com/articles/film/84749/no-one-knows-about-persian-cats-film-review.

Frith, S. (1978). *The Sociology of Rock.* London: Constable and Company Ltd.

Frith, S. (1989). 'Introduction.' In S. Frith (ed.), *World Music, Politics and Social Change*, 1–7. Manchester: Manchester University Press.

Frith, S. (1996). *Performing Rites: on the Value of Popular Music.* Cambridge, MA: Harvard University Press.

Glass, B. (2010). 'No One Knows about Persian Cats Soundtrack Review.' *Working Author* (8 June). http://www.workingauthor.com/no-one-knows-about-persian-cats-soundtrack-review.

Gothic Goddess Media. (2010). *Gothic Goddess Media Interviews Maral Afsharian* (June 26) http://digg.com/news/entertainment/Gothic_Goddess_Media_Interviews_Maral_Afsharian.

Hebdige, D. (1983). 'Posing … Threats, Striking … Poses: Youth, Surveillance, and Display.' *SubStance*, 11 (4).

Hochman, S. (2010). 'Persian Music Iconoclast Mohsen Namjoo Rocks Through "Strange Times".' *Spinner* (15 June). http://www.spinner.com/2010/06/15/mohsen-namjoo-strange-times.

Holslin, P. (2010). 'Theocracy bites: Indie-rockers Hypernova Won't Return to Iran Any Time Soon.' *San Diego CityBeat* (14 July). http://www.sdcitybeat.com/sandiego/article-7933-theocracy-bites.html.

Huq, R. (2006a). *Beyond Subculture: Pop, Youth and Identity in a Postcolonial World.* London: Routledge.

Huq, R. (2006b). 'European Youth Cultures in a Post-colonial World: British Asian Underground and French Hip-hop Music Scenes.' In P. Nilan and C. Feixa (eds.), *Global youth? Hybrid identities, plural worlds*, 14–31. London: Routledge.

Irving, K. (1988). 'Rock Music and the State: Dissonance or Counterpoint?' *Cultural Critique* 10: 151–70.

Kafai, Y. B. and K. A. Peppler. (2011). 'Youth, Technology, and DIY: Developing Participatory Competencies in Creative Media Production.' *Review of Research in Education* 35: 89–119.

Karami, Arash. (2011). 'Kiosk: "Hey Man, Pull Over".' *Frontline: Tehran Bureau* (April 19). http://www.pbs.org/wgbh/pages/frontline/tehranbureau/2011/04/video-kiosk-hey-man-pull-over.html.

Kaufman, G. (2007). 'Meet Iran's Hypernova: a Rock Band from a Country that Arrests Rock Bands.' *MTV* (6 April). http://www.mtv.com/news/articles/1556532/20070405/hypernova.jhtml.

King, R. (2007). 'What is Underground?' *Zirzamin* (14 January). http://zirzamin.se/?q=node/77.

Lashkari, S., M. Golestan, and A. Kooshanejad. (2011). *Persian Hip-hop and Alternative Music Forum. Performance and Discussion*. Oxford: Oxford University Press.

League for the Defence of Human Rights in Iran, The International Federation for Human Rights (2013). *Rising Poverty, Declining Labour Rights* (report 2013). http://www.fidh.org/IMG/pdf/iran_report_en.pdf.

Levine, M. (2008). *Heavy Metal Islam*. New York: Three Rivers Press.

Lutfi, M. (2007). 'Iran's Underground Music Revolution.' *Asharq Alawsat* (26 May). http://www.asharqalawsat.com/english/news.asp?section=3&id=9082.

Magee, P. (2010). 'Bust Blog Interview: Roxana Saberi, Iranian-American Journalist and Screenwriter of No One Knows About Persian Cats.' *Bust Magazine* (23 April). https://bust.com/blog/bust-blog-interview-roxana-saberi-iranian-american-journalist-and-screenwriter-of-no-one-knows-about-persian-cats.html.

Mansouri, M. (2011). The underground rises. *Frontline: The Tehran Bureau* (24 May). http://www.pbs.org/wgbh/pages/frontline/tehranbureau/2011/05/best-music-writing-2011-honoree-the-underground-rises.html.

McKay, G. (2005). 'The Social and (Counter)Cultural 1960s in the USA, Transatlantically. Summer of Love: Psychedelic Art, Social Crisis and the Counterculture in the 1960s.' *Tate Liverpool Critical Forum* 8: 35–62.

Memarian, O. and T. Nesvaderani. (2010). Iran primer: the youth. *Frontline: Tehran Bureau* (27 October). http://www.pbs.org/wgbh/pages/frontline/tehranbureau/2010/10/irans-youth.html.

Meraji, S. (2010). 'Hypernova: an Iranian Rock Band in Brooklyn' (9 April). http://www.npr.org/templates/story/story.php?storyId=125780177&ft=1&f=1039.

Miller, L. (1999). *Music and Song in Persia*. Richmond, Surrey: Curzon Press.

Mowlaei, M. M. (2007). An Interview with Dr. Mehdi Semati: Iranian Underground Music, a Music to Stay (Translated by Nina Jamshid Nejd). *7-Sang Persian E-Zine*. http://www.7sang.com/languages/english/2007/12/iranian-underground-music-a-music-to-stay.html.

MTV. (2007). 'Hypernova: Rockers Without Borders.' *MTV* (6 April). http://www.mtv.com/videos/news/142229/hypernova-prove-you-can-rock-in-iran.jhtml#id=1556595.

Nasri, G. (2008). 'Immigrant rock band Hypernova on U.S. Tour.' *Payvand Iran News* (13 November). http://www.payvand.com/news/08/nov/1127.html.

Newman, M. Z. (2009). 'Indie Culture: in Pursuit of the Authentic Autonomous Alternative.' *Cinema Journal* 48 (3): 16–34.

No One Knows about Persian Cats – Official Trailer (2010). YouTube (March 17, 2010). https://www.youtube.com/watch?v=5gLq3E4pRuU.

Nooshin, L. (2008). 'The Language of Rock: Iranian Youth, Popular Music, and National Identity.' In M. Semati (ed.), *Media, Culture and Society in Iran: Living with Globalization and the Islamic State*, 69–93. New York: Routledge.

Petersen, F. (2007). 'Iranian Rock Band has a New York Moment.' *The New York Times* (28 March). http://www.nytimes.com/2007/03/28/arts/music/28band.html?_r=3&oref=slogin.

Reshad, K. (ed.) (2008). *Urban Iran.* New York: Mark Batty Publisher.

Reverbnation. (2008). *Introduction to Khal Punk.* http://www.reverbnation.com/artist/song_details/738741.

Sadighi, R. (2009). 'The Underground Double Bind.' *Tehran Avenue* http://www.tehranavenue.com/article.php?id=901.

Satrapi, M. (2008). *Persepolis.* DVD. Sony Pictures Home Entertainment.

Shahabi, M. (2006). 'Youth Subcultures in Post-revolution Iran: an Alternative Reading.' In P. Nilan and C. Feixa (eds.), *Global Youth? Hybrid Identities, Plural Worlds*, 111–29. London: Routledge.

Shuker, R. (2012). *Understanding Popular Music.* Abingdon: Routledge.

Siddiqi, A. (2005). 'Khatami and the Search for Reform in Iran.' *Stanford Journal of International Relations* 6 (1). http://www.stanford.edu/group/sjir/6.1.04_siddiqi.html.

Siletz, A. (2010). 'Subversive Music: Interview with Kiosk's Arash Sobhani.' *The Iranian* (23 June). http://www.iranian.com/main/2010/jun/subversive-music.

Silverman, C. (2012). *Romani Routes: Cultural Politics and Balkan Music in the Diaspora.* New York: Oxford University Press.

Solomon, T. (2005). '"Living Underground is Tough": Authenticity and Locality in the Hip-hop Community in Istanbul, Turkey.' *Popular Music* 24: 1–20.

Tafreshi, F. (2011). Interview with author. Email correspondence (12 June).

Thornton, S. (1996). *Club Cultures: Music, Media and Subcultural Capital.* Middletown, CT: Wesleyan University Press.

Weinstein, D. (2006). 'Rock Protest Songs: So Many and So Few.' In I. Peddie (ed.), *The Resisting Muse: Popular Music and Social Protest*, 3–16. Aldershot: Ashgate.

Widdicombe, S. and R. Wooffitt. (1995). *The Language of Youth Subcultures: Social Identity in Action.* Hertfordshire: Harvester Wheatsheaf.

Williams, R. (1963). *Culture and Society 1780–1950.* Harmondsworth: Penguin.

XXXBLACK LINEXXX

EWSLETTER KOLEKTIF SXE 'ULTRAMILITANCE' BANDUNG

#1

STRAIGHT HARDCORE AND RED

11. 'DIY OR DIE': DO IT YOURSELF PRODUCTION AND THE STRUGGLE FOR AN AUTONOMOUS COMMUNITY IN THE BANDUNG HARDCORE PUNK SCENE

SEAN MARTIN-IVERSON

Abstract

The city of Bandung, Indonesia is home to a substantial hardcore punk scene; within this scene, a small but assertive DIY hardcore current strives to build a creative community that operates according to anti-capitalist DIY principles. Drawing on ethnographic research in the Bandung scene, I explore the value practices and social organization of this community, focusing especially on three specific DIY projects: the Kolektif Balai Kota [City Hall Collective], an open, consensus-based collective that organizes non-profit hardcore shows; the Endless DIY Store, a local independent distributor of DIY records, zines, and other products; and Inkoherent DIY Nutritionist, a record label that releases localized, affordable versions of albums by international DIY bands. Through such projects and the social relations in which they are embedded, the 'DIY kids' [*anak DIY*] are building a cultural commons of shared means, knowledge and value as an alternative to the alienating logic of the capitalist market. While the autonomy of this DIY community remains partial, precarious and contested, the values it expresses and realizes point towards alternative ways of organizing cultural production and social life. Such practices of radical social creativity are important parts of the continuing political significance of punk in Indonesia and elsewhere.

Keywords: DIY production, value politics, cultural commons, Indonesia, hardcore punk

Sean Martin-Iverson is an Associate Lecturer in Anthropology and Sociology at The University of Western Australia. This paper is based on his doctoral research project, 'The Politics of Cultural Production in the DIY Hardcore Scene in Bandung, Indonesia.' Sean has ongoing research interests in underground music scenes, the politics of creative labour, global social movements, and contested urbanism in Indonesia.
E-mail: smartiniverson@graduate.uwa.edu.au

'DIY OR DIE': DO IT YOURSELF PRODUCTION AND THE STRUGGLE FOR AN AUTONOMOUS COMMUNITY IN THE BANDUNG HARDCORE PUNK SCENE

Introduction: DIY hardcore in Bandung

The city of Bandung, Indonesia is home to a notable hardcore punk scene, which is marked by both a history of radical political expression and, especially in the context of neoliberal 'post-authoritarian' twenty-first century Indonesia, a considerable degree of commercialization. Within this scene, a small DIY hardcore[81] community, centred on the Kolektif Bali Kota [City Hall Collective], strives to uphold the Do It Yourself principles and practices of production that they identify as the authentic core of punk. Drawing on global anarcho-punk and DIY hardcore currents, these 'DIY kids' [*anak DIY*] organize themselves on the basis of the twin values of autonomy [*kemandirian*] and community [*komunitas*], which together constitute a DIY ethic of collaborative, non-profit production. In this chapter, based on ethnographic research in the Bandung scene, I describe several DIY hardcore projects from Bandung, seeking to demonstrate the social logic of the DIY ethic as the basis for an autonomous community of production, and critically analyse its political potential as part of an anti-capitalist movement.

Indonesian hardcore punk, and especially the Bandung scene, is marked by a relatively recent history of assertive political expression and action; in the late 1990s, during the decline and fall of the Suharto dictatorship, a militant anarcho-punk movement took their anti-authoritarian protest to the streets as well as the stage. In the 2000s, however, the scene was marked by a turn to a depoliticized, market-oriented lifestyle politics (Martin-Iverson 2012; Pickles 2007). While Luvaas (2012) celebrates this entrepreneurial spirit as an expression of DIY creativity and agency, for the *anak DIY* it represents a betrayal of the anti-capitalist principles of DIY punk. Their commitment to independent, non-profit production is a critical response to this process of commercialization and the perceived failure of the spectacular forms of subcultural and protest politics that preceded it.

The Bandung DIY hardcore scene takes inspiration from global and especially North American models of DIY production and exchange through a network of small, independent labels, distributors, and other enterprises that operate to a large extent outside the corporate music and cultural industries (Gosling 2004; Moore 2007; O'Connor 2008; Spencer 2005; Thompson 2004). Examples of such enterprises in the Bandung scene include Inkoherent DIY Nutritionist, a record label that releases localized, affordable

---

81 'Hardcore' in this context refers to hardcore punk, a punk-derived music genre and subculture with aesthetic influences from extreme metal and connotations of a more stringent commitment to the DIY principles of punk independence.

CD-R versions of albums by international DIY bands, and the Endless Independent Store, a local independent distributor of DIY records, zines, and other products from Bandung and around the world. For much of the 2000s, a central institution for the scene was the Kolektif Balai Kota (BalKot) – an *ad hoc* collective that organized non-profit hardcore punk shows, often featuring touring international bands.

O'Connor (2008) and Moore (2007) describe DIY production in terms of a struggle for creative autonomy, but the meaning of this DIY autonomy is contested. For the *anak DIY*, the autonomy of DIY hardcore punk comes through a collective refusal of commodified, alienated labour. Like other DIY punks, Bandung's *anak DIY* stress the use value of hardcore punk products and performances – their social role as forms of expression and communication – against their economic exchange value as commodities for sale on the market (Thompson 2004). Furthermore, against the more individualist definitions of 'Do It Yourself' that have taken hold in the wider scene, the *anak DIY* particularly emphasize the collective social value of DIY production.

While DIY production can in part be considered a system of petty commodity production, it also displays many features of gift exchange (Godbout 1998; Graeber 2001, 151–228; Gregory 1982; Mauss 2002; Sahlins 1972). DIY production is largely free from immediate entanglement in capital accumulation and the commodification of labour, and contributes to establishing a cultural commons of shared means. It can thus be considered a practice of commoning (Hardt and Negri 2009; Linebaugh 2014; De Angelis 2007, 238–9) or self-valorization (Cleaver 1989; 1992; Negri 1991), producing qualitative forms of cultural value and social relations independently from the capitalist value system. On this basis, DIY punk can be positioned as a form of anti-capitalist struggle (Holtzman, Hughes and Van Meter 2007; O'Hara 1999; Ovetz 1993; Rosen 1997).

The *anak DIY* in Bandung are attempting to establish a system of production and social organization that is autonomous from the global circuits of capital accumulation. While in practice their autonomy remains partial and contested, the values expressed and realized through DIY hardcore do point towards an alternative way of living, starkly at odds with the authoritarian capitalism that dominates social life in Indonesia and around the world. I thus consider DIY hardcore to be a form of value struggle, in De Angelis' (2007) terms an ongoing struggle to escape from capitalist circuits of value and establish an autonomous community based on the alternative social values of the DIY ethic.

Autonomy, Community and the DIY Ethic

The Bandung DIY hardcore community is guided by a set of principles and practices which they refer to as the DIY ethic or *etika DIY*. While there is no single, stable definition of this ethic, the *anak DIY* describe it in terms of the twin values of autonomy [*kemandirian*] and community [*komunitas*]. DIY autonomy can be compared to the anarchistic ethic of independent living and self-expression which O'Hara (1999) calls 'the philosophy of punk.' Most centrally, the DIY ethic refers to a set of principles and practices of independent cultural production enacted through underground networks. The *anak DIY* are significantly influenced by global DIY networks in developing their understanding of DIY, but they put a stronger emphasis on the collaborative and communal aspects of DIY production, especially when compared to the dominant North American DIY hardcore scenes (Gosling 2004; Moore 2007; O'Connor 2008). While individualist and entrepreneurial interpretations of DIY are certainly present in the wider Indonesian scene (Luvaas 2012; Martin-Iverson 2012), the *anak DIY* associated with the Kolektif Balai Kota adopt a more resolutely anti-capitalist approach.

In positioning DIY as a practice of non-alienated production, the *anak DIY* exclude profit-seeking and the employment of wage labour as much as possible from their DIY hardcore activities. They contrast this approach with what they identify as the growing dominance of a capitalist business ethic in the wider scene. For example, in a leaflet produced for the opening of his DIY store (described below), Methui condemns the commercialization of hardcore punk associated with a 'big business mentality' that violates the DIY ethic. Instead, he argues that DIY hardcore should be a collective endeavour for realizing an autonomous, alternative way of life.

While in part a defence of underground authenticity against 'selling out' to mainstream appropriation, this critique also reveals the positioning of DIY production as an interpersonal form of autonomy. As BalKot activist Tremor puts it:

> DIY is like an alternative so that we don't have to just spend all our money on corporate products. Yeah, and … the BalKot kids are no longer dependent because everyone can do sharing with each other. Like it's a way to make something for ourselves … So we reduce our consumption of products that we don't really need, and learn how to make stuff ourselves. For our own use, and not products for sale, y'know? (Interview with Tremor, 2004, my translation)

The DIY ethic thus includes a valorization of production for use rather than market exchange, as Thompson (2004) and Holtzman, Hughes, and Van Meter (2007) argue, but this use value is not understood in purely individual or aesthetic terms. The *anak DIY* connect their personal autonomy to the collective activity and self-organization of the DIY community as a whole. This emphasis on collectivity in part reflects the influence of communal values within Indonesian political culture more generally, but the *anak DIY* sharply distinguish their approach to *komunitas* from the authoritarian discourses of social harmony associated with the Indonesian state (Bourchier 1998). Some of the *anak DIY* do draw parallels with traditional Indonesian commoning practices, such as the local volunteer labour practices known as *gotong royong* [mutual aid], but in doing so they tend to emphasize the local rather than the nationalist aspect of such practices, as BalKot activist Rahar does:

Sean: What would you say is the relationship between DIY and Indonesian culture?

Rahar: In some cases, like some DIY screen-printing industry, they are very Indonesian. Run by their self and their friends. You know, like, you know the terms of *gotong royong*? Yeah, that's – I think the relationship, it's just only about that. Some DIY production usually involves their friends and their local friends, like their neighbourhood. But for me there is not yet a big impact on the society. Probably just a small, a small community like in family or just like in collectives like this. (Interview with Rahar, October 2004, original in English)

DIY production emphasizes the positive aspect of labour as self-organized and socially productive creative activity, in opposition to the alienating and sacrificial logic of capitalist production (Marx 1973, 610–16; Vaneigem 2006, 107–16). The *etika DIY* is not simply an assertion of individual creative autonomy; rather, it is an ethic of participatory production which also forms part of a collective movement away from a system of production dominated by capital accumulation and alienated labour. The DIY struggle for autonomy can certainly lead to a form of self-marginalization, as the autonomous community becomes an isolated and inward-looking underground, yet it is also this very marginality that enables them to carve out a space for non-alienated production. Such marginal autonomous spaces can also serve as liberated zones for engaging in broader anti-capitalist struggles (Cleaver 1989; Holtzman, Hughes, and Van Meter 2007; Ovetz 1993; Shukaitis 2010; Wright 2000).

'By the Kids, For the Kids': The Kolektif Balai Kota

A central institution for Bandung's DIY hardcore community is the organizing collective known as the Kolektif Balai Kota, named for their regular meeting place on a flight of steps outside Bandung's city hall or *Balai Kota*. It is a fairly small group without formal membership; weekly meetings usually attract between fifteen and thirty people, who gather to organize hardcore punk shows and other DIY activities, hold discussions on key issues for the scene, and also socialize. BalKot participants are mostly young men (and a few women) in their late teens and early twenties; well educated but with low incomes, many are students or recent graduates precariously employed in the culture and service industries. Most people involved in BalKot are also engaged in various other DIY projects, such as performing in DIY hardcore bands, operating micro-scale music labels and distros, or producing zines, artwork, or band merchandise. BalKot serves as a central meeting place and networking hub for the *anak DIY*, helping to bring together various DIY activities, projects, and enterprises into a coherent community. The collective is rather marginal in relation to the broader Indonesian hardcore scene, but also stands out as a bastion of DIY principles.

The major collective activity of BalKot is to organise non-profit, non-sponsored shows for local and touring DIY hardcore bands, though the group also plays a role in coordinating other activities of the DIY community. Skill-sharing workshops are occasionally organised through BalKot on topics such as screen-printing and badge-making. On a few occasions, the BalKot steps have also been used as a performance space, such as for touring Australian solo punk musician Steve Towson in 2004. BalKot meetings are also used for discussions on DIY principles, the state of the scene, the relationship between punk and anarchism, and broader social, political, and philosophical issues. BalKot is also a place to hang out, chat, and gossip with friends, swap music, zines, merchandise, and books, keep in touch with scene and activist news and events, and meet up before going to shows.

BalKot itself is part organizing collective and part social gathering; the organizational and political work of the BalKot collective is embedded in a context of personalised DIY activities and exchanges. Some participants have argued that a more stable and organised approach is needed, modelled on anarchist infoshops, the anarcho-punk social centres found in many European cities, and long-standing DIY institutions such as 924 Gilman Street in Berkeley, California or ABC No Rio in New York.[82] However, BalKot activists also value the open, informal, and non-hierarchical nature of the group. The demand for practical organization asserts itself most strongly in the immediate lead up to a show, with venues to book, publicity to produce, and funds to raise.

Organizing DIY shows, for both local and touring bands, is the central activity of BalKot; the *anak DIY* put a great deal of effort and resources into organizing these shows, which are vital for bringing the community together and demonstrating DIY principles in action.[83] BalKot shows are explicitly intended to serve as examples of the self-organization of the DIY community; run 'by the kids, for the kids,' these shows serve as a focal point for their collective organization and decision-making processes. DIY shows organized by BalKot range from small, intimate studio performances to the more ambitious and larger shows put on for visiting international DIY acts, usually held in student or community halls. As well as organizing shows in Bandung, BalKot activists played a key role in the emergence of a regional DIY touring network in the early 2000s, coordinating with neighbouring scenes and DIY bands from around the world.

All BalKot shows are run on a strictly non-profit, no sponsorship basis. Much of their funding comes from ticket sales, but these are kept relatively low at between Rp 5000–6000.[84] Where costs are low, as with the solo performances by Rachel Jacobs (acoustic punk from New York) and Steve Towson (from Australia), BalKot will gladly organize free shows, often in impromptu venues. BalKot completely rejects commercial sponsorship, which is a major source of funding for shows and festivals in the wider scene. The *anak DIY* regard such sponsorship as the line of demarcation between a DIY and a commercial show, and publicity material for their shows often includes statements such as 'sponsored by: no one' and 'no sponsorshit!' or parodies of sponsors' logos.

If there are any proceeds left over from a DIY show they are put back into BalKot and the DIY community, being used to support subsequent shows and other BalKot events. However, ticket sales do not always fully cover costs and BalKot does not have an

---

82 In 2005–6 such a DIY space was established in Bandung, supported by a fundraising show and album organized by the KTS social centre in Freiburg, Germany, but this project proved to be short lived.

83 See Martin-Iverson (2014) for a more-detailed discussion of the ways in which DIY values are expressed through hardcore punk performances in the Bandung scene.

84 Equivalent to less than AU $1.00.

accumulated reserve of funds, so the collective must rely on various additional fundraising techniques and voluntary contributions from the DIY community. The most important and consistent source for pre-show funding is BalKot's 'pay to play' policy, in which each band is expected to contribute Rp 100,000 to the show, although they are usually refunded some proportion of their contribution from money raised through ticket sales. Touring international bands are exempt from this contribution and may even receive some payment to help defray their travel costs, though not usually enough to make a profit; most treat their Indonesian tours as something of a 'working holiday,' exchanging their performances for the hospitality and organizational work of local groups like BalKot.

BalKot shows are very much participatory endeavours, without firm divisions among the performers, organizers, and audience. While participation cannot be said to be completely equal, it is not divided into rigidly distinct roles; most of the more involved community members will take on various roles as musicians, organizers, promoters, ticket sellers, photographers, journalists, and members of the audience. While BalKot shows would be accounted failures by commercial standards, they succeed in forging a sense of solidarity and asserting the autonomy of the DIY community. DIY shows possess substantial social value for the *anak DIY* as collective expressions of cultural creativity and social intimacy. It is BalKot's role as the main vehicle for organizing DIY hardcore shows, as well as the regularity of its weekly meetings, that grants the collective its part at the heart of the Bandung DIY community.[85] However, the community itself is wider and more diffuse than BalKot, constituted by a range of overlapping, personalized relationships of production, exchange, collaboration, and friendship.

Inkoherent DIY Nutritionist: Producing Relationships through a DIY Micro-label

The archetypal DIY punk enterprise is a small, independent record label, often started by one or more band members in order to release their own music and that of their friends. While not able to completely ignore commercial considerations, these labels are primarily motivated by social and artistic rather than economic goals (Moore 2007, 457–61; O'Connor 2008, 24–8; Spencer 2005, 323–43). They operate based on friendship and trust rather than legal contracts, and there is little to no demarcation between the operations of the enterprise and the personal tastes, relationships, and attitudes of the individuals involved. DIY labels are often launched and directed by a single person or small group, but they are also motivated by the desire to make a contribution to the DIY hardcore community and are embedded in its collective activities.

This is demonstrated by the Bandung label Inkoherent DIY Nutritionist, founded in 2004 by Ari 'Ernesto' from BalKot and the DIY hardcore band Domestik Doktrin, operating until 2006. A small-scale DIY enterprise, from 2004 until 2006 Inkoherent released a series of CD-R versions of albums by international DIY bands that toured Indonesia, specifically

---

85 Since I conducted my fieldwork, the collective has shifted its location and focus of activity several times, experienced various changes in membership, and been disbanded, re-established, and disbanded again. Yet the mode of organization of which it is an exemplar remains vital to the value practices of DIY hardcore in Bandung.

Barackca (from Hungary), a Pack/S.O.L. split release (Switzerland/Germany), Secret 7 (Singapore), My Disco (Australia), and Sabot (Czech Republic), burning them in small batches of 50 to 100. By copying and distributing localized, affordable versions of these recordings, Ernesto sought to help build relationships between the local *anak DIY* and these touring bands:

> What I want to achieve is for people here in Indonesia to be able to get to know these bands. Because, especially right now, I'm releasing bands that will be coming to Indonesia, like Barackca and maybe later My Disco from Australia. I want people here to know those bands, because although they're international bands maybe they aren't too well known. But I want people here to get to know them, and not just know about the big hardcore punk bands from the US. So I want to supply information to people here, that's all. (Interview with Ari 'Ernesto,' 2004, my translation)

Inkoherent was launched as a personal project of Ernesto, and indeed he funded the first release, the 2004 Indonesian tour edition of Barackca's *Open Your Mouth*, out of his own pocket, but it was always reliant on input from the wider DIY hardcore community. Inkoherent releases were discussed at BalKot meetings so that they could be properly coordinated with the organization of the shows, and Ernesto brought in various friends and fellow BalKot activists to help out with the design, production, and distribution. One of these volunteers, Frans, took on most of the responsibility for organizing the label's 2005 Pack/S.O.L. release, and became Ernesto's partner in the label. Marking this shift towards shared responsibility, Inkoherent adopted a new logo featuring a pair of skulls. Further demonstrating Inkoherent's collaborative approach, their third release, for the 2005 tour by Singapore's Secret 7, was a joint effort with the Jakarta DIY label Stop N Go.

Inkoherent releases were directly connected to the shows organized by BalKot and the Indonesian DIY Tour Network of which it was a part. Ernesto and Frans especially wanted to help transform the relationship of local *anak DIY* with international bands from one of distant consumption to a more interactive one of mutual communication. Though published informally and without royalty payments, Inkoherent releases were produced with the support of the bands. The releases helped to promote and support their Indonesian tours, and bands were given between ten and fifty copies to distribute themselves. This was intended to facilitate cross-scene exchange rather than be a form of economic compensation, and Pack and S.O.L. reciprocated the fifteen Inkoherent CDs they received by providing twenty-five copies of their original CD recordings for local distribution.

The choice of producing records in a CD-R format was intended to reconcile a range of competing goals – affordability, accessibility, ease of initial production, and facilitating subsequent reproduction and sharing – while still producing valued and personalized objects with distinctive aesthetic qualities. Although much DIY hardcore distribution has now moved online, Internet access was (and still is) unevenly distributed in Indonesia, and so Ernesto decided that Inkoherent should utilize an affordable hardcopy format. Although cassettes were the dominant recording format in Indonesia at the time, he decided to go with a digital format which enabled both inexpensive DIY production – the CD-Rs could be burned in small batches at home – and ease of further copying and circulation within the local scene.

The *anak DIY* also value many of the aesthetic and communicative features associated with physical records, such as artwork, detailed liner notes, and the inclusion of stickers, comics, leaflets, and other bonus materials, as well as the more direct and personal social interaction associated with hand-to-hand distribution. Although produced in an inexpensive DIY format – the materials cost around Rp 3500 per CD[86] – a fair amount of attention and work went into the design and packaging. Several Inkoherent releases used 'vinyl-look' CDs and were packaged in DVD cases, differentiating them from other Indonesian DIY CDs which tended to be distributed in thin plastic envelopes. Inkoherent packaging included cover art and graphic design by local scene artists (including Ernesto's bandmate Ken Terror, Ucok Homicide, and Frans from Inkoherent), along with lyrics sheets, explanatory notes, and contact details for the bands. The limited production and restricted distribution also contributed to a certain exclusivity and intimacy, highlighted by the hand numbering of the releases as 'Indonesian tour limited editions.' Both the sense of exclusivity and the close association with a specific experience of live performance added to the value of these records within the local DIY community, yet this value was not fully reflected in their price (Rp 10,000–12,000).[87]

While the value of Inkoherent recordings derives in part from adherence to hardcore aesthetics, the label is more concerned with upholding the DIY ethic through producing cultural artefacts that facilitate the establishment and maintenance of community relationships, using freely given rather than alienated wage labour in its direct production activities, and generally aiming to strengthen the autonomy of the DIY community rather than operating as a self-interested business. Ernesto also expressed a desire to develop Inkoherent beyond a record label into various other forms of DIY education:

> It's called Inkoherent – not *Records* and not *Tapes*, but simply *'DIY Nutritionist'.*
> What this means is that we can be a *nutritionist*, like a supplier of health for the DIY
> community in Indonesia. *It's figurative speech, yeah?* So, it's possible that in the future
> we won't just release tapes and CDs and stuff like that. We'll also release other things.
> Maybe we can do books, or even art exhibitions, paintings – stuff like that. (Interview
> with Ari 'Ernesto,' 2004, my translation; italicised passages originally in English)

Inkoherent never fully achieved these goals, winding up after its fifth release, Sabot's *Doing It Ourselves* in 2006, as Ernesto prepared to study in the Netherlands. However, the band tours it supported did help to establish wider relationships of cultural, artistic, political, and social exchange. With the end of the Inkoherent label, the remaining stock was given over to BalKot, Ultimus, and the IF Venue (an art and performance space managed by Frans) to distribute. In 2009, Frans briefly revived the Inkoherent name for

---

86 Equivalent to around 50 cents Australian.
87 Roughly AU $1.50–2.00.

a series of two photography zines, containing portraits of local artists and scene members and documenting their influences and inspirations.

DIY projects like Inkoherent tend to be rather transient; many are little more than a logo affixed to a band's self-released record, though they may grow from this into more long-term projects. Successful DIY record labels may become professionalized businesses over time, especially if they significantly expand their roster and seek wider distribution, as has happened to several underground labels in Bandung. A few may develop into relatively well-established and ongoing concerns while retaining a commitment to the DIY ethic; examples from the Bandung area include For the Kids Records and Pin Rose 150. More typically, however, a DIY label will have a few releases and then fade away, or crash and burn. Thompson (2004, 139–57) sees this as a kind of success through market failure – a refusal of commercial success which may undercut longevity but which also demonstrates a self-destructive punk authenticity. On the other hand, many DIY labels do aim for sustainability, hoping to make an ongoing contribution to their scene or community without becoming subordinated to a market logic. Certainly, this was the initial intent for Inkoherent DIY Nutritionist. While Inkoherent did not achieve all of Ernesto's initial goals, the label did make an important contribution to the Bandung scene, serving as a model for local DIY production while strengthening connections with global DIY networks. Judged by the criteria of the *etika DIY* rather than that of the capitalist marketplace, Inkoherent can be considered a modest success.

Endless Independent Store: Distributing relationships through a DIY enterprise

While independent record labels are often identified as the bedrock institutions for underground music scenes, distributors also play a vital role as significant vectors for both assertions of autonomy and commercial compromise (Hesmondhalgh 1999; O'Connor 2008, 35–43; Spencer 2005, 338–40). A DIY distributor – typically called a 'distro' in DIY hardcore, though this term has acquired rather commercial connotations in Bandung – may develop from a label or band engaging in self-distribution or an individual's desire to trade some of their personal record collection, or may be established as a dedicated standalone enterprise. DIY distributors are typically embedded in local scenes, but the exchange of records, zines, and other DIY media also serves to link different individuals, enterprises, and communities together into an extensive global DIY network.

In Bandung, punk distros played an important role in the development of the local scene in the 1990s; associated with underground labels and studios, distros such as Reverse, Riotic, and Harder also established storefront locations which became important hangout spots and organizing centres for the scene. By the 2000s, the infrastructure and networks established by such distros had given rise to a flourishing indie music and fashion industry (Luvaas 2012; Martin-Iverson 2012). However, the committed DIYers at BalKot tend to view this distro industry as evidence that the wider scene has 'sold out' and become alienated from the DIY punk values of autonomy and community.

Within the DIY hardcore scene itself, distribution tends to take place through informal hand-to-hand exchanges at collective merchandise tables at shows, or through a practice known as *lapak*, whih is setting out goods on a mat or box at a meeting, show, or other event. Long-distance DIY distribution takes place largely through mail-order, sometimes using catalogues included in zines and newsletters, though now usually online. However, attempts are also made to transform these transactions into more personalized forms of correspondence, such as by including letters or personal notes, scene reports, leaflets, artworks, and gifts with the packages and orders.

A significant example of an attempt to run a more substantial and sustainable distribution service according to the DIY ethic is the Endless Independent Store, an enterprise including a small storefront and a mail-order service established by Domestik Doktrin guitarist Methui in 2004.[88] Although in the wider underground scene distros have become synonymous with retail outlets, Endless' possession of a storefront is atypical for DIY hardcore distributors. The store is actually based in the small front room of Methui's grandmother's house, rather than rented commercial property. While Endless has some similarities with the early punk distros of Bandung, it is quite distinct from the commercial distros in its organization and intent. Indeed, Methui deliberately avoids using the term 'distro' for his own enterprise due to the connotations of hipster capitalism that it has acquired in the Bandung scene:

> As for why I've set up this *DIY store*, it's in order to help some bands and people that maybe still see DIY as the best path for the hardcore punk scene, or for grind and crust as well. And generally, I don't call it a distro because there's this perception in Bandung that distros are, well, they've become dedicated to selling t-shirts that might cost even more than the outlet price, or at big shops. That's what they're dedicated to, y'know? So that's why I'm providing this DIY store myself, because people who come here can do as they please. And when it comes to buying something, I do trades. I don't have fixed prices. (Interview with Methui, 2004, my translation)

Endless stocks a modest collection of cassettes, CDs, and even a few vinyl records, along with zines and newsletters, videos of DIY shows, and a small selection of band merchandise. The store operates on a rather informal basis, and is in many ways an outgrowth of Methui's personal collection. Endless does not see much 'walk-in' business; rather, most exchanges are organized through mail-order with existing contacts, informal orders, or hand-to-hand trades made with friends, or sold from *lapak* or merchandise tables at shows. Methui gets much of his stock directly from local DIY hardcore bands, as well as from DIY labels and distributors such as Inkoherent, Teriak Records (from Depok), Stop N Go Records (Jakarta), and Uglysmokers Tapes (Malaysia). However, he also has a personal exchange network that extends much further, trading records and zines with friends and contacts in the Netherlands, Russia, Australia, and the United States. The role of Endless is

---

88 In 2006, Methui replaced Endless with a more substantial DIY record store/distro enterprise called Full Speed Ahead, located at the Ultimus bookshop.

thus in large part to give other *anak DIY* access to Methui's exchange network, facilitating translocal exchanges as well as circulating local products within the Bandung scene.

In 2004, Endless hosted a performance by New York acoustic punk Rachel Jacobs, though the performance itself actually took place in Methui's grandmother's dining room. As well as contributing to Endless' role as a local DIY community institution, this event helped Methui to develop the store's role in facilitating translocal DIY communication and exchange; Alex from Art of the Underground, a DIY label and distro based in Buffalo, New York, accompanied Rachel Jacobs on the tour and brought along a collection of records and other merchandise to sell and trade. Alex and Methui also exchanged some stock with each other in order to facilitate ongoing relations.

In operating Endless, Methui draws on a network of contacts around the world, established through letter writing, online conversations, and references from others, with zines, webzines, band tours, and social media serving as important points of first contact. More generally, DIY distribution relies on personal relationships of trust and establishing a good reputation within DIY hardcore networks, especially when using the traditional long-distance DIY exchange method of sending cash or trades through the post. A good personal reputation is especially important for Indonesian DIYers who want to engage in transnational exchanges, as the Indonesian scene is rather notorious for mail-order and credit card fraud (*carding*), and so many international labels and distros are rather wary of doing business with Indonesians with whom they do not have an established relationship.

In drawing on his own social networks in and beyond the local scene to build Endless as a sustainable, ongoing distribution enterprise, Methui is seeking to demonstrate that the *etika DIY* is a viable alternative to what he calls the 'mainstream system' of market production and exchange, albeit on a smaller and more intimate scale:

> Sometimes there are people who see hardcore punk and the DIY ethic as something that can be used for mass production, for sale to a bunch of consumers, at prices that are like, y'know, really expensive. I don't agree with that. However, with DIY we can compete with, like, the *major label* ethic, with the distribution of the releases that we publish with a DIY concept. With the DIY concept, maybe it can be even better than the *major label* or the so-called *mainstream* system, because you can release what's important to you. And DIY is really important in the hardcore punk scene, because with DIY we can communicate directly with people, or individuals – with everyone, with all the people here, and also with other scenes. (Interview with Methui, 2004, my translation)

Gifts, Commodities, and DIY Exchange

'Do It Yourself' suggests production for personal use, and this is encouraged by the *etika DIY*, but most of the goods produced by the *anak DIY* are intended for exchange. Furthermore, DIY products are usually given a monetary price and used to calculate value for trade or sale. However, despite its monetization, DIY exchange does not follow a specifically capitalist logic, and the boundaries between economic enterprises and informal trading or gift-giving between friends is rather blurred. Although DIY exchange remains entangled in the wider market economy, it is also informed by an ideal of non-commercial gift exchange. While Thompson (2004, 122) argues that 'the gift stands as the preferred punk object that exchange betrays,' it is money, not exchange as such, that threatens DIY values.

Money is both a necessary and a disavowed element in DIY production and exchange. DIY hardcore is not fully self-sustaining, and relies on the input of money and commodities from outside. Money enters DIY circuits as cash payments for DIY products and donations for specific DIY projects, and is also used to purchase the non-DIY goods and services which are required for DIY production. There is a certain shame associated with monetary transactions conducted within the community itself, though this is moderated when they can be presented as a collective contribution, as with the money gathered to help with BalKot shows. Still, monetary contributions are not highly valued within the DIY community compared to contributions of time, effort, and creative labour; while Ernesto and Frans spent their own money to produce Inkoherent releases, this is rarely mentioned; rather, it is their contributions of labour and ideas which are emphasized by themselves and others in the community. Directly exchanging DIY cultural products for each other is generally considered a more authentically DIY mode of transaction than a one-way sale for cash, though monetary prices are often used to calculate a roughly balanced transaction. As Methui emphasises with regard to his DIY store, a preference for trading in kind and a flexible approach to pricing are seen as bringing exchanges closer to the values of the *etika DIY*.

The use of money within DIY exchange connects DIY enterprises to the wider market economy, and serves as a vector for the further commodification and alienation of their own products. Money is thus both a necessary way of contributing value to the community and a reminder that they have not achieved the independence and self-sufficiency they seek. This ambivalence reflects the dual function of money under capitalism as both a specific medium of exchange and a generalized measure of value (Marx 1973, 163–8; 1976, 188–227). As a universal equivalent, money establishes relationships between things (and people) but also tends to dissolve these relations into its own logic of universal abstraction (Marx 1973, 221–8; 1976, 227–44; Simmel 1990). Through the imposition of wage labour, money serves as the central form of capitalist political power (Cleaver 2000, 153–8; Negri 1991, 21–40). Money can be domesticated within other systems of value, but not without exerting its own disruptive influence (Graeber 2001, 91–115; 2011; Gregory 1997; Maurer 2006).

For the *anak DIY*, the abstract value of money brings the risk of autonomy *from* the DIY community while threatening the autonomy *of* the DIY community by connecting it to the wider market. The *anak DIY* accept the role of money as a medium of exchange – if somewhat grudgingly – but reject its apotheosis as the supreme social value. The *anak DIY* seek the autonomy to deploy money as a tool, facilitating their exchanges, while subordinating it to their own goals and values. Yet the circulation of money cannot be so readily disentangled from its accumulation, and so they also express an anxious criticism of their own use of money. Demonstrating this attitude, I once received a Rp 1000 note in change from a DIY *lapak* vendor with the message 'money, why are you so valuable?' written on it in pen.[89]

Thompson (2004, 150–1) argued that DIY punk constitutes a form of petty commodity production, in which commodities are produced in order to be exchanged for other commodities, and this does capture something of its logic. Whereas capitalist production starts and ends with money, with commodities playing a mediating role (M – C – M'), petty commodity production starts with the desire to obtain commodities as specific use values, and uses the production and exchange of other commodities as a method to achieve this (C – M – C'). For Negri (1991, 138), this kind of small-scale circulation of money represents the subordination of money to working-class self-valorization, in distinct and antagonistic opposition to its function as an expression of capitalist power. However, this circuit of commodity exchange can also be understood as a subordinate stage in a wider system of value production dominated by the accumulation of capital (Marx 1976, 247–57). Indeed, Thompson saw DIY production as intensifying the contradiction between use value and exchange value which Marx (1976, 125–31) analysed as an internal contradiction of capitalist commodities. Thus, for Thompson, DIY punk production expresses a desire to free the aesthetic use value of commodities from their economic exchange value, without being fully able to escape from the capitalist commodity form. Holtzman, Hughes, and Van Meter (2007, 45) also argue that DIY production expands use value at the expense of exchange value, though they are more optimistic in seeing this as 'a first step in the process of going beyond capital.'

While resisting the reduction of their exchanges to an abstract and universal exchange value, the *anak DIY* do use money to calculate relatively balanced exchanges, assigning a quantitative exchange value to their products. In this sense, DIY production can be considered a form of petty commodity production, existing on the margins of the wider market economy, remaining dependent on it and at least partially bound up with its economic logic without being directly organized for capitalist accumulation. However, the concept of petty commodity production does not fully capture the principles or practices of the DIY economy. As with the economists' 'myth of barter' (Graeber 2011, 21–41), petty commodity production is less a prehistory of the capitalist market than it is a projection of capitalist values onto other value systems, though it can also capture some of the processes through which they are enclosed by and subordinated to the circuits of capital accumulation. In the case of DIY hardcore production and exchange, I argue that the elements of barter or petty commodity production reflect an incomplete and contested attempt at an exodus from the capitalist value system.

However, DIY productive activities are not motivated primarily by a desire to obtain goods, although this is not a negligible factor; rather, the dominant motivation is the desire to

---

89 In Indonesian, 'uang mengapa kau begitu berharga?' Ironically, from my point of view, this message itself served to radically transform the value of the note; no longer a measure of abstract exchange value, it now has a place in my collection of research materials as a unique communicative artefact. Of course, this is also influenced by the fact that Rp 1,000 is a rather small amount of money.

engage in creative and socially-productive activity, to communicate and share one's work with others. DIY production is not so much organized around the pursuit of distinct use values as it is a form of qualitative exchange value – as associated with anthropological understandings of gift exchange (Godbout 1998; Graeber 2001, 151–228; Gregory 1982; Mauss 2002; Sahlins 1972). While stressing that they are coeval systems that exist alongside and in relation to each other, Gregory made a sharp distinction between gift and commodity exchange, arguing that the former is based on: 'the *personal relations* between people that the exchange of things in certain social contexts creates. It is to be contrasted with the *objective relations* between things that the exchange of commodities creates' (1982, 8).

Gift exchange can itself be considered a form of symbolic or moral economy (Cheal 1988, 12–19; Mauss 2002, 83–5), but Godbout (1998, 130) and Graeber (2001, 8–9) suggest that it can only be understood by moving beyond 'economic' logic altogether. Rather than calculating an equal and immediate exchange, systems of gift exchange are often characterized by deferred, imbalanced, indirect, or incommensurable exchanges, leading to ongoing relations of mutual obligation. There is also a degree of continuity between gift exchange and more total or generalized forms of reciprocity (De Marcellus 2003, 7–9; Godbout 1998; Graeber 2001, 158–63; Mauss 2002; Sahlins 1972, 193–4).

The *anak DIY* use exchange to open and maintain specific social relationships within a personalized network and also to support a wider sense of the DIY hardcore community. At least in their individual, direct exchanges, however, they tend to favour more immediately balanced forms of reciprocity. Such balanced reciprocity typically involves some degree of calculation of exchange value and can shade into forms of barter or market exchange, and is thus often associated with relations of social distance (Graeber 2011, 29–34; Sahlins 1972, 194–5, 219–20). However, the DIY concern with balance can also be explained with reference to their value of autonomy. Gift-giving compels reciprocity and generates ongoing obligations, and while these often constitute mutual relations of indebtedness, they can also be marked by forms of competition and domination. Through balanced exchange, the *anak DIY* seek to retain their individual autonomy and avoid the creation of ongoing debts and obligations, along with the concomitant status hierarchies.

The calculated autonomy of such balanced reciprocity undermines the DIY ideal of community solidarity, potentially closing off the potential to establish lasting relationships, though it retains a gift-like character as a vector for sociability in its denial of competitive self-interest (Sahlins 1972, 220). Individual DIY exchanges are also embedded in wider, collective relations of reciprocity; while individual relations of debt and obligation are resisted, DIY production relies on a collective obligation to engage with others that is ongoing, personalized, and immeasurable in economic terms. There is a strong ethic of participation and mutual aid in DIY hardcore, challenging commodification while seeking to balance the principles of autonomy and community.

In practice, the *anak DIY* continue to use money as a mediator and balancer of exchange while also attempting to enact a gift-like logic of personalization and continuing reciprocity against the alienating logic of the market. Like many other cultural artefacts, DIY hardcore products remain associated in significant ways with those who have produced them, even as they circulate through exchange networks. In contrast to commodities, the power of gifts is that they remain to some degree inalienable even as they are exchanged. Weiner (1992) referred to this as the paradox of 'keeping-while-giving,' but this apparent paradox is the very basis for the value of gifts and DIY hardcore products alike – their ability to establish mutual, unresolved relationships. A vital aspect of DIY production is the reciprocal pleasure of sharing one's creations with the wider DIY community. This kind of exchange cannot be reduced to the kind of reciprocal sacrifice which Simmel (1990, 82–90) and Appadurai (1986) describe as the essence of exchange relationships. While there may be a degree of conflict between the desire to keep and the desire to receive, there is also a desire to give and establish community (De Marcellus 2003, 7–9; Godbout 1998; Hyde 1983).

DIY value is located in the relationships established through exchange and the experience of participatory production and consumption which the exchange of products mediates. DIY exchanges are not simply about accumulating value – whether abstracted as money or in terms of the individual 'use values' of commodities; instead, there is a strong desire to keep DIY products in circulation and thereby to encourage further DIY production. The qualitative value of the social relations that are established or maintained through DIY production, exchange, and use is mobilized against the quantitative market value of DIY products as alienated commodities; thus, the DIY value system works against the commodification of hardcore and towards the establishment of a DIY hardcore commons.

DIY Production and the Hardcore Commons

Behind the apparently balanced exchanges of DIY products lies a huge amount of valued but 'unaccounted for' creative and organizational labour, given relatively freely and without the expectation of direct recompense. The price of a DIY hardcore product does not come close to capturing its social value, and according to DIY principles it should not do so. Not only are the production and distribution practices of DIY hardcore embedded in the social relationships they establish, but these practices are valued primarily through and for these social relationships. As an ethic of participatory production and shared value, DIY goes beyond the logic of exchange to establish a cultural commons, a shared sphere of products, skills, knowledge, resources, and value as against the enclosures of capital (De Angelis 2007, 238–47; Hardt and Negri 2009; Linebaugh 2014). In addition to the shared space and material resources of the DIY community, commons in this sense also refers to the production and mobilization of relations of commonality, as in common values, common interests, common networks of communication, common culture, and a common movement (De Marcellus 2003; Hardt and Negri 2009, 139). Such commons are produced and reproduced through an active, collective, and non-alienated labour process that Linebaugh (2014, 13–15) calls 'commoning.'

Despite being subjected to various processes of commodification and enclosure, artistic forms of cultural production have a particular affinity with such commoning practices and the ethic of the gift (Godbout 1998, 82–7; Hyde 1983). Hyde (1983, 143–9) argues that artistic creativity is received as a gift from the commons – a gift to be returned through further artistic production which increases the value of the commons. However, while the cultural commons draw upon the logic of the gift, they do not rely on direct reciprocity but on a general relationship of interdependence and collaboration (Hyde 1983, 77–84). Cultural value is a product of the 'mutual artistic labour, the independence of collaborative networks and the creative ecology' of artistic communities (Shorthose and Strange 2004, 49–50).

DIY production is a self-conscious commoning practice, mobilizing the cultural commons of hardcore punk as part of a struggle for autonomy and community beyond the limits of the capitalist value system. Still, DIY products remain in a contradictory position, as both the objects of balanced economic exchanges between autonomous individuals and gifts to the community, contributing to the production of a shared commons. Thompson (2004, 149–57) argues that DIY punk enacts a double failure – a wilful refusal of commercial success, combined with a failure to break free from the commodity form. In this view, the struggle for DIY autonomy is an intensification of the internal contradiction characteristic of market exchange, an antagonistic relationship in which 'commodities as use-values confront money as exchange-value' (Marx 1976, 199). However, the *anak DIY* refuse to accept the limited choice of 'sell out or die' (Hesmondhalgh 1999, 51) the market offers to independent music; instead, they strive to establish their own autonomous community of production, redefining the meaning of 'success' and 'failure.' As the BalKot-affiliated DIY hardcore band Bones Brigade puts it, echoing a common DIY hardcore slogan, the choice can rather be seen as 'DIY or DIE':

> It's true! We can start! Are we gonna get going? Do it together!!
> Why do we need sponsors, when we've got friends to help us?!
> Help each other and do it independently!!!
> Wahh!! Now that's cool!!!

> Explanation:
> What do you get from DIY, from a community or scene like this?? Some people say 'poverty'!!! Sorry for the difference of opinions, but I think that's wrong! I get new friends, experiences, and learn how to design t-shirts and stickers from my friends, how to sell t-shirts *hand to hand*, and a lot more. Yes, it's true that I won't get rich doing stuff like this!! But in my opinion success isn't just about having money but it's about having lots of friends, experiences, and having the chance to make history. ('DIY or DIE' by Bones Brigade, 2004)[90]

The Bandung DIY hardcore scene and similar communities of DIY hardcore production express and enact desires for autonomy and sociality which cannot be reduced to the values of the market. DIY production is organized around the collective accumulation of shared

---

90 Taken from a self-released CD-R split with Jakarta DIY band Bahasa Bayi. English lyrics as original; explanation my translation from Indonesian.

social and cultural value, associated with the production and circulation of the common. In this sense, such commons constitute a form of self-valorization of collaborative labour, in opposition to the self-valorization of capital (Cleaver 1989; 1992; Negri 1991). Kropotkin (1968) views this kind of decentralized, cooperative labour as both fundamental to human nature and as the basis for a potential anarcho-communist society. Similarly, Graeber (2011, 94–103) argues for the social importance of 'baseline communism' – everyday relations of mutuality that cannot be collapsed into the logic of exchange. The commons of DIY hardcore takes on an anti-capitalist political dimension to the extent that it seeks to expand this everyday communism into spheres of activity normally claimed by the capitalist market.

It must be acknowledged that DIY production remains a limited, precarious, and constrained alternative; given its continued dependence on and enclosure within a wider capitalist economy, DIY production can be viewed as a form of self-exploitation as well as self-organization (Shukaitis 2010; Wright 2000, 128–30). The cultural and creative industries function in part by appropriating value produced by independent underground scenes and communities, drawing them into marketized channels of distribution and control (Arvidsson 2007; Böhm and Land 2009; Shorthose and Strange 2004, 50–3). More generally, the appropriation of value through the enclosure of the commons – what Marx (1976, 873–6) calls 'primitive accumulation' – is an integral if contradictory part of contemporary capitalism (Caffentzis 2010; De Angelis 2007, 136–41; Harvey 2011). In Indonesia, as elsewhere, the DIY hardcore community overlaps with a more commercial scene, and value in various forms – products, aesthetics, skills, relationships, money, publicity, and so on – flows between them; thus, ultimately, labour that was dedicated to the production of the DIY commons also generates value for capital.

Thus, the DIY economy is an example of a politics of value – not in the narrowly economic sense of competing to appropriate value through exchange, but rather as the struggle to define what is valuable (Graeber 2001, 88; De Angelis 2007, 24–5). While not entirely free from entanglements in the market economy, the Bandung DIY community and the various projects and enterprises associated with it vigorously assert their autonomy not only from the major labels, but also from the logic of capital accumulation itself. In seeking to extricate their products from the market economy, the *anak DIY* have constructed an embryonic alternative value system which is both emergent in their everyday practices and consciously constructed as a political project. The values of the *etika DIY* are defined and established through the political and social activities of the DIY community, and mobilized against the alienating values of capitalist production. Although the autonomy of the DIY value system is compromised by capitalist processes of appropriation and dispossession, within its own limited sphere it is remarkably successful at challenging the alienation of the market. DIY practices of production and exchange establish a commons of DIY hardcore as a shared and flexible – if neither completely open nor fully autonomous – community of collective means.

References

Appadurai, A. (1986). 'Introduction: Commodities and the Politics of Value.' In A. Appadurai (ed.), *The Social Life of Things*, 3–63. Cambridge and New York: Cambridge University Press.

Arvidsson, A. (2007). 'Creative Class or Administrative Class? On Advertising and the Underground.' *Ephemera* 7 (1): 8–23.

Böhm, S. and C. Land. (2009). 'No Measure for Culture? Value in the New Economy.' *Capital & Class* 97: 75–98.

Bourchier, D. (1998). 'Indonesianising Indonesia: Conservative Indigenism in an Age of Globalisation.' *Social Semiotics* 8 (2/3): 203–14.

Caffentzis, G. (2010). 'The Future of "The Commons": Neoliberalism's "Plan B" or the Original Disaccumulation of Capital?' *New Formations* 69: 23–41.

Cheal, D. (1988). *The Gift Economy*. London and New York: Routledge.

Cleaver, H. (1989). 'Marginality and Self-valorization.' *Common Sense* 8: 22–7.

Cleaver, H. (1992). 'The Inversion of Class Perspective in Marxian Theory: from Valorisation to Self-valorisation.' In W. Bonefeld, R. Gunn, and K. Psychopedis (eds.), *Open Marxism II: Theory and Practice*, 106–44. London: Pluto Press.

Cleaver, H. (2000). *Reading 'Capital' politically*, 2nd ed. Edinburgh: AK Press.

De Angelis, M. (2007). 'The Beginning of History: Value Struggles and Global Capital.' London and Ann Arbor: Pluto Press.

De Marcellus, O. (2003). 'Commons, Communities and Movements: Inside, Outside and Against Capital.' *The Commoner* 6. http://www.commoner.org.uk/demarcellus06.pdf.

Godbout, J. T. (1998). *The World of the Gift*. Montreal and Kingston: McGill-Queen's University Press.

Gosling, T. (2004). '"Not For Sale": The Underground Network of Anarcho-Punk.' In A. Bennett and R. A. Peterson (eds.), *Music Scenes: Local, Translocal, and Virtual*, 168–83. Nashville: Vanderbilt University Press.

Graeber, D. (2001). *Towards an Anthropological Theory of Value*. New York and Houndmills: Palgrave.

Graeber, D. (2011). *Debt: the First 5,000 Years*. Brooklyn: Melville House.

Gregory, C. A. (1982). *Gifts and Commodities*. London and New York: Academic Press.

Gregory, C. A. (1997). Savage Money: the Anthropology and Politics of Commodity Exchange. Hoboken: Gordon and Breach.

Hardt, M. and A. Negri. (2009). *Commonwealth*. Cambridge, MA: Belknap Press.

Harvey, D. (2011). 'The Future of the Commons.' *Radical History Review* 109: 101–7.

Hesmondhalgh, D. (1999). 'Indie: the Institutional Politics and Aesthetics of a Popular Music Genre.' *Cultural Studies* 13 (1): 34–61.

Holtzman, B., C. Hughes, and K. Van Meter. (2007). 'Do It Yourself … and the Movement Beyond Capitalism.' In S. Shukaitis and D. Graeber (eds.), *Constituent Imagination: Militant Investigations // Collective Theorization*, 44–61. Oakland and Edinburgh: AK Press.

Hyde, L. (1983). *The Gift: Imagination and the Erotic Life of Property*. New York: Vintage Books.

Kropotkin, P. (1968). *The Conquest of Bread.* New York and London: Benjamin Blom.

Linebaugh, P. (2014). *Stop, Thief! The Commons, Enclosures, and Resistance.* Oakland, CA: PM Press.

Luvaas, B. (2012). *DIY Style: Fashion, Music and Global Digital Cultures.* London: Berg.

Martin-Iverson, S. (2012). 'Autonomous Youth? Independence and Precariousness in the Indonesian Underground Music Scene.' *The Asia Pacific Journal of Anthropology* 13 (4): 382–97.

Martin-Iverson, S. (2014). 'Running in Circles: Performing Values in the Bandung "Do It Yourself" Hardcore Scene.' *Ethnomusicology Forum* 23 (2): 184–207.

Marx, K. (1973). *Grundrisse.* Harmondsworth: Penguin.

Marx, K. (1976). *Capital: Volume One.* London: Penguin.

Maurer, B. (2006). 'The Anthropology of Money.' *Annual Review of Anthropology* 35: 15–36.

Mauss, M. (2002). *The Gift.* London and New York: Routledge.

Moore, R. (2007). 'Friends Don't Let Friends Listen to Corporate Rock: Punk as a Field of Cultural Production.' *Journal of Contemporary Ethnography* 36 (4): 438–74.

Negri, A. (1991). *Marx Beyond Marx: Lessons from the Grundrisse.* Brooklyn: Autonomedia.

O'Connor, A. (2008). *Punk Record Labels and the Struggle for Autonomy: the Emergence of DIY.* Lanham, MD: Lexington Books.

Ovetz, Robert. (1993). 'Noize Music: the Hypostatic Insurgency.' *Common Sense* 13: 5–23.

Pickles, J. (2007). 'Punk, Pop and Protest: the Birth and Decline of Political Punk in Bandung.' *RIMA* 41 (2): 223–46.

Rosen, P. (1997). '"It Was Easy, it Was Cheap, Go and Do It!" Technology and Anarchy in the UK Music Industry.' In J. Purkis and J. Bowen (eds.), *Twenty-first Century Anarchism,* 99–116. London: Cassell.

Sahlins, M. (1972). *Stone Age Economics.* Chicago: Aldine.

Shorthose, J. and G. Strange. (2004). 'The New Cultural Economy, the Artist and the Social Configuration of Autonomy.' *Capital & Class* 84: 43–59.

Shukaitis, S. (2010). 'Sisyphus and the Labour of Imagination: Autonomy, Cultural Production, and the Antimonies of Worker Self-management.' *Affinities* 4 (1): 57–82.

Simmel, G. (1990). *The Philosophy of Money,* 2nd ed. London and Boston: Routledge.

Spencer, A. (2005). *DIY: The Rise of Lo-fi Culture.* London and New York: Marion Boyars.

Thompson, S. (2004). *Punk Productions: Unfinished Business.* Albany. New York: State University of New York Press.

Vaneigem, R. (2006). *The Revolution of Everyday Life.* London: Rebel Press.

Wallach, J. (2008). *Modern Noise, Fluid Genres: Popular Music in Indonesia, 1997–2001.* Madison: The University of Wisconsin Press.

Weiner, A. B. (1992). *Inalienable Possessions: the Paradox of Keeping-While-Giving.* Berkeley: University of California Press.

Wright, S. (2000). '"A Love Born of Hate": Autonomist Rap in Italy.' *Theory, Culture, & Society* 17 (3): 117–35.

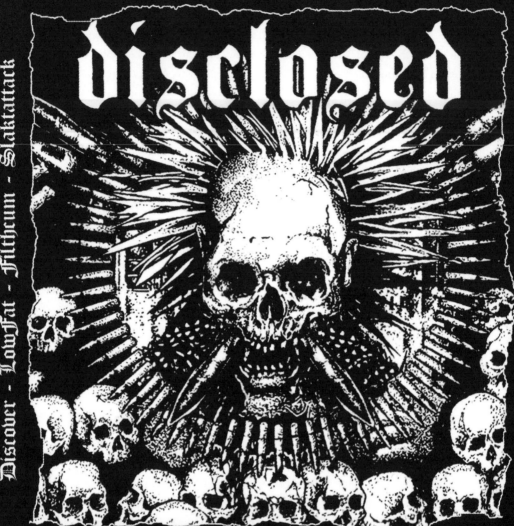

12. A PROFANE EXISTENCE? DIY CULTURE, SONIC EXTREMISM, AND PUNK IDENTITY IN TWENTY-FIRST CENTURY MALAYSIA

MARCO FERRARESE

Abstract

This chapter demonstrates how Malaysian punk has manifested, adhering to the features of the global parent punk culture defined as 'anarcho-punk.' Such an effect is not casual, but guided by specific determining factors related to the distribution of subcultural capital in Malaysia. Ethnographic fieldwork in Kuala Lumpur's punk house *Rumah Api* and textual analysis of Malaysian fanzine *Shock and Awe* demonstrate that in the Malaysia of the 2010s the fractured knowledge of the wider gamut of punk has shaped local punk 'authenticity' based on the deregulated flows of global subcultural capital, and the influence of foreign touring punk bands who mostly categorize as 'anarcho-punk.' These increasing contacts foster integration with the global scene but also hinder the self-reflective development of Malaysian punks who, conversely, prefer to adopt such institutionalized forms of foreign punk identity rather than develop their own.

Keywords: Malaysian punk, global anarcho-punk, punk music globalization, Kuala Lumpur, Southeast Asian popular culture

Marco Ferrarese is a musician, travel writer, and author of the novel *Nazi Goreng* (2013), the memoir *Banana Punk Rawk Trails: A Euro-Fool's Metal Punk Journeys in Malaysia, Borneo and Indonesia* (2015), and several journal articles and book chapters on the globalization of heavy metal and punk in Malaysia. He has been living and researching in the Southeast Asian region since 2009. Currently, he teaches languages at the Hebei Normal University of Science and Technology, Qinhuangdao. Besides traveling and writing, he plays guitar in thrash-core band WEOT SKAM from Penang, Malaysia.
E-mail: mferrarese80@gmail.com

A PROFANE EXISTENCE? DIY CULTURE, SONIC EXTREMISM, AND PUNK IDENTITY IN TWENTY-FIRST CENTURY MALAYSIA

Introduction

I am standing behind a line of black-clad Malaysians pumping their fists in the air and headbanging at the centre of the Soundmaker club, an independent performance space on Penang Island. On stage, a Malaysian band in jeans and black t-shirts emblazoned with the logos of several international hardcore punk bands plays a series of relentless songs as their singer screams into the microphone. Up next is a crust band clad in black leather jackets with iron spikes and patches representing a cornucopia of internationally famous Western hardcore bands' logos, such as Final Conflict, Mob47, Anti Cimex, and Minor Threat. Crust or D-beat, a subgenre of hardcore punk, reifies strong political themes and developed from the music scenes of 1980s United Kingdom and Scandinavia. But I am in Malaysia. Certainly, the globalization of punk music to Southeast Asia is far from a novelty (Baulch 2007; Hannerz 2005; Martin-Iverson 2012); however, there has been less focus on understanding the ways in which 'foreign' punk has impacted the imagination of Southeast Asian youth as a powerful agent of globalization. This chapter aims to describe how contemporary Malaysian punks construct and perform punk in early 2010s Malaysia.

In order to illustrate my arguments with clear empirical examples, this chapter presents several case studies. Based on the definition of the local music scene as a community that engages in local music activities over a specific time lapse and delimited by a precise space, and which appropriates music and cultural signs from other places but re-elaborates them through locality (Peterson and Bennett 2004, 8), the case studies I illustrate are not represented in people or bands but in the physical representations of what Malaysian punks established in their country. In this sense, I refer in particular to the self-proclaimed punk house *Rumah Api* in Kuala Lumpur and to *Shock & Awe*, a printed fanzine assembled by prominent thinkers among the Malaysian punk scene.

The case studies described here will demonstrate a few main things; firstly, that punk in Malaysia adheres to the features of the global parent punk (sub)culture defined as 'anarcho-punk'. Such a fact is not random, but guided by specific determining factors related to the distribution of subcultural capitals in Malaysia. Secondly, these case studies will attempt to show that in Malaysia the fractured knowledge of the wider gamut of punk influenced the participants' choices in terms of their construction of a 'punk authenticity' based on the locally available features of the global punk parent culture's production. Third, we will try to show that the construction of contemporary Malaysian punk's identity is influenced by the arrival of foreign punk groups, who can be best categorized as anarcho-punk or socio-politically active. These increasing contacts foster integration within the global scene but also hinder the self-reflective development of Malaysian punks who, conversely, prefer to adhere to such institutionalized forms of foreign punk identity.

By referring to Arjun Appadurai's (1990) definitions of mediascapes, ideoscapes, and ethnoscapes, I will explain how and why Malaysian punk had come to replicate a single model of the parent punk culture. In order to do so, I will present ethnographic descriptions of my informants' lives and subcultural practices, outlining the key issues that arose from my interviews and ethnographic observations. Furthermore, I will observe discourses extracted from relevant passages in Malaysia's prominent punk fanzine *Shock & Awe*. The contents of this fanzine, self-published in a DIY style, have provided a profound insight into how Malaysian punks behaved within their scene, and how they expressed their own local views as influenced by the global parent punk culture.

Theoretical Framework

Appadurai defines mediascape as the global distribution and electronic capabilities of media, and ideoscape as the images of the world created by the media. In other words, audiences around the world today experience media as a complicated interconnection of print, electronic screens, billboards, and celluloid, and are thus prone to confuse between the reality and fiction of what they observe. The more an audience is situated in one of the world's geographical peripheries, 'the more [likely] they are to construct "imagined worlds" which are chimerical, aesthetic, even fantastic objects, particularly if assessed by the criteria of some other perspective, some other "imagined world"' (1990, 299).

In this sense, and as confirmed by early research in the region (Baulch, 2002, 2003; Pickles, 2007; Wallach, 2008, 2010), Southeast Asian extreme music scenes constructed their 'imagined world' of music by being exposed to a series of extreme music media and cultural production in the form of imported recordings, fanzines and videos. In the case of Malaysia, evidence of the reception and local production of Western underground music materials since the 1980s is documented by both scholars (Lockard 1998) and pioneer Malaysian underground musicians (Kidd 2012). Conforming to the development of most music scenes around the world (Bennett 2004), the Malaysian extreme music scene first developed locally using the means and examples of other more-established and influential music scenes around the world to create its own imagined idea of extreme music, which largely eschewed the use of local languages or local folk instruments. This development is akin to that of the punk, metal, and reggae music scenes in 1990s Bali (Baulch 2007; 2003) which 'gestured elsewhere,' refraining from defining particular geographical elements into their subcultural identities. However, recent research on the Indonesian DIY punk subculture (Martin-Iverson 2011) subverted this conclusion by evidencing how Indonesian punks were, rather than acting in simple 'mimesis' of a foreign subcultural model, active participants and decision makers in the global underground punk networks.

This particular case evidences how the idea of extreme music had spread through a network of interconnected communities around the world, and shaped according to

Figure 12.1: A punk in Kuala Lumpur conforms to the genre's stereotypical mohawk hairstyle (picture by the author).

different local situations. In this regard, Arjun Appadurai's concept of ethnoscapes –the contemporary mobility of peoples across nations affecting the world's social and political relationships to an unprecedented degree (1990, 297) – is helpful for understanding the dynamics of today's Malaysian extreme music scene. Based on my fieldwork experiences, I observed how many extreme Western and Asian bands increasingly toured and intermingled in Malaysia. Consequently, the whole 'imagined world' of extreme music started to be affected by these fleeting ethnic relations. These interactions are too short to give the Malaysian extreme music scene accurate and long-lasting impressions of foreign extreme music instances; on the other hand, they are also very relevant for challenging the imagined expectations that Malaysians have of foreign punk music. In fact, very few Malaysians could otherwise experience live international punk bands if not by travelling out of their country. This situation is crucial to understanding how all of the ethnically diverse groups that engage in punk music performance in Malaysia do so by conforming to precise sets of 'authentic rules' based on globally consolidated ideas of punk as a community that bears more desirable living conditions than those offered by the 'hegemonic mainstream society.'

Further theoretical interpretation is required to address why collectivities would want to reproduce such models. Social groups sharing common practices represent what Bourdieu (1984; Bourdieu and Johnson 1993) defined as the 'field of social interaction.' He specified that individuals compete with others to accrue distinction in their respective fields

(Maton 2008, 54). The 'authenticity' of a practice is arguably one of the most important attributes that individuals strive for in order to accrue subcultural capital and distinction within a field. Bourdieu (1993) suggested that notions of authenticity are employed to verify the value of an individual's cultural capital, and are founded upon one's perceived possession of privileged cultural knowledge. He also noted how critical appraisal for the authenticity of an artistic product holds the dual role of rewarding the 'orthodox' (authentic practice within the field) and condemning the 'heretical' (inauthentic practice leading outside of the field). Likewise, Bourdieu specified that consumption practices allow players within the same field to form distinct identities by competing for status endogenously, learning the tempos and unwritten rules through time and experience (Maton 2008, 54). The final objective in any field is the accumulation of capitals: they are both the process within and product of a field. This theorization has been expanded to subcultures, where individuals accumulate subcultural capital based on their level of interaction and engagement within a music scene (Kahn-Harris 2007; Thornton 1995).

Considering the Malaysian punk scene as a field of social interaction, my research outlines how its participants desire to fit within the global rules as set by foreign instances of punk music. By doing so, Malaysian punks today create their own imagined idea of what 'authentic punk' is, adopting behaviours, ideas, and music scene politics from the 'orthodox' and 'true' foreign examples of the parent punk culture they are exposed to. This argument could partially support the idea that, after globalization, punk music could have become another instance of what George Ritzer (2004, 3) defined as a form of 'nothing,' or an empty, centrally conceived and controlled form which is relatively devoid of distinctive content. Such 'empty templates' are filled with objects which are not characteristic of any particular culture – like chain stores instead of shops selling local, unique products (Ritzer and Ryan, 2002, 2) – and indicate 'a trend in the world as a whole in the direction of nothing' (Ritzer 2004, 6). Punk performance in early 2010s Malaysia seems to verify in similar ways: the unequal flows of Western punk's imagescapes in fact tend to reproduce an indigenous version of punk that adopts globally authenticated codes of performance rather than 'fills' the empty container of punk with local meanings. Performers then refuse to refer to any particular locality, referencing authenticated global codes of performance instead (Weinstein 2011).

This is particularly notable: since its inception, punk in the West has symbolized a 'something,' or a full form that is indigenously conceived and controlled, and rich in distinctive content. However, my ethnographic observations reveal that punk in Malaysia, a fast-developing nation, accepted the parent Western punk culture as a globalized 'nothing,' adopting and replicating Western punk symbols and using the common language of English as the dominant tongue in the local punk cultural production. Furthermore, as a consequence of unequal global distribution of subcultural capitalist flows (Kahn-Harris 2007, 13) and the majority of visiting anarcho-punk ethnoscapes, punk in contemporary Malaysia has embraced and replicated the politically active, globally authenticated examples of anarcho-punk, thus eschewing other instances and sub-genres of punk which have instead represented important milieus of the parent genre throughout its development in the 1990s and 2000s. The case studies provided aim to explain how punk in Malaysia, far from being a mere globalized 'nothing,' has been culturally translated from a limited number of worldwide punk models which have invariably formed its current structure, philosophy, and existence.

Anarchy in Kuala Lumpur

Malaysia was the first Southeast Asian nation to produce rock, punk, and metal bands, as early as 1982,[91] and together with Indonesia has one of the most active hardcore punk and extreme metal scenes in the world today (Wallach 2011). Based on the scene reports from Asia that French traveller Luk Haas (1995) published in San Francisco's seminal punk fanzine *Maximumrocknroll*, Malaysia at large remained virtually untouched by the explosion of punk in the 1970s and hardcore-punk in the 1980s. Nevertheless, thanks to imported British magazines and tapes, a punk scene generated in the rural and Islamic state of Terengganu from the late 1970s. Joe Kidd, the most active member of this early scene, moved to capital Kuala Lumpur in 1988, becoming a journalist and promoter, and prime mover of an early punk scene that enjoyed major label attention and great popularity throughout the 1990s. The fate of Malaysian punk changed in the early 2000s with a governmental ban on black metal music that affected the whole gamut of underground music performance (Azmyl 2009).

Nevertheless, since the 1990s, Malaysia's capital city Kuala Lumpur has been the main centre of local punk and heavy metal music scenes. The Central Market, an area close to the backroads of Chinatown and its peculiar tourist enclave Petaling Street, was indicated as the favourite hang out of Malaysia's early punk and metal scenes in the writings of pioneer Malaysian punk musicians (Kidd 2012; Wolf 2013). During my fieldwork in 2013 and 2014, Kuala Lumpur still constituted one of the most up-and-coming places for extreme music production in the country. Today, however, punks have moved away from gathering in public spaces because of the existence of a dedicated subcultural hangout space called Rumah Api [Fire House].

Of all punk venues in Malaysia, Rumah Api, situated in Kuala Lumpur's northeastern district of Ampang, is the only one that can be categorized as an 'anarcho-punk house.' In fact, its appearance potently resembles that of the anarcho-punk squat houses found in many European countries. Rumah Api's affiliation with foreign forms of punk, and in particular political anarcho-punk, is very evident from the building's main facade. The front wall depicts a drawing of an anarcho-punk and a straight edge skinhead happily shaking hands. In the West, straight edge skinheads profess clean living from the intoxication of alcohol and drugs, and promote positive social change (Haenfler 2006); on the other hand, anarcho-punks embrace a lifestyle based on militant discourses of anarchism as valid alternatives to capitalist society, promote world peace, and generally write lyrics that express positive political change or denounce the horrors of contemporary society (Thompson 2004).

91 The band Blackfire from Kangar in Perlis, at the time still known as Metal Ghost, is indicated as the first Southeast Asian metal band (http://www.metal-archives.com/bands/Blackfire/72457).

Figure 12.2: Rumah Api's peculiar entrance (picture by the author)

As if these signs of affiliation with the militant and politically conscious anarcho-punk movement were not enough, Rumah Api's punks also etched another clear statement of subcultural affiliation on the door leading upstairs to the living quarters: 'This space is run by punks for punx.' The message is further reified by a number of anarchic symbols and slogans such as 'DiYor Die' that adorn the sides of the walls, as illustrated in Figure 12.2 above. It is interesting to note how Rumah Api's dwellers used the nomenclature 'punx,' which refers to urban slang originating in the West Coast of the United States which implies the existence of a very tightly-knit crew of punks. In the European punk scene, punks and other alternatives must physically occupy such spaces to settle their local communities. They must defy police forces until their subcultural group can claim that space for itself. For this reason, in Europe squats are usually old abandoned buildings, without running water or electricity (they are illegally wired by the occupants), situated in peripheral areas of cities or carved out of abandoned structures in the city centres.

From the outside, Rumah Api seems to aptly conform to the style of European squats, but the occupants pay rent for the use of this space. Thus, Malaysian punks clearly practice the 'imagined world' of punk, but can enact their subcultural resistance only by conforming to the basic rules of city living. In addition, Rumah Api stands at the opposite side of the road from Ampang's district major balai polis [police station] that has so far had no problems with the numerous musical events the punks organize. The following is a detailed description from my Fieldwork Diaries:

Rumah Api has two storeys: on the first floor, a few couples live in a shared apartment centred around a common living room, a kitchen and bathroom area.

I have been particularly surprised to observe a number of westerners staying here. Most of them are Europeans travelling through Southeast Asia from or on their way to China or Australia. It seems that Kuala Lumpur's punks had attracted a subculture of global travellers who, as I inquired, know about this place from Australian punk friends who visited Kuala Lumpur previously. Most of them are not even punks: they just came here to have a free place to stay, and some have stayed for a long time.

(Fieldwork diary, 2 October 2013)

The spaces provided by Rumah Api have been both physically and ideologically shaped by its residents based on an interpretation of the punk identity strongly based on the parent culture of European and North American anarcho-punk. The strong presence of a number of punk foreigners who fleetingly arrive into this Malaysian punk space is symbolic of the direct influence of a foreign punk ethnoscape (Appadurai 1990). These punks connect Rumah Api to their translocal punk networks, thus guaranteeing a continuous flux of foreigners who come from a limited circuit of anarcho-punks used to communal living in squatted spaces around the world. Although Malaysia is a country with a very different social, political, and historical background from the United Kingdom, where anarcho-punk originated (Glasper 2007), the case of Rumah Api brings forward remarkable questions about authenticity. For example, how could anarcho-punk – or political punk in general – come to be chosen as the matrix upon which Malaysia's most 'authentic' instance of punk developed? And why, of all the facets of the punk gamut, is anarcho-punk – and political punk in general – the sub-genre of global punk that has found most fertile ground in Malaysia? The evidence of Rumah Api's case study seems to support an important argument that emerged from the study of Burmese popular music (Maclachlan 2011, 4): that the cultural imperialism of the West, in this case punk, has not forced vulnerable populations to subject to it. Quite the opposite – Malaysian punks, akin to Burmese pop musicians, seem to have gone to great lengths to acquire the codes of a Western-centred punk parent culture, its ideological signifiers, and its core beliefs. In this perspective, Malaysian punk seems to reflect and adopt the unwritten rules of global punk, but as for why anarcho-punk was chosen, of all genres, is a question I examine in the next section.

Submitting to 'True' Punk?

After almost forty years of existence, punk has become a global entity that has not frozen into a single defined existence, but has instead fractured into dozens of sub-genres and styles. Today, punk has ultimately become a commercial commodity marketed both within and outside a mainstream and an 'underground' audience that claims to be more 'authentic' based on the self-perceived 'truth' of its own subcultural practices and affiliations (Hannerz 2013). Furthermore, punk, like other forms of popular music, travelled to almost every developed and developing nation thanks to the power of global media distribution and the internet. This situation created legacies based on the idea of punk as a translocal, globally interconnected community divided into hundreds of local 'music scenes' (Dunn 2008; O'Connor 2002).

In this perspective, the case of Rumah Api seems to epitomize a Malaysian punk instance of what Arjun Appadurai defined as the effect of the mediascapes (1990), or the global distribution and electronic capabilities of media, and ideoscapes, or the images of the world created by the media. In this regard, if Rumah Api constitutes the paramount Malaysian example of living life in the 'punk style,' it has to be stressed that the idea of 'authentic' punk in the Malaysian scene is constructed over an ideoscape of British, American, and European punk cultural production that reached Malaysia in the 1990s. As outlined in the previous section that likened Rumah Api to a European punk squat, the features adopted by Malaysian punks seem to refer to European anarcho-punk influences. This evidence is illustrated in Figure 12.3 below, which depicts the entrance to Rumah Api's gig room. The punk residents used strong slogans to decorate the wall and thus reify their own political stances that adhere to those globally spread by the parent anarcho-punk subculture. Specifically, I want to underline how the slogans are written using a font that resembles the one made famous around the world on the artwork of seminal British anarcho-punk band CRASS, and later employed throughout the years as a readily recognizable sign of anarcho-punk affiliation, for example in the logo of influential North American fanzine and collective *Profane Existence* from Minneapolis, United States (Thompson 2004). With these examples, I seek to present how global punk symbols that carry authentic meanings in the West are employed in Malaysia as a submission to what Ritzer (2004) would call a 'nothing-fication' of globalized punk.

As shown in Figure 12.3 below, the messages themselves are a list of negations of the stereotypical horrors of industrial society (racism, sexism, homophobia, drugs, alcohol, violence) as reified in most global anarcho-punk cultural production. On the other hand, by considering the troubled relationships of Malaysian extreme music with the authorities ('Black Metal is a Choice' 2006; Azmyl 2009; BBC 2001), I also argue that Rumah Api's punks might use these slogans in an attempt to protect their space from police control and 'exorcise' it by explicitly declaring how their group practice 'clean living.' This might not be the case, though, as by analysing the fanzine *Shock & Awe*, produced by a number of people who have ties with the organization of Rumah Api, similar influences are confirmed.

A discrete level of familiarity with global punk literature clarifies that *Shock & Awe*'s editorial structure heavily resembles that of stalwart Californian fanzine *Maximumrocknroll*, globally recognized as the most influential printed punk fanzine (Thompson 2004). It is also the one that, if not openly supporting the anarcho-punk cause, is well known for its critical outlook on scene politics. Taking a look at *Shock & Awe*, its formula comprises personal columns that emphasize the critical discussion of troubled punk identities and

Figure 12.3: Punk slogans written in the typical anarcho-punk font made popular by British band Crass decorate the entrance of Rumah Api's show room (picture by the author).

ethics of the authentic DIY lifestyle, followed by band interviews, and record and fanzine reviews. It is by reading the columns that the Malaysian choice of politicized DIY hardcore as a prominent model of punk authenticity comes to the fore:

> I am in favour for Infest reunion because it is Infest. Full stop! We can talk about how certain bands played a huge influence on the hardcore scene. I mean yeah, SPAZZ is all fun and stuff. But this is Infest. If you call yourself a hardcore lifer since the '90s and don't have either *Slave* or *No Man's Slave* as your deserted island records then you should re consider [*sic*] yourself as a hardcore lifer because I don't think any self respecting hardcore lifer would miss out on those two monuments to kick ass hardcore records. (*Shock & Awe* 2013, 6)

The author raises two important points. First, a band like Infest[92] gets a primary marker of 'authenticity.' Their lyrics exhibit angst, socio-political issues, and music-scene politics, mostly delivered in a very accusatory tone. Compared to their peers, Infest showed increasingly fervent political stances and imagery, using images of war and poverty to illustrate their album covers, in contrast to their era's common hardcore punk trend of depicting pictures of the bands playing live.

---

92 Los Angeles band Infest were active from 1986 to 1991, and, although they never coined the term, have been indicated as the forefathers of the "powerviolence" subgenre of hardcore punk. They blended the ethos, speed, and song structure of straight edge hardcore with the sonic aggression of straight edge hardcore bands such as Detroit's Negative Approach.

Consequently, such standards of politically-charged hardcore punk – or 'powerviolence' – ground the Malaysian punk scene in its foundations of 'authentic punk.' As described in the same column, the concept of being 'authentically punk' both prescribes an individual's mandatory deep research for the correct authentic parent punk culture's sources, and also harshly criticizes those members of the Malaysian punk scene who lack such a rigorous and compulsory submission to the established and dogmatic rules of punk authenticity:

> Remember when a notorious local tape label released that Infest boot? No? Does it make me wonder why most local powerviolence bands failed to deliver the violence? How about that chubby cunt, who was never a fan of Infest, that told me that nobody is listening to Infest a few years back but recently proceed [*sic*] to acquire a clothing item with Infest logo on it? [*sic*] Here's the deal chub, if I ever came across with you with that Infest cap you better watch out because I'm going to fetch my pliers and proceed to extract your teeth one by one with it. (*Shock & Awe* 2013, 6)

Not complying to the scene's rules or the same models, and thus not showing true punk 'authenticity,' is regarded as a practice that would warrant physical aggression. Belonging to the scene therefore seems to require a mandatory compliance to authenticity, to being 'true' and not a 'poseur' who deserves punishment for their faulty behaviour. The above example – a recurrent theme in all issues of *Shock & Awe* I observed – clearly exemplifies how in Malaysia punk authenticity equals punk identity, and how it is constructed on Western forms of DIY socio-political hardcore punk music which were initiated by the current of British anarcho-punk. Based on my fieldwork, I argue that the reason this genre of punk shaped Malaysians' idea of punk authenticity is related to the ways in which the parent punk culture's mediascape was distributed in the country, favouring the importing of selected instances of punk music genres.

A Limited View of Worldwide Punk

In his study on punk authenticity and performance, Eric Hannerz (2013) mentions that he individuated about sixty different categories of performing the punk identity. Indeed, punk is a multi-faceted corpus of music genres and cultural production that comes in very divergent types. If on the one hand it could be argued that the common denominator of all instances of punk is a rebuttal of mainstream society's approved rules – so vehemently refused since punk's early beginnings as testified by songs such as Wire's 'Mr Suit' (1977) the Sex Pistol's 'Anarchy in the UK' (1977) and countless others – on the other it is clear that anarcho-punk and political punk are also not the only ways in which punk music brings about such resistance. One clear example is a form of punk that became popular in Europe and the United States in the 1990s defined as 'garage punk' by some critics, as it took some of the themes of American garage rock music of the 1960s and injected them with muscular punk guitar power. The term is quite limited to aptly describe the diverse gamut of bands and styles that mutated the face of underground punk music after the commercial success of Nirvana and grunge (Azerrad 1994). Eric Davidson, singer of the New Bomb Turks and one of the protagonists of this scene, defined this form of music by coining the umbrella term 'gunk punk' (Davidson 2010), one that encompasses a spectrum of genres and bands as diversified as the Lazy Cowgirls, the Gories, the White Stripes, the New Bomb Turks, Guitar Wolf, and the Dwarves, to cite just a few.

Gunk punk was very different from any other form of pre-existent punk, as it eschewed the submission to any form of totalizing political ideals with which punk had usually been paired with. Gunk punk was transgressive punk as it did not conform to any of the music scene's rules, and also eschewed the clean living of straight edge and the political resistance of anarcho-punk. The most important characteristic of the gunk punk bands was that they renounced the label 'punk' in the first place. American and European record labels such as Crypt, Estrus, Sympathy for the Record Industry, Rip Off, Reptilian, and several others gave 1990s punk a definite facelift, disdaining the rigors of politically charged hardcore and late 1980s punk, and looking back at the basics of rock and roll, the blues, and the garage sounds of the 1950s and 1960s that gave life to the original proto-punk and punk bands of Detroit, New York, and London. Gunk punk was not really concerned with politics, anarchism, or social change; it dealt with the simplicity of youth filtered through a North American popular culture influence, glorifying sex, drugs, and rock and roll as life's pleasures.

Gunk punk changed the face of global underground punk in North America and Europe. It arrived in Asia, and most particularly in Japan, where bands such as Teengenerate, Guitar Wolf, and the Jet Boys embodied a globalized Asian version of very Western-centred forms of high octane rock and roll (Davidson 2010). In Malaysia, however, gunk punk never really arrived. Veteran punk rocker Joe Kidd told me during our interview that Kuala Lumpur's punks 'used to print New Bomb Turks t-shirts, but somehow, the music did not stick because Malaysians preferred more politically charged forms of punk.'[93] The scarcity or non-existence of a gunk punk subculture in Malaysia is confirmed by Man Beranak, Rumah Api's main organizer, who, like most other Malaysian punks I interviewed, was not aware of the garage punk explosion of the 1990s.[94]

This digression is intended to show the global importance of an instance of the parent punk culture that did not directly impact nor is represented in Malaysia, where punk seems to embrace a very specific set of attitudes and ideals. As my fieldwork experiences and the evidence of local punk materials show, to be punk a Malaysian must refer to the authenticity of anarcho-punk and socio-political subgenres of punk music from the West. This is confirmed in the words of Rozaimin, a politically active skinhead from Penang interviewed during my fieldwork. He reported that:

> It is the norm. If you are a punk, you must believe in anarchism; but if you are an
> anarchist, it does not mean that you must be a punk. You know what I mean? If you
> are punk, you must believe in it. I also do not agree when skinheads in Malaysia call

93 From an interview I conducted on 5 December 2013.
94 Fieldwork Diaries, 2 October 2013.

themselves traditional and are not political. I told them that if they are, they must be SHARP,[95] against racism, because we have the Boneheads[96] here. You must be white or black, left or right. You must choose a side.

Punk in Malaysia is associated with political activism and anarchism. It is therefore of note that the few Malaysian bands who have toured in Europe, such as Kuala Lumpur's Tools of the Trade or Seremban's Daighila, organized their tours through anarcho-punk circuits. By observing the dates of the very few European tours of Malaysian bands, it can be seen that the vast majority of their gigs were held in venues that classify as anarcho-punk squats. Consequently, the few Malaysian bands who are able to go to Europe continue to experience only one side of the underground punk touring circuit. This side has no access to the club and festival circuit, forcing Malaysian punk bands to experience only political punk cultures and spaces, further cementing their limited authentication of punk with anarcho-punk.

The authentication of punk as a rebellious and political musical form makes Malaysian punks embrace everything that appears to have a DIY attitude as punk. During my fieldwork, I interacted with many punk music fans and observed numerous live bands that had very few features to share with DIY anarcho-punk. Most often, they encompassed instances of grindcore and other genres of music which tapped into the heavy metal spectrum. I argue that this happens because Malaysian punks identify such forms of music as authentic based on their overtly political lyrics and context. For example, one of my respondents, Marvin Gayle, a self-proclaimed punk rocker from Kuching, organized a festival that can be more aptly described as a grindcore festival.[97] Grindcore is indeed an evolution of political British anarcho-punk of the late 1980s, mixed with the extremity of thrash metal and hardcore (Mudrian 2004).

As the sonic extremity and anarcho-punk inclinations of the Malaysian punk scene start to surface on the global punk map, reaching other international music scenes and being configured as an interesting territory for international touring bands. This, however, based on my fieldwork, has only deepened the consolidation of Malaysia as an extension of the global anarcho-punk circuit.

The Influence of Anarcho-punk Ethnoscapes

When landmark British anarcho-crust veterans Doom played in Malaysia on 25 February 2014, the scene greatly rejoiced. Facebook posts exhibited great excitement and anticipation for this event and also a certain level of national pride in seeing Malaysia hosting an international band of such a level of underground distinction. The show drew more than six hundred attendees, marking a definite success in the history of Malaysian extreme live music. This particular case not only supports my argument of anarcho-punk's

---

95 SHARP is an acronym for 'skinheads against racial prejudices' and is a current of Skinhead Oi! Music with political leftist views formed in the United Kingdom during the 1980s.

96 Boneheads are identified as a Malaysian skinhead group of ethnic Malay heritage that sympathizes with extreme right-wing ideologies as portrayed by Western Neo-Nazi groups.

97 Fieldwork Diaries, 14 September 2013.

importance in the Malaysian scene but certainly also reflects how, during my fieldwork, I experienced an increase of arrivals, and consequential influence, of foreign punk bands of varying degrees of success in Malaysia. In fact, between 2013 and 2014 the number of Western bands coming to perform was higher compared to what I observed in previous years (Ferrarese 2012).

Consequently, the whole imagined idea of extreme music, and in this case of punk, solidified based on these fleeting ethnic relations. In fact, such interactions are too short to give Malaysian punks an accurate and long-lasting impression of the foreign extreme music instances; on the other hand, they are also very relevant for challenging the imagined expectations that Malaysians created based on mediated forms of foreign extreme music. In fact, my observations reflected that very few Malaysians are able to experience international instances of extreme music scenes, as they are unwilling to travel out of the country for this purpose.

However, the construction of a particular kind of punk 'authenticity' in Malaysia is certainly related to the kind of bands that arrive and affect the local music scene with their sonic examples. These music performances cannot be considered as just fleeting encounters, as one could argue regarding the short time that foreign musicians spend within the local punk scene. In fact, I am not the first to argue that extreme live music performances are able to both sanction authenticity in a space of experience (Overell 2010) and create liminal encounters that immerse the participants in 'the process of morphing and transfiguration' (Ensminger 2013, 2).

By observing the recent history of Malaysian punk gigs I observed and recorded during my fieldwork, it is easy to argue that the majority of anarcho-punk or inspired bands who usually play in Malaysia are foreign. And based on the accounts of foreign bands who toured the region previously and have referred positively to the experience with other bands, Malaysia shaped its presence on the global punk map as a receptive territory for anarcho-punk. What I want to emphasize is, however, a crucial factor defining this 'ethnoscape.' I have observed first hand how it is the budding, less-successful, or less-known Western anarcho-punk and political punk bands that come to tour in Southeast Asia and Malaysia. They try to expand their possibilities for success where Asian promoters are willing to book them. Internationally respected bands on commercially established punk labels only come to these regions in the context of large festivals, when commercial profits are adequate. Conversely, the 'ethnoscape' constituted by anarcho-punk bands that come to this part of the world is imbued with the desire to explore and play music for what they consider the 'punks of the third world.' These are bands that tour the region without thinking of economic rewards.

In December 2013, the Swedish band Crutches toured Indonesia, Malaysia, and Singapore together with Apparatus, one of the three or four Malaysian bands who have toured Europe in recent years.[98] The tour flyer reproduces and continues the visual legacy of symbols related to the anarcho-punk mediascape. It is not casual that the vowel 'A'

---

98 Fieldwork Diary, 16 October 2013.

Figure 12.4: Flyer for Crutches and Apparatus Southeast Asian tour.

contained in the word 'war' is presented inside a circle, the signifier of anarchy.

This detail signifies the need of the Malaysian artists who designed this flyer to clearly sanction the punk authenticity of the bands. In this way, the flyer not only attracts the attention of Malaysian, Indonesian, and Singaporean punk fans who are used to understanding punk under these politicized, anarchic terms; it also continues a tradition imbued with precise anarcho-punk visual significance. In a sense, the bands become 'qualified' to draw the punk scene's interest. The flyer's text is also presented in English, the authenticating language of the Western punk parent culture.

Such interpretation prompts the consequential reflection that the arrival of such foreign anarcho-punk bands had helped Malaysian punks' search for authenticity in this particular fringe of extreme political punk. Studying Malaysian anarcho-punk band Apparatus, the signifiers of their main influences are very apparent: their clothing style follows the canons of the genre, they have song titles such as 'Another Night of Holocaust' (following the warfare and nuclear war themes used in anarcho-punk lyrics), and their music is in line with anarcho-punk global productions. In a way, it seems that, more than trying to come up with something more Malaysian and unique, Apparatus, like many other Malaysian punk bands and fans, preferred to adhere to the musical structures and lyrical images that are stereotypical of the parent genre. As evidenced by the other cases alluded to in this chapter, in Malaysia the punk stereotypes seem to convert into signifiers of 'authenticity.'

Conclusion

The case studies described in this chapter have outlined how punk in Malaysia mostly followed a global mediated image of one sub-genre of punk: anarcho-punk. They have also illustrated how, by adhering to such instance of global punk, Malaysian punks reclaim and recognize their own 'punk authenticity.' In this regard, if we had to consider what is original as 'authentic' or related to the folkloric traditions of a people, the case of Malaysian punk would fail in showing any authentic value. On the other hand, by considering Malaysian punk as a global product of an imperialist punk culture, a musical instance of globalizing nothing (Ritzer and Ryan 2002), then the authenticity of its practices would become, conversely, very understandable. Malaysian punk, in fact, seeks legitimacy from the parent Western punk culture. At this point in time, the Malaysian punk scene seems very concerned with the imitation of a foreign parent cultural other, or the replication of a Westernized punk 'non-thing' (Ritzer and Ryan 2002). This reproduction arguably takes place because Malaysian punk has still not reached a level of local cultural production able to impress and influence the parent punk culture. It still has to produce music and trends able to influence the scene at an international level and become an accepted part of it.

The power of punk's parent culture could be better understood through Bourdieu's theories of cultural capital and education (2006). Considering the global parent punk culture as that with a higher level of cultural capital, the Malaysian punk scene would constitute a globalized example of inefficient pedagogic transmission. In fact, based on the different cultural, historical, and political backgrounds of the parent punk culture of the West, the Malaysian 'punk students' still appear to be unable to clearly understand the messages that their 'punk teachers' tried to get across. Like how Bourdieu referred to economically disadvantaged pupils – in the sense of lacking authentic educational sources of any particular culture – Malaysian punks cannot compete with the parent culture in terms of credentials because of their disadvantaged music scene, which lacks resources and global distribution channels. Thus, the parent punk culture remains in a dominant position, exerting a model of authenticity that Malaysian punks strive to follow. Rather than challenging the system, they attempt to contribute to it by meritocratic means: in fact, the more they conform to the parent culture by adapting their own cultural production to the global, the more they feel 'authenticated.'

In other words, because of an unequal distribution of cultural flows between developed and developing nations (Appadurai 1996), the Malaysian instance of punk still looks for ways to educate itself through the observation of mediated ideoscapes and 'punk ethnoscapes' represented by visiting exponents of the foreign parent culture. Consequently, based on an unequal power relation, I argue that it would be reprimanding to categorize Malaysian punk as 'non-authentic' only because it constructs its own punk identity based on a foreign parent punk culture. The risk, however, is that by pursuing an authenticating meritocracy reified by foreign cultural forms, Malaysian punk risks remaining bound to a foreign idea of punk authenticity, thus failing to develop its own possibility of cultivating a different, localized indigenization that could transform it from a globalized 'nothing' into a pro-active 'something.'

References

Appadurai, A. (1990). 'Disjuncture and Difference in the Global Cultural Economy.' *Theory Culture Society* 7: 295–310.

Appadurai, A. (1996). *Modernity at Large: Cultural Dimensions of Globalization*. St. Paul: University of Minnesota Press.

Azerrad, M. (1994). *Come As You Are: The True Story of Nirvana*. New York: Main Street Books.

Azmyl, Y. (2009). 'Facing the Music.' In S. G. Yeoh (ed.), *Media, Culture and Society in Malaysia*. New York: Routledge.

Baulch, E. (2002). 'Creating a Scene.' *International Journal of Cultural Studies* 5 (2): 153.

Baulch, E. (2003). 'Gesturing Elsewhere: The Identity Politics of the Balinese Death/Thrash Metal Scene.' *Popular Music* 22 (2): 195–15.

Baulch, E. (2007). *Making Scenes: Reggae, Punk, and Death Metal in the 1990s*. Bali: Duke University Press.

BBC. (2001). *Herbal Cure for Malaysian Metal Fans* (13 August). http://news.bbc.co.uk/2/hi/asia-pacific/1489407.stm.

'Black Metal is a Choice.' (2006). *The Star* (28 January). http://www.thestar.com.my/news/nation/2006/01/28/black-metal-is-a-choice/

Bourdieu, P. (1984). *Distinction: A Social Critique of the Judgement of Taste*. London: Routledge.

Bourdieu, P. (2006). 'The Forms of Capital.' In H. Lauder et al. (eds.), *Education, Globalization and Social Change*. Oxford: Oxford University Press.

Bourdieu, P. and R. Johnson. (1993). *The Field of Cultural Production: Essays on Art and Literature*. Columbia University Press.

Davidson, E. (2010). *We Never Learn: The Gunk Punk Undergut, 1988–2001*. New York: Backbeat Books.

Dunn, K. C. (2008). 'Never Mind the Bollocks: The Punk Rock Politics of Global Communication.' *Review of International Studies* 34 (1): 193–210.

Ensminger, D. (2013). 'Slamdance in the No Time Zone: Punk as Repertoire for Liminality.' *Liminalities: A journal of Performance Studies* 9 (3).

Ferrarese, M. (2012). 'Malaysian Rocks: an Introduction to the Contemporary Malaysian Extreme Music Underground, 2010–2011.' In J. Lee and J. Hopkins (eds.), *Thinking through Malaysia. Culture and Identity in the 21st Century*. Kuala Lumpur: SIRD.

Glasper, I. (2007). *The Day the Country Died: A History of Anarcho Punk 1980 to 1984*. London: Cherry Red Books.

Haas, L. (1995). 'Scene Report Southeast Asia: Further Travels of Luke Haas.' *Maximumrockandroll*, 147 (August).

Haenfler, R. (2006). 'Straight Edge: Clean-living Youth, Hardcore Punk, and Social Change.' Piscataway, NJ: Rutgers University Press.

Hannerz, E. (2005). 'Punk Not Die!: A Minor Field Study on the Performance of Punk in Indonesia.' *Asian Survey* 25 (7): 745–59.

Hannerz, E. (2013). *Performing punk: Subcultural Authentications and the Positioning of the Mainstream*. Uppsala: Uppsala Universitet.

Kahn-Harris, K. (2007). *Extreme Metal: Music and Culture on the Edge*. Oxford, New York: Berg Publishers.

Kidd, J. (2012). 'A Brief History of the Malaysian DIY Hardcore-punk Scene (1994–1997).' *Shock & Awe* 5–9.

Lockard, C. A. (1998). *Dance of Life: Popular Music and Politics in Southeast Asia*. Honolulu, HI: University of Hawaii Press.

Maclachlan, H. (2011). *Burma's Pop Music Industry: Creators, Distributors, Censors*. Rochester, NY: University of Rochester Press.

Martin-Iverson, S. (2011). *The Politics of Cultural Production in the DIY Hardcore Scene in Bandung, Indonesia*. Perth: School of Social and Cultural Studies, University of Western Australia.

Martin-Iverson, S. (2012). 'Autonomous Youth? Independence and Precariousness in the Indonesian Music Scene.' *The Asia Pacific Journal of Anthropology* 13 (4): 382–97.

Maton, K. (2008). 'Habitus.' In M. Grenfell (ed.), *Pierre Bourdieu – Key Concepts*, 49–66. Durham: Acumen.

Mudrian, A. (2004). 'Choosing Death: the Improbable History of Death Metal and Grindcore.' Los Angeles: Feral House.

O'Connor, A. (2002). 'Local Scenes and Dangerous Crossroads: Punk and Theories of Cultural Hybridity.' *Popular Music* 21 (2): 225–36.

Overell, R. (2010). 'Brutal Belonging in Melbourne's Grindcore Scene.' In N. K. Denzin (ed.), *Studies in Symbolic Interaction*, 101–21). Bingley: Emerald Group Publishing.

Peterson, R. A. and A. Bennett. (2004). 'Introducing Music Scenes.' In A. Bennett and R. A. Peterson (eds.), *Music Scenes: Local, Translocal and Virtual*, 1–15. Nashville: Vanderbilt University Press.

Pickles, J. (2007). 'Punk, Pop and Protest: The Birth and Decline of Political Punk in Bandung.' *Review of Indonesian and Malaysian Affairs* 41 (2): 223–46.

Ritzer, G. (2004), *The Globalization of Nothing*. Thousand Oaks, CA: Pine Forge Press.

Ritzer, G. and M. Ryan. (2002). 'The Globalization of Nothing.' *Social Thought & Research* 25 (1/2): 51–81.

Thompson, S. (2004). *Punk Productions: Unfinished Business*. Albany, NY: State University of New York Press.

Thornton, S. (1995). *Club Cultures: Music, Media, and Subcultural Capital*. Oxford: Polity Press.

Wallach, J. (2008). *Modern Noise, Fluid Genres: Popular Music in Indonesia, 1997–2001*. Madison, WI: University of Wisconsin Press.

Wallach, J. (2010). 'Distortion-drenched Dystopias: Metal and Modernity in Southeast Asia.' In R. Niall and W. Scott (eds.), *The Metal Void: First Gatherings, Critical Issues*, 357–66). Oxford: The Inter-Disciplinary Press.

Wallach, J. (2011). 'Unleashed in the East: Metal Music, Masculinity, and "Malayness" in Indonesia, Malaysia, and Singapore.' In J. Wallach, H. M. Berger, and P. D. Greene (eds.), *Metal Rules the Globe: Heavy Metal Music Around the World*, 86–103. Durham, NC: Duke University Press.

Weinstein, D. (2011). 'The Globalization of Metal.' In J. Wallach, H. M. Berger, and P. D. Greene (eds.), *Metal Rules the Globe: Heavy Metal Music Around the World*. Durham, NC: Duke University Press.

Wolf, F. (2013). *Social Carbon Copy: Stories From the Road 2000–2002*. Kuala Lumpur: Doyerown Books.

MAXIMUMROCKNROLL

3   DECEMBER 2016 $4.99 IN THE US

THE ALL CHINA ISSUE

FEATURING SCENE REPORTS PAST AND PRESENT, INTERVIEWS, PHOTOS, AN ANNOTATED DISCOGRAPHY, AND MORE

TANG CHAO

HONG SE BU DUI

13. THE PUNK SUBCULTURE IN CHINA

JIAN XIAO

Abstract

This chapter presents a study of the punk phenomenon in China. Overall, I argue that it exists in China as a subculture. By using the concepts of space, style, and network from previous subcultural studies, it explores the collective actions of punk musicians in aspects of their dress, performance, political aspirations and interactions at different levels. It is found that Chinese punk musicians have created their own spaces for gathering while being constrained by the declining performance opportunities in large venues. Influenced by imported Western punk music and culture, similarities can be found in the music and clothing styles between Chinese punk musicians and the Western punk bands that they regard as idols. Their anti-government political aspirations lead punk musicians to break rules when performing. Interactions between punk musicians happen at both local and international levels. In this process, divisions of sub-groups emerge due to a differing identification with punk values and beliefs.

Keywords: Chinese punk, subculture, space, style

Jian Xiao recently received her PhD in Media and Cultural Studies from the Department of Social Sciences, Loughborough University, United Kingdom. Her thesis was on exploring the punk phenomenon in China. She has one article about online punk communities in China forthcoming in the *Chinese Journal of Communication*, and one about punk authenticity in China forthcoming in *Punk & Post Punk*. Her research interests focus on new media and cultural studies. She has previously worked as an overseas journalist for several Chinese publications, mainly writing articles related to art, fashion, and travel. E-mail: jx.jianxiao@yahoo.com

THE PUNK SUBCULTURE IN CHINA

Introduction

> Chinese punk is the Chinese style of punk. Due to the specific country context, Chinese punk is relatively implicit and less straightforward. Certain behaviours related to violence and anti-government [*sic*] cannot be explicitly shown. Chinese punks can only criticise and express their views secretly. Their way of 'talking bullshit' has become a particular way of criticising socialistic modernism. (Definition of *Chinese Punk*, from the website *Baidu* by Kuking, 2014)

In 1996, a group of Beijing musicians first heard Western underground music, from bands such as East Bay, Chicago, or DC punk, brought over by an American, O'Dell, and these musicians later formed the first Chinese punk band – Underbaby (O'Dell 2011).[99] Since then, the punk phenomenon in China has expanded to different cities and developed its own cultural formation. However, this has not been without controversy, as can be seen from the documentary film *Beijing Punk* which was banned in China. It explores the lives of punk musicians and issues regarding dress, performance, and their political attitudes and opposition of the government.

Although it has developed for almost twenty years, the Chinese punk phenomenon has received little attention within and outside of China. In contrast, punk phenomena in the West have been studied for many years. Early scholars from the University of Birmingham Centre for Contemporary Cultural Studies (CCCS) defined the British punk phenomenon as a counter-culture, exploring its symbolic meanings in opposing the mainstream culture (Hall and Jefferson 1976; Hebdige 1979). Recent years have witnessed the scope of punk research becoming wider both theoretically and empirically (Furness 2012; Leblanc 1999; Williams 2011). To further expand the current punk research, this chapter will present a study on the punk phenomenon in a non-Western social context, i.e. China, and discuss how it exists in China as a subculture.

In this chapter, the theoretical background regarding subculture studies will be provided to contextualize the punk phenomenon in China. Following this, the development of punk music will be presented, focusing on the use of live houses as performance spaces and bars or small restaurants as gathering spaces for Chinese punks. The discussion will then move onto the punk style itself, with a focus on performance and political aspirations. Finally, the analysis will focus on how members of the Chinese punk group form a network for supporting and interacting with each other and how this process shapes their punk identities as well as creates division within the punk group, leading to a summative discussion of the existence of Chinese punk as a subculture.

---

99 We have undertaken a free translation of the songs and band names to demonstrate the importance of the language and words for punk as an intentional manifestation and, in most cases, a social critique.

Subcultural Studies: From CCCS to Post-subcultural Studies

Subcultural studies have had a long history and have experienced considerable changes as a result of critical debates over the years in the Anglo-American area. The 1920s to the late 1960s witnessed the original studies associated with subcultures by the Chicago School. Established in 1964, the Centre for Contemporary Cultural Studies at Birmingham University (CCCS) was famous for its contribution in analysing youth subculture from its social and cultural conditions. In particular, Hebdige (1979) examined the Western punk phenomenon in the well-known book *Subculture: The Meaning of Style* and explained it as a resistance to the mainstream through style.

Through the lens of leisure activities conducted by post-war youth, CCCS theorists aimed to examine the social structure of that period of Britain. This objective led to an explicit CCCS framework, studying the collective features of a group and explaining power relations within a subculture. The exploration in this aspect is conducted in three ways: first, the emphasis on class division, particularly the construction of working-class culture, provides the base of the argument of the relation between subcultures and social structure. Second, the dominant culture has been discussed within the theoretical framework of hegemony. Third, the power relation within subculture is structured through the subordinated subculture resisting the dominant parent culture symbolically.

Criticisms of CCCS' work have been made in a body of work known as 'post-subcultural studies,' which questions and readdresses the previous subcultural theory and the empirical research undertaken by CCCS subcultural analysts (Weinzierl and Muggleton 2003; Shildrick and MacDonald 2006). Although it has been argued that post-subcultural studies are not unified, two main strands in this field can be identified (Weinzierl and Muggleton 2003). In Weinzierl and Muggleton's opinion, the first strand criticizes the CCCS work and establishes a new framework. An example of this is Thornton's (1997) use of Bourdieu's work to theorize the concept of subculture capital and ideologies. The main criticism is that the CCCS concepts of 'resistance' and 'incorporation' are too limited, ignoring the internal stratification of subcultures, the subcultural participation in commerce, and the significant role of the media in subcultural formation (Gelder 1997). Muggleton (2005) also points out that the second strand abandons CCCS theories completely and attempts to replace the term 'subculture' with other terminologies such as 'subchannels' (Singh 2000), 'temporary substream networks' (Weinzierl 2000), and 'neo-tribes' (Bennett 1999; 2005). Meanwhile, by applying the urban tribes theory, 'tribe' identities are also explored (Winge 2003).

Post-subculturalists shifted CCCS' focus on the collective meanings of a group to stressing the influence of individuals' choices and creativity in leisure phenomena. Nevertheless, this trend is criticized as offering 'little more than new empirical examples of something already theorized in terms of generic social process' (Williams 2011, 42). As the CCCS approach is still of value in explaining subcultural phenomena, for example when regarding the relationship between cultural formation and social structure in contemporary times (Shildrick and MacDonald 2006), future research needs to be undertaken with substantial empirical evidence to avoid the problem of being over-theoretical due to the lack of indigenous perspectives from subculturalists concerned.

Williams' Approach to Subcultural Studies: Redefining Subculture

As a researcher studying the Straightedge subculture in America for many years, Williams (2011) 'placed communication and culture at the center of his symbolic interactionist theory of subculture' (Blackman 2014, 507). Based on his ethnographic studies, Williams provides a definition of subculture:

> Subcultures refer to culturally bounded, but not closed, networks of people who come to share the meaning of specific ideas, material objects, and practices through interaction. Over time, their interaction develops into a discourse and culture that shapes, but does not determine, the generation, activation, and diffusion of these ideas, objects, and practices. (2011, 39)

Williams' conceptualization does not emphasize the formation of subcultures originating from class culture. Instead, shared interests become the primary reason of an aggregate of subculturalists. To this extent, this is in harmony with post-subcultural theory. However, Williams' model is different since he further asserts that subculture members' shared interests also led them to identify themselves as different from – usually in some form of antagonistic relationship with – normal, 'square' society (8).

Compared to the post-subcultural scholars who regard the society as being fragmented, Williams prefers to view it as being normal and different. Further, Williams argues that the term subculture is problematic if used to 'classify people who comprise a social network or a population segment (e.g. scene or gang), rather than a cultural phenomenon that refers to sets of shared values and beliefs, practices, and material objects' (38). In this respect, the formation of subcultures is not limited to the static or assumed categories such as location, age, or class.

Without a rigid framework, Williams' theorization with different dimensions can direct subcultural research into new areas that remain unexplored within the CCCS model. For instance, subcultural practices in the online setting are explored; different dimensions of resistance are conceptualized. By framing the society as 'normal' and 'different' rather than 'mainstream' and 'marginalized,' the possibilities of exploring contemporary society with a less static structure can be actualised.

It can be seen that the Anglo-American theorists discussed above approach subcultural phenomena differently. CCCS subcultural studies focus on the power relation between subculture and its parent culture, with the inclusion of individual biographies of a subculture member in order to reveal the underlying reasons for the formation of subcultures in a particular period. Opposing CCCS subcultural studies, post-subcultural studies direct their research into competing areas, focusing on the individual basis of a subculture member rather than their assumed collective one. Benefitting from ethnographic approach, Williams abandons the categories of class and age in defining subculture for a process of sharing and interacting as the focus of his approach while asserting the perspective of relating to social structure.

Concepts in Subcultural Studies Relevant to this Chapter

The main purpose of this chapter is to examine a punk phenomenon in a non-Western context, i.e. China. Inspired by the subcultural approach from Western literature on subcultural studies, particularly those from CCCS studies and Williams, it will adopt the conceptualized space, style and collective network to contextualize the punk phenomenon in China through gaining empirical evidence from Chinese punks.

CCCS theorists regard certain spaces, such as street corners or open roads, as sites for working-class youths to conduct subcultural practices to resist their parent culture, although the subcultures can only offer this since, according to Willis (1981), those youths will eventually leave and return to their vocational schools or dead-end jobs. In a broader sense, space serves to shape social interactions. As earlier research typically focuses on specific geographical spaces (Baron 1989; Cohen 1972), recent studies include virtual space as an area to examine subcultural practices or translocal interactions (Hodkinson 2002; Williams 2006; Williams and Copes 2005).

Style, particularly clothing style, can be regarded as the essential subcultural component for CCCS theorists in explaining symbolic resistance through appropriation. As mentioned earlier, Hebdige (1979) was particularly famous for his conceptualization of the meaning of style in punk subculture. Clothing style was also interpreted as a form of 'distinctive individuality' (Muggleton 2002). Style as practice, nevertheless, is argued to have gone far beyond consuming music; examples can be seen in the practice of body modification in primitive subcultures (Williams 2007).

While returning to the issue of group coherence and commitment explored by CCCS theorists, scholars (Hodkinson and Lincoln 2008; Williams 2011) focus on the aspect of 'increased knowledge, flexibility, participation, and collectivity transmitted through a subcultural network' offered by the new form of subcultural communication (Blackman 2014, 507). The earlier section has shown that Williams (2011) uses 'network' to define subculture and stresses the formation of culture as being a consequence of members' interactions. In this sense, examining subcultural networks can facilitate an understanding of the structure of a subculture.

By adopting the concepts of subcultural space, style, and network, this chapter explores the punk phenomenon in China, focusing on its embodiment of dress, performance, and political aspirations, as well as its internal structure developed through different levels of interactions.

Methodology

In O'Reilly's (2012) introduction, ethnographic research can solve the problems of validity since it focuses on the 'native's' perspective (Fetterman 2010, 20–2). Therefore, conducting ethnographic research became a favoured means to explore the Chinese punk subcultural phenomenon, with a particular focus on the articulations of subcultural experiences by the native punk subculture members.

In 2013, I conducted thirty-seven semi-structured interviews with Chinese punks while also meeting others who I did not interview (e.g. at punk performances and informal gatherings). Participant observation and interviewing were the two main methods I employed in this research. With the goal of discovering the lived experiences of Chinese punks, I attended punk performances and informal gatherings organized by my participants. In particular, I chose to travel to where they lived or worked to conduct the interviews and, if allowed, observe their daily activities. By doing this, I was not confined to a particular location or a particular subgroup but could collect findings from different research areas, ranging from the city centre to the suburbs, and from large-scale to small-scale cities, and obtain thoughts and opinions from distinctive subgroups.

Overall, the distribution of punk bands tends to be diverse in China. While there are over ten punk bands in Beijing, two or three bands can be found in each of the other cities, such as Shanghai, Wuhan, and Changsha. It is difficult to classify punk styles in China. Among those I interviewed, I met skinhead oi! punk style, hardcore style, and street punk style, for example. In line with the diverse forms of punk music, other related styles such as dress and performance style varied.

Space for Punk Performance and Gathering

One issue regarding studies on subcultural activities is related to social space (Cressey 1932; Baron 1989; Leblanc 1999). Williams (2007) concluded that those studies 'highlight the significance of bounded geographical spaces for embodied, situated social action' (582). In China, punk musicians are typically active in performing at different live houses and gathering in different bars established by senior punks. Those spaces with distinctive features shape how punk musicians perform and interact with each other as well as with audience members. Specifically, the situation of punk music being gradually marginalized in the Chinese music scene is happening in China, which nevertheless, in turn, generates new practices from punk musicians creating spaces for their gatherings.

Several live houses exist in Beijing for punk performances, although none of them specialize in it. Two years ago, the live house D-22, which performed mostly punk style, was closed and transformed into a live house called XP, which embraces mostly alternative music performances and holds fewer punk music performances. According to my participant Mr L, the closing down of D-22 was a consequence of financial difficulties, since punk performances were not as popular as before. This move was particularly significant since it suggested a tendency of punk-style performance to become marginalized in China's music scene.

Among different live houses, the Mao live house is the most desirable for all kinds of musicians including punk musicians due to its professionalism and the high standard of its sound system. Due to its popularity, it can be difficult for punk bands that want to perform there since punk performance is not profitable. Comparatively, the other live house, School, though being small and with a lower quality sound system and performance equipment, has shown its enthusiasm for holding punk performances. Not only does it hold a series of the paid monthly punk-only performances but also a series of free monthly punk-only performances, initiated by other punk bands. More importantly, since both the owner and manager of School have previously or currently performed in punk bands, this place demonstrated an informal yet intense mode of social networking and interaction among punk musicians. Regarding other live houses, one called Old What was mentioned by several punk musicians. While some criticized its extremely low standard as a live house, some praised it for its intimate performing environment and the enjoyable interactions that happen there between audiences and musicians.

Given the fewer performances in live houses, old punk musicians started to establish bars and create their own spaces for networking with others. It is not unusual to find punk musicians gathering in bars rather than performing; they discuss ideas and entertain themselves by simply hanging out together. In Beijing, Mr L's restaurant has particularly served this purpose. With different kinds of punk music playing, the door covered by heavy curtains, low lighting, and rock-themed posters, the restaurant creates an underground atmosphere. Mr L, who is also an punk musician over 35 years old, is famous for long being on the scene and has also become a key figure in networking and socializing with other punk bands. In the suburbs of Beijing, punk events happen quite frequently and the key organizer is a 30-year-old punk musician with a considerable reputation who has stayed on the punk scene for a long time. Similarly, he too opened a new bar in order to socialize with other musicians. The same thing has happened in other cities, including Shanghai and Wuhan where two bars were established independently.

The bar opened by a senior punk musician in Wuhan is located in an area filled with bars and skateboarding shops owned by other former punk musicians. One of my interviewees, a young punk musician, spoke frankly to me about her desire to enter this circle before becoming part of one punk band. In this sense, although some punk musicians have stopped playing in bands, they still identified themselves with punk and are recognized by others as being punk. In Wuhan, former punk musician Mr D established a place called Our Home, which is similar in concept to the punk practice of squatting. The house was rented at a cheap price from a nearly-abandoned area, and became the birthplace of an autonomous style community. But this is an exceptional case and there is no other similar squatting phenomenon in other cities in China.

The constructed space for punk musicians is significant in shaping their performance as well as their daily practices. Although punk musicians are less favoured by the big live houses, the small ones provide them opportunities to interact intensely with audience members. Thus, the site not only allows an intense emotional release due to the intimacy, but also enables an influence on audience members through expressing punk beliefs, values, and political attitudes in the means of speaking and singing on the stage. Meanwhile, a growing number of bars or restaurants serve an important role in forming punk norms since they are relatively closed spaces for allowing social interactions to happen among punks as a group themselves. Through hanging out with other punk musicians or fans, activities such as holding gigs and tours and creating albums and music videos are discussed and scheduled; political views, punk cultures, and the DIY philosophy are exchanged and shared, leading to a mutual reaction to all the different forms of authority. Within such intimate and safe environments, a coherent pattern of thinking is easily formed. Moreover, the special case of an autonomous community being built in Wuhan suggests the possibility of someone following punk philosophies in order to guide their way of living in China.

Punk Style, Performance, and Political Aspiration

The above section has discussed where Chinese punks choose to gather and perform. This section will look at the forms of punk practices as manifested in China.

One of the core concepts in studying subcultures for CCCS theorists is the meaning of style, focusing particularly on choice of clothing. As the conceptualized visual style is critical to understanding Chinese punks, the musical style as practice should also be considered as a crucial component for them, since Western punk culture has impacted the development of punk music in China to a great extent. For instance, the Western music genre is generally adopted or imitated by almost all of the punk bands in China. During my field trip, I even received one suggestion from a band that preparing a question such as 'who is your music idol?' was necessary for the interviews with Chinese punk musicians.

The other competent of style, that of the punk visual style, has become a means of playing out punk identity as well as creating a sense of group belonging, although different spaces of performance have witnessed some variety in this aspect. In my visit to the punk-only performance in Mao, a notice associated with the ticket rule came out as 'those who wear a Mohawk can enjoy free entrance,' which was supposed to encourage the audiences to adopt a punk dress style. For punk musicians, seeing audiences wearing punk dress is an encouragement for judgement if the environment is familiar enough. Nevertheless, the encouragement of the dress codes in that particular event was a failure since there were very few people who had a Mohawk or wore a leather jacket. Comparatively, more audience members were willing to have or wear a Mohawk hairstyle or leather jacket in School, perhaps unsurprisingly given that it is believed to be a hub for punks in Beijing. Punk musicians expressed surprise when they observed a full house of people dressed as punks at the annual Punk Music Festival. 'I have no idea where those punks come from. I never met them before but I am also very happy to see them,' said one punk musician. As analysed before, Mao, as a relatively commercial venue, attracts a greater variety of audiences, while School is less popular with the general public. In other words, the latter environment is more encouraging for punks in conducting the practice of wearing punk-style clothing.

It is the nature of punk performance, which challenges the norms of conventional musical performance and contains strong political messages, to create conflicts between their own ideals and the demands of commercial imperatives. Ideally speaking, punk musicians prefer performing in a completely trustworthy environment. This includes sincere enthusiasm from the organizer for promoting punk music and emotional synchronization as well as a mutual understanding with the audience. However, this preference normally results in a mismatch with reality since not enough resources are available to support punk music performance, given its decreasing popularity in China. On a practical level, there are chances for punk performances, either at music festivals with a mixture of different styles, or in commercial performances for companies. Thus, the main concerns for punk musicians have become whether or not the performance is motivated by commercial reasons and how to practice their own norms in those mixed performances.

The politically driven punk performance in China often encounters strict government controls and constraints. It is worth noting that one particular norm of punk performance –political speech before performances – invites scrutiny and prohibition by the government. Accompanied by this feature, their anti-authoritarian desire can lead punk musicians to break rules that have been established by the government, especially in mixed performance events (i.e. events featuring performances of various genres and styles). Here, I present a story shared by one punk musician: while his band was invited to attend a performance consisting mostly of popular music bands organized by the local government, they broke the performing norms by expressing social injustice on the stage, thus invoking a disturbance among audience members. The consequence of being fined was that the band received no payment; nevertheless, the members felt happy because they had shown their power to defy the government.

The motivation to seek opportunities to express political attitudes while performing can be seen explicitly in another practice – organizing activities such as the Punk Music Festival. Held every August in Beijing, this festival is an event that combines leisure, punk beliefs, and political expression, fitting closely with what could be regarded as the ideal performance environment that Chinese punk musicians pursue. With participants actively dressing and performing as punks, the organizers encourage audience members to criticize the government on stage along with the musicians. The appeal of an event like this is its creating an environment with equal chances of free expression, and the associated actions of pogoing and moshing which serve to release emotions and break social boundaries between people, becoming an existence opposing that of the outside world with its hierarchies and controls. To better understand the practices of organizing a punk festival and challenging the performance rules discussed earlier, an explanation can possibly be found in how O'Hara (1999) defined punk philosophy associated with anarchy: 'a belief formed around the anarchist principles of having no official government or rules, and valuing individual freedom and responsibility (who doesn't?)' (71).

Punk Networks in China

As mentioned earlier, Chinese punk musicians interact with each other in different forms of spaces. In fact, it is this resulting group dynamic that has shaped the punk practices which have been discussed in the previous section. The next part of this chapter will focus on differing levels of interactions within the Chinese punk group and the issue regarding the division of subgroups as a result.

Interacting with local and overseas punks

The punk support network in China allows the formation of two frames of reference for subculture members to establish shared core values, which frequently assist the members in their life stages. The first of these emerges from the process of the localization of punk music and its culture in China attributed to the interactions within the local Chinese punk group. The second is more about Chinese punk musicians interacting with punks in Anglo-American countries and finding out what they believe and how they behave. These two frames of reference can overlap and inevitably impact each other, resulting in a relatively static frame of reference in the punk group.

Mr L's skinhead oi! punk band was established in Beijing in 1999 and is known by most other punk bands. The intense connection of his band and other groups was exhibited in several aspects: first, the introduction to my participant Mr J's band shown on its website was written by Mr L. Second, another participant, Mr C, has taken on the shared responsibility of organizing the Punk Music Festival, which was originally created by Mr L. Third, several other participants such as Miss K and Mr F became acquainted through him. The interviews with them and many other punk musicians have shown that themes such as emphasizing visual resistance or including anti-government comments in songs have been mostly shared, with the musicians referring to each other by name.

The period when punk shows were popular in China has gone. As a consequence, the punk group remains relatively small and somewhat marginalized within the wider music scene. Regarding the composition of subculture members, the age range of my participants is from 19 to 37. It was noted that there are a number of punk musicians who are still very active over the age of 30. The number of young people (i.e. below 25) who join the group has declined over the years. For those who attempt to participate, having an interest in punk music and a punk lifestyle serves as the main reason for people wanting to join the punk group. It is argued however that the opportunity of joining such a culturally-bounded group is limited. One feature that was identified from various participants is the desire to keep the punk performance 'independent' so that they have the freedom to choose the content to express and the style. For instance, the musicians were found to be proud of the non-commerciality of punk and resisted opportunities to participate in more commercial or mainstream activities, for example if a band was invited to participate in a pro-government style of performance.

Outside the local punk interactions, Chinese punks also interact with those in Anglo-American countries. The Western punk-related lifestyle is particularly appealing to musicians who once experienced performance tours in European countries, and almost half of my participants have overseas experience and contacts abroad. Typically, Western countries are considered to be democratic, to have free speech, to be environmentally-friendly, and to be diverse, while China is described as being heavily polluted, constrained, commercial, and singular. While Western society is seen as independent, normal Chinese society is viewed as being brainwashed and blindly following the status quo.

Mr L, for instance, has a strong connection with German punks as a result of his band's tour of Germany in 2007. In the interview, Mr L mentioned the treatment while performing in Germany, i.e. being treated to free drinks and the environmentally friendly festival theme. More importantly, he was welcomed by German punks. In contrast, he initially experienced visa refusal for 'unspoken political reasons' from the Chinese government when applying to travel to Germany to perform, but gained financial help from German punks to cover the financial loss. Because of the help received from the German punks, this interviewee stated, 'I don't know which my real country is, China or Germany.' Through frequent interaction with German punks, particularly in comparing the situations in the two different countries over such issues as government reactions to graffiti, he has formed a strong critical stance towards China resulting in his argument that the establishment of a new society operating without a government is necessary. Another participant, Mr F, described the cyber environments of the Western countries and China as being in opposition. According to him, Thailand is an example of a democratic Eastern country following the Western model. He was willing to use the concept of an ideal country, with European countries quoted as being that ideal. For Miss K, Western people knew what they were going to achieve even when they were squatting (in the punk movement, punk musicians squat in deserted houses to live in a state of anarchism or hold music festivals). Comparatively, Chinese people or punks have already lost their direction, and the general public is brainwashed.

To summarize, interactions between punks can be seen in different cities, particularly Beijing and Wuhan, through music performances, music festivals, or simply hanging out to discuss and share interests. On the one hand, interacting with other punks locally provides a frame of reference, such as attitudes to visual appearance and the Chinese government. On the other hand, interaction between Chinese punks and Western punks provides a frame of reference guiding Chinese punks to appreciate the attitudes and lifestyles of Western punks.

The division of subgroups within the punk group
Although frames of reference exist in the Chinese punk group for guiding the overarching practice, subtlety can be seen in variations in specific areas among the

different bands. Sometimes, these differences can invite conflict within and between them. Nevertheless, this process suggests that Chinese punk musicians as a group have multiple facets and therefore further reveals the focal concerns that are mutually shared yet approached differently, such as specific practices regarding the issues of localization and lifestyle choice.

In Beijing, one focus of many disagreements among different punk musicians is the debate about whether the lyrics should be sung in English or Chinese. Normally, this was discussed along with other issues – for instance, the punk musician's economic or educational background. When I talked to one punk musician, he expressed the belief that those who insisted on singing in Chinese had more potential to be successful. Moreover, he criticized those who sang in English as having no background of high-level education, thus not only losing their Chinese identity but also trying too hard to emulate Western punks. Since some of the musicians criticized were from wealthy backgrounds, this background would also be criticized for being mismatched with songs appealing for equality and freedom, as they were perceived to represent a higher social class. When I first stayed in Beijing, I went to the monthly punk-only event, which was not free. At a later stage, a free monthly punk-only event emerged, organized by the punk musicians who held opposing attitudes to those who organized the non-free punk-only performances. It seemed like an assertion of battle for the territory, resulting in the formation of subgroups within Chinese Beijing Punk. In a broader sense, it involves how punk musicians locate the concept of localization in the punk group, which originated in Western countries and further generates the issue of being an authentic punk.

The other issue in which opinions differ concerns that of dressing as a punk. Although punk musicians typically agree over clothing style being an important means to play out identity, I still encountered different attitudes regarding 'when to dress like a punk.' More specifically, their differing attitudes can be seen particularly in their ways of dealing with non-performing occasions. While Mr L insisted on a skinhead to maintain his identity, even in his working time, another punk musician, Mr DF, believed that wearing punk style clothing was not necessary since he valued the 'inner side' of living as a punk and emphasized the contrast between the visual appearance and inner belief. To those punk musicians who have professional jobs without relation to music, wearing professional clothes is deemed to be the only choice in normal situations.

As discussed, punk bands are distributed widely in different areas or cities in China. The division between these bands is not only a result of geographical difference, but can sometimes be attributed to the opposing choices of punk lifestyle. For instance, the motivation of a group of punk musician who moved to the suburb of Beijing was to escape from the city centre where most of the punk bands gathered and a punk circle had formed. Returning to a 'utopian place' was the hope, as this could fulfil the desire for creating an intimate and free environment for punk musicians. Moreover, the suburb also provided a relatively quiet place for musicians to reflect on how to live as a punk.

For the punk musicians who live in the small cities of China, their main concern was to keep their punk identities alive. Compared to the punk musicians who live in large cities and possess all the resources they needed, they believe that their non-stop but struggling punk practices, such as planning performances or maintaining their clothing styles, have proved their own authenticity of being punks. Apart from having established a set of beliefs and values to justify their choices of living, punk musicians who live in suburbs or small cities are inclined to use the term 'marginalized' to describe their situations. This can be seen from the example of one participant expressing to me, 'it is good to see that there are people who care about marginal people like us.'

Conclusion

In the limited press discussions of punk phenomena in China, one article includes it as a general form of Chinese alternative music and a music subculture (A. A. 2013). DeHart (2013) is nevertheless reluctant to deem punk music a subculture since he believes that the lack of suitable political and economic conditions slows its development and expansion in China. It is true that punk bands remain small in number and are loosely distributed in different cities. However, one cannot ignore not only the reality of the formation of punk styles, performances, and spaces for punk practices but also the interactions within punk groups at different levels.

Thus, informed by previous subcultural studies, this chapter adopted the ideas of conceptualized space, style, and network to examine the punk phenomenon in China. Chinese punks perform in large and small-scale live houses, and gather in bars or restaurants established by senior punk musicians. While the bigger live houses are reluctant to accommodate punk performances due to their low profitability, the smaller live houses provide intimate and familiar spaces for punk musicians to perform and interact. The status quo of performance opportunities reducing has led to an increase in the number of bars or restaurants opened by members from the punk group, aiming at providing private spaces for social interactions between punks. In those spaces, punk musicians schedule their tours or gigs, exchange ideas about instruments or albums, and express political opinions.

Heavily influenced by Western punk music and its culture, Chinese punk musicians imitate music styles from famous bands as well as clothing styles associated with particular genres of punk music. Comparatively, small live houses have witnessed more audience members that wear punk-style clothing due to the familiar environment, while in larger venues fewer people choose to dress as punks mainly because of the diversity of the audiences there. Punk performance in China faces pressure and control from the government. This situation can be attributed to punk musicians' political aspirations. Acts such as the breaking of rules in mixed performance settings and making political speeches before their performances facilitate punk musicians' pursuit of freedom.

Through interacting locally and internationally, punk musicians form a network where two frames of reference, involving punk style and political attitudes formed through local interactions, as well as appreciating the attitudes and lifestyles of Western punks formed through international interactions, guide their practices. Locally, Chinese punks have informal gatherings that happen in specific places such as bars opened by punk musicians or park corners. In different cities or among different subgroups, punk musicians interact with each other and maintain a network, even occasionally manifesting in conflict. The division of subgroups has emerged due to differing opinions and the according practices over such matters as language use when singing, the importance of dressing as a punk, and general lifestyle choices. Ultimately, the process of differentiation is rooted in their respective identifications with punk culture as well as beliefs about how to develop them through their daily practices.

The distinctive social context has shaped the punk phenomenon in China in a particular way, despite the fact that as a body of practices and ideals it is largely imported from the West. While it is important to acknowledge that punk culture can be politically radical for its rooted anti-authority ambitions in China, the subtlety in its manifesting features that are unique to Chinese punks should also be noted. In essence, what is ultimately revealed is how a subculture is shaped by its surrounding society. Perhaps further exploration of how local factors can influence a subculture may offer another perspective from which a detailed picture of punk practices and their attached meanings could be viewed.

Author's Note: the participants' names were not provided in this study in order to protect their identities.

References

A. A. (2013). 'Subcultural sounds.' http://www.economist.com/blogs/analects/2013/05/music-festivals.

Baron, S. W. (1989). 'Resistance and its Consequences: The Street Culture of Punks.' *Youth and Society* 21: 207–37.

Bennett, A. (1999). 'Subcultures or Neo-tribes? Rethinking the Relationship between Youth, Style and Musical Taste.' *Sociology* 33 (3): 599–617.

Bennett, A. (2005). 'In Defence of Neo-tribes: a Response to Blackman and Hesmondhalgh.' *Journal of Youth Studies* 9: 255–9.

Blackman, S. (2014). 'Subculture Theory: an Historical and Contemporary Assessment of the Concept for Understanding Deviance.' *Deviant Behaviour* 35 (6): 496–512.

Cohen, P. (1972). 'Sub-cultural Conflict and Working Class Community.' *Working Papers in Cultural Studies*, 2 (Spring). CCCS, University of Birmingham.

Cressey, P. G. (1932). *The Taxi-dance Hall*. New York: Greenwood Press.

DeHart, J. (2013). 'Punk in Asia: Rebelling from Burma to Beijing.' http://thediplomat.com/asia-life/2013/04/punk-in-asia-rebelling-from-burma-to-beijing.

Fetterman, D. (2010). *Ethnography: Step-by-step*, 3rd ed. London: Sage.

Furness, Z. (2012). *Punkademics: the Basement Show in the Ivory Tower*. Wivenhoe, Brooklyn, Port Watson: Minor Composition.

Gelder, K. (1997). 'Introduction to part three.' In K. Gelder and S. Thornton (eds.), *The Subcultural Reader*. London, New York: Routledge.

Hall, S., and T. Jefferson. (1976). *Resistance through Rituals: Youth Subcultures in Post-war Britain*. London: Hutchinson.

Hebdige, D. (1979). *Subculture: the Meaning of Style*. London: Methuen.

Hodkinson, P. (2002). *Goth: Identity, Style and Subculture*. Oxford: Berg.

Hodkinson, P. and S. Lincoln. (2008). 'Online Journals as Virtual Bedrooms? Young People, Identity and Personal Space.' *YOUNG* 16 (1): 27–46.

Kuking. (2014). *Chinese Punk*. http://baike.baidu.com/view/1152078.htm.

Leblanc, L. (1999). *Pretty in Punk: Girls' Resistance in a Boy's Subculture*. New Brunswick, NJ: Rutgers University Press.

Muggleton, D. (2002). *Inside Subculture: the Postmodern Meaning of Style*. Oxford: Berg.

Muggleton, D. (2005). 'From Classlessness to Club Culture: a Genealogy of Post-war British Youth Cultural Analysis.' *YOUNG* 13: 205–19.

O'Hara, C. (1999). *The Philosophy of Punk: More Than Noise!!*. Oakland, CA: AK Press.

O'Dell, D. (2011). 'Inseparable: the Memoirs of an American and the Story of Chinese Punk Rock.' Lulu.com. http://www.lulu.com/shop/david-odell/inseparable-the-memoirs-of-an-american-and-the-story-of-chinese-punk-rock/paperback/product-21623973.html

O'Reilly, K. (2012). *Ethnographic Methods*. London: Routledge.

Shildrick, T. and R. MacDonald. (2006). 'In Defence of Subculture: Young People, Leisure and Social Divisions.' *Journal of Youth Studies* 9 (2): 125–40.

Singh, A. (2000). 'Live, Streaming Subculture.' *Springerin* 3: 17.

Stahl, G. (2003). 'Tastefully Renovating Subcultural Theory: Making Space for a New Model.' In D. Muggleton and R. Weinzierl (eds.), *The Post-Subcultures Reader*. Oxford: Berg.

Thornton, S. (1997). 'The Social Logic of Subcultural Capital.' In K. Gelder and S. Thornton (eds.), *The Subcultural Reader*. London and New York: Routledge.

Ueno, T. (1997). 'Techno-orientalism and Media Tribalism: on Japanese Animation and Rave Culture.' *Third Text* 47: 95–106.

Vestby, S. (2007). 'Signs and Sounds: Identity Projects and Postmodern Bricolage in a Chinese Punk Rock Community.' Unpublished MA thesis. Telemark University College.

Weinzierl, R. and D. Muggleton. (2003). 'What is 'Post-subcultural Studies' Anyway?' In D. Muggleton and R. Weinzierl (eds.), *The Post-Subcultures Reader*. Oxford: Berg.

Weinzierl, R. (2000). *Fight the Power: a Secret History of Pop and the Formation of New Substreams*. Vienna: Passagen-Verlag.

Williams, J. P. (2006). 'Authentic Identities: Straightedge Subculture, Music and the Internet.' *Journal of Contemporary Ethnography* 35: 173–200.

Williams, J. P. (2007). 'Youth-subcultural Studies: Sociological Traditions and Core Concepts.' *Sociology Compass* ½: 572–93.

Williams, J. P. (2011). *Subcultural Theory: Traditions and Concepts*. Cambridge: Polity Press.

Williams, J. P. and H. Copes. (2005). '"How Edge Are You?" Constructing Authentic Identities and Subcultural Boundaries in a Straightedge Internet Forum.' *Symbolic Interaction* 28 (1): 67–89.

Willis, P. E. (1981). *Learning to Labour: How Working-class Kids Get Working-class Jobs*. New York: Columbia University Press.

Winge, T. M. (2003). 'Constructing "Neo-tribal" Identities through Dress: Modern Primitives and Body Modifications.' In D. Muggleton and R. Weinzierl (eds.), *The Post-Subcultures Reader*. Oxford: Berg.

INDEX